Schweizer Anglistische Arbeiten
Swiss Studies in English

Begründet von Bernhard Fehr
Herausgegeben von Andreas Fischer (Zürich), Henri Petter (Zürich),
Werner Senn (Bern)

Band 120

Thomas Honegger

From Phoenix to Chauntecleer

Medieval English Animal Poetry

francke
verlag

Die Deutsche Bibliothek – Cataloguing in Publication Data

Honegger, Thomas:
From Phoenix to Chauntecleer : medieval English animal poetry /
Thomas Honegger. – Tübingen ; Basel : Francke, 1996
(Schweizer anglistische Arbeiten ; Bd. 120)
Zugl.: Zürich, Univ., Diss., 1994/95
ISBN 3-7720-2432-7
NE: GT

This thesis was accepted as a doctoral dissertation by the Faculty of Arts of the University of Zürich in the winter semester of 1994/95 on the recommendation of Professor Dr. Andreas Fischer.

Published with support of the Swiss National Science Foundation.

Illustrations by Lilla Hangay
Printed by Laupp + Göbel, Nehren
Bound by Braun + Lamparter, Reutlingen
Printed in Germany

ISSN 0080-7214
ISBN 3-7720-2432-7

DEDICATUS

AUCTORI LIBRI NATURAE

Acknowledgments

I wish to express my deepest gratitude to all those who have contributed in one way or another to this study in matters animal.

In particular, I would like to thank my supervisor, Professor Dr. Andreas Fischer (Zurich), whose valuable advice and personal encouragement have been highly appreciated. It was thanks to his seminar on 'Animals in Medieval English Literature' that I picked up the scent – and though he did not 'carry the hound to the hunt', he had the wisdom to let me chase after the prey.

I also want to acknowledge my great indebtedness to Professor Dr. Paul Michel (Zurich). His courses, his publications on animal symbolism and, not least, his inspired as well as inspiring guided tour of the Grossmünster cloisters have been a source of inspiration and encouragement in the bleaker hours of academic research.

Furthermore, my sincere thanks are also due to Professor Dr. Kenneth Varty (Glasgow), Dr. Brian Levy (Hull) and Dr. Paul Wackers (Nijmegen) for their valuable comments on, and suggestions for, the chapter on *The Vox and the Wolf*.

Moreover, I wish to thank Andrew Torr, MA, who read and corrected my manuscript with the greatest care and sagacity and who offered essential comments and advice.

On a more personal note, particular thanks are due to my parents, for their unwavering belief in my work and their encouragement and interest.

Finally, a word of praise and appreciation must go to Lilla Hangay, whose cover and chapter illustrations have made a decisive contribution to the visual attractiveness of the book.

Thomas Honegger
Spring 1996

Table of Contents

Introduction

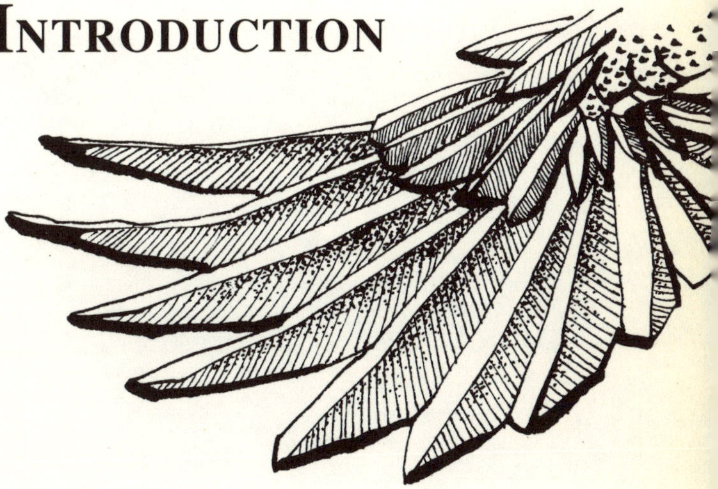

I. Introduction

> "And God made the beasts of the earth after his kind, and cattle after their kind, and every thing that creepeth upon the earth after his kind: and God saw that it was good." *Genesis* 1,25[1]

1. Aim, Scope, and Methods

The aim of this study is to analyse the function of animals in medieval English vernacular literature by discussing the most important 'animal poems' over a period of 700 years (i.e. between c. A.D. 700 and c. A.D. 1400). Even though many critics have repeatedly discussed the role of animals in various contexts, notably in allegorical and fable literature, no comprehensive study based on an overall analysis of the different poems which make use of animal protagonists has yet been undertaken. Thus, my study is intended to fill this gap, by pointing out the typical characteristics of the different genres of 'animal literature', and by providing an integrated analysis of each work. The presentation of the individual poems and their respective genres will enable us to uncover some of the often subtle and intricate connections between the various animal poems separated by place and time, and to appreciate the usually gradual – yet sometimes sudden – development within a genre which may, at first sight, appear rather heterogeneous. Thus, the study will, on the one hand, sharpen our perception of the typical individual and 'original' traits of the poems. On the other hand, we will also achieve a more conscious awareness of the common features of these works, so that the rather nondescript label 'animal literature' will acquire new significance.

I have limited the scope of this study to those literary works in which animals play a major role, namely *The Old English Physiologus*, *The Old English Phoenix*, *The Middle English Physiologus*, *The Owl and the Nightingale*, *The Thrush and the Nightingale*, *The Cuckoo and the*

[1] All English quotations from the Scriptures are taken from *Holy Bible: The New Scofield Reference Bible – Authorized King James Version.* 1967. Edited by C.I. Scofield. London: Oxford University Press.

Nightingale or The Book of Cupid, *The Parlement of Foulys*, *The Vox and the Wolf*, and *The Nun's Priest's Tale*. Thus, it is not my intention to take into consideration every occurrence of animals in vernacular English literature nor do I want to examine (once more) the often entangled and intricate relationship between English vernacular poems and their Latin, French, or Italian parallels and sources.[2] The wider literary environment of the individual poems will be taken into consideration where necessary, yet the main emphasis will be consciously placed upon the analysis of the role and function of animals in the selected works. This limitation is justified, insofar as the English vernacular poems discussed in this study are, on the one hand, more or less typical representatives of the different (international) genres of animal poetry, and may thus serve well as the basis of our analysis. On the other hand, they are also typically 'English' poems, displaying characteristics found nowhere else in European literature.[3]

In order to gain an insight into the literary lives of animal protagonists, we must not be afraid to ask seemingly simple questions. It is often harder to find an answer to those than to spend one's time pondering complex and apparently more challenging problems. Therefore, in spite of the wide variety of texts which feature animals in one way or another, the same simple questions have to be put time and again, namely: what is the function of the animals in this particular text? Why did the author settle on animals as protagonists and not on human beings or inanimate objects, as is the case in many fables and debates? And why did the author choose these particular animals and not others?

In order to find satisfactory answers to these questions, I will first briefly discuss the typical characteristics of the literary genre of each poem, its sources and parallels. Most of the works I deal with belong to literary genres for which the use of animals was not yet, or is still not, self-explanatory. In order to facilitate a critical discussion of the individual

---

2 As is well known, the literature written in the English vernacular is no more than the tip of an iceberg whose bulk consists of Latin and, after the Norman conquest, French texts. Both Latin and French texts written on English soil have thus to be included in the term 'medieval English literature', and make necessary the subcategory of 'medieval English vernacular literature' (i.e. literature written in the English vernacular). Our discussion of the sources and parallels of the individual texts will prove the indebtedness of English vernacular literature to its Latin and French cousins time and again. Unfortunately, the body of English vernacular literature has lost some of its substance as it has passed down to us. Wilson (1970) records the traces of many of the lost medieval vernacular works in England, and thus provides us with valuable information for our task.

3 Thus, for example, the fact that most of the Middle English bird debate poems have only birds as protagonists, and no human participants in the debate proper, is unique in medieval European literature.

works, I have arranged them into chapters which contain all the poems of the same or an affiliated genre. Following a rough chronology, I will start with the *Physiologus* tradition, then move on to the bird debate poems, and conclude with the beast fable and the beast epic. This order not only does justice to the chronological aspect, but it also has the great advantage of acquainting the modern reader with those medieval concepts which provide the basis for most – if not all – further developments in this field.

2. Historical Background

"What are we first? First animals; and next
Intelligences at a leap"
George Meredith (1828-1909), *Modern Love*, sonnet 30, ll. 1-2

The Human Perception of Animals before Christianity

A study of animals in medieval English vernacular literature is not so much a study of the real animals themselves, but rather an inquiry into the history and development of the human perception and conception of animals, and the relationship between human beings and beasts.[4] The rise of the hominids from their animal origins must have been a long and slow process, without sharp and sudden 'jumps'. There is no unique event which can be said to sever the link between the modern 'homo sapiens' and his or her animal ancestors.[5] Thus, for a long time – at least up to the early hunters and gatherers – the mental boundaries separating 'man' from 'animal' were by no means fully established.[6] Animals not only stand in close connection to

4 Munsterberg's (1980:99) comment on the bird poems is also true of other animal poems: "What these poems really record is man's changing view of his world, and in this sense, the subject is man himself." The most recent and also most comprehensive discussion of the relationship between medieval man/woman and animals is the study by Salisbury (1994).

5 See Potts (1991:56): "[T]races of the events and processes involved in becoming human span the entire fossil history of hominids. Those events at the end of this history are no less fundamental than those at the beginning."

6 See Maag (1983:8), who writes that, in the early societies of hunters and gatherers, "das Daseinsgefühl jener Menschen noch so sehr mit dem Tierreich verbunden ist, dass sich ihr Selbstbewusstsein noch nicht als ausschliesslich menschliches Bewusstsein hat konstituieren können. [....] Menschen [leben] in der Überzeugung [...], dass Tiere eine andere Erscheinungsform gleichzeitig lebender Menschen sein können." Harkort (1970:19) locates the origin of the anthropomorphisation of animals in this early period.

man – as indicated in the early Upper Paleolithic cave paintings – but at the same time they are also linked to the sphere of the divine.[7] As long as Maag's (1983:9) axiom of identity ('Every thing and every being is identical only with itself') has not yet gained universal validity, it is possible for a god to assume animal form, or for an animal to become the 'alter ego' of a human being.[8] In the centuries which are characterized by the rise of technologically and socially advanced civilizations based on agriculture and the domestication of animals, there is an increasing awareness of, and emphasis on, the gap which separates human beings from animals.[9] In the western world, the step from the shamanistic view of the world towards a more 'objective' one can be clearly seen in the teachings of the Greek philosophers of the sixth century B.C.[10] Furthermore, the settled way of life gave rise to a new way of looking at things which greatly differed from the shamanistic view of life in general, and of animals in particular. The wild

---

The curious composite beings that unite both human and animal elements can be seen as pointing in this direction, too. On composite beings, see Ackermann (1991:61) and Bossard (1991:14 and 33).

Stoob (1991:175-179) distinguishes three levels in the relationship between human beings and animals. On the first level, the hunters and gatherers experience their common dependency on nature as the predominant characteristic which links them to the carnivorous or predatory animals. On the second level, the agricultural revolution changes man's relationship with nature, since human beings now start to dominate nature. Those animals which are potential or partial competitors for food are increasingly subjected to moral judgment. Finally, the third level would ideally reestablish the original relationship between the hunters and gatherers and the animals on a higher level.

7 The Germanic animal symbolism relevant to this study and its connections with the human and the divine is discussed by Müller (1968) and Naumann (1991). Beck's (1965) is a more specialized study of Germanic boar symbolism.

8 On gods and demons in animal form, see Ackermann (1991:48-49). On the consequences of the increasing importance of the 'axiom of identity' in religion, see Maag (1983:11): "[Je] weiter das Identitätsaxiom für die gesamte Mentalität des Menschen zwingend wird, desto unmöglicher wird die doppelte, die tiermenschliche Göttervorstellung. Damit hat das Tier für den Menschen einen ganz grossen Teil seiner religiösen Relevanz eingebüsst."

9 The distance between man and animal in Anglo-Saxon times, however, was not yet as great as that in modern western civilization. See Metcalf (1970:75): "[D]ie alten Engländer standen inmitten der Tierwelt, nicht gesondert daneben." Animals were seen anthropomorphically: "Tiere dachten und empfanden wie Menschen" (Metcalf 1970:75). They were also always related to the human world: "Wann immer Tiere vorkommen, werden sie auf die Menschenwelt bezogen" (Metcalf 1970:75).

10 On the function of animals in shamanism, see Henking (1983). On the Greek natural philosophers, see Klingender (1971:82-84) and also A. Clark (1975:13-17) and Rowan (1991:284).

beasts which were the fellow-travellers of the hunters and gatherers disappeared from the ordered and often enclosed human universe of the village, and were noticed only when they encroached upon human territory.[11] Klingender (1971:84) sees the Aesopian fable as the product of this "disenchantment which took the magic out of the old animal imagery[.]"[12]

Christianity and the Religious-Allegorical Tradition

The establishment of Christianity as the main religious and cultural force within the majority of western civilizations rekindled the discussion of the status of human beings with regard to animals and monsters.[13] Since God created Adam and Eve "ad imaginem suam" (*Liber Genesis* 1,27[14]) and since they possessed immortal souls, they and their progeny had to be regarded as standing above all other creatures in the hierarchy of mortal beings. Thus, throughout the Middle Ages, the touchstone for humanity was the possession of a soul – this being the only valid criterion.[15] While the immortal soul set mankind apart, animals were still fellow creatures, insofar as they had been created at the beginning of the world, had dwelled peacefully with Adam and Eve in Paradise and had also participated involuntarily in the Fall.[16]

---

11 See Stoob (1991:196): "Durch selektive Wahrnehmung wird die Ausnahme, das Eindringen der Wildtiere in menschliche Siedlungen und Behausungen, zum zentralen Motiv." The exclusion of wild animals from the human universe as a result of the civilizational process seems to go hand in hand with the decrease in popular animal tales. Thus, Harkort (1970:13) notes that popular animal tales ('Tiervolkserzählungen') occur much more frequently in primitive societies than in technologically more developed ones.

12 Klingender (1971:93) notes that in *The Physiologus*, however, the animals "lost the veneer of philosophical sophistication with which the ancient naturalists had invested them and regained the imaginative appeal of folktales."

13 On the status of monstrous beings, see page 83ff. of this study. Linzey and Regan (1988) provide a general introduction to the Christian attitude towards animals in the light of the relevant biblical texts.

14 All references are, if not otherwise indicated, to the *Biblia Sacra Iuxta Vulgatam Versionem* (1983).

15 Salisbury (1994:162) notes that "in the high medieval world view [people had an] increasing tendency to define humanity and bestiality by actions." In spite of Salisbury's (1994) view that there was a certain blurring of the distinction between human and animal from the twelfth century onwards, the possession of an immortal soul remained the ultimate criterion for humanity. How to prove the rather elusive existence of this immortal soul, however, was another question.

16 Klingender (1971:154) quotes the apocryphal first century A.D. *The Life of Adam and Eve*: "The beasts, over whom thou didst rule, shall rise up in rebellion against thee, for

They were again going to live in peace with each other and with man in the Kingdom of God.[17] Thus, animals were considered part of the fallen yet divine creation imbued with meaning by its maker.[18]

For medieval literary man, who was either a cleric or a monk, animals were primarily part of the religious-allegorical cultural 'code'.[19] Cultural codes, however, are likely to change over the centuries. Thus, a medieval cleric would have difficulty in correctly reading a modern cultural code such as traffic signs. He might be able to guess the meaning of some of them, but without a helping hand he would never be able to arrive at the correct interpretation. We are in a similar situation when it comes to the meaning of animals in medieval literature. We may call each other 'ass', 'bitch', 'pig', 'fox', etc. in certain situations; we still refer to such a strange notion as the ostrich's presumed habit of sticking its head into the sand when sensing danger; or, especially in advertisements, we encounter animals as a means of creating favourable associations with certain products. Yet, this is practically all that is left of the rich and variegated tradition of animal symbolism.[20] Our modern culture has no use for the sophisticated allegorical and moral interpretations of animals. The beautifully carved or painted beasts and birds found in medieval manuscripts, or in the Romanesque, Gothic, and even later churches, remain nothing but beautifully carved or painted animals to

---

thou hast not kept my commandment[.]" With regard to the animals' loss of speech as a consequence of the Fall, Klingender (1971:154) refers to the likewise apocryphal *The Book of Jubilees or The Little Genesis* (also first century A.D.), which reports: "And on that day was closed the mouth of all beasts, and of cattle, and of birds, and of whatever walks, and of whatever moves, so that they could no longer speak: for they had all spoken with one another with one lip and one tongue[.]" See also JOSHUA SYLVESTER, who, in his early seventeenth century translation of *The Divine Weeks and Works of Guillaume de Saluste Sieur du Bartas*, writes: "Before that *Adam* did revolt from thee,/And (curious) tasted of the sacred Tree,/He lived King of *Eden*, and his brow/Was never blanck't with pallid feare, as now:/The fiercest Beasts, would at his word, or beck,/Bow to his yoake their self-obedient neck" (Sylvester 1979:268, ll. 197-202). On the consequences of the Fall, see also Linzey and Regan (1988:17).

17 See, for example, *Isaias Propheta* 11,6: "habitabit lupus cum agno et pardus cum hedo accubabit[.]" On the importance of animals as part of the concept of the 'Golden Age' in Antiquity, see Toynbee (1983:277-281).

18 On the medieval attitude towards nature in general, see Ganzenmüller (1914).

19 This is, of course, not true for medieval man/woman in general. For most people, as Salisbury (1994:128) has shown, "the functions of animals as labor and food continued to dominate the medieval imagination."

20 Rowan (1991:280), however, thinks that "one could be provocative and state that animal symbols appear to be [still] sufficiently important to humans to be placed on a level similar to God and sex."

most modern onlookers. Our ears are no longer attuned to this symphony in stone, wood, glass, and paint; the score is spread out in front of our eyes, yet we cannot transform it into music. This is not only due to the fact that modern man looks upon animals in a different way from medieval literary man – at least since the publication of DARWIN's *On the Descent of Man* (1871) and the books of his successors.[21] Animals, in the Middle Ages, were not seen as representing different aspects of the evolutionary force. For the time between A.D. 700 and A.D. 1400, we must assume – for our present purpose – the predominance of a religiously inspired 'devolutionary' view of animals and nature in general, i.e. the belief that the whole of sublunar creation fell from the original status of perfection after the Fall of Man. This 'devolutionary' view of the world stands, of course, in contrast to the modern concept of 'evolution'.[22] Those medieval scholars who dealt with animals did not yet have modern scientific methods and concepts at their disposal – and if they had had them, they would most probably not have used them. Theirs was a view of the world which is almost completely forgotten nowadays. Nature, the whole of creation, was, to them, a gigantic book written by the prime author of the universe, a revelation of the eternal truths for those who could 'read' the religious-allegorical code.[23] The English vernacular *Physiologus* tradition which is of importance for this study (comprising *The Old English Physiologus*, *The Old English Phoenix*, and *The Middle English Physiologus*) has its roots in this 'code'. Thus, in order to understand the basic Christian ideas about the function of animals in literature, we have to relearn the allegorical code by means of the *Physiologus* ABC.

The Secular Traditions

With the development of courtly society and the establishment of secular centres of learning and culture, new literary traditions were slowly established.[24] Soon, they started to counterbalance the predominantly

21 On DARWIN's scientific environment and the repercussions of his theories, see the preface to the 1966 German edition of *On the Descent of Man* by G. Heberer (1966).

22 See C.S. Lewis (1964:220).

23 This learned approach stands in contrast to the primitive one, as Munsterberg (1980:98) notes: "The primitive and the folk were preoccupied with the actual bird [or beast], because it had a direct bearing upon their lives. Medieval poets looked for revelations, reading birds [and beasts] as if they were signs which God had created to make his many teachings visible."

24 For a discussion of the animal fable tradition, which has been a popular genre since Antiquity, see page 173ff. of this study.

religious-allegorical use of animals in literature.[25] We can roughly distinguish four (mostly courtly) secular traditions.

The first one exploits the allegorical dimensions of animals for non-religious aims. Thus, the form of the 'bestiary', for example, is applied for very secular purposes, as can be seen in RICHARD DE FOURNIVAL's (†1260) *Li Bestiaires d'Amours*.[26] There, the poet makes use of the technique of interpreting the different animals in order to woo his courtly lady – who, ironically, wards off his advances by the same means.

On a different level, political poetry also profits from the symbolic potential of animals and harks back to the socio-critical roots of the beast fable, as can be seen in LANGLAND's political poem *Richard the Redeles*.[27] And finally, there is the richly varied heraldic use of animals in the later Middle Ages, which can be seen as a distant relative of the Germanic

---

[25] In order to illustrate the relevance of this development, I would briefly like to sketch the changes in the perception of the fox as an example. The fox itself did not change over the seven centuries (A.D. 700 to A.D. 1400) covered by this study. The real fox in its entirety and its scientific classification seems to have been of no interest to the English vernacular authors. Their interest was clearly limited to the discussion of what were, from the human perspective, its most central natural characteristics, namely its cunning and wiliness. These central traits then dominated human perception of the fox for centuries – and thus it is presented to us time and again as sly and cunning. Yet, even though all the different authors stress the same characteristics, we get a slightly different picture from each work, depending on the poet's approach. Thus, although the overall human perception of the fox remained basically stable, it nevertheless underwent a noticeable but gradual change, which can be seen in the fox's role in the different poetic traditions. *The Old English Physiologus*, probably because of its limited or fragmentary scope, does not provide us with a chapter on the fox, but the missing information can easily be inferred from one of the various contemporary Latin manuscripts of the *Physiologus* tradition; see, for example, the edition of the *Codex Bongarsianus 318* by Steiger and Homburger (1964). There, we find the interpretation of the fox as 'figura diaboli' – and it is this interpretation which is to be found in *The Middle English Physiologus*. Those of the English vernacular debate poems which make use of animals, however, seem to recruit their protagonists almost exclusively from the realm of birds, so that the fox does not occur in any of the known animal debates. It makes its re-appearance in the beast fable and the beast epic traditions, where it emerges as the approximate counterpart to the roguish hero of the continental *Renart* cycle. It – or now rather 'he' – is still the cunning and wily animal, but no longer the 'figura diaboli' of *The Physiologus*. The fox has been secularized, so to speak.

[26] The first troubadour to use religious animal symbolism in secular poetry was RIGAUT DE BERBEZIEUX (see Jauss 1977:180). A modern edition of *Li Bestiaires d'Amours* was published by Segre (1957). On RICHARD DE FOURNIVAL, see also Jauss (1977:187).

[27] See the edition by Skeat (1873). See also Klingender (1971:371). On the socio-critical roots of the Aesopian fables, see, for example, Salisbury (1994:106-107).

'totemistic' traditions. Klingender (1971:460) comments on this development:

> [F]or the medieval knight the beast-crest which he wore on his helmet, or the animal embroidered on his surcoat, to which Beowulf and his contemporaries still looked for magical protection, proclaimed a completely new and ethical ideal – the adoption of a chivalrous virtue to which the bearer of arms committed himself and his descendants.

Of the texts analysed in this study, the 'bird debates' (especially *The Owl and the Nightingale*, *The Parlement of Foulys*, and, to a lesser extent, also *The Thrush and the Nightingale* and *The Cuckoo and the Nightingale*) make 'secular' use of the symbolic dimensions of their protagonists.

The second secular tradition of importance treats animals from an (almost) purely practical point of view. It has its early forerunners in the 'practical textbooks' on hunting, fishing, animal medicine, etc. which enjoyed great popularity in the Hellenistic era and also in the days of the Roman Empire.[28] Even though this practical literary genre does not feature prominently among the vernacular writings of medieval Europe, we must assume the (orally transmitted) existence of what C.S. Lewis (1964:146) calls "practical zoology which had nothing to do with the Bestiaries." Skills like hunting, fishing, and the art of falconry did not normally have a place in the monastic universe – CHAUCER's Monk is the unworthy exception to this rule.[29] Such mundane pleasures, together with secular love, were the domain of the courtly man.[30] Thus, treatises on hunting in general or falconry in particular are products of the non-monastic secular environment of the courts. These works often combine straightforward natural history with first-hand experience. One of the earliest and, for centuries, best examples of this new category of 'practical textbooks' is FREDERICK (Fredericus) II's *De arte venandi cum avibus* (c. A.D. 1250).[31] Besides imparting the necessary knowledge for taming and training falcons and other birds of prey, FREDERICK makes critical use of the Aristotelian zoological works which were, by then, again available in the west, and often

---

28 See Balss (1947:11).

29 On the theme of the 'hunting cleric', see Rooney (1993:122-127).

30 On the status of hunting in medieval society, see Rooney (1993).

31 See the facsimile edition of the Ms. Pal. Lat. 1071, Bibliotheka Apostolica Vaticana, which was published in 1969. According to Rooney (1993:8, fn. 2), the Latin *De arte bersandi* (before A.D. 1250) is the earliest medieval hunting manual and the *La Chace dou cerf* (c. A.D. 1250) the first manual in a European vernacular.

contrasts ARISTOTLE's information with his own experience – which makes it a unique work for its time. GASTON III PHOEBUS, COMTE DE FOIX's *Livre de Chasse* (before 1391) is an example of a later treatise on hunting which also gives natural historical and practical information on the various species of game.[32] As far as Middle English is concerned, there are four hunting manuals still in existence, namely *The Art of Venery* by WILLIAM TWICI or TWITI (written sometime during the reign of Edward II, 1307-1327), which survives in both Anglo-Norman and English versions, *The Master of Game* (written c. 1406-1413 by EDWARD PLANTAGENET, DUKE OF YORK, and based on GASTON III PHOEBUS' treatise), *The Boke of Huntyng* (also written in the first decade of the fifteenth century), and *The Tretyse off Huntyng* (mid or late fifteenth century).[33] The tradition of (more or less) practical knowledge with regard to hunting also finds expression in Middle English literary texts, as Rooney (1993) has shown. Probably the best known application of specialized hunting knowledge is to be found in *Sir Gawain and the Green Knight*.[34] Yet in this instance, the realistic and detailed accounts of the deer, boar, and fox hunts acquire an additional 'symbolic' dimension in the narrative context of the parallel seduction scenes. Among the texts selected for this study, however, we have none which belong to this category.

The beast epic is the third secular tradition. It links up, on the one hand, with the shadowy beast tale tradition and, on the other hand, with the Aesopian fables. Its most famous representative, the *Roman de Renart*, very likely started out as a parody of the courtly epics. The beast epic tradition was open to various influences, and in the second half of the thirteenth century, we notice the incipient moral allegorization of this originally exclusively secular genre.[35] In Middle English vernacular literature, *The*

---

32 See the facsimile edition of MS. Français 616 of the Bibliothèque Nationale Paris, which was published in 1976. See also Klingender (1971:473).

33 Rooney (1993:7-20) provides a more detailed discussion of these Middle English hunting manuals. She (1993:19) concludes her analysis of the Middle English hunting manuals as follows: "We may conclude that the major preoccupations of the Middle English hunting manuals are not with the practical procedures of the hunt, but with the details of terminology, correct hunting calls, and categorisation of animals which are of little practical use."

34 See Tolkien and Gordon (1967:31-33, ll. 1126-1177; 37-38, ll. 1319-1371; 39-41, ll. 1421-1475; 43-45, ll. 1558-1622; 47-48, ll. 1690-1749; and 52-53, ll. 1893-1921). Rooney (1993:159-193) devotes an entire chapter to the discussion of the hunting passages in *Sir Gawain and the Green Knight*.

35 See Jauss (1977:50-123).

Vox and the Wolf and *The Nun's Priest's Tale* are representatives of this tradition.

The scientific classification of plants and animals constitutes the fourth secular tradition, which supplements both the religious symbolic and the secular (courtly) approaches to animals. In the western world, it had its origin in the writings of ARISTOTLE (fourth century B.C.).[36] The Christian predilection for the religious symbolic view of the world, however, relegated the scientific approach to second or third position. ARISTOTLE's works fell into oblivion in the Christian west; yet, the Arabic scholarly tradition kept them alive by means of translations and commentaries, so that in the thirteenth century, they made their re-entrance into western scholarship in this form. The extant texts are almost exclusively in Latin, so that no medieval English vernacular work of this tradition is known for the period of time covered by this study. Thanks to the rediscovery of the Aristotelian natural historical treatises, the scientific classification of nature increasingly gained in importance, even though it was centuries before it could claim predominance over the religious symbolic approach. It was in the field of botany that 'scientification' made rapid progress. For zoology, however, it proved more difficult to break free of its imaginative heritage.[37] The 'scientification' of our relation to nature and the increasing scepticism towards religious doctrine prepared the way for the assumption of a common origin for both man and animal. The religious concept of the 'soul', being of no scientific value today, has lost most of its importance, so that, even though we all feel the mental gap between ourselves and animals, modern science and philosophy no longer offer any clear 'test of humanity'.[38]

Since only relatively few Old and Middle English texts have survived, we only have representatives of the religious-allegorical/symbolic tradition, the beast epic, and some which belong, to a limited extent, to the secular-symbolic tradition.

---

36 See the edition by Barnes (1984). Balss (1947:9) comments on ARISTOTLE: "Bei ihm sind – mit Ausnahme der Abstammungslehre – schon alle Gebiete und Probleme behandelt, die auch die Biologie der Neuzeit bearbeitet[.]"

37 See Klingender (1971:491): "[I]t took centuries to free zoological textbooks from the supposed character-traits and habits which human beings had projected since time immemorial into the animal world."

38 See Rowan (1991:286).

THE *PHYSIOLOGUS* TRADITION

II. The *Physiologus* Tradition

"But ask now the beasts, and they shall teach thee; and the fowls of the air, and they shall tell thee[.]"
Job 12,7

1. Introduction

Turning our attention to the first tradition, i.e. the one of *Physiologus*, that found expression in the vernacular, we enter the world of the monastic scriptoria, where the rhythmic scratching of the goosequills on the parchment and the gentle shuffling of sandaled feet are the only sounds to be heard. Here the emphasis is not on animals native to the British Isles, animals which were known to the people from first-hand experience, but on exotic or even imaginary animals which populated the margins and illustrations of the manuscripts. The *Physiologus* tradition stresses the allegorical interpretation of its subjects, and thus has a tendency to move away from its originally (at least partially) naturalistic roots.[39]

With the (Re-)Christianization of the British Isles from A.D. 597 onwards, and the establishment of monasteries and churches, a new and, for our topic, crucial development set in. The spread of Latin literacy enabled England once more to join the civilized western world, after having been cut off from the mainstream of European culture for about two centuries.[40] Along with a host of different manuscripts, which were mainly of a clerical, liturgical, or scholarly nature (see Ogilvy 1967), there must have appeared a rather small Latin work on approximately forty animals, including some chapters on stones and plants, which is known to us by the title *The Physiologus*. In its different (enlarged) versions and editions, it enjoyed such great popularity throughout the Middle Ages that it was considered to be the

39 Brunner-Traut (1968:14) notes that the analysis of several *Physiologus* chapters yields the following result concerning its development: "(Naturbeobachtung –) Mythos – Naturlehre – Allegorie – das etwa ist das mehrstöckige Gebäude unseres Volksbuches[.]"

40 For a more detailed discussion of the effects of the (Re-)Christianization of England, see Mayr-Harting (1972).

most popular book of all, after the Bible.[41] Unfortunately, we have no definite idea as to when this 'menagerie on parchment' reached the shores of Anglo-Saxon England. All we know is that it must have arrived before the presumed date of composition of *The Old English Physiologus* (to be found in Krapp and Dobbie 1936:169-174 as *The Panther*, *The Whale*, and *The Partridge*), which is the oldest surviving vernacular adaptation in western Europe, and also before the compilation of *The Exeter Book* (Krapp and Dobbie 1936), which includes both *The Old English Physiologus* and *The Old English Phoenix*; this means sometime between A.D. 600 and c. A.D. 970.[42] The Latin *Physiologus*, from which all the known vernacular versions in the western world originated, certainly broadened the minds of its readers and showed a new way of looking at the world in general and at animals in particular. The oldest surviving Latin *Physiologus* manuscripts (Burgerbibliothek Bern, MS. 233 and MS. 318) date from the eighth or ninth century.[43] Yet, traces of what is most probably a Latin version can already be found in AMBROSIUS' *Hexaëmeron*, which points to a Latin *Physiologus* translation from the Greek original before A.D. 386.[44] Since *The Physiologus* is of such great importance for the understanding of the texts discussed both in this chapter and in later ones, a closer look at its history and characteristics is indispensable.

A Brief History of the *Physiologus* Tradition

Apart from odd chapters in various books on animal literature and an article on *The Physiologus* in *Paulys Real-Encyclopädie der classischen Altertumswissenschaften* by Perry (1941), there are four important works which provide an in-depth discussion of the history and the development of *The Physiologus*. The most recent ones are L. Frank (1971) and Henkel (1976). Lauchert (1889) and Wellmann (1930) are the oldest works consulted. Since the most recent authors have also taken the findings of their predecessors

---

41 See T.H. White (1959:232): "'Perhaps no book,' says E.P. Evans, 'except the Bible, has ever been so widely diffused among so many people and for so many centuries as the *Physiologus*.'" See also McCulloch (1960:15), Mermier (1989:70), and Seel (1992:89).

42 For the dating of *The Old English Physiologus* in relation to the other vernacular versions, see L. Frank (1971:24). For the dating of *The Exeter Book*, see Blake (1990: 1-2).

43 See Curley (1979:xx), George and Yapp (1991:2), Henkel (1976:21), McCulloch (1960:72), and T.H. White (1959:232).

44 See L. Frank (1971:13).

into account, we will mostly rely on them, and refer only occasionally to the less recent publications on the topic

It is generally assumed that the Greek original which was to become the model for the subsequent Latin versions was written in Alexandria, sometime in the second century A.D.[45] Alexandria was, at that time, the centre of learning, offering a wealth of Greek knowledge and traditional lore of the ancient East, allied to a taste for the allegorical exegesis of the Scriptures and nature.[46] Though no extant copy of the original Greek *Physiologus* is available to us, we are nevertheless able to make a well-founded guess at its form and content, based on the later Greek editions and the various extant translations into Latin and the vernacular languages. Thus, it contained approximately forty-nine chapters, forty-one of which dealt with animals or mythological beings, six with stones (including the pearl), and two with trees.[47] Many of the chapters were headed by a quotation from the Scriptures which either explicitly mentioned the subject to be treated in the following text, or contained a reference, or was linked to it in some other way.[48] Then, the typical chapter would open with the standard introductory sentence: 'The Physiologus has said concerning ...', continue with a description of the subject's natural habits, which was followed by the allegorical interpretation of the characteristics mentioned, and end with 'And so the Physiologus has spoken well concerning ...'.[49] The constant mention of this unknown authority called (the) 'Physiologus' (Greek for 'the one who knows about nature') is responsible for the fact that subsequent generations referred to the originally untitled work as *The Physiologus*.[50] Though we have no conclusive evidence, it is thought that the otherwise unknown PHYSIOLOGUS was the author of a book on the characteristics of animals, plants, and stones.[51] Thus, the work which we call *The Physiologus*

---

45 For an in-depth discussion of this problem, see Henkel (1976:2-3).

46 See Curley (1979:xvii), L. Frank (1971:4), and McCulloch (1960:17).

47 For a detailed list of the individual chapters, see L. Frank (1971:6).

48 See L. Frank (1971:10), Sbordone (1936), and Treu (1981). See also George and Yapp (1991:6), who characterize the pattern of a reconstructed *Physiologus* chapter as beginning with a quotation from the Scriptures, followed by a fact of 'natural history' about the habits or properties of the animal, and concluding with the moral, which is sometimes supported by additional biblical quotations.

49 See Treu (1981:15-16) and Wirtjes (1991:lxxii).

50 Curley (1979:x-xi) discusses the changing use of the Greek term 'physiologos' up to the beginning of the Christian era.

51 See Henkel (1976:12).

actually takes its title from an author of that name, who is quoted as the authority on the nature of animals, mythological beings, plants, and stones.

The text of each chapter can itself be divided into two quite distinct parts. On the one hand, we first get a description of some of the subject's (supposed) characteristic traits (often superscribed with the word 'natura' in later Latin versions), and afterwards there is an allegorical interpretation of these characteristics (the 'significatio', in the later Latin versions). Henkel (1976:12) therefore calls *The Physiologus* "die christliche Bearbeitung eines rein naturkundlich orientierten Werkes eines 'Naturkundigen'[.]" Henkel (1976:12-20), and especially Wellmann (1930), deal with the question of the possible authorship and the sources of the original *Physiologus*.[52] The rather complex, and ultimately rather inconclusive task of establishing the identity of the author and the connection between the various sources yields little useful information for our purpose. McCulloch (1960:19) reports that "[m]any of the *Physiologus* tales were the common property of the ancient world." The work of the Egyptian writer BOLOS OF MENDES (around 200 B.C.) on the nature of animals, plants, and stones, which was a distant ancestor of *The Physiologus*, provided an early focus for the various literary and oral traditions.[53] BOLOS' writings combined natural philosophy with mysticism, and depicted the world as a "Kosmos von Syn-[sic] und Antipathie" (Seel 1992:86). Considering the background of *The Physiologus*, it is, therefore, quite natural for it to contain many exotic animals, plants, or stones native to the region or mythology of the Near or even the Far East.[54]

Henkel (1976:18) makes an important observation about the way in which the author of *The Physiologus* edited his sources:

> Die Tierberichte des *Physiologus* lassen aber gegenüber den antiken Quellen und Parallelbelegen eine eindeutige Bearbeitungstendenz erkennen, die dahin zielt, die Geschichten für die Auslegung brauchbarer zu machen.

B. White (1954:21) adds that *The Physiologus* "was a typical product of Alexandrian-Judaeo-Christian theology and it was original only in its

52 It seems that even the medieval audience refused to accept the anonymity of this very popular work and thus ascribed it to many a famous person, such as ARISTOTLE, SOLOMON, AMBROSIUS, etc. (see Henkel 1976:39).

53 See Curley (1979:xxi), L. Frank (1971:5), Henkel (1976:15), McCulloch (1960:18), and Wellmann (1930:56).

54 For example the panther, the ant-lion, the hyena, the Peridexion tree, the diamond, the siren and the onocentaur, etc.; see L. Frank (1971:6) and McCulloch (1960:16-17). The prevalence of the exotic 'animals' has already been noted by Schmidtke (1968:55).

deliberate and extensive use of animal imagery to illustrate Christian doctrine."

Although the further development of *The Physiologus* is of no immediate concern to us, it is, nevertheless, of some importance for the discussion of the later works dealing with animals which were influenced by the tales and lore disseminated by the different versions of this work. The first significant changes in the relevant Latin versions of *The Physiologus* were effected through the inclusion of material found in ISIDORE's *Etymologiae* (c. A.D. 630). This great encyclopaedia referred, among other sources, to the information on animals originally taken from PLINY's († A.D. 79) *Naturalis Historia*, which had found its way into the Middle Ages via SOLINUS' *Polyhistor* (c. A.D. 218).[55] The greatest alteration, however, took place in the twelfth century, when the original number of chapters doubled. Most of these additions were taken from ISIDORE's *Etymologiae*. These enlarged versions of the Latin *Physiologus* are known as 'bestiaries', and their moving ever further away from the original source led to the modern critic's recognition of the bestiary as a genre of its own.[56] The most significant change of all occurred when the bestiaries started to incorporate chapters with no moral or spiritual exposition and dropped the biblical quotations, thus breaking, at least partially, with the pattern established by *The Physiologus*.[57] At the end of this development, we have, especially in England, the richly illustrated bestiary manuscripts which were intended less to illustrate points of Christian doctrine than to entertain both eye and mind with their exotic and often fantastic pieces of natural lore, and thus to satisfy what B. White (1954:23) calls the "human need for fantasy".[58] *The Physiologus* reached the climax of its popularity in the western world in the twelfth and thirteenth centuries, but subsequently disappeared as an independent text. Its subject matter, however, lived on in the bestiaries and, often after dropping the 'significatio' part, in the vast encyclopaedias.

After this short survey, we can summarize the relevant facts concerning the original *Physiologus* as follows:

---

55 See McCulloch (1960:28) and T.H. White (1959:233).

56 See also Henkel's (1976:24) definition: "Der Übergang zum Bestiarium erfolgte da, wo dieses Traditionsgut in irgendeiner Weise verändert wird; sei es durch zusätzliche Kapitel, Änderungen der Auslegung usw."

57 See McCulloch (1960:35) and A. Payne (1990:10).

58 For a more extensive discussion of the development from *The Physiologus* to bestiary and its consequences, see McCulloch (1960), Schmidtke (1968:62-65), and T.H. White (1959:230-270).

1) Many of the chapters were preceded by a quotation from the Scriptures (i.e. the Septuagint), and were thus based on the ultimate authority, the Word of God.[59]

2) Each chapter could be divided into a 'natura' and a 'significatio' part, thus reflecting the idea that the 'res' (i.e. the 'things' of this world) could be interpreted allegorically.

3) Many of the animals, mythological beings, plants, and stones were native to the Near or Far East. Therefore, most of them were not known in the West from first-hand experience.[60]

In order fully to appreciate the Old and Middle English texts which were the product of the *Physiologus* tradition, it is necessary to discuss in detail some of the notions which constitute the basis for the points mentioned above.

The Allegorical and Typological Interpretations

During the early formative period of Christianity, i.e. the first two or three centuries A.D., the proponents of the new religion often found themselves confronted with the problem of explaining the Scriptures to a pagan, yet nevertheless philosophically well-informed audience. People with such an intellectual background as those in the Hellenistic East were not very likely to accept the new religion without at least some critical questioning. Christianity's Jewish heritage added considerably to this problem, yet at the same time provided a solution in the form of the allegorical method of interpretation. First of all, there arose the question of how the texts of the Old Testament, which were still considered valid, could be reconciled with those of the New Testament. Secondly, the inclusion of the Old Testament within the corpus of fundamental Scriptures forced Christianity to find a solution to the problem with which every religion based on an ancient corpus of texts is confronted. Michel (1991a:206-207) describes the situation as follows:

59 For the typical structure of the *Physiologus* chapters, see Perry (1941:1096); for examples, see the translations by Curley (1979), Seel (1992), and Treu (1981), or the Greek 'originals' in Lauchert (1889:229-279) and Sbordone (1936).

60 See Schmidtke (1968:94): "Überhaupt ist anzumerken, dass die mittelalterliche Tierauslegung einen stark exotischen Einschlag hat, was allerdings bereits durch die Hauptquelle, den *Physiologus*, bedingt ist; die patristische Exegese steuerte dagegen eher Auslegungen vertrauterer Tiere (Hund, Hahn, Taube etc.) bei."

> Die im Textkorpus (in der Bibel) niedergelegten Texte stammen aus fernen Zeiten, während der Leser sich in einer Epoche befindet, die religionsgeschichtlich weitergeschritten ist, und in der andere lebenspraktische Erfordernisse anstehen. Anderseits hat der heilige Text einen bleibenden normativen 'An-Spruch'. Es stellt sich immer neu die Aufgabe, das Überkommene behutsam zu aktualisieren.

Even the earliest patristic writers already felt compelled to deal with this problem. Actually, "[d]er Drang nach dem Verstehen der Heiligen Schrift stellte die Christenheit vor die grösste [...] interpretatorische Aufgabe schlechthin, die damals von der Menschheit angegangen wurde" (Ohly 1958:2). The Bible, however, was not the only work which held a normative claim to the truth. The followers of the Stoa had already started to develop the allegorical method, in order to preserve the validity of Greek myths, as handed down by HOMER and HESIOD.[61] In pagan allegory, however, an event signified some abstract truth, and the literal level was often seen as not much more than a fancy disguise.[62] The Hellenistic Jew PHILO OF ALEXANDRIA (c. 25 B.C.-A.D. 40) then applied the allegorical interpretation to the Torah, thus conferring a quality of universality on Jewish law and history, and setting the pattern for the first Christian exegetes.[63] Most Christian exegetes, especially BASIL and AMBROSE, stressed – at least in theory – the importance of the literal meaning as the basis of all allegorical interpretation, and thus differed on a very important point from the pagan tradition.[64] The problem of how to adapt the oldest parts of the Bible (the Old Testament) to contemporary conditions could be satisfactorily solved by falling back upon the allegorical interpretative methods applied to the Torah. The fusion of two such different text corpora as the Old and the New

---

61 Smalley (1983:2) comments on this development: "The allegorical interpretation marks a stage in the history of any civilized people whose sacred literature is 'primitive'." On the allegorical interpretation of HOMER and VIRGIL, see Donahue (1960:65).

62 For the difference between pagan and Christian allegorization, see Donahue (1960:66), Schmidtke (1968:71), and Smalley (1983:viii). See also Klingender (1971:150), who writes about PHILO's view of the phenomena of nature as not existing for their own sake, "but only as clues to the deeper truths to which human thought must penetrate by the twin roads of rational abstraction and allegorical interpretation."

63 PHILO, quoting from the Scriptures, took events from the lives of the patriarchs, and then added an allegorical explanation. See Wellmann (1930:3).

64 The two most prominent representatives of the 'literal approach' were BASIL and AMBROSE. They defended the precedence of the literal truth of the Scriptures over the allegorical interpretation and, for example, affirmed the literal truth of disputed passages of the *Liber Genesis* and rejected the allegorical interpretation by ORIGEN and PHILO. See Klingender (1971:151).

Testaments, however, could not be achieved even with such a versatile method as the allegorical interpretation. Thus, the second pillar on which the biblical exegesis rests was erected: the typological interpretation. This type of interpretation, unlike the allegorical one, which links the literal level of a text to a spiritual level via allegorization, establishes a connection between a historical event, person, gesture, etc. before the birth of Christ (i.e. mostly an event from the Old Testament) with a somehow similar event, person, gesture, etc. after the birth of Christ (i.e. mostly from the New Testament). The event in the Old Testament is seen as the 'typus' or the 'figura', a prefiguration which finds its fulfillment in its 'antitypus' in the New Testament.[65]

ORIGEN (c. A.D. 185-254), who lived and taught in Alexandria and the surrounding cities, was one of the greatest proponents of the allegorical way of interpreting the Scriptures. His time and place of teaching roughly coincide with the assumed date and place of origin of *The Physiologus*, which points towards its early Christian exegetical background. Indeed, as stated above (page 20), *The Physiologus* was a product of the Alexandrian-Judaeo-Christian branch of theology. It is thus necessary to deepen our acquaintance with the exegetical methods outlined above, so that we are familiar with the methods which are also vital to the understanding of the allegorizations of *The Physiologus* proper, and of its vernacular translations.

The Allegorical Method of Interpretation[66]

The preceding chapter has touched upon some basic notions, which need to be made more explicit. First, we will deal with the suppositions which made the allegorical interpretation of a text like the Bible not only possible, but also very desirable.

1) The Bible was believed to be a divinely inspired piece of writing.
2) The Bible had a claim to universal truth, i.e. all of it was considered to be relevant for all men throughout all ages.
3) Both the early Christian and the medieval readers lacked a historical point of view in their appreciation of the Bible.
4) Several passages of the biblical text were obscure, contradictory, or even absurd if taken at face value.

---

65 Michel (1991a) gives a short and succinct overview of the allegorical and typological interpretative methods.

66 The following chapter is mainly based on Leclercq (1963), Michel (1991a), Ohly (1958:1-25), Schmidtke (1968), and Smalley (1983).

Whereas the given fact of the divinely inspired character of the Scriptures raised no problems, we have to consider more closely the idea of the 'universal relevance' of the Bible, which was, of course, closely connected to the first point; it implies that no part of the Bible is without relevance to the reader. Leclercq's (1963:94) observation concerning the monastic attitude towards the Scriptures also holds true for our discussion: "[The Bible] ist [...] nicht zuerst eine Quelle der Erkenntnis und wissenschaftlichen Forschung, sondern ein Mittel zum Heil; sie vermittelt das 'Heilswissen', 'salutaris scientia'." Thus, the reader may make use of every part of the Scriptures in his attempt to gain eternal salvation, and if the usefulness is not apparent at first glance, then it is clearly the reader's fault, and it is his duty to search for the underlying message.

The problems which arise when one tries to answer contemporary questions with the help of scriptural passages, especially those of the Old Testament, were made even more complex by the ahistorical point of view. The thought of considering the Old Testament to be exclusively or primarily the history of the Jews, or more precisely the Israelites, and therefore of abstracting from the historical facts and events in order to attain the relevant interpretation, was alien to the early Christian and the medieval readers alike. The Scriptures, along with many other Latin classical works, were treated rather like a contemporary text.[67] This lack of a historical point of view caused both the early Christian and the medieval readers to stumble over passages which hold no pitfalls for a modern audience.[68] Thus, seemingly absurd passages, metaphorical expressions from Hebrew poetic diction, and anthropomorphic descriptions of God, could not be summarily explained away as the product of a religion and culture distant in time and space. Thanks to its claim to universal truth, the Bible existed in an eternal 'hic et nunc', and there was no easy way out.

It is, therefore, all the more understandable that even the earliest patristic writers were at pains to find methods which led to an adequate understanding of the Bible. The Christian allegorical and typological methods of interpretation were the fruits of their labour. Later authors continued to develop and reflect on the allegorical method, and even though

---

67 C.S. Lewis (1964:68) observes that the exegetes had the "determination to find in all old texts what [their] own age accepts as Wisdom."

68 Though medieval man largely lacked a historical point of view in our sense of the word, he nevertheless had a way of his own of looking at things. See Ohly (1958:15): "Das vermeintlich perspektivelose Mittelalter hat die eigene, ihm gemässe Art der Perspektive in der spirituellen Transparenz des Seienden. [....] Sie ist die Perspektive im wahrsten Sinne, indem sie durch das Sichtbare auf das Unsichtbare, durch das 'Significans' auf das 'Significatum' hindurchschaut."

the various exegetes often differed in matters of secondary importance, they all observed the same basic set of rules. This allows us to present the allegorical method in an abridged and simplified manner, yet one which is adequate for our purpose.

The symbolic quality of the language provides the starting point for the more complex notion of the symbolic quality of things: words (i.e. sounds or the written letters or signs) have the ability to express things or ideas. The relation between word and thing, however, is quite arbitrary and, at least theoretically, up to the user (there is no inherent necessity to call a chair a 'chair'). The human sphere of influence normally ends with the choice of names or labels for the 'res'. The 'res' themselves are given, and man's power over them, at least since the Fall, is very limited. The Bible, however, possesses an additional dimension. Not only do the words of the Scriptures signify something (i.e. a thing, an idea, or an event), but these things, ideas, or events in turn stand for an idea or an event on a spiritually higher level. Because of this, biblical language can be said to have a twofold quality: on one level, we read the words which refer to the 'res' of the human world; and on another level, we have the same 'res' of the human world which refer to spiritual matters. Thus, God talks to man, not only via the words of the Bible, but also with the help of the 'res-code'.[69] It may be noticed that, up to this point, the Christian allegorical interpretation can correctly be applied only to the Bible, since it is the only book with both human and divine authorship.[70] It is, furthermore, important that only dogmatically sound ideas can be illustrated or sustained by means of allegorization. Allegorical interpretation can never be used as a means of conclusively proving the dogmatical correctness or incorrectness of a point of view, or for introducing a new dogmatic truth.[71] All it can do is to help

---

69 See Ohly (1958:11-12): "[D]ie Bedeutung der Worte ist durch den Menschen gesetzt und dient der Willensäusserung des Menschen. Die Bedeutung des Dinges aber ist durch Gott gesetzt. Durch das Wort spricht der Mensch zum Menschen, durch das Ding spricht Gott zu dem Menschen, und das Wort Gottes in den Dingen gibt es zu verstehen[.]"

70 For the twofold authorship of the Bible, see Bloomfield (1958:77) and Smalley (1983:300). For the limitation of the Christian allegorical method to the Scriptures, see Bloomfield (1958:79): "ST. EUCHER OF LYONS is apparently the only patristic author who admitted that secular works could have levels of meaning. All the other Fathers or theologians I have been able to examine, when they do not tacitly assume its applicability only to Scripture, reserve the method exclusively for biblical exegesis." On the use of the allegorical method in secular writings in the later Middle Ages, see Huppé and Robertson (1963) and Kaske (1960).

71 Especially the exegetes and theologians of the twelfth and thirteenth centuries stressed this point. See Smalley (1983:xv): "ST. THOMAS demonstrated that these [i.e. the allegorical interpretations] could not serve in theological argument: 'theologia symbolica

reconcile the obscure and difficult passages of the Scriptures with the truths already established. In order to take the two interpretative steps from sound/word to the 'res', and subsequently from the 'res' to the spiritual meanings, the help of the 'septem artes liberales' was considered to be necessary.[72] The following graphic illustration shows how these 'scientific implements' were used so that the correct allegorical interpretation was attained. Here, I am indebted to Paul Michel, whose depiction of the allegorical interpretative process provided the starting point for my own version.[73] The illustration is an idealized model and does not correspond to the often unreflected application of the allegorical method in exegetical works.[74] It does, however, give us a fairly good idea of the basic concepts underlying the allegorical method of interpretation.

non est argumentativa'[,]" and Smalley (1983:261): "[LANGTON] has a test for the content of allegory. It must conform to the Christian faith. [....] Hence allegory is regarded as illustrating and confirming established theological truth. It does not constitute proof in itself[.]" On the primacy of the literal sense, see also Donahue (1960:78).

72 Kolb (1970:586) comments: "Nicht schon das frühe Christentum, sondern erst die späteren Kirchenlehrer (wie HIERONYMUS, AUGUSTIN, CASSIODOR) haben der christlichen Lehre zu ihrer Aufschliessung und Systematisierung das ausserbiblische Wissensgut zugeführt, das sich das Mittelalter für seine eigenen geistigen Intentionen zunutze machte."

73 See Michel (1991a:211).

74 See Bloomfield (1958:81): "Finally, the assumption of the organized use of the symbolic [i.e. the allegorical] method in medieval literature is essentially simplistic. It imposes a non-historical order and system on what was in fact disordered and unsystematic."

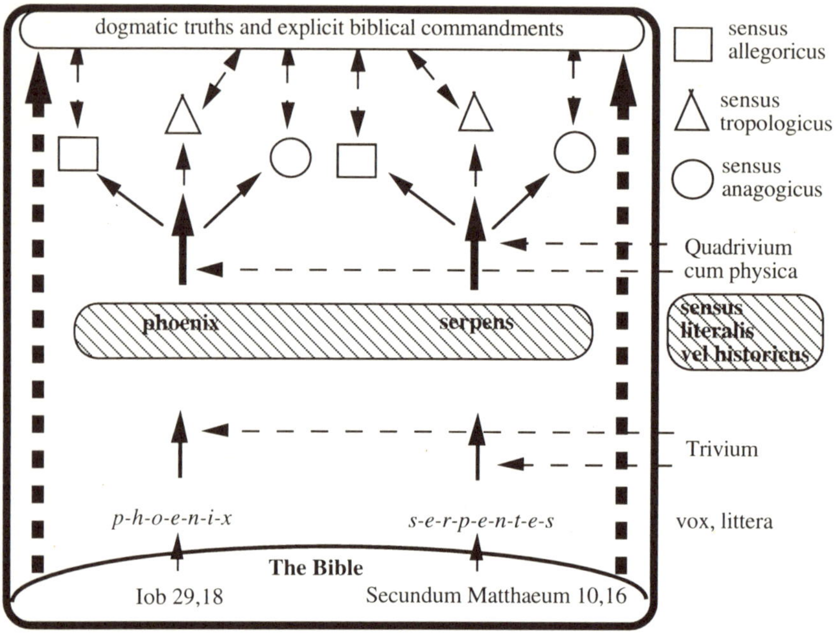

Once more, we notice the overwhelming importance of the Bible for our task. The Scriptures not only provide the basis of the literal and allegorical interpretation, but at the same time they are the object of the exegetical endeavour. Even the use of the allegorical method itself was assumed to be proven by the Scriptures. The model allegorizations in *Ad Corinthios I* 10,1-6 and *Ad Galatas* 4,21-31 provided the biblical examples, and thus justified the use of the allegorical method. In addition, the exegetes applied the very same technique of allegorical interpretation to some biblical passages, and thus provided a justification for its further application.[75] The basic concepts of faith gained directly from the Bible enable the exegete to interpret the less clear passages by means of the concepts already safely established. This is represented in the graphic depiction above by the bold

75 The biblical passages chosen were, for example, *Secundum Matthaeum* 2,11 (the gifts of the three magi were interpreted as the three 'sensus spirituales') and *Secundum Iohannem* 2,1-10 (the transformation of water into wine at the Marriage of Kanaa was seen as the bestowal of new spiritual meaning upon the Old Testament). Michel and Schwarz (1978) is an illuminating introduction to the way in which medieval exegetes worked.

broken line. We have, for example, the concept of corporal resurrection, which is mentioned explicitly in the New Testament (*Ad Corinthios I* 15) and therefore has to be accepted as a dogmatic truth. On the other hand, we have the passage concerning the 'phoenix' in the Old Testament.[76] Its relevance for the Christian reader is not quite clear, and, if the claim of the universal validity of the Bible is to be kept up, then an interpretation is needed. The exegete now has the task of relating this passage, which is rather obscure in its spiritual dimension, to one of the categories of truths already established, which provide the basis for the 'sensus allegoricus', the 'sensus tropologicus' (sometimes called the 'sensus moralis'), and the 'sensus anagogicus'.[77] The 'sensus allegoricus' illustrates, often by typological interpretation, the importance of a passage in the context of the plan of salvation ('Heilsgeschichte') and its relevance for Christian teachings.[78] Thus, the 'phoenix' in our table can be allegorically seen as the 'typus' of Christ, since both rose from the dead after three days.[79] The 'sensus tropologicus (vel moralis)' provides the Christian with guidelines for his or her behaviour in this world, and thus relates the passage in question to the 'simplex moralitas' already in existence, i.e. the precepts which can be found on the literal level (for example the Ten Commandments in *Liber Exodi* 20,3-17). Finally, we have the 'sensus anagogicus', which hints at things to come, i.e. the eschatological dimension. All of these 'sensus' may be found in a single biblical passage or word.[80] AUGUSTINE OF DACIA († 1282) sums up the different dimensions of the Scriptures in his famous gnomic verse:

> Littera gesta docet, quid credas allegoria,
> Moralis quid agas, quo tendas anagogia.[81]

---

76 See Kantrowitz (1964:2), who refers to this particular pre-Vulgate reading of *Liber Iob* 29,18.

77 I use the term 'allegorical' as an equivalent to 'spiritual' and as the umbrella term for all three 'sensus spirituales'. For the allegorical interpretation proper, the term 'sensus allegoricus' is employed.

78 For a more detailed examination of the typological method, see page 31f.

79 The three day span from the death to the resurrection of the phoenix, however, is not biblical and can only be found in the *Physiologus* tradition.

80 The best known example to illustrate the fourfold meaning of a word is 'Jerusalem'. On the literal level ('sensus historicus'), it denotes the city of Jerusalem in Israel; on the spiritual level, it stands for a) the Church ('sensus allegoricus'), b) the human soul ('sensus moralis vel tropologicus'), and c) the 'Heavenly Jerusalem' or 'City of God' ('sensus anagogicus').

81 See Michel (1991a:212). I am aware of the fact that the gnomic verse is an anachronism in our context. Yet, since it expresses the relevant ideas in a succinct way, I have chosen

Thus, the Bible constitutes the alpha and omega of the allegorical universe, and we will now proceed to examine some of the intervening letters of this 'allegorical alphabet'.

The textual sciences of the 'artes', i.e. grammar, rhetoric, and, to a lesser extent, dialectics, which were later united in the so-called 'trivium', were applied on the level of the 'vox' or 'littera'; they were used in the process of eliciting the meaning of difficult words or idiomatic expressions.[82] A medieval reader would first try to establish the use of the word *s-e-r-p-e-n-t-e-s* in the text. Was it a metaphor, a rhetorical figure, or an idiomatic expression? Which 'serpens' was meant in *Secundum Mattheum* 10,16? Was it the 'serpens antiquus' (= 'Satanas' in *Apocalypsis Iohannis* 12,9), the 'serpens' which seduced Eve (for example *Liber Genesis* 3,1), the 'serpentes' which were encountered by the Israelites in the wilderness (see *Liber Numerorum* 21,6-7), or the 'serpens aeneus' forged by Moses to cure the stung Israelites (*Liber Numerorum* 21,9), to name just a few of the possibilities? The same thing happened with the word 'phoenix'. Here, however, the exegete had to deal with the additional problem of homophony. The Greek word of the *Septuagint*, 'phoinix', could be translated as either 'palm tree' or 'bird phoenix'. Since both versions would have made sense, it was up to the exegete, if he was aware of the homophony, to decide which version was more suitable.[83] After having (more or less) established the meaning of the word in question by means of an investigation into its use, the reader would then proceed to the level of the 'res'. Things and events are located on the level of the 'sensus litteralis vel historicus', which means they are, on this level, taken at face value. The 'trivium', having provided the meaning of the word, now has to be supplemented by the knowledge of the 'quadrivium cum physica', i.e. the ancient and medieval equivalents and predecessors of the natural sciences. The 'quadrivium cum physica', or "Dingbedeutungskunde" (Ohly 1958:7), is now called upon to provide the necessary information concerning the 'res' in question.[84] As a rule of thumb,

---

to include it here. ST. THOMAS AQUINAS gives us yet another version of this quatrain and thus testifies to its popularity: "Littera gesta docet;/ Quid credes, allegoria,/Moralis, quid ages;/Quid speres, anagogia" (Klingender 1971:266).

82 M. Gerhardt (1970:234) comments on the difficulties which the exegetes-cum-translators were likely to encounter: "Les traducteurs [...] ne sont pas toujours sortis des difficultés que présente le vocabulaire, surtout celui de l'Ancien Testament."

83 Some of the pre-Vulgate Latin translations of the Bible give, for *Liber Iob* 29,18, the reading 'bird phoenix', whereas the Vulgate decided in favour of 'palma', i.e. 'palm tree' (see Kantrowitz 1964:2).

84 I have added the 'physica', since the 'quadrivium', comprising 'geometria', 'arithmetica', 'astronomia', and 'harmonia (musica)', does not include the biological and

every 'res' has as many meanings as it has characteristics. Smalley (1983:258) comments: "The spiritual interpretation must be based on the properties of the thing it signifies. The exegete shows his science by knowing these properties, his skill by adapting them." This is now the point at which, in our special case, *The Physiologus* comes in. It is, indeed, primarily a collection of knowledge of the 'quadrivium cum physica' type. The biblical quotations at the beginning of many chapters provide the 'sensus litteralis vel historicus', and the 'natura' part, extracted from the works of authors who combined animal lore, myth, and scientific information, supplies the information on the characteristics of the 'res'. This information was nearly always taken out of books and hardly ever acquired by first-hand experience, a problem with which we will deal later on.[85] The 'significatio' part is the spiritual interpretation of the 'sensus litteralis vel historicus', on the basis of the information given in the 'natura' part. The 'literary' quality of the whole procedure cannot be stressed too strongly. Passages or words in 'the Book' (the Bible) are explained with the help of information gathered from other books (which, in turn, are more often than not compilations, too) and interpreted, using categories gained from 'the Book', in an allegorical way. Thus, it is rather a 'bookish' affair, and the reality of the physical world hardly ever intervenes.

The Typological Method of Interpretation

Even the early exegetes developed the method of typological interpretation, in order to harmonize the often differing corpora of the Old and the New Testaments.[86] They made use of the fact that the Old Testament often displays structural or even verbal parallels with the New Testament.[87] The passage about Abraham's intended sacrifice of Isaac (*Liber Genesis* 22,1-14), for example, showed not only structural parallels with the passion of Christ, but also implicit verbal parallels, at least in the Latin commentaries.

---

zoological branches of knowledge that are relevant for us. For the discussion of the terms 'trivium' and 'quadrivium', see Piltz (1982:25-26); for 'physica', see Piltz (1982:113-114).

85 This phenomenon is obviously not limited to the occidental tradition. Eisenstein (1990:183) notes a similar development in medieval Arabic-Islamic zoology.

86 Another application of the typological method was its use in the early missionary efforts of the Christians towards the Jews. It was also employed as an apologetic instrument with which to set Christianity apart from its Jewish origins. Furthermore, it could be used to complete the often defective tradition of the New Testament, by projecting parallel scenes from the Old Testament on to the gaps in the textual tradition of the Gospels (see Michel 1991a:213-215).

87 See Leclercq (1963:123).

Thus, on the one hand, Isaac had to carry the wood for his own sacrifice (*Liber Genesis* 22,6), which is the 'typus' for Christ's carrying the cross (for example *Secundum Iohannem* 19,17; structural parallel). On the other hand, Isaac was laid between the 'cornua' of the altar, whilst Christ's limbs were transfixed onto the 'cornua crucis' (this originally structural parallel was later extended into a verbal parallel by the commentaries, which made the implicit verbal parallels explicit).[88] Michel (1991a:214) uses the term "gesteigerte Rekapitulation" to characterize the relation between the two text corpora; this expresses the notion that an event or thing in the New Testament is somehow similar to another event or thing in the Old Testament, which can be seen as a shadowy predecessor of a thing or event to come. The New Testament event or thing is considered to be of greater salvational value than its Old Testament counterpart, since it is the fulfillment of the Old Testamental announcement. The historicity of the Old Testament event or thing, however, is not doubted, and possesses, if it is of interest, a historical value of its own.[89] Thus, the Old Testament is looked upon as an anticipation of the New Testament, which is, in turn, used as a guideline for interpreting the Old Testament. The following graphic illustration shows the basic concept of the typological interpretative method 'in nuce'.[90]

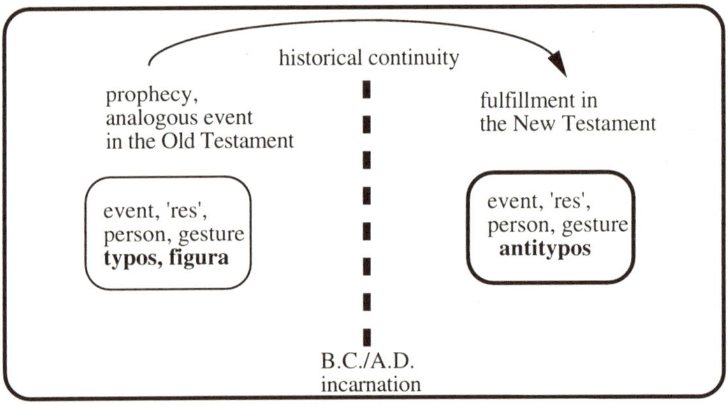

[88] A detailed typological interpretation of this passage can already be found in OTFRID OF WEISSENBURG's *Liber Evangeliorum* (Erdmann 1957:72-74, ll. 31-86), composed c. A.D. 870.

[89] The ahistorical point of view, which made the historical evaluation of the Old Testament obsolete, has been mentioned above, page 25.

[90] The graphic illustration is an adaptation from Michel (1991a:215).

The 'Liber Naturae'

Although the Christian allegorical method was, at first, strictly limited to the interpretation of the Bible, it was only a question of time until new subjects were found to which it could be applied. This was all the more so, since the pagan Alexandrian method of allegorization had already disconnected itself from the texts, and had been used for interpreting the 'res' of the visible world. Since the Christian exegetes insisted on the validity and divine authorship of the biblical texts, and thus also valued the 'littera', in contrast to their pagan predecessors, they could not simply unfasten the ties which tightly bound the allegorical method to the Scriptures.[91] Allegory was not to be underestimated, and once it was used outside the dogmatically sound biblical framework, it was a potentially dangerous tool.[92] The notion of the 'Book of Nature', however, provided the necessary means to bridge the gap between the universe of the Bible and the human world.[93] TERTULLIAN (A.D. 160-220) was among the early Christian proponents of this notion.[94] We would have neither *The Old English Phoenix*, nor *The Old English Physiologus*, nor *The Middle English Physiologus* in its current form, if it were not for the mediating notion of the 'Book of Nature'. Even though most of the passages relating to the idea of nature being a book written by God were from post-Anglo-Saxon times, they nevertheless reflect, to a considerable degree, the changing presuppositions of the *Physiologus* tradition. Traces of the new idea, or of the older Alexandrian notion, could already be found in the reconstructed original version of the Greek *Physiologus*. Nearly all of the chapters are based on a Scriptural passage, yet

---

91 See Curtius (1961:308). Schmidtke (1968:128) writes: "Streng genommen rechtfertigt die Theorie vom geistlichen Sinn der Schrift nur die Auslegung der in der Bibel erscheinenden 'res'. Da aber sowohl Schöpfung als auch Bibel als Werk Gottes erschienen, war im Bereich der Naturdinge der Übergang von den in der Bibel angesprochenen Dingen zu der Gesamtheit der geschaffenen Dinge als Möglichkeit von Anfang an angelegt, konnte bibelfremder Stoff relativ leicht in den Prozess allegorischer Naturbetrachtung einbezogen werden." On this point, see also Curley (1979:xiii-xv).

92 ORIGEN, one of the greatest proponents of Christian allegory, and the Calabrian abbot JOACHIM OF FLORA were both accused of heresy and are just two prominent examples of the dangers which lie in the use of the allegorical and typological methods of interpretation. For JOACHIM OF FLORA, see Smalley (1983:287). However, as ÆLFRIC already pointed out in his *Preface to Genesis* (Crawford and Ker 1922:76-80), reading the Bible without the relevant allegorical or typological 'know-how' could also lead to problems.

93 For a discussion of the book as a symbol, see Curtius (1961:306-352, especially 323-329).

94 See Schmidtke (1968:123).

the biblical foundation of at least some of the subjects remains doubtful (for example the chapters on the 'Serra' or on the 'Ichneumon'). These could, indeed, be the first tentative and exploratory steps in the direction of a more liberal use of the allegorical method. The biblical foundation of such an application to the 'res' of this world was given in *Ad Romanos* 1,20: "invisibilia enim ipsius a creatura mundi per ea quae facta sunt intellecta conspiciuntur[.]"[95] Schmidtke (1968:119) comments on this passage:

> Die Auslegung auf die Gesamtheit der erschaffenen Welt war deshalb seit patristischer Zeit allzeit als Möglichkeit gegeben. [....] Die Römerbriefstelle bot Anlass und Legitimation zur Übernahme verwandt erscheinender Vorstellungen der hellenistischen Philosophie in den christlichen Bereich.

Thus, we find the doctrine of the possibility of knowing God by means of His creation with patristic and medieval Doctors of the Church, though after its first appearance, it took several centuries for the idea of contemplating the world in an allegorical way to be generally accepted.[96]

The term 'Book of Nature' may very well evoke the wrong associations with modern readers, and it is therefore necessary to clarify its meaning for the Middle Ages. The exegetes did not suddenly begin to allegorize their immediate surroundings – or at least, if they did, we do not know about it.[97] Actually, the term 'Book of Nature' holds the key to the understanding of their way of allegorizing nature. The exegetes turned first, and often exclusively, to the available books on animals, plants, stones, etc. to learn about nature.[98] This should not strike us as too strange a thing to do, since a

---

95 "For the invisible things of him from the creation of the world are clearly seen, being understood by the things that are made[.]"

96 See Schmidtke (1968:127): "Die gedankliche Verbindung von Bibelallegorese und symbolischer Auffassung der Welt scheint bei AUGUSTIN noch nicht völlig vollzogen zu sein."

97 This final phase in the development of the Christian allegorical method can be observed in the anecdote about Anselm of Canterbury, which is related in the *Vita Anselmi* by the monk EADMER OF CANTERBURY (see Schmidtke 1968:142): while Anselm is travelling overland, a hare seeks refuge from the hunting dogs beneath his horse. Anselm immediately interprets this incident allegorically, and compares it with the situation of our soul after death, which will be beleaguered by devils. On the allegorical interpretation of real-life events by Anselm, see also Ganzenmüller (1914:175). The late fourteenth century poem *By West, Under a Wilde Wode-Side* (Luria and Hoffman 1974:162-166), which is a meditation on the theme of 'mercy', also starts from a (supposedly) 'animal' real-life event.

98 See T.H. White (1959:257): "The reaction of the patristic writers, when puzzled by an animal, was to reach for the nearest copy of PLINY, not to examine the animal itself, and,

large portion of our knowledge of natural subjects stems from books, too. The difference, however, lies in the quality of the books at one's disposal, and the mental attitude towards the information gained from the written sources.

Sources

An average monastery library during the Dark Ages could not be expected to contain more than a dozen-odd volumes, most of which were of a clerical character.[99] The most reliable works on animals, however, were ARISTOTLE's books, which were not known in the West until the thirteenth century.[100] Yet, assorted fragments of Aristotelian knowledge were handed down to the medieval scholars via the works of PLINY THE ELDER († A.D. 79), SOLINUS (c. A.D. 218), and, most important of all, ISIDORE OF SEVILLE (c. A.D. 630). Together with *The Physiologus*, the various commentaries on the Scriptures, and the Bible itself, they represented practically all the possible written sources from which a medieval reader before A.D. 1220 could gather information on a zoological subject. Prior to the translation of ARISTOTLE's works, "they had had little else but encyclopaedias compiled in the late Empire and early middle ages, when natural science had long been in decline, marvel, legend and symbol with a small admixture of fact" (Smalley 1983:308).

---

if PLINY's two thousand sources failed them, they would seek for a linguistic relationship in the animal's name."

99 Larger monasteries and, later on, cathedral schools, of course, had a greater number of works available. For an outline of the books known to the English between A.D. 597 and 1066, see Ogilvy (1967). See also Wilson (1958).

100 The relevant works *De generatione animalium*, *Historia animalium*, *De motu animalium*, *De partibus animalium*, and *De progressu [*or: *incessu] animalium* were translated from Greek into Latin by the Flemish Dominican WILLIAM OF MOERBEKE, who lived c. A.D. 1215-1286 (see Grant 1974:40). His translations were preceded by MICHEL SCOTUS' work *De animalibus* (no later than 1220). Since the Aristotelian writings had been saved from oblivion by the Arabian scholars, Europe first came into contact with ARISTOTLE's works in Arabic translation. Thus, MICHEL SCOTUS' treatise is a translation from Arabic into Latin of the Aristotelian zoological works *Historia animalium*, *De partibus animalium*, and *De generatione animalium*. A modern English translation of ARISTOTLE's works on animals can be found in Barnes (1984).

Mental Attitude

For several centuries, the focus of the intellectual elité's endeavours was on the interpretation, explanation, reading, and copying of the Scriptures. Christianity developed, as perhaps only the Jewish civilization had done before, into a 'culture of the Book'. The high esteem which 'the Book' enjoyed, influenced attitudes towards books in general. The arduous, time consuming task of copying or compiling a book added to this. C.S. Lewis (1964:5) expresses medieval man's attitude towards books as follows:

> If their culture is regarded as a response to environment, then the elements in that environment to which it responded most vigorously were manuscripts. [....] [T]he Middle Ages depended predominantly on books.

Indeed, as Smalley (1983:308) puts it, "[s]cientific studies [were] an affair of the library rather than the laboratory." The fact that the medieval compiler took his science impartially from the poets and the philosophers did not help much to improve the quality of scientific knowledge from a modern point of view. The same hermeneutical approach was used for both natural history and fiction, and "beide [waren] in einer Gesamtvorstellung von der Welt unter theologischen Prämissen aufeinander bezogen" (C. Meier 1978:117). The medieval model of the world and the universe was not based on an empirical inquiry into the immediate environment, but "built out of the real, or supposed, agreement of any ancient authors – good or bad, philosophers or poets, understood or misunderstood – who happened, for whatever reason, to be available" (C.S. Lewis 1964:19). Thus, "[t]he most spectacular differences between the Medieval Model and our own concern astronomy and biology" (C.S. Lewis 1964:219). The medieval model of biology, and of animals in particular, relied, as we have seen above, on the authority of books, whereas our model is supported by a wealth of empirical evidence. The focus was on the Bible, and the world was more often than not seen through the grid provided by the Scriptures.[101] "The Bible was the most studied book of the middle ages" (Smalley 1983:xxvii), and the study of the Scriptures – in the 'original' Latin tongue – was considered to be the highest branch of learning. Thus, for example, BEDE was not primarily known as the author of the *Historia ecclesiastica gentis Anglorum*, but rather

---

101 The notions which had originally been shaped by the biblical tradition lived on, and exerted their influence even after the Scriptures had lost their predominant position. Thus, as Harrison (1960) has shown, the 'Birds of Paradise' were identified with the phoenix in the sixteenth century and for a long time after. Literature and myth had obviously prepared the explorers to see new and hitherto unknown birds within the framework of traditional knowledge.

for his commentaries on the Bible.[102] In the monasteries, the prescribed and repeated daily reading of the Latin Bible, either as part of the divine service, or as the 'lectio' during meals, or for private study, caused both the language and the content of the Scriptures to permeate medieval thought. The monks meditated on the words of God, and assimilated the Scriptures by means of 'ruminatio', i.e. the repeated, slow, and almost meditative reading of the Bible.[103] Yet, the monks were not the only ones who studied the Bible in detail. Smalley (1983:xxx) states that "[t]eachers in the middle ages regarded the Bible as a school book par excellence." This meant that the 'clerici' had also made first-hand acquaintance with the Scriptures. Laymen, however, handicapped by illiteracy, had to make do with what they could glean from sermons. Indeed, the Church had a safe monopoly on learning, and we can rule out Bible study by laymen until about 1300. Thus, it is possible, for our purpose, to assume a fairly extensive and intensive knowledge of the Bible for monks as well as for clerics throughout the Middle Ages. A single reference to an animal name in the Bible was sufficient to recommend it to the constant attention of commentators and scholars, whereas a familiar animal such as the squirrel was often neglected, because the Bible did not mention it.[104] Yet, it would be wrong to think that all knowledge of animals was reduced to this special form of literary erudition. C.S. Lewis (1964:146) observes that "there was a practical zoology which had nothing to do with the Bestiaries."[105] However, this first-hand knowledge was probably handed down by word of mouth, only very rarely finding its way into a (monastic) scriptorium and on to parchment. A manuscript like FREDERICK II's *De arte venandi cum avibus* (c. A.D. 1250) was the great exception to this rule.[106] This treatise, the first one based

---

[102] See Smalley (1983:xxvii).

[103] See Leclerq (1963:88). It may be interesting to note that the monks took a term normally used to describe a characteristic action of the cow, in order to describe their meditative reading.

[104] See M. Gerhardt (1970:234). At least once, however, the squirrel was also allegorically interpreted, as Huppé and Robertson (1963:25) observe: "ALEXANDER NECKAM attributes symbolic values to the squirrel, even though there is no squirrel in the Scriptures."

[105] See, for example, the passage in *Sir Gawain and the Green Knight* (Tolkien and Gordon 1967:37-38, ll. 1325-1361 and 1967:44-45, ll. 1605-1614), where the skilful drawing of the slain deer and boar is described.

[106] Grant (1974:658) praises *De arte venandi cum avibus* as "a masterpiece of objective and concise scientific description. [The author] relied mostly on his own personal experience for the details of the bird habits and structure. Indeed, in the preface to his treatise, he was quite critical of ARISTOTLE[.]"

mainly on empirical observation, was written in the cosmopolitan atmosphere of the Norman Sicilian court, where the Greek, Arabic, and Latin cultures met. Furthermore, it was about a topic which did not belong to the monastic sphere of life.

The most important factor in the discussion of medieval zoological knowledge, however, is not its literary or practical quality, but its purpose: it all depended on the genre of the text and on its focus. No one would use a bestiary as a hunting manual, nor would anyone use the latter for edificational purposes.[107] Henkel (1976:145) observes that

> im Bereich der nicht primär geistlich ausgerichteten Wissensvermittlung die *Physiologus*-Geschichten deutlich als nicht der natürlichen Wirklichkeit entsprechend gekennzeichnet werden und durchaus als 'fabula' [...] aufgefasst werden können.

The *Physiologus* tradition used even doubtful knowledge gained from 'scientific' works to illustrate truth on a higher level, and to edify its audience. As T.H. White (1959:244) puts it: "In the ages of faith, people believed that the Universe was governed by a controlling mind and was capable of a rational explanation. They believed that everything meant something."[108] Thus, the focus was on the 'signifié', and not so much on the 'signifiant'. Indeed, one could say that, as soon as a 'res' or a quality thereof stood for a higher truth, its material existence became, for the exegete, relatively unimportant. He was perpetually in search of suitable material with which to illustrate the divine truth explicitly related by the Bible. Therefore, spiritual truth provided the starting point for and basis of the allegorical interpretation of a 'res'-quality. This was a new situation. The earlier exegetes had dealt with animals mentioned in the Scriptures, which were thus sanctified even on the literal level. They then had to create the structure of the allegorical interpretation on the basis of the literal level. This older model of allegorical interpretation was thus based entirely on the Bible, and the 'scientific' branches of knowledge played an inferior, supporting role. This changed from the very moment when the exegetes left the strictly confined biblical framework, in order to 'read' in the 'Book of

---

107 See M. Gerhardt (1970:238-239).

108 Eisenstein (1990:122) points out a parallel in the Arabic-Islamic world where the ninth century standard work on animals (the *Kitāb al-hayawān* by AL-GAHIZ) was not primarily designed for the study of the different species, but rather to provide a "Beweis der Existenz des Schöpfers, die aus seiner Schöpfung ersichtlich ist, und ein Lobpreis der Weisheit Gottes, der nichts völlig Nutzloses geschaffen hat[.]"

Nature'.[109] Even though this was also assumed to have been written by God, it was difficult to read, and one always had to cross-check the findings with the Scriptures.[110] Its credibility and authority were, therefore, inferior to those of the divinely-inspired Scriptures themselves. From this, it follows that the 'Book of Nature' might serve as a storehouse for illustrations of dogmatic truths, but it could never be used as the basis of an allegorical deduction of such a truth. Considering these basic differences between the two applications of the allegorical interpretation, it is all the more understandable, then, that the exegetes had to fall back on the only secure knowledge when interpreting the 'Book of Nature', namely the spiritual truths of the Bible. Thus, the illustrations taken from natural history came to be based on the theologically solid foundation of the Scriptures. If the natural historical examples turned out to be wrong, this did not diminish the validity of the spiritual truths which formed their basis; the collapse or rejection of the 'natura' part did nothing to endanger the truth expressed by the 'significatio'. In the *Physiologus* tradition, the 'natura' part originally depended on the 'significatio', and not the other way round. This was what ST. AUGUSTINE implied in his often-quoted statement about the characteristics of the pelican. At the same time, we can observe the exegete's awareness of the possible difficulties which the allegorization of doubtful natural scientific information may have caused, and his efforts to anticipate them.[111]

> Vos sic audite, ut si verum est congruat; si falsum est non teneat. [....] Fortasse hoc verum, fortasse hoc falsum sit; tamen si verum est, quemadmodum illi congruat, qui nos vivificat sanguine suo, videte. Congruit illi quod matris caro vivificat sanguine suo filios suos: satis congruit.[112]

---

109 Apart from the application of the allegorical method to the 'res' of this world, there was always the temptation to start with the allegorical interpretation of literary works other than the Bible (as had been done by the Stoics). Thus, ST. THOMAS AQUINAS, at a time when the allegorical mode was highly esteemed, "specifically denie[d] a spiritual sense in writings other than the Bible" (Bloomfield 1958:77, fn. 17).

110 Ohly (1976:7) observes that "[n]ur 'philologisch' genau gelesen und recht verstanden, offenbart das Buch der Natur dem in ihm als Gottes Schöpfung erfahrenen Deuter sein Geheimnis. Es kommt an den Tag beim Achten auf das Zusammenstimmen der doppelten Offenbarung Gottes in seinem Schöpfungswerk und in der Schrift der Bibel."

111 For an in-depth discussion of the relation between natural scientific information and allegorization, see C. Meier (1978).

112 The quotation is taken from Henkel (1976:140-141), and can originally be found in the *Enarrationes in Psalmos*, Vol. III, Ps. CI, 7-8, sermo 1,8. CCSL 40, Turnholti 1956.

Lauchert (1889:78) reports another significant statement by ST. AUGUSTINE, this time related to the eagle:

> Dieses Beispiel vom Adler, wie das vom wachsenden Mond, soll uns unsere Auferstehung zur Unsterblichkeit nicht beweisen (denn in der sinnlichen Natur gibt es nur eine gleichnisweise Auferstehung, die wieder der Veränderung und Vergänglichkeit unterworfen ist), aber sinnbildlich bedeuten.[113]

Matters became more complex, as soon as the 'significatio' part was omitted, a development which had already set in with the excerpts found in the glossary of ANSILEUBIUS and ISIDORE's *Etymologiae*.[114] There, we find the 'natura' parts of many an animal mentioned in *The Physiologus*, stripped of its 'significatio'.[115] This development reached its climax in the great encyclopaedias of the thirteenth and subsequent centuries, which included more and more 'natura' chapters without the 'significatio' part, and thus shifted the focus from the spiritual interpretation of the 'natura' to the 'natura' itself.[116] Though many of the 'scientific works' thus created were used as quarries from which to take illustrative material for allegorizations, and often still included spiritual interpretations, this step away from the biblical foundation could not be reversed; the 'natura' parts could now also be used to illustrate worldly wisdom.[117]

ST. AUGUSTINE's most important work on the allegorical interpretation of the Scriptures, the *De doctrina christiana*, is available in German translation by Mitterer (1925).

[113] Lauchert (1889:78, fn. 2) adds the Latin original: "Data est enim similitudo, quantum de re mortali potuit trahi ad rem utcumque significandam immortalem, non ad demonstrandam."

[114] Lauchert (1889:91) mentions ANSILEUBUS, who mostly selected the 'natural scientific' information and omitted both the biblical references and the spiritual interpretation. For an evaluation of ISIDORE's incorporation of several *Physiologus* 'naturae', see Henkel (1976:143-144) and Lauchert (1889:96).

[115] See Curley (1979:xxix).

[116] For the great encyclopaedias, see Curley (1979:xxix), and Schmidtke (1968:90), who writes: "Wesentlich frei von geistlichen Auslegungen im Bereich der Mitteilung von naturkundlichem Wissen scheint die dritte und umfangreichste Enzyklopädie 'de natura rerum' des 13. Jahrhunderts, das *Speculum naturale* des Dominikaners VINZENZ VON BEAUVAIS, zu sein." The same is true for ALBERTUS MAGNUS' *De animalibus libri 26*, which shows a complete division between natural science and natural symbolism (see Schmidtke 1968:91).

[117] See Ohly (1976:105), who observes a more general use of the allegorical method: "Die Allegorie will in dem Buch der Natur durch Offenbarung und Erfahrung [emphasis added] vorgegebenes Wissen wiederfinden." See also Klingender (1971:343): "In the

Although the further development is of no direct importance for the discussion of the *Physiologus* tradition, it does add considerably to the understanding of the development and origin of other traditions relevant to our study later on, and is thus outlined here, too.

The loosening of the formerly strong ties between 'natura' and 'significatio' prepared the development of the modern natural sciences. It is true that the great medieval encyclopaedias, which were often seen as the first heralds of a new scientific attitude, were still deeply rooted in the exegetical tradition and, like ISIDORE before them, they referred to ST. AUGUSTINE to justify their undertaking.[118] The fact, however, that the knowledge of nature was now more and more accessible independently of any preconceived spiritual interpretation led, in the long run, to the reinforcement of the already growing tendency towards lifting the 'Book of Nature', at least in practice, on to the same level as the Scriptures. Thus, we find a "wechselseitige Erschliessung der beiden Bücher: Bibel und Welt" (C. Meier 1978:117). Furthermore, we can observe that the 'natura' parts were used more and more to provide the basis of the allegorizations, and that an increasing "Entflechtung von 'erfahrensbedingter Faktenbeschreibung und glaubensbedingter Schrift- und Dingauslegung'" (C. Meier 1978:121) took place, in favour of the former. This development had several consequences. First, we notice that increasing emphasis was placed on the accuracy of natural scientific information. Christel Meier (1978:119) comments:

> Analog zu dem Argument, die christliche Allegorese gründe im Literalsinn auf historischer Faktizität und hebe sich dadurch von entsprechender Heiden- und Poetendeutung ab – was 'in praxi' nicht immer zutraf –, muss auch die naturkundliche Grundlage wissenschaftlich verifizierbar sein, um die Wahrheit der erschlossenen Signifikanz zu garantieren.

The second change is already apparent in *The Old English Phoenix* (Blake 1990), as we will see in greater detail later on. If we compare the 'natura' from the 'Phoenix' chapter of the reconstructed original *Physiologus* (for example Curley 1979:13-14 or Seel 1992:14-15) with the 'natura' part of the

---

circles of courtiers and lesser nobility, the Bestiary stories were, from the thirteenth century onwards, interpreted in a new and purely secular sense."

118 ST. AUGUSTINE, in the second book of *De doctrina christiana* (Mitterer 1925), laid down the principles of a Christian encyclopaedic science (see Henkel 1976:154 and 157). The great medieval encyclopaedias of the thirteenth century were: *De naturis rerum* by THOMAS OF CHANTIMPRÉ (c. A.D. 1245), *De proprietatibus rerum* by BARTHOLOMEW ANGLICUS (c. A.D. 1230-1240), and *Speculum quadruplex sive maius*, mostly by VINCENT OF BEAUVAIS († A.D. 1264).

Old English poem, the difference becomes obvious. Whereas the *Physiologus* 'natura' is rather short, and more or less sticks to the main facts and characteristics relevant to the 'significatio', we have a redundancy of natural scientific information in *The Old English Phoenix*. This demonstrates that the 'natura' no longer has the exclusive function of providing the necessary information for the 'significatio'. Irrespective of the 'significatio', it has a value of its own. The third consequence is the logical extension of the tendencies listed above: the 'significatio' is omitted, and the 'natura' remains in its own right, unaided by any supporting spiritual truths.[119]

Conclusion

Even though we have not been able to discuss in detail all the points touched upon in this chapter, we now have the necessary theoretical foundation to deal with the Old and Middle English texts belonging to the *Physiologus* tradition. In order to discuss some of the problems in greater depth, we will return to them in the course of our analysis. The following graphic illustration depicts the structure of an ideal *Physiologus* chapter and will serve as a point of reference for our analysis of the Old and Middle English texts.

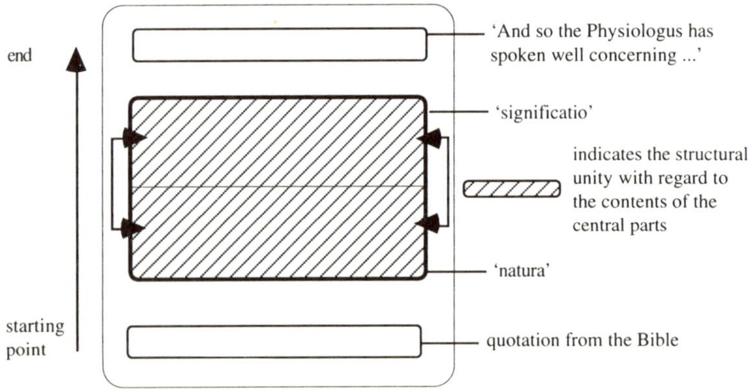

[119] Kolb (1970:602) comments on this: "Das Buch Gottes, das die Natur, und das Buch Gottes, das die Heilige Schrift ist, werden nicht mehr ineinander gelesen; das eine wird zur Interpretation des anderen nicht mehr, weil sie eines Ursprungs und eines Geistes sind, herangezogen wie früher; sondern jedes hat seinen Eigenwert und seine Eigenart für sich."

Thus, the model chapter begins with a quotation from the Bible which explicitly mentions the subject (here: an animal). The 'natura' part then provides the relevant 'scientific' information concerning the animal (appearance, feeding habits, habitat, special characteristics, etc.). The characteristics mentioned in the 'natura' are then explained with regard to their spiritual content and allegorically interpreted. The chapter closes with the standard sentence 'And so the Physiologus has spoken well concerning ...'.

2. *The Old English Physiologus*

Introduction

The *Physiologus* tradition is represented in England by three items, the so-called *Old English Physiologus*, *The Old English Phoenix*, and *The Middle English Physiologus*. Even though the first of the two Old English poems displays some interesting individual traits, it is much better suited than the intricately structured *Old English Phoenix* to serve as an example of the typical characteristics of the *Physiologus* genre. I have therefore decided to discuss it first.

Author, Date, Manuscript, and Sources

The so-called *Old English Physiologus* consists of three poems and has been handed down in folios 95b-98a of *The Exeter Book* (Krapp and Dobbie 1936:169-174). It is believed to have been composed in the late eighth or in the ninth century by an unknown author, and along with *The Old English Phoenix*, it is the oldest Old English text which interprets animals in an allegorical way.[120] *The Old English Physiologus* clearly belongs to the *Physiologus* tradition, even though its direct source is unknown and it only deals with three animals, namely the panther, the whale, and (most probably) the partridge; since the third poem has been handed down as a fragment and the name of the animal is not mentioned, we have no factual evidence that it is actually about the partridge. Lothar Frank (1971:37) summarizes the results of research into the source of *The Old English Physiologus* as follows: "Unter diesen Bedingungen kann zur Quellenfrage nicht mehr gesagt werden, als dass dem ae. Bearbeiter ein ziemlich alter lat. *Physiologus*-Text als Grundlage gedient haben muss." Neither the fact that the oldest surviving Latin *Physiologus* manuscript dates from the eighth or

[120] See L. Frank (1971:36).

ninth century, nor the certainty that the whole occidental *Physiologus* tradition goes back to the Latin versions of the Greek original, is of much help to us.[121] Thus, our information about the immediate source of *The Old English Physiologus* is a little sparse, to say the least. We may, nevertheless, assume that a Latin *Physiologus* version was the model for the Old English poem.

Critics on *The Old English Physiologus*

The scholarly debate about the nature of *The Old English Physiologus* has so far been largely dominated by three questions:[122]

1) Are the three poems part of a complete cycle, or are they the fragments of a much larger work?

2) Do the fragments on folios 97b and 98a belong to one and the same poem?

3) Which bird is the subject of the third poem?

Questions 2) and 3) are closely linked to the first; if the bird in question was indeed the partridge, then we would have a complete *Physiologus* 'en miniature', with a representative from each sphere of life (panther: earth; whale: water; partridge: air).[123] The foliation of *The Exeter Book* points towards the loss of a single leaf between folio 97b and folio 98a. It is, therefore, very likely that the two fragments belong to the same poem.[124] Since the introductory lines 1a-8a of *The Panther* can be interpreted as a kind of general introduction to an abridged *Physiologus* cycle, which comes to an end with the "Finit" in line 16b of *The Partridge*, we can conclude that no other animals were included. Lauchert (1889:111) and also L. Frank (1971:43) observe that *The Panther*, *The Whale*, and *The Partridge* were consecutive chapters in the early *Physiologus* versions. Thus, the Old English poet/translator may have selected these passages for his adaptation and omitted the preceding and following chapters. In connection with the fact that the traditional interpretation of the partridge sees the righteous as the children of God, to whom we also have a reference in *The Partridge* (see "on bearna stæl", Krapp and Dobbie 1936:174, l. 11b), it is very likely that

---

121 See Henkel (1976:21).

122 The authors consulted are Cordasco (1949), L. Frank (1971), Lauchert (1889), and Peebles (1911). For an overview, see L. Frank (1971:37-47).

123 Bradley (1982:353) adds the phoenix from *The Old English Phoenix*, which is "a creature uniquely associated with the fourth and last of the elements, fire[.]"

124 See L. Frank (1971:42).

the partridge is indeed the subject of the fragmentary poem. Inspired by the idea that the three animals are representatives of the three spheres of life, an attempt has been made to find a similar analogy on the allegorical level. Thus, Christ (in *The Panther*), the devil (in *The Whale*), and man (in *The Partridge*), who stand at the centre of the allegorical interpretation, are considered to constitute a complete cycle on the 'significatio' level, which parallels that of the 'natura' parts.[125] According to this theory, the poet consciously selected these chapters and thus interfered with the original text to a greater extent than was normal.

To this day, it has always been the author/translator who has been held responsible for the selection of the three poems. No explicit thought has been given to the possibility that the compiler of *The Exeter Book* may have selected the appropriate passages from a more complete, but now lost, Old English version of *The Physiologus*. By adding the general introductory lines 1a-8a of *The Panther* and the final "Finit" of *The Partridge*, he could have fused the three poems into a coherent whole. Yet, for sake of simplicity and since we have no evidence of any interference by the compiler on this level, I will herafter speak only of 'the poet'.

The Focal Points of *The Old English Physiologus*

Before starting to analyse the individual poems, it is necessary to give an account of the criteria according to which they will be judged. The model of the allegorical interpretation provides the basic parameters for our approach; we will compare the structure of the poems and the function of the animals treated with our idealized model (page 42). The differences thus ascertained should help us to achieve a better understanding of the Old English version of *The Physiologus*.

Discussion of the Poems

The Panther

(*The Exeter Book*, fol. 95b-96b, Krapp and Dobbie 1936:169-171)

In order to analyse the structure of the first poem, I have compiled a list containing all the relevant information given and subdivided the poem into four parts: 1) General Introduction (ll. 1a-8a), 2) 'natura' (ll. 8b-54b), 3)

[125] See L. Frank (1971:45-47). According to Bradley (1982:353), the allegorical theme of *The Old English Phoenix*, i.e. the "destiny of the righteous human soul", would fit in, too.

'significatio' (ll. 55a-68b), and 4) Epilogue (ll. 69a-74b). The structure of the poem with regard to its contents can be depicted as follows:

[General Introduction]	
ll. 1a-8a	multitude of animals in the world
['natura']	
ll. 8b-10a	it (yet unnamed) is known to mankind
ll. 10b-12a	**habitat**
ll. 12b-13a	**name**
ll. 13b-15a	source of knowledge: written authority
ll. 15b-18b	**temperamental disposition** towards other animals, with special reference to the dragon
ll. 19a-20a	**colouring**
ll. 20b-25a	comparison to Joseph's coat
ll. 25b-30a	**colouring** of the panther's fur
ll. 30b-34b	**temperamental disposition**
ll. 35a-42a	after feeding, it **sleeps for three days**
ll. 42b-43b	pleasant **roaring**
ll. 44a-48b	pleasant **smell**
ll. 49a-53a	men are attracted by this smell
ll. 53b-54b	wild animals are attracted by the smell
['significatio']	
ll. 55a-58a	God benign to all creatures except dragon: **'temperamental disposition'**
ll. 58b-61a	dragon ~ ancient enemy (Satan)
ll. 61b-64a	He (Christ) rose from death after **three days**
ll. 64b-65b	this (death and resurrection?) ~ **sweet smell**
ll. 66a-68b	men are attracted by this smell
[Epilogue]	
ll. 69a-74a	St. Paul: good things given to men by God so that they are saved
ll. 74b	good things (?) ~ **sweet smell**

The General Introduction and the 'natura' Part (ll. 1a-8a & ll. 8b-54b)

Being the first poem in the triad, *The Panther* starts with a 'general introduction'. The description of the panther itself begins as late as line 8b and opens with the oral epic formula "we [...] hyrdon" (l. 8b).

The poet organizes the information of the 'natura' part in a rather special way. The preceding introduction (ll. 1a-8a) gives a very general comprehensive view of the creatures inhabiting the earth and the air, yet does not explicitly mention the water-dwelling animals. The poet then 'zooms' in on a particular animal and, while at first concealing its identity, he informs the audience about its habitat.[126]

Comparing the listing of the 'scientific' facts and the other information given in the 'natura' part to a standard *Physiologus* chapter (see page 42), we get the following differences:

1) The biblical basis in the form of a scriptural verse related to the topic is missing. We do, however, have a rather tedious and allegorically irrelevant scriptural link in the form of the comparison of the panther's fur to Joseph's coat.[127]

2) The source of the information given in the 'natura' passage is not explicitly named as 'Physiologus', but more generally alluded to as the writings of "wisfæste weras" (l. 14a).

Apart from these two structurally deviant points, the poem is in keeping with our model, as shown on page 42. There are, however, some poetic peculiarities in the first two parts which deserve closer examination. First, we notice the double theme of the animal 'being known/famous' and 'living in a far away land' (ll. 10a-11a). A medieval audience would very likely believe strange tales and exotic lore, according to the principle: the farther away it is, the more fantastic it may be. This adds considerably to the credibility of what follows, and the reference to the "wisfæste weras" (l. 14a) provides the necessary authoritative underpinning of the information. Secondly, the poet repeats the information concerning the panther's gentle overall disposition and its exceptional hostility towards the dragon (ll. 15b-

---

126 Lines 1a-12a display a certain affinity with the riddles of *The Exeter Book*. Their subjects are often animals, too.

127 The "wundrum scyne/hiwa gehwylces" (ll. 19b-20a) must have functioned as the cue to connect the panther's many-coloured fur with Joseph's coat. This comparison remains on the literal level and is already to be found in the Greek and Latin *Physiologus*. It nicely illustrates how the content and words of the Bible permeated the minds of early Christian and medieval clerical authors, so that a single word would call forth scriptural associations. On this point in general, see Leclercq (1963) and Smalley (1983).

18b and again in ll. 30b-34b). Although we possess no exact knowledge of the poet's direct source, it seems very likely that this repetition of the theme of the panther's temperamental disposition, which is of great importance for the 'significatio', was necessary because the poet inserted the extended 'biblical comparison' of the fur to Joseph's coat. After these poetic, yet allegorically irrelevant verses, the author had to return to the main line of argument by refocussing on the allegorically relevant facts.

The 'significatio' Part (ll. 55a-68b)

The allegorical interpretation of the 'natura' part takes place in the 'sensus allegoricus', i.e. it connects the 'scientific' facts with events from the plan of salvation such as the death and the resurrection of Christ. The allegorical interpretation more or less proceeds along the lines set out in the 'natura' part: we have the explicit interpretation of the panther's temperamental disposition and its enmity towards the dragon, the comparison of the panther's three-day rest with Christ's three-day sojourn in the grave (with the panther's cave being paralleled to the grave), and the logically rather dubious allegorization of the sweet smell as the (message of the) resurrection, which attracts people from all over the world. Comparing the factual content of both the 'natura' and the 'significatio', we notice an almost complete correspondence: there are only two items in the 'natura' part which are not interpreted in the 'significatio'. The first and more important omission concerns the panther's fur: lines 19a-30a do not add anything relevant to the development of the poem, but are essentially of a digressive quality. This is corroborated by their circular arrangement; i.e., they begin with the beauty of the fur's colour and conclude on the same level. The second item not allegorized is the "woþa wynsumast" (l. 43a). Yet, since the poet concentrates on the "stenc" (l. 44b), which is causally connected with the roar and which essentially fulfils the same function, we could actually regard the "woþa wynsumast" (l. 43a) as having been taken into consideration.

The Epilogue (ll. 69a-74b)

Although the final verses of *The Panther* (ll. 70a-74a) can be interpreted as summing up the allegorical view of the world, they seem to have their origin not so much in the affinity of their contents to what has been said in the 'significatio', as in the fact that the first words of St. Paul in the 'epilogue' ("Monigfealde sind geond middangeard", l. 70) are similar to those of the 'general introduction' ("Monge sindon geond middangeard", l. 1). Like the 'digression' (ll. 19a-30a) before, they testify to the poet's highly allusive biblical frame of mind, and do not seem to belong to the allegorical argument proper. This almost verbatim repetition of a line brings us to the stylistic analysis of the poem.

Stylistic Peculiarities

In spite of the fact that *The Panther* lacks the stylistic and structural complexity of a poem like *The Old English Phoenix*, it nevertheless possesses some stylistic characteristics which display a kind of rudimentary similarity to the more sophisticated ones of *The Old English Phoenix*. Thus, for example, the poet changes from calling the panther 'deor' (for example l. 12b, l. 19a, and l. 25b) to "se þeodwiga" (l. 38a), thereby anticipating the allegorical interpretation. He then reverts once more to the 'animal level' in line 43b ("wildres muð"), before finally beginning the allegorical interpretation of the 'natura'. Apart from this correspondence with regard to the contents, there is a certain stylistic parallelism between the 'natura' and the 'significatio'. Line 16b reads "butan dracan anum", which is repeated verbatim in line 57b. Also, line 41b, "on þone þriddan dæg", is taken up again in line 61b as "ond þy þriddan dæge". Although these obvious stylistic parallels can be accounted for as traits of the typical stylistic inventory of Germanic heroic poetry, they may also owe their origin to the fact that the poet thus highlights the two central themes, namely the antagonism between God and devil, and the resurrection of Christ.

Conclusion

In its focal limitation, *The Panther* is a typical example of the *Physiologus* tradition. Even though it is not explicitly marked, we have a clear division of the poem into two main parts, namely the 'natura' and the 'significatio'. The selection of the 'natura' characteristics has obviously been influenced by the intended allegorical interpretation. Two facts corroborate this: on the one hand, we find hardly any allegorically superfluous information in the 'natura', while on the other hand, traits which do not fit into the positive view of the panther are relegated to a subordinate position or even omitted completely. Thus, the poet draws a veil of judicious silence over the panther's carnivorous nature, and stresses the allegorically valuable fact that men are attracted (ll. 49a-53a). The "deor efne swa some" (l. 53b), which also follow the sweet smell and which are likely to be the real panther's prey, are only mentioned in the form of an incidental remark.[128] Fur-

[128] The dietary habits of the real panther, which are problematic on an allegorical level, have sometimes been not simply omitted, but changed. Thus, the author of the Middle High German *Physiologus* turns the carnivorous panther into a vegetarian (see L. Frank 1971:127).

thermore, the 'natura' lacks the necessary bulk to stand alone, and even details which do not seem to correspond directly with parts of the 'significatio' would nevertheless fit in, if an interpretatory effort were made. The appeasement of the panther's hunger, for example, could be and, as Schmidtke (1968:363) points out, has been otherwise interpreted as Christ's being "durch die ihm zugefügten Qualen und Verspottungen gesättigt[.]" Yet, the brevity of the 'natura' has another very important effect: there is no need for the poet to repeat every single characteristic he is going to allegorize; it suffices to mention the key word(s). This technique of allegorizing influences the selection and presentation of the 'scientific' information to a far greater extent than the method of restating the allegorically relevant 'natura' points within the 'significatio' itself.[129] The poet of *The Old English Physiologus* seems to favour this apparently more transparent method of reference, so that he prefers to divide up the 'natura' into allegorizable pieces, as we can see in the poem of *The Whale*, rather than increase the level of complexity to the point where he would have to restate the allegorically relevant traits.

The Whale

(*The Exeter Book*, fol. 96b-97b, Krapp and Dobbie 1936:171-174)

The listing of the informational structure of *The Whale* will give us a first impression of its composition. The headings in square brackets indicate the possible divisions of the poem.

[Epic Introductory Formula & Introduction of Subject]

ll. 1a-3b	topic of the poem: "fisca cynn" (l. 1b) => "hwale" (l. 3b)
ll. 4a-6a	seafarers mentioned, **temperamental disposition** towards men
ll. 6b-7b	'scientific' name of the whale

['natura I']

ll. 8a-10b	outward appearance
ll. 11a-12b	**deception** of sailors
ll. 13a-23b	detailed description of sailors
ll. 24a-31a	**reaction** of the whale => **destruction** of sailors

['significatio I']

ll. 31b-37b	**deception** of men through demons

[129] See the chapter on *The Old English Phoenix*.

ll. 38a-47a	**reaction** of the devil => **destruction** of men
ll. 47b-49a	refer back to 'natura'
['natura II']	
ll. 49b-50b	introduction of a new characteristic
ll. 51a-62a	sweet **smell** attracts other fish, which are then **caught** in the **fangs** of the whale
['significatio II']	
ll. 62b-79b	sweet **smell** of vain desire attracts men, who are then **caught** in **hell**
ll. 80a-81b	refer back to 'natura'
[Epilogue]	
ll. 82a-88b	moral adhortation

Epic Introductory Formula and Introduction of Subject (ll. 1a-7b)

The poet links the second poem of the cycle to the first with the help of the poetic introduction (ll. 1a-3a), now moving on from the category of 'deor' to the "fisca cynn" (l. 1b). The whale itself is introduced immediately afterwards, and is briefly characterized by means of its disposition towards man. The introductory lines conclude with the 'scientific' term for the whale.[130] The central role of the seafarers is prepared for, and will become fully apparent in the subsequent 'natura'. As in *The Panther*, we also find that the introduction of *The Whale* lacks the usual biblical reference(s), though the identification of the biblical Leviathan (*Liber Iob* 40,20) with the whale and the adventure of Jonah (*Iona Propheta* 2,1f.) would have provided the poet with sufficient scriptural material to draw on. This makes it very likely that the poet consciously foregoes biblical references in order to achieve a greater effect on another level, as we will see later on.

The 'natura I' Part (ll. 8a-31a)

The first 'natura' begins traditionally enough. The poet describes the strikingly deceptive appearance of the whale in some detail, in order to make the deception of the seafarers more acceptable. The audience will

130 The term "Fastitocalon" (l. 7b) actually designates the giant sea-turtle. See L. Frank (1971:190, fn. 2). Its application to the whale is probably due to the confusion of the lesser known sea-turtle with the whale, which was better known to the Anglo-Saxons and exhibited similar characteristics.

hardly question any of the information given, as long as the poem deals with wonders and wondrous events in the fabulous East. The whale, however, is probably too familiar a creature to be treated without at least some realism. Thus, the audience, among whom we may find some seafarers, too, is likely to expect some good reasons for the sailors' being taken in by a whale. Then, however, the 'narrative digression' (ll. 13a-23b) takes over and dominates the whole of 'natura I'. In spite of the fact that the whale is the explicit subject of the poem, the narrative focus of 'natura I' centres on the sailors. The poet elaborates on their stay on the whale's back, even though this narrative extension does not contribute any further to the passage's allegorical value. The poet seems intentionally to subordinate the allegorical importance of the passage to its emotional effect, which he heightens by deliberately postponing the inevitable climactic disaster. He obviously warms to the task of painting the idyllic scene of the unsuspecting sailors sitting around the warming fire, while the audience, nerves tense, awaits the impending doom to come. Lines 24a-31a revert to the whale, and bring the climactic contrast to the preceding narrative passage. It is interesting to note that the whale is depicted as an actively malicious and plotting animal (vs. the whale in *The Middle English Physiologus*), which may be due to its identification with the devil later on.[131]

The 'significatio I' (ll. 31b-49a) and Stylistic Peculiarities

The allegorical interpretation of the first 'natura' part in the 'sensus moralis' follows immediately, while the characteristics discussed are still fresh in the memory of the audience. The poet can do without explicitly referring back to the 'natura' and keep the relation between the two parts on a very low level of complexity (which stands in marked contrast to a poem like *The Old English Phoenix*). The seafarers are equated with men 'high and low', the deceptive appearance of the whale is paralleled to the snares of the devils, and the bottom of the sea obviously stands for hell itself (see the parallel between l. 29b "grund geseceð" and l. 45b "helle seceð").

Parallels which would link the two parts on a stylistic level are of no great importance, though a close reading yields such minor parallels as "gewiciað" (l. 19a), taken up again in "wic geceosað" (l. 37b), "fæste" (l. 25b), repeated in l. 41a, and the aforementioned "grund geseceð" (l. 29b), which is

[131] Bausinger (1991:163) observes, concerning the moral abilities of animals: "Moralisches – und auch unmoralisches – Handeln ist menschliches Handeln, und wenn dieses in der Gestalt von Tieren präsentiert wird, dann handelt es sich entweder um naive Projektion oder gezielte Übersetzung." In our case, it is most likely a variation of the latter, i.e. a 'gezielte Übersetzung' of the devil's qualities into animal terms.

paralleled in "helle seceð" (l. 45b). The structural parallels are so clear that the stylistic ones are redundant.

The fact that the poet does not exploit the allegorical possibilities of the extended description of the seafarers corroborates the assumption that it has to be seen as a narrative digression irrelevant to the spiritual interpretation. It also illustrates the author's efforts to achieve transparency and clarity. The wish to retain a clear structure must have induced him to split up the 'natura' section and to deal separately with the two elements, to make them more 'audience-friendly', so to speak. Although the poet makes no explicit use of the wealth of allusive possibilities provided by the sea-imagery, the audience may very well have been sufficiently sensitized to detect the rich symbolic undertow.[132] The 'significatio I' ends with a reference to the first 'natura', and thus, by reverting to the 'natura' level, the poet leads up to the second 'natura'.

The 'natura II' (ll. 49b-62a)

The second 'natura' excels through its succinctness. Neither biblical nor narrative digressions or allusions divert the audience's attention from the 'scientific' report about the whale's way of procuring food for itself. The connection between the first 'natura' and the second is established not only by means of the figure of the whale, but also through the continuation of the deception-theme. Once more, the whale is depicted as luring its victims to their doom, though this time the participants are all members of the animal kingdom. The equation of the whale with the devil(s) in the 'significatio I' may have prompted the author to use "aglæcan" (l. 52a, meaning 'monster' or 'demon') to refer to the whale.

The 'significatio II' (ll. 62b-81b) and Stylistic Peculiarities

The 'significatio' transfers the information given in the 'natura' on to the level of human behaviour. Thus, we have the equation of fish ~ men, sweet smell ~ sinful earthly joys of the body, and whale ~ devil(s). The "wynsum stenc" (l. 54b) of the 'natura II' is taken up as the "swetne stenc,/leasne willan" (ll. 65b-66a). This refers back to the 'natura' by means of repetition, and at the same time provides the interpretation on the level of the 'sensus moralis'. The same technique can be observed in lines 76a-77b: the "[...] þa grimman goman bihlemmeð/[...] fæste togædre", which takes up the final lines of the 'natura II', "hlemmeð togædre/grimme goman" (ll. 62b-63a), is

---

132 For a discussion of fish-symbolism and the symbolic value of the sea, see Haas (1991). For a well-versed example of an allegorical interpretation of the sea and the ship by MASTER ACHARD, Abbot of St. Victor, see Owst (1966:68).

interpreted as the closing of the "helle hlinduru" (l. 78a). The "muð ontyneð" (l. 53b) of the 'natura II' is also taken up again in "helle ontyneð" (l. 68b), and thus reinforces the parallel between the whale's pharynx and the abyss of hell. The iconographic tradition of depicting the entrance to hell as the gaping jaws of a dragon-like monster may also have given additional reason to take up again the picture of the clashing jaws.[133] The final lines of the 'significatio II' again revert to the 'natura II' level and conclude with the same image that ushered in the allegorical interpretation: the fish caught in the whale's jaws.

The Epilogue (ll. 82a-88b)

Although the scribe obviously omitted at least one-and-a-half lines, we are still able to get the drift of the epilogue. The poet draws the general moral for the audience and ends on a solemn, yet joyful note which stands in marked contrast to the grim image that provided the conclusion to the 'significatio II'. The poet juxtaposes the more or less fatalistic quality of events in the 'natura' parts, where man's role is reduced to passive suffering, to the alternative course of action open to the Christian on the level of the 'significatio'.

Conclusion

The Whale, by and large, exhibits the same characteristics as *The Panther*. We have a limitation to the allegorically relevant 'scientific' facts, and these are interpreted in the immediately following 'significatio' parts. Apart from the 'narrative digression', the poet's composition of the 'natura' parts of *The Whale* is strongly influenced by the intended allegorical interpretation. The 'narrative digression' does not add any factual knowledge of the whale, but shifts the focus of attention away from the whale and on to the men. From an allegorical point of view, it is of a purely ornamental quality. The predominant position of the 'significatio' is most clearly shown by the fact that the 'natura', which provides the 'scientific' information on the whale, is split into two. Instead of at least a structurally coherent description, we get two individual pieces of lore obviously selected because they suit the purpose of the allegorical interpretation. This breaking-up of the original unity of the 'natura' part drastically reduces its independence, and demonstrates the overall supremacy of the 'significatio'.

---

133 See Kennedy (1952:220): "The jaws [...] are the gates of hell, the yawning Hell-mouth represented in the drawings of the Junius MS. that was used so often later on the medieval stages of mystery and miracle play."

The Partridge

(*The Exeter Book*, fol. 97b-98a, Krapp and Dobbie 1936:174)

The fragmentary character of this poem greatly limits our opportunities to gain useful information. Nevertheless, the surviving lines hint at the following structure:

[Introduction and Naming of the Subject]

l. 1a	oral epic formula
ll. 1b-2a	**genus** (bird)

['natura']

- - - - - - -	(missing)

['significatio']

ll. 3b-4b	introduction to the words of God
ll. 5a-11b	God promises adoption of those who abandon sin

[Epilogue]

ll. 12a-16b	moral adhortation

The Epic Introductory Formula and the Naming of the Subject (ll. 1a-2a)

Like the similar line in *The Panther* (l. 8b), the introductory words which refer to an oral source of the poem are part of the formulaic heritage taken over from the oral poetic tradition, and must not be taken at face value. The introduction of the subject follows the established pattern of first naming the genus, i.e. here 'fugol' (see 'deor' and 'fisc' before). Then, the name of the animal itself would most probably have been given.

The 'natura' Part

Owing to the loss of one or more pages, we have no reliable information about the content of the missing 'natura'.

The 'significatio' (ll. 3b-11b)

God Himself is speaking, promising to accept us as His children if we abandon sin and evil. These 'words of God' are not taken directly out of the Bible, but are a fusion of several passages (see *Isaias Propheta* 55,7; *Ad Corinthios II* 6,17-18; and *Ad Hebraeos* 2,10-11). The central notion of leaving the life of sin and returning to God is in accord with the traditional allegorical interpretation of the partridge, and thus corroborates the conjecture that the partridge is the subject of the poem.[134]

The Epilogue (ll. 12a-16b)

As before in the epilogue of *The Panther*, the author admonishes the audience to strive for heavenly reward by shunning sin during their life on earth, and thus gaining a place in heaven.

General Conclusion

The Old English Physiologus as a whole displays a clear structural composition, which corresponds to a large degree with the idealized model presented on page 42. The following depiction illustrates the typus found in *The Old English Physiologus*:

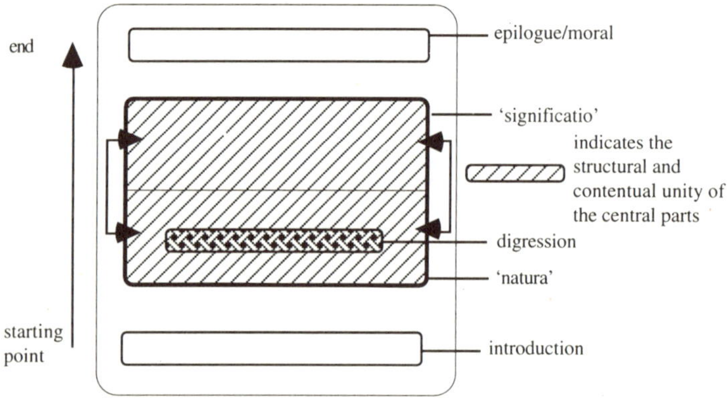

implicitly assumed biblical frame

The two main parts, i.e. the 'natura' and the 'significatio', accord with each other to such a degree that the metaphor of the two sides of the same coin could be appropriately used. Unlike the 'natura' of *The Old English Phoenix* – as we will see – the 'natura' parts of *The Old English Physiologus* are highly dependent on the 'significatio' parts. This rigid correspondence is only partially broken up by the digressions within the 'natura' passages, which have no counterparts in the 'significatio' sections. The function of the animals, therefore, remains limited to providing the peg on which to hang the interpretation. The overall layout of the poems is characterized by an

[134] For an overview of research on this aspect, see L. Frank (1971:39-40).

'audience-friendly' structuring of information. The poet only selects characteristics which can be interpreted consistently, i.e. ones that remain within the same 'sensus'. In addition, he limits himself to the allegorization of the relevant traits, and once on the spiritual level, he pays no attention to details. In combination with the introduction and the moralizing epilogue, these characteristics may suggest the origin or intended use of the poems as parts of a sermon or a sermon 'in nuce'. However, since we lack any further circumstantial evidence to support such conjecture, we had better confine ourselves to what we have: the poems themselves.

3. *The Old English Phoenix*[135]

Author, Date, and Manuscript

The complete *Old English Phoenix* has come down to us in one single manuscript, preserved on folios 55b-65b of *The Exeter Book* (Krapp and Dobbie 1936:94-113).[136] As is the case with the majority of Old English poetry, the author of *The Old English Phoenix* remains unknown. Since the poem has much in common with those assigned to CYNEWULF and with *Andreas*, it seems likely to have been composed in the ninth century.[137]

The Source(s)

Establishing the identity of the source(s) of *The Old English Phoenix* seems to be a relatively straightforward matter. The author mainly used the Latin poem *Carmen de ave phoenice* (Blake 1990:92-96) by LACTANTIUS († A.D. 340) for the 'natura' part of his poem, and AMBROSE's *Hexaëmeron* (Blake 1990:96-97) for the 'significatio' part. In addition, he may have incorporated ideas on and references to the phoenix by the Fathers and other Christian writers.[138] Scholars who have looked into this matter do not mention the Latin *Physiologus* as a possible direct source for the poem, and

---

135 All references are to the edition by Blake (1990).

136 In his introduction to what is up to now the most recent edition of *The Old English Phoenix*, Blake (1990:1-8) gives a short discussion of the age and language of both the manuscript and the poem.

137 See Blake (1990:24).

138 For a detailed discussion of the possible sources of and influences on *The Old English Phoenix*, see Blake (1990:8-24). One of the earliest Christian writers to use the phoenix was CLEMENT (c. A.D. 100) (see Broek 1972:4).

indeed, the fact that *The Old English Phoenix* does not include the notion of the worm which develops into a phoenix in three days supports the assumption that *The Physiologus* did not figure among its immediate sources. As Broek (1972:214) observes: "Only the *Physiologus* and the texts related to it say that the worm developed into a phoenix within three days." This might lead us to question the inclusion of this poem under the heading 'The *Physiologus* Tradition', but I can put forward four reasons for doing so.

First, the very idea of interpreting animals allegorically was mainly propagated by *The Physiologus* and the texts related to it. The immediate source, LACTANTIUS' *Carmen de ave phoenice* (Blake 1990:92-96), shows no signs of an attempted allegorical interpretation.

Secondly, the structure, with its implicit division into 'natura' and 'significatio', shows undeniable parallels with *The Physiologus*, and it is very likely that *The Physiologus* provided the structural model, even if indirectly, via AMBROSE's *Hexaëmeron* (Blake 1990:96-97).

Thirdly, the phoenix is seen as a symbol of Christ in both *The Old English Phoenix* (see ll. 646b-649b) and *The Physiologus*. Yet at the same time, the phoenix in *The Old English Phoenix* is also seen as a symbol of the resurrection of the blessed (ll. 381a-392b). This has its parallels in the treatises of the western Fathers. Thus, *The Old English Phoenix* comprises ideas from both the Fathers and *The Physiologus*.

Fourthly, the phoenix is one of the traditional *Physiologus* animals.[139]

For all these reasons, it seems justified to me to include *The Old English Phoenix* among the texts discussed in this chapter.

Since we can identify the direct source(s) of *The Old English Phoenix* with a degree of probability close to certainty, we have the rare opportunity of approaching the poem from the very beginning of its poetical conception. In the following discussion, we will try to find answers to the four central questions which arise when dealing with the poem:

1) Why did the poet choose LACTANTIUS' *Carmen de ave phoenice* as his source for the 'natura'?
2) What major alterations were made by the poet?
3) What are the underlying and governing principles of the poem?
4) What is the function and role of the phoenix in the poem?

The answers to questions 1) and 2) will provide the necessary information for our discussion of 3) and 4). Before proceeding to the poem itself, let us first turn our attention for a moment to some of the critics who have written

---

139 See Curley (1979:13-14), Lauchert (1889:237-238), and Seel (1992:14-15).

on *The Old English Phoenix*, and who may provide some answers to our questions.

The Critics on Some Aspects of *The Old English Phoenix*

The Choice of the Source

The answer to the first question is relatively easy. Cross (1967:137) states: "The English poet wished to write a poetic homily on the significance of the Phoenix and took the *Carmen de ave phoenice* as the fullest and most suitable historical description of the bird." Recalling the graphic illustration of the process of allegorical interpretation (page 28), we can note the following; the biblical legitimation for a poetic treatment of the phoenix is provided by two passages of the pre-Vulgate version, i.e. *Liber Iob* 29,18: "Dicebamque: In nidulo meo moriar et sicut phoenix multiplicabo dies", and *Psalmi Iuxta Hebraicum* 91,12: "Justus florebit velut phoenix" (Kantrowitz 1964:2).[140] It is now the poet's task to provide the necessary information from the 'quadrivium cum physica' field to make possible the step from the 'sensus literalis' to the 'sensus spiritualis'. To the poet and his contemporaries, the phoenix must have been an exotic, yet nevertheless real bird, which made the choice of source for the 'natura' an important issue.[141] We have indications of the use of LACTANTIUS' poem in schools in general, and of its availability in England in particular.[142] Since, as we have seen above (page 36), ancient poets and scholars alike were consulted on zoological matters, enjoying more or less equal authority, the *Carmen de ave phoenice* can indeed be seen as the best available source for the 'natura' of the phoenix. Thus, we can credit the author with choosing the most complete

---

[140] The official *Vulgate* translations read: "dicebamque in nidulo meo moriar et sicut palma multiplicabo dies" (*Liber Iob* 29,18) and "iustus ut palma florebit" (*Psalmi Iuxta Hebraicum* 91,12). The differing translations arose from the fact that the Greek word for 'phoenix' and 'palm' was identical. Medieval writers usually knew only the reading 'palm' for the relevant passage in *Liber Iob*, but we know of at least one Latin commentary which links this verse in *Liber Iob* with the phoenix (attributed by BEDE to PHILIP THE PRESBYTER) and which may have been known to the poet of *The Old English Phoenix* (see Blake 1990:21).

[141] See Kantrowitz (1964:1).

[142] See Glauche (1970:8). Cross (1967:149, fn. 35) observes that the *Carmen de ave phoenice* "may well have been the most available description, since we know that LACTANTIUS was one of the authors whose works were in the York Library, according to ALCUIN, and that he was quoted and named by ALDHELM[.]"

historical account of the phoenix, and thus fulfilling his duty as a responsible exegete.

Alterations and Additions

Emerson (1926) was one of the first critics to focus on the changes, omissions, and additions attributed to the Old English poet, and his seminal article provided the point of departure for many subsequent critics.[143] The alterations made by the Old English poet, as discussed by Emerson (1926), can be grouped into:

1) Omissions: references to classical divinities and myths, as well as allusions to the names of exotic peoples and places, are omitted.
2) Christianization: references to classical divinities and myths are, if not omitted, replaced by their biblical equivalents and by references to God.
3) Extensions and additions: for example the seed-corn simile (ll. 240b-259a) and the entire 'significatio' part (ll. 381a-677b).

Cross (1967:130) adds a fourth point:

4) The transfer into a different poetic idiom, i.e. the idiom of the Old English poetic tradition.

We will have a closer look at these alterations in connection with the discussion of the underlying principles of the poem.

The Underlying and Governing Principles

Emerson (1926:26) attributed changes 1 to 3 listed above to the Old English poet's intention to "thoroughly Christianise[...] the source before him." This point of view has been challenged by Cross (1967), who opposes the notion of interpreting *The Old English Phoenix* as a kind of "Lactance moralisé" (Cross 1967:129). He rightly calls our attention to the fact that the omission of references to classical pagan divinities and myths was not a prerequisite for the Christian allegorization of the poem. However, as Cross (1967:130) states,

> [t]he Old English poet cannot do other than omit the names in transferring the ideas to a different poetic idiom, especially in such a clearly didactic poem, which assumes an audience less knowledgeable than the author.

Also, the 'Germanization' of the poem, or at least the use of epithets stemming from the vocabulary of Germanic heroic poetry in order to refer

---

[143] For example Blake (1962) and Cross (1967).

to the phoenix (for example "þegn", l. 288a and "æþeling", l. 354b), can be seen as a consequence of its transfer into the Old English poetic idiom. Yet, the fact that the poet intended to Christianize his model remains undisputed; the various critics only differ as regards the degree to which he achieved his purpose.

Blake (1990:26) stresses the modification of the source by the poet, so that the 'natura' part, based on the *Carmen de ave phoenice*, prepares for the allegorical interpretation in the second part. Indeed, Blake (1990:28) even goes as far as to claim that "for the Old English Christian poet of *The Phoenix* the bird is merely a symbol of a divine truth. The poem was written in order that we might realise what this truth was", and comes to the logical conclusion that the 'natura' part can be considered only in the light of the allegorical interpretation. Therefore, "[i]t has no existence in its own right" (Blake 1990:31). This attitude towards the phoenix as a bird, according to Blake (1990:28-29), allowed the author to handle his source with great freedom: he was able to take only that which served his purpose. This point of view raises some questions concerning the correspondence of the first part of the poem with the second one. As Blake (1990:33) notes, the poet obviously "failed to select and arrange his material satisfactorily, for the overlapping interpretations sometimes confuse the reader." Thus, in his final appraisal of the poem, Blake (1990:35) sees *The Old English Phoenix* as

> a valiant attempt by a sensitive poet to produce an Old English poem out of a mixture of a late classical Latin poem and some Christian themes. The attempt is not altogether successful for the poet has not been ruthless enough in selecting and arranging his material.

Kantrowitz (1964:1), on the other hand, stresses the natural scientific value of the poet's source: "To the poet and his contemporaries that fabulous creature was a real bird existing in the real world[.]" He was, thus, not completely free to select from his source only those things which he would use later. Kantrowitz nevertheless credits the poet with being in more or less complete control of the poem. According to her, the poet went beyond his immediate source and fused different symbols from Christian allegory into a whole. Since she takes a different point of departure from Blake (1990), Kantrowitz (1964:13) reaches a more positive assessment of the poet's achievement:

> [T]he poem is not merely a 'loose paraphrase' of its source, but a reworking of the material which both increased and changed the allegorical possibilities of its original through the poet's selection and addition of details relevant to Christian thought. [....] Speaking

> within traditional allegory, he provides the general interpretation. Our part is to understand the details.

Cross (1967:145), the third and most recent critic (since the introduction of Blake 1990 is more or less identical to the one in the first edition 1964), takes *The Old English Phoenix* to be

> an effective medieval homily on the Phoenix, in which LACTANTIUS' *De Ave Phoenice*, the fullest description of the bird, was adapted as a Christian historical explanation, and ideas taken from patristic exegesis and polemic, as well as the Physiologus literature, were elaborated to provide distinguishable tropological, anagogical, and typological explanations, so to present a fourfold interpretation of a real and scriptural bird.

The Role and Function of the Phoenix

As a consequence of the differing points of view, the role and function of the phoenix itself in the poem is judged differently. Emerson (1926:19) credits the Old English poet with originality in using the symbolism of the phoenix at length, and emphasizes the importance of its symbolic value. For him, the phoenix "is a symbol of the life of the righteous here and hereafter" (Emerson 1926:27), which embraces the whole life of man. Apart from this, it also symbolizes Christ, an idea first found in the Greek *Physiologus*.[144] Blake (1990:12 and 18-19) reminds us of the widespread use of the phoenix as a symbol of the resurrection of mankind in the writings of the Fathers, and does not consider the exploits of the Old English poet to be as original as Emerson did. Blake (1990:28) sees the phoenix as being "merely a symbol of a divine truth." As a symbol, it stands not only for the traditional notion of the resurrection of all men on Doomsday, but also for the belief that all good men will go to heaven. Finally, it symbolizes Christ, too. Thus, Blake (1990:33) sees the role of the phoenix as a symbol imbued with several layers of meaning. Kantrowitz (1964:1) relates the phoenix to the other Christian allegorical symbols, i.e. the apple, the silkworm, the eagle, and the seed grain. In her opinion, the phoenix is the focal point in the real world around which the other symbolic items cluster. In order to be able to judge the validity of either theory, we will now have a closer look at the poem itself.

---

[144] See Emerson (1926:31, fn.).

The Focal Points of the Poem

There are, in my opinion, three centres of interest around which the different parts of the poem are to be grouped:

1) The first prominent centre of interest is God. Blake (1990:27) writes that "God dominates the poem which is firmly and unashamedly Christian." God is explicitly and repeatedly named as the creator of the heavenly land (l. 84), of the phoenix (ll. 281a-282a), and of heaven and earth (ll. 129b-131a). Even such a passage as the one which centres on the phoenix (ll. 291a-318b) is, in the end, used to enhance the glory of God (l. 319), and thus shifts the focus from one centre of interest to the other.

2) The second important centre of interest embraces the essential dogmatic belief in the resurrection of the dead at the time of the Last Judgment, and the moral consequences derived from this eschatological point of view. Indeed, the poet implicitly introduces the central notion of the resurrection in lines 48a-49b, in connection with his description of the day of the Last Judgment: "Dryhtnes dōmes þonne dēaðræced,/hæleþa heolstorcofan onhliden weorþað." This is long before the phoenix is even mentioned (see ll. 85a-86b).

3) The third centre of interest is, of course, the phoenix itself. Although it is used to illustrate the central dogmatic truth of the resurrection of the dead, its allegorical possibilities are not exhaustively treated. Besides its importance on the allegorical level, it has a value of its own as an exotic part of God's creation and as a bird that exists in the real world.

In order to come to terms with the rather complex structure of *The Old English Phoenix* and the function of the phoenix within this setting, we will examine the poem from the point of view of focus. To facilitate the analysis of the text, I have divided it into three parts, namely 'introduction' (ll. 1a-84b), 'natura' (ll. 85a-380b), and 'significatio' (ll. 381a-677b).

Discussion of the Poem

The 'Introduction' (ll. 1a-84b)

God

God, especially the God of the Old Testament, can indeed be seen as the main focus of the otherwise seemingly unmotivated adaptation of the ideal landscape description taken from the *Carmen de ave phoenice*. Firstly, God Himself and references to His work replace the pagan deities and the allusions to their spheres of influence.[145] In addition, the poet replaces the allusions to pagan mythology with their biblical equivalents, which also help to shift the focus on to God.[146] Furthermore, the poet adds traits to the adapted form of the ideal landscape, which make the reinterpretation of the land as the 'Garden of Eden' an obvious step.[147] He also subjects the originally 'timeless' grove to the eschatological perspective of the Bible, which means that it, too, will perish at the end of time.[148]

The Resurrection of the Dead

The poet refrains from explicitly mentioning the resurrection of the dead. However, he does report the opening of the graves in connection with the Last Judgment (ll. 48a-49b). In this way, even though he does not begin the poem in the typical *Physiologus* manner, he succeeds in introducing what is, for the poem, the central dogmatic truth before the phoenix is even mentioned. Thus, he fulfils the methodological criteria of the allegorical interpretative method, which first establishes the biblical foundation before starting the 'natura' (see the graphic illustration on page 28).

---

145 References to God Himself, His power, and His work can be found in l. 6a, ll. 9b-10b, l. 36b, l. 46b, l. 68b, l. 79b, and l. 84b.

146 Thus, the firestorm caused by Phaeton (*Carmen de ave phoenice* Blake 1990:92, ll. 11-12) and the flood of Deucalion (*Carmen de ave phoenice* Blake 1990:92, ll. 13-14) are rendered as the apocalyptic conflagration (*The Old English Phoenix* ll. 38b-41a) and the biblical deluge (*The Old English Phoenix* ll. 41b-43a).

147 The most obvious parallel with the biblical paradise is the fact that the land of the phoenix is irrigated by rivers (*The Old English Phoenix* ll. 62b-68a). This reminds the audience very much of the irrigation of Eden by the four rivers, Phison, Geon, Tigris, and Eufrates (*Liber Genesis* 2,10-14).

148 See ll. 40b-41a, ll. 47b-48a, and ll. 82b-84b.

The Phoenix as a Bird

As we have seen above, the first 84 lines introduce a variety of elements to the audience, but not the phoenix proper. Yet, it would be wrong to assume that these introductory lines are, therefore, of no relevance at all to the function of the phoenix itself, even though the main centres of interest are God and the notion of the resurrection of the dead. The adaptation of the ideal landscape description from the *Carmen de ave phoenice* serves as a means of establishing the biblical-Christian setting of the phoenix as a bird. In addition, the adoption of the theme of the 'wondrous land far away to the East' heightens the audience's level of acceptance for the wondrous things and events to come. As has been convincingly shown by J.B. Friedman (1981:36-37) and Simek (1992:115), the medieval theories about the influence of climate and planets upon humans, animals, and plants provide a 'scientific' explanation for the strangest of creatures. Therefore, to an average medieval audience, it was more or less a matter of course to assume that the people, animals, and plants of the East, which lived in such different climatic and planetary conditions, differed from their counterparts in the more temperate regions of the earth.

The 'natura' Part (ll. 85a-380b)

God

As the name suggests, this part of the poem comprises the 'natural scientific' information on the phoenix, which is thus the main focus of attention. Yet, God also remains very much present and, at times, comes close to dominating the poem. The references to God as the creator, which were already present in the introduction, are now specified and multiplied. Thus, the sun (l. 95a), heaven and earth (ll. 130a-131a), melodies (l. 138), the phoenix-tree (ll. 175a-179a), the 'winsome' plants (ll. 196a-197b), and the phoenix itself (ll. 281a-282a, l. 319, ll. 327b-330b, ll. 355b-360b, and ll. 377a-380b) are the creations of God or owe their special qualities to Him. The effect of this repeated and reinforced interpretation of nature as the creation of God is quite obvious: everything can be seen as a "tācen Godes" (l. 96a, emphasis added), and the way to an allegorical interpretation is thus prepared.

The Resurrection of the Dead

At first sight, one has difficulty in making out the elements which are connected to the notion of the resurrection of the dead; this is mainly due to the symbolic terms in which they are couched. Thus, neither the worm (l. 232a), nor the eagle (l. 235b and l. 238a), nor the seedgrain (ll. 250b-252a) is explicitly related to the resurrection of the dead. Yet, all three are either biblical symbols of resurrection and renewal or used as such in exegetical commentaries.[149] Thus, the 'resurrection-connection' does exist, though in a more implicit than explicit manner, and is easily discernible to a theologically trained audience.

Besides these links which are more implicit than explicit, in the 'natura' part we find other elements which shift the focus on to the theme of resurrection. This is done in a roundabout way, by establishing parallels and links between the 'natura' part and those passages of the 'significatio' that place emphasis on the notion of the resurrection of the dead. Thus, the poet uses the verbal technique of anthropomorphizing, on the one hand, certain elements in the 'natura' part. For example, he repeatedly calls the phoenix's nest "hūs" (l. 202b, l. 212a, and l. 217a). On the other hand, he uses 'natura' expressions to denote ideas on the spiritual-human level, such as "nest" (l. 451a) for the protection provided by God against evil. Anthropomorphizations of a different kind are found in the many instances in which the poet uses words from heroic poetic diction to refer to the phoenix, such as "þēodne mǣrum" (l. 165b), "lēofne lēodfruman" (l. 345a), "gūðfrecan" (l. 353a), and "æþeling" (l. 354b). The use of these terms may be explained as the consequence of the poet's transfer of a Latin poem into the Old English poetic tradition. In addition, however, they provide further links with the allegorical level, where the good Christian is seen as "Dryhtnes cempa" (l. 452b). In this way, the poet establishes additional connections between the different sections of the poem and includes aspects which are of secondary importance here, but which add to the overall structure of the poem. Blake (1990:26) interprets these as unmistakable signs that "the English poet's descriptions are always affected by the allegorical implications." An apt example is line 242a, where the newborn phoenix is described as being "synnum āsundrad". This is most probably interference from the allegorical level, since the resurrected will be shriven and purged of their sins (see ll. 525b-526a and ll. 544a-545b), whereas we do not know of any sins on the part of the phoenix.

---

149 Kantrowitz (1964:4-13) offers an illuminating discussion of the various Christian symbolic meanings of the (silk)worm (~resurrection of the soul, see BASIL's and AMBROSE's *Hexaëmeron*), the eagle (~renewal, see *Psalmi Iuxta Hebraicum* 102,5: "qui replet in bonis desiderium tuum renovabitur ut aquilae iuventus tua"), and the seedgrain (~resurrection, see *Ad Corinthios I* 15,36-37: "insipiens tu quod seminas non vivificatur nisi prius moriatur et quod seminas non corpus quod futurum est seminas sed nudum granum ut puta tritici aut alicuius ceterorum").

Even though the often ambiguous qualities of the 'natura' part caused critics like Blake (1962 and 1990) and Kantrowitz (1964) to reach quite different conclusions concerning the function of the phoenix, there can be hardly any doubt that the principal focus of this part of the poem is on the bird itself. Thanks to the preparatory work performed in the 'introduction' (ll. 1a-84b), the poet had to change or omit very little of the 'scientific' information provided by his Latin source. The wondrous qualities and actions of the bird are either seen as special graces bestowed by God (see ll. 377a-380b), or interpreted so as to fit into the Christian framework (see ll. 90a-96a). The strongest argument in favour of the assumption that the main focus of this part is on the bird itself is the fact that the 'natura' part is virtually teeming with possibilities for allegorical interpretation. However, the great majority of these are not fully exploited – at least, not explicitly. Thus, to list some examples, neither the phoenix's bathing twelve times in the sea-cold water (ll. 106a-110b) nor the fact that it thrice claps its wings (ll. 144b-145a) is ever taken up on the allegorical level. In this context, it seems especially important to me to point out the rather lengthy passage which provides a description of the phoenix (ll. 291a-318b). Here, the poet obviously quite closely follows his model (*Carmen de ave phoenice* Blake 1990:95, ll. 124-149). Although the description of a bird would have provided a skilled scholar with ample possibilities for an interpretation on the spiritual level, as HUGO DE FOLIETO († 1172) demonstrated some centuries later, the poet lets the opportunity slip.[150] Like other characteristics mentioned in the 'natura' part, the description of the phoenix does not appear to be influenced in any way by the allegorical interpretation; it is what Kantrowitz (1964:3) calls "eighth-century science". Even the association of the phoenix with such potential Christian symbols as apple (l. 230b), worm (l. 232a), and eagle (l. 235b and l. 238a), which, with the exception of the worm, are not found in the *Carmen de ave phoenice* (Blake 1990:92-96), and which strengthen the embedding of the phoenix in the Christian allegorical setting, is not primarily based on the allegorical properties of these objects. Kantrowitz (1964:5) stresses the fact that the development of the reborn phoenix from the "æples gelīcnes" (l. 230b) to the "wyrm" (l. 232b) and then into the likeness of an "earnes brid" (l. 235b) is in accordance with medieval zoological ideas on the generation of birds. The use of the seedgrain metaphor is of special interest, too, and illustrates the poet's predilection for a multi-dimensional approach. By reversing the usual sequence of the two

[150] For a discussion of HUGO DE FOLIETO's allegorical interpretation of the dove, see Ohly (1968).

arguments, which are of equal importance in the resurrection tracts, the poet emphasizes the predominance of the phoenix as the centre of interest.[151] Thus, the seedgrain argument is relegated to the position of a supporting metaphor, even though it enhances the import of the notion of the resurrection of the dead.

The 'significatio' Part (ll. 381a-677b)

God

If we were to classify a passage according to the frequency of an idea expressed or referred to, we would be obliged to place the main stress in the 'significatio' on God. Yet, quantity is not the only criterion. The sheer numerical predominance of God is reinforced by the poet's habit of relating almost everything to God as its creator, protector, author, judge, or aim. The choir of the righteous (ll. 632a-654b) accomplishes the final fusion of the three different aspects under the all-encompassing idea of God. The resurrected phoenix is interpreted as a symbol of the risen Christ (~ God), who was the first one to conquer death, and who thus points forward to the resurrection of the dead.

The Resurrection of the Dead and the Phoenix

Owing to the complex and intertwined character of the 'significatio' section, we have to examine these two centres of interest simultaneously. Unlike the 'significationes' of *The Old English Physiologus*, that of *The Old English Phoenix* does not restrict itself to a one-dimensional allegorical interpretation of the traits mentioned in the 'natura' part; in the course of analyzing the 'significatio', I encountered the following links between the different parts with regard to the contents and structure.

1) Explicit interpretation of a 'natura' trait.
2) Incorporation of 'natura' passages within the 'significatio'.
3) Parallels with regard to the contents.
4) Stylistic parallelism.
5) Verbal links between two levels.

The following discussion of this list gives typical examples of this linking, without making any claim to being exhaustive.

---

[151] See Kantrowitz (1964:12).

1) Explicit interpretation of a 'natura' trait

The verbally explicit and more or less systematic allegorical interpretation of the characteristics discussed in the 'natura' part is a typical trait of the original *Physiologus* tradition. Even though the 'significatio' of *The Old English Phoenix* includes several verbally explicit allegorical interpretations, it still differs from an average *Physiologus* 'significatio', since it lacks a thorough, systematic interpretation of many traits mentioned in the 'natura' part of the poem.[152] On the other hand, the poet's highly selective approach, explicitly interpreting only the most significant traits, brings him more into line with the original *Physiologus* tradition. There, the 'natura' part contains a pre-selected number of characteristics, from which more or less all the superfluous elements have been omitted.

In *The Old English Phoenix*, we find all three 'sensus spirituales' among the verbally explicitly marked allegorical interpretations.[153]

a) 'sensus allegoricus': in lines 646b-649b, the phoenix is interpreted as signifying the 'child of God', i.e. Christ.
b) 'sensus moralis vel tropologicus': the nest-building (l. 451 and ll. 465b-469b) is seen from the moral point of view; i.e., the interpretation tells the audience how to lead a virtuous life (ll. 452a-465a).
c) 'sensus anagogicus vel eschatologicus': in lines 534b-538b, we are given the spiritual interpretation of the phoenix's resurrection as the resurrection of the blessed at the time of the Last Judgment.

Apart from the traditional 'sensus spirituales', there are several hybrid levels which comprise aspects and elements of two 'sensus', or in which the standard category has been modified. Thus, in lines 387a-392b the "fugles gecynd" (l. 387a) is projected on to the moral-anagogical level; i.e., the nature of the phoenix is not further specified, but is seen as providing the model for gaining happiness in this world with the help of God (moral aspect), while at the same time securing bliss in heaven (anagogical aspect). A good example of a modified interpretation is the allegorization of the phoenix's self-incineration on the level of the individual 'sensus anagogicus'

---

[152] I am aware of the fact that the average *Physiologus* 'significatio' does not always interpret every single trait mentioned in the 'natura' part. See, for example, the description of the elephant's trunk in Seel (1992:63-65), which is not allegorized in the 'significatio'. However, these instances are the exceptions to the rule.

[153] The poet usually marks the allegorical interpretation with introductory words like 'characteristic X fela gelīces Y [...] bēacnað Z on the allegorical level' (see ll. 387b-389a) or 'as X swā Y' (see l. 437b).

(ll. 381a-386b). There, the author connects the 'natura' characteristics with the fate of each blessed soul immediately after death.

2) The incorporation of 'natura' passages within the 'significatio'

The 'significatio' of *The Old English Phoenix* often has the tendency to repeat entire 'natura' sections. This stands in contrast to the often very sparse and abbreviated form in which the traditional *Physiologus*, as well as *The Old English Physiologus* 'significationes', relate back to the 'natura'. Thus, after relating the expulsion of Adam and Eve from the Garden of Eden, it would have sufficed to say "Is þon gelīcast, [...] þisses fugles gefær" (ll. 424a-426a) in order to point to the 'sensus allegoricus' of the phoenix's departure from paradise. Apart from the fact that repetition is a typical characteristic of the Old English poetic tradition, the repetition of the relevant 'natura' passages not only allows the poet to arrrange the 'natural scientific' information according to his (exegetical) wishes, but also helps to shift the focus onto the desired centre(s) of attention. The latter two points call for a more detailed discussion.

First, let us examine the way in which the poet arranges the information given in the 'natura'. The structural concept underlying the interpretation of the 'natura' part makes itself known immediately after the rather general and non-committal beginning (ll. 381a-392b) of what I take to be the 'significatio'. In lines 393a-423b, the poet switches to the historical biblical level, i.e. in this instance the biblical account of the creation of mankind, the Fall, the expulsion from paradise, and its re-opening for the saints after the (only implied) harrowing of hell. The poet then adds suitable 'natura' passages to relate the biblical events to the story of the phoenix and thus refers to its 'sensus allegoricus' dimension. It is very important to notice that the divine plan of salvation, as related in the Scriptures, provides the line along which the spiritual dimensions of the 'natura' are unfolded, as has been shown by the example above, and not vice versa. This, of course, stands in marked contrast to the procedure usually found in the *Physiologus* tradition, where the 'significatio' follows the pattern established by the 'natura'.[154] Recalling the graphic illustration of the allegorical method of interpretation (see page 28), we may recognize the import of this observation. Up to this moment, the poet has dealt with the phoenix more or less on a 'scientific' level, and has done without the explicit biblical foundation of the bird. Yet now, he builds his allegorical interpretation on the basis of the sound biblical framework which the historical biblical passage provides. His first step is to use apt 'natura' passages to illustrate the

[154] Though, of course, the average *Physiologus* 'natura' has, more often than not, been designed so as to meet the demands of the 'significatio'.

biblical report. Only after thus pointing out the parallels and creating a strong link between the two texts, which he reinforces by referring to Job and quoting rather freely the explicit mentioning of the phoenix in the Bible (ll. 552a-569b), is the poet fully able to use the 'natura' level as a starting point for allegorical interpretations.[155] Yet, even then he does not revert to successively interpreting each 'natura' characteristic, but adheres to the course of following the divine plan of salvation; this brings us to the second point.

The question of the centre(s) of interest is closely linked to the way in which the poet structures his material. The selective incorporation of 'natura' passages, be it in a summary-like form or be it almost as detailed as in the original 'natura' part, simplifies both the poet's and the audience's interpretative task a great deal. The 'significatio' can be read more or less independently of the 'natura' part, since all the relevant passages are repeated. Even though the author indirectly encourages the audience to undertake a closer allegorical reading of the 'natura' passages by placing the relevant 'natura' parts right next to the biblical passages, he stops short of the complete 'allegorical dissolution' of the 'natura' part which would relegate the phoenix to a very subordinate place. Therefore, we can indeed say that "he provides [only] the general interpretation", and it is up to the audience "to understand the details" (Kantrowitz 1964:13). As a consequence, the original 'natura' part retains its 'scientific' status. Furthermore, the repetition of selected pieces within the context of the 'significatio' allows the poet to omit all the traits which would either disturb or fail to contribute to the main centres of interest of the 'significatio', which are the notion of the resurrection of the dead and the idea, derived from it, of gaining eternal bliss through a virtuous life and good deeds on earth. Adherence to the overall eschatological focus of the 'significatio' and to a selective approach to the 'natura' part reduces the danger of losing sight of the broad lines, which, considering all the possible allegorical interpretations offered by the unshortened account of the 'natura' part, could easily happen. Thus, in a roundabout way, the poet of *The Old English Phoenix* arrives in the 'significatio', at least in this respect, at the very same point from which the traditional *Physiologus* 'natura' chapter departs: the selection of the traits relevant to the illustration of a dogmatic truth.

[155] An example of a 'natura' passage providing the starting point for the allegorical interpretation can be found in ll. 575b-588b.

3) Parallels with regard to the contents

Apart from the allegorical interpretations explicitly introduced, the 'significatio' contains a number of more implicit pointers towards the spiritual dimension of the 'natura' part. Parallels on the level of content belong to this category, and include similar or identical actions, events, etc. Thus, for example, the singing of the phoenix towards the sun (l. 124) is paralleled by the singing of the saints and their praising of God (ll. 615b-617b). The fact that God has been linked verbally to the sun gives additional support to this interpretation, and illustrates how complex the structural connections can be.[156]

4) Stylistic parallelism

Lines 611a-615a provide the best example of parallelism on a stylistic level. In order to describe the heavenly paradise, the poet uses the very same rhetorical device of negation already employed in lines 50a-62a, in connection with the description of the phoenix's paradise. Similarity of style does not automatically establish a correspondence on the allegorical level, but it certainly enhances the audience's willingness to find one.

5) Verbal links between two levels

Verbal links are employed in two slightly different ways. On the one hand, we have verbal parallelism, i.e. the reapplication of an originally 'natura'-level word on the level of the 'significatio', often in a metaphorical sense. As already mentioned above under point 3), 'Parallels with regard to the contents', God, who is called "wlitig wuldres gim" in line 516a, is thus equated with the sun (= "wuldres gim", l. 117b), which in turn triggers the idea of connecting the singing phoenix – on an allegorical level – with the singing saints. On the other hand, the poem provides some examples of 'verbal switching', i.e. the use of a 'natura' word in place of the apt 'significatio' expression, and vice versa. Apart from adding a metaphorical touch to the passage in question, this guides the audience, with beacon-like certainty, to the related sections. A very typical example is the use of 'hūs', or 'nest': the poet several times calls the phoenix's nest in the 'natura' part "hūs" (l. 202b, l. 212a, and l. 217a), whereas he metaphorically uses "nest" (l. 451a) in a human context.

An analysis of the explicit allegorizations and the implicit linking of passages reveals differences in the application of these techniques; the poet limits the use of explicit allegorical interpretation to passages which:

---

156 See below, under 5) 'Verbal links between two levels'.

a) help to establish the structuring of the 'significatio' along the lines of the divine plan of salvation,
b) provide, if interpreted in the 'sensus moralis', guidelines for a virtuous life and therefore for the achievement of eternal bliss, and
c) are related, in the 'sensus anagogicus', to the resurrection of the dead and the Last Judgment.

In this way, explicit allegorization strengthens the overall eschatological focus of the 'significatio', since a) and b) exhibit a more or less pronounced eschatological perspective, too.

The wide range of stylistic and other means used for creating implicit connections shows no perceptible limitation. The poet applies the various techniques of linking to achieve a richer and more complex, though implicit allegorical pattern. The poem consequently presents itself to the audience in a twofold, yet harmonious way: on the one hand, since the main focus of attention is on the moral and eschatological aspects of the phoenix and the Bible, the general message is quite clear: lead a virtuous life (see the biblical models mentioned in ll. 443a-446b) and perform good deeds, so that at the time of the Last Judgment, you will be among the chosen followers of God. On the other hand, the implicit intricate patterning allows the poet to exploit the 'natura' part in its entirety. This stands in contrast to the piecemeal use of passages for the explicit allegorizations. By alluding to the various levels of meaning, he evokes associations which often show a far greater depth than a passage analysed in the harsh light of an allegorical interpretation which tells us exactly what is what and which is which. Any attempt to logically disentangle this skillfully tied Gordian knot without destroying it is bound to fail.

Conclusion

This brings us back to the central question, for us, of assessing the role and function of the phoenix in the poem. Taking the above observations into account, we can depict the function of the phoenix in the following manner:

The Function of the Phoenix

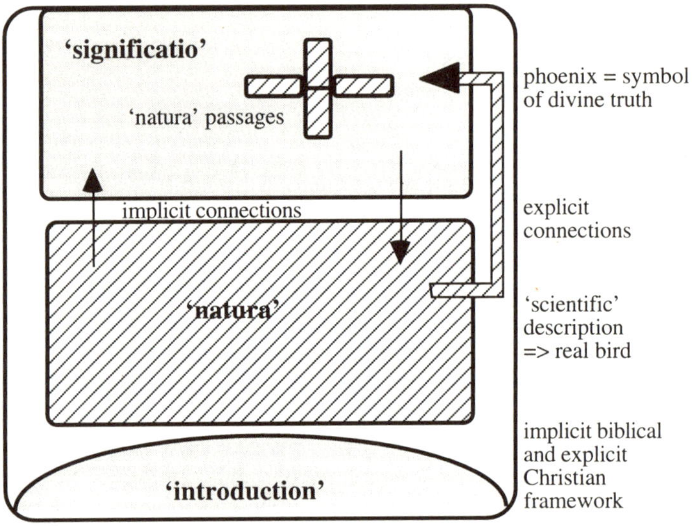

By means of implicit parallels and by explicitly naming God, the introductory part of the poem establishes the biblical-Christian framework which encompasses the entire poem. Within this frame, however, the different parts show a certain degree of independence with regard to the function of the phoenix. In the 'natura', the phoenix is obviously considered to be a real bird possessing some characteristics which display striking parallels with certain dogmatic truths that are not yet explicitly stated. The accepted scriptural and worldly reality of the bird prevented the poet from using the phoenix exclusively as an illustration, and made him include spiritually irrelevant (since it was not allegorized) 'scientific' information from his source. Thus, the 'natura' part gives us a 'scientific' description of the bird, and even though the influence of the 'significatio' part becomes apparent, it would be wrong to deny that interest in the real bird prevails in this part of the poem. This changes as soon as we move on to the 'significatio' part, where the poet uses the information made available in the 'natura' part as the quarry yielding the data needed to illustrate the spiritual truths. Only in this context does it seem justifiable to me to speak of the phoenix as being "merely a symbol of a divine truth" (Blake 1990:28).

To sum up, we can state that the main function of the phoenix with regard to the poem as a whole is, indeed, to illustrate the divine truths. Yet, this does not rule out partial shifts of focus and the performance of secondary functions. Thus, we have a variety of meanings on several levels. On the one hand, the phoenix is a real bird; on the other, it symbolizes the virtuous on earth, is used as the symbol of the blessed, and functions as a 'sign' that points to the resurrection of the dead (both immediately after the individual's death, and on Doomsday). Finally, the phoenix is the symbol of the resurrected Christ.

In my opinion, the poet succeeds in creating an original, multilayered work, which is clear in its principal statements, while implicitly preserving the great wealth of intricate allegorical possibilities.

4. *The Middle English Physiologus*[157]

Introduction

The work which will be the subject of the last part of this chapter has, until recently, been known by the name of *The [Middle English] Bestiary*.[158] Yet, since it is basically a late thirteenth century Middle English version of the eleventh century Latin *Theobaldi 'Physiologus'*, I feel justified in following Wirtjes (1991), who published a new critical edition of this work under the title *The Middle English 'Physiologus'*.[159] The space and time needed to discuss all of the thirteen chapters would be out of proportion to the contribution of new insights, so I have limited my analysis to a closer examination of *The Spider*, *The Whale*, *The Siren*, *The Panther*, and *The Dove*. These five chapters have been chosen because of both their representative and their original qualities, and because they provide an opportunity of comparing *The Whale* and *The Panther* with their equivalents in *The Old English Physiologus*.

[157] All references are to the edition by Wirtjes (1991).

[158] See Bennett and Smithers (1968:165-173).

[159] Concerning the dependence of *The Middle English Physiologus* on the *Theobaldi 'Physiologus'*, see L. Frank (1971:63).

Author, Manuscript, and Sources

Written by an unknown author, *The Middle English Physiologus* is part of British Library MS. Arundel 292 (folios 4a-10b), where it rubs shoulders with the Middle English *Meditation on Death* in verse and the Latin prose *Fables of Odo de Cheriton.*[160] Since the poet of *The Middle English Physiologus* attempts to match THEOBALD's variety of metrical forms, we find alliterative long lines, couplets, common metre, septenaries, and combinations thereof.[161]

The relation between the individual chapters and their immediate source, i.e. the Latin *Theobaldi 'Physiologus'*, is discussed at length in L. Frank (1971:62-202) and Wirtjes (1991:lxxix-xci). We will refer to the *Theobaldi 'Physiologus'* (critical edition by Eden 1972) in the analysis of the individual poems.

General Characteristics

The Middle English Physiologus shows the typical division into one or more 'natura' parts and their 'significatio' counterparts.[162] The author indicates the beginning of each subdivision by means of the Latin subtitles 'natura X' or 'significacio' (sic). These subtitles are mostly incorporated into the body of the text, and there is no introductory biblical quotation or reference. The characteristics presented in the 'natura' parts are obviously adapted to meet the interpretatory demands of the 'significatio' and, with few exceptions – for example *The Spider* (Wirtjes 1991:12-13) – have little intrinsic poetic or 'scientific' value. Apart from the repetition of a key-line or a central expression, an analysis of the 'significatio' parts yields few stylistic links with the corresponding 'naturae'; the parallels on the level of content are too straightforward to profit from a more subtle form of linking on the stylistic level. The overall structural simplicity, the repeated direct addressing of the audience in the 'significatio' parts – for example l. 35, l. 63, ll. 118-119, and l. 209 – and the pronounced tendency towards an interpretation on the level of the 'sensus moralis' (eleven out of thirteen 'significatio' parts are either entirely or at least partially moralistic) point to the use of the individual chapters in the context of sermons.[163]

---

[160] See Wirtjes (1991:xiii). A very useful translation of ODO's fables has been done by Jacobs (1985).

[161] See Wirtjes (1991:liv).

[162] See, for example, *The Lion* (Wirtjes 1991:3-4) or *The Snake* (Wirtjes 1991:6-7).

[163] For the use of animals in sermons during the High and Late Middle Ages, see Owst (1966:154): "[T]he homilists were indebted [for illustrations] to books of moralized animals and properties of things." See also Owst (1966:195): "Most popular of all

The following graphic depiction illustrates the basic set-up of an idealized chapter with a twofold 'natura' and 'significatio'. This twofold-structure is due to the fact that the 'natura' parts in *The Middle English Physiologus* are in most cases not immediately followed by a spiritual interpretation.[164] The identical pattern of some fields indicates that those 'natura' characteristics are allegorically interpreted in the 'significatio'.

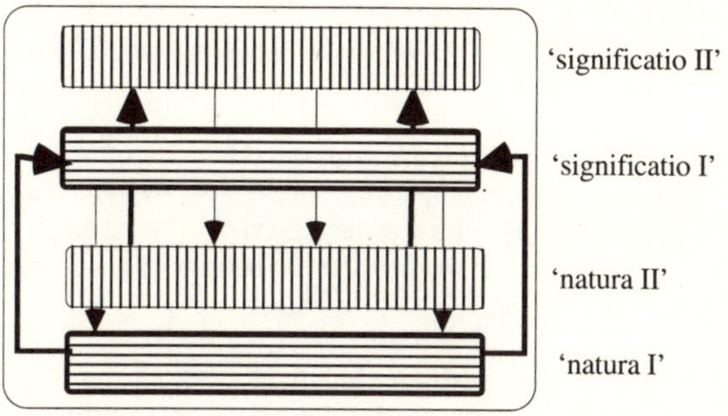

implicitly assumed and virtually existing biblical frame

The Middle English Physiologus keeps the 'natura' parts together, and thus differs from *The Old English Physiologus*, which has each 'natura' in its chapter on the whale immediately followed by its 'significatio'. The main structural principle is, therefore, not a matter of coherence with regard to contents (i.e. the literal and spiritual dimensions of the same account) but of form ('natura' vs. 'significatio'); the arrows in the illustration indicate the degree of mutual influence. The selection of the characteristics presented in the 'natura' parts is, to a great extent, affected by the intended spiritual interpretation. The inclusion of only allegorically relevant traits within the 'natura' points towards such an influence, although it cannot be rendered visible within the text. The connection of the 'natura' and the 'significatio' is conspicuous and needs no futher explanation.

---

created things in pulpit moralization were the beasts, birds and fishes of the animal kingdom."

164 See, for example, the chapter *The Lion* (Wirtjes 1991:3-4, ll. 1-26) where we find three subsequent 'natura' parts which are then allegorically interpreted.

Discussion of the Poems

The Spider
(Wirtjes 1991:12-13, ll. 313-334)

The chapter on the spider is well suited to illustrate the Middle English poet's ability to exploit the limited freedom which his Latin model grants. Even though he does not make up an entirely new chapter, he either adds or omits ideas and descriptions. Wirtjes (1991:lxxxvi) considers this chapter to be "one of those that are furthest removed from THEOBALD; in fact, the ME *Physiologus* is not really a translation of the Latin here." L. Frank (1971:176) rates it as:

> das eindrucksvollste Beispiel im ganzen me. Bestiary für das [...] Bestreben dessen Verfassers, die vom lat. Dichter zumeist in sachlich knapper Form gehaltene 'Berichterstattung' in eine detaillierte, wirklichkeitsnahe und lebendige Schilderung umzugestalten.

The short chapter VII, *De Araneo* (Eden 1972:52-55) in the *Theobaldi 'Physiologus'*, which goes back to the *Dicta Chrysostomi*, provides the starting point for the Middle English version. Although it does feature the interpretation of the spider as a deceitful and treacherous man, it directs its special attention to the ultimate futility of earthly (ill-)doings (see Eden 1972:54, ll. 16-18). The Middle English chapter on the spider, however, shifts the focus and concentrates on the comparison of the spider with morally objectionable man, who betrays his fellow-men.

'natura' (ll. 313-328)

The section headed "Natura [a]ranee" (Wirtjes 1991:12) begins with a three-line introduction which explicitly renders what has, until now, been only the implicitly presupposed symbolic function of the "Seftes" (l. 313); this introduction shows only a marginal connection with the 'natura' itself.[165] The fact that such a statement occurs as late as the seventh chapter points towards the independent use of the individual chapters. The 'natura' proper starts at line 316 and consists of a vivid and detailed account of where and how the spider weaves its web, and how it afterwards lies in wait for the fly to get caught. The moment the poet focusses on the killing of the fly, the detailed, yet somewhat detached description gains in intensity and

[165] According to L. Frank (1971:176), these lines are "ein wertvoller Beleg für die der gesamten *Physiologus*-Literatur zugrunde liegende christlich-symbolische Naturauffassung [... der] im lat. *PT* [*Physiologus Theobaldi*] kein Vorbild [hat]."

immediacy. The act of killing is rendered by means of expressions which have strongly negative connotations. Thus, the spider bites "Bitterlike" (l. 326) and becomes the fly's "bane" (l. 326); these expressions have no counterparts in the Latin source. The Middle English author also indulges in a factually correct, yet rather gruesome account of the blood-drinking, whereas THEOBALD euphemistically, but at the same time probably ironically, calls the fly "[d]ulcis et utilis esca" (Eden 1972:52, l. 6) and refrains from giving such horrible details at all.

'significatio' (ll. 329-334)

The 'significatio' of the spider chapter exemplarily illustrates the technique of only allegorizing the most important points. The spider ("wirm", l. 329) is equated ("bitokneð", l. 329) with deceitful man. The biting, blood-drinking, and devouring are identified with inflicting injury, vexing, and working evil; thus, the focus is on the abominable nature of the act of deceiving. The poet passes implicit judgment by placing deceitful man on the same level as the spider, and omits what is, for this moral interpretation, the irrelevant allegorization of the web-weaving.

Conclusion

As the following graphic 'summary' of the chapter on the spider shows, the poem differs in the aforementioned points from the idealized model:

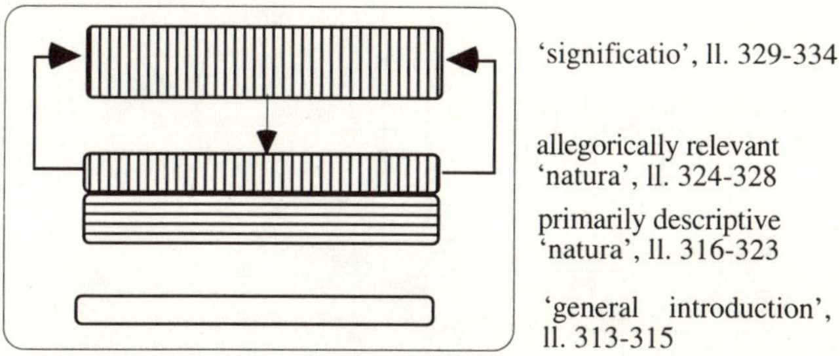

The two most important differences are the addition of a 'general introduction' and the subdivision of the 'natura'. The 'general introduction' may be seen as an attempt to justify the inclusion of such a 'leiðe wirm' among the otherwise more pleasant and sizeable animals of *The Physiologus*.[166] Within the 'natura', we can discern a twofold division: on the one hand, we have a passage that provides an accurate and even lovingly

[166] See also L. Frank (1971:178): "Der erstmals im lat. *PT* erscheinende Abschnitt von der Spinne ist dem ursprünglichen *Physiologus* ganz fremd."

detailed account of the spider's web-weaving; on the other, there is the dramatic rendering of the fly's death. The vivid language and the carefully observed details confer a poetic quality on the whole 'natura', and testify to the poet's great narrative skill. His strength lies not so much in the construction of striking and intricate allegorizations, as in the imparting of the central spiritual and moral truths. In other words, he is a better spiritual adviser and preacher than he is an intellectually-minded theologian.

The Whale
(Wirtjes 1991:13-15, ll. 335-390)

In contrast to his free handling of the chapter on the spider, in this chapter the poet sticks to the Latin model – or at least tries to do so. Accordingly, and also because of some misinterpretations of the Latin original on the Middle English poet's part, the structure of this chapter is more complex than usual. The following illustration is intended to help us analyse the poem. As before, the identical patterns of some fields indicate the fact that 'natura' traits are allegorically interpreted in the 'significatio'; those fields that have individual patterns indicate the lines that stand on their own.

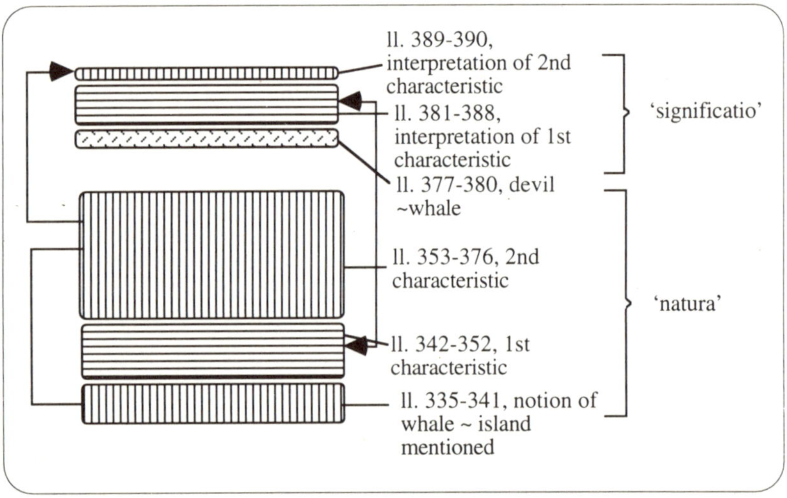

'natura' (ll. 335-376)

The poet introduces the whale by 'quoting' from the Latin original, and fuses the "cetus,/Monstrum grande satis" (Eden 1972:56, ll. 1-2) into "Cethegrande" (l. 335). Lines 337-340 tell us then, that the floating whale displays a striking similarity to an island and contains the direct address to the audience, which is a typical characteristic of the Middle English poet's style. The poet then changes track and continues with the whale's remarkable ability to lure small fish into its mouth by exuding a sweet smell. Bigger fish, however, cannot be deceived. The allusion in the Latin model to the biblical story of Jonah is not included.[167]

Whereas the Old English chapter on the whale had each 'natura' directly followed by its allegorical interpretation, we do not find any such deviant structuring in the Middle English version. Here, the division between the 'natura' and the 'significatio' is kept intact. The 'island-theme', which was abandoned or, depending on one's point of view, prepared for in the opening lines, is taken up again in lines 353-376, yet without being marked by means of a Latin subtitle as the second 'natura'. In contrast to the corresponding chapter in *The Old English Physiologus*, the whale's surfacing is motivated by the equinoctal gales, which make it impossible to remain on the bottom of the sea (ll. 355-362). The very same gales explain why the seafarers moor their ships on this supposed island. This impression of an impersonal 'fate' is intensified in lines 374-376. Whereas we have a clearly malicious intention governing the actions of the whale in lines 24a-31a of the Old English poem, the Middle English account of the very same incident remains neutral, insofar as it does not imply that the whale's actions are prompted by malice: its submerging is nothing more than a natural reaction to the fire on its back, a response which is in full accord with its emerging from the depths of the sea because of the storms. At least in its relationship with man, the whale is not depicted as an actively deceitful being. Thus, the 'natura' level remains separated from the morally explicit 'significatio'.

'significatio' (ll. 377-390)

The rather short allegorical interpretation begins with four lines (ll. 377-380) which are a faulty and, therefore, sometimes unclear rendering of the Latin verses:

> Viribus est Zabulus quasi cetus corpore magnus,
> Ut monstrant magni, quos facit ille, magi.
> Mentes cunctorum, qui sunt ubicunque, virorum
> Esurit atque sitit, quosque potest, perimit.
> (Eden 1972:58, ll. 23-26)

[167] See Eden (1972:56, l. 12).

These can be translated as follows:

> The devil is as great in strength as the whale in body: this is shown by the power of the wizards whom he creates. He hungers and thirsts for the minds of all men everywhere, and he destroys those he can.
> (Eden 1972:59)

Knowing the original Latin text, we can guess the Middle English poet's intention in lines 377-378: he adopted the notion of the devil's great strength, yet omitted the explicit comparison with the whale's bulk. However, the exact logical connection between lines 377 and 378 remains unclear. The train of thought of the Latin model has been transformed into a vague and hazy associative connection between the power/skill of the "wicches" (l. 378) and the aforementioned 'mikel wil & maȝt' (see l. 377) of the devil. The next two lines (ll. 379-380) are an example of an original misinterpretation. The Latin lines can obviously be seen as the allegorical interpretation of the whale's way of alleviating its hunger. Yet, its Middle English counterpart still remains on the level of characterizing the devil and mistranslates the Latin original, so that it is not the devil which hungers and thirsts for the minds of men, but the men themselves who are pained by hunger, thirst, and "mani oðer sinful list" (l. 380). It may strike the contemporary reader as strange that hunger and thirst are mentioned in the same breath as other, sinful, desires. Yet, things become clearer if one looks at *The Later Genesis* (Timmer 1948), where Adam complains "nu slit me hunger 7 þurst" (Timmer 1948:96, l. 801b): hunger and thirst are among the consequences of the original sin. Before the Fall, man had never experienced the piercing physical pain of these two basic needs, and since the devil seduced Adam and Eve to commit the original sin, he is correctly blamed with causing hunger and thirst. Thus, although the 'mistranslation' makes sense, the link with the 'natura' is lost and we thus have four somewhat disconnected lines (ll. 377-380) standing in front of the 'significatio' proper.

Owing to the Latin original, the allegorical interpretation of the two traits is limited to the basic correspondences. Lines 381-388 (or, alternatively, lines 381-386) render the spiritual dimension of the first characteristic ('swete onde'). Here, the Middle English poet transfers the image of the sweet breath on to the allegorical level and once more takes up the image of 'ðe little & ðe mikle fisses', which he explicitly equates with those who are weak and strong in faith. The allegorical interpretation of the second characteristic, however, has shrunk to a mere two lines (ll. 389-390) – or four, if we take lines 387-388 also to refer to the second characteristic.

Apart from the link on the level of vocabulary (line 389: "festeð" and line 369: "festen"), no explicit connection is established.

Conclusion

As before in the chapter on the spider, the poet does not exhibit any extraordinary innovative power on the allegorical level; he seems to be content to follow his Latin model, sometimes taking the liberty of embellishing this or that characteristic in the 'natura' or clarifiying the correspondences between the 'natura' and the 'significatio'. Yet, he never attempts to exploit additional details to strengthen his allegorical interpretation, but rather aims to keep the relation between the 'natura' and the 'significatio' as simple as possible, while stressing the moral dimension, even if this means shifting the focus of the original (see *The Spider*).

Before continuing with the discussion of *The Siren*, it is now necessary to say a word or two about the status of monsters and similar creatures.

Digression on the Status of Monsters and Other Fabulous Beings

Up to now, we have encountered animals which are more or less familiar even to a modern reader, or which would at least belong to a known genus (for example, the phoenix is still clearly recognisable as a bird); the strangeness of the animals has been limited to individual characteristics which could still somehow be accounted for. An entirely fabulous being, however, constitutes a challenge to the modern reader's model of the world. Yet, taking the very limited availability of reliable 'scientific' works into account, it is all the more astonishing that monsters appear so rarely in medieval works on animals.[168] It is also in accordance with the medieval writer's respect for the authors of Antiquity that we have very few monstrous newcomers, as Lecouteux (1982:265) states: "L'étude des traditions tératologiques nous a appris que les écrivains médiévaux respectent leurs sources et n'ont pratiquement pas créé de monstres." Thus, the question of the origin of monsters and fabulous beings is of little importance to us.[169]

---

[168] On the availability of reliable 'scientific' works, see C. Gerhardt (1988:156) and T.H. White (1959:257). The fact that monsters appear relatively rarely in works on animals does not mean that the Middle Ages showed no interest in monsters. On the contrary, there are specialized works which deal exclusively with them (for example the *Liber Monstrorum*).

[169] For a psychological attempt to explain the origin of monstrous beings, see, for example, Ackermann (1991). Lecouteux (1982:304-306) traces the genesis of many a monstrous

The Realism of Monstrous Creatures

Monstrous or fabulous creatures constituted a real aspect of the medieval man's model of the world. Approaching the world with different questions in mind, the medieval scholar found different answers which, in turn, influenced his view of the universe. The fundamental difference between the modern scientific model and the 'medieval' one is a matter of focus.[170] Modern science tries to explain the structure and nature of the universe without recourse to any postulation of God. Natural science exists aside from theology, and transcendental questions are relegated to the realm of philosophy and theology. Things were different during the Middle Ages and well into the Renaissance: the objection that 'this is not possible' had little force when applied to fabulous creatures. Two obstacles rendered such an argument powerless: first, the systematic classification of nature had not yet been (re-)discovered, and even when scholars attempted something of that sort, they were well aware of their limited human perspective; secondly, the belief in an actively intervening God made it easy to see Him as the source of all seemingly unfathomable events and beings.[171] Thus, medieval science had no fundamental objections which would rule out the existence of composite creatures and monstrous races. Yet, the step from merely having no objections to actually accepting the reports of these beings needs some explanation. Most of the fabulous and monstrous creatures which were known to medieval scholars were handed down via the Bible itself, via the works of the poets of Antiquity, or via the 'scientific' writings which incorporated the sum of the geographical, biological, and ethnographical knowledge of the time. Whereas the authority of the Scriptures was beyond question, the information contained in the writings of Antiquity could be subjected to a certain critical examination. However, the criteria for such an evaluation differed from modern heuristic methods. Medieval scholars had three criteria at their disposal when judging a text; we can label these

---

creature to the manner of describing unknown animals ('has a head like an ox and a tail like a lion' => 'has an ox-head and lion's tail') and to textual misunderstandings.

170 I am aware that there was no such thing as 'the medieval model of the world'. See, for example, Cronin (1941:194), who refers to the changing models over the centuries. In accordance with C.S. Lewis (1964), I use this term to denote a reconstructed and idealized model which will allow us to point out the most fundamental differences.

171 See J.B. Friedman (1981:2), C. Gerhardt (1988:157), Schmidtke (1968:155), and Simek (1992:126). On the function of monsters and fabulous beings, see below (page 91f.).

'auctores', 'ratio', and, last and least, 'experientia'.[172] Let us now try to apply this 'critical' method to the siren.

First and foremost, the siren is a biblical creature (*Isaias Propheta* 13,22: "sirenae in delubris voluptatis"); this fact alone would suffice to vouch for her reality. Yet, the siren is also known from the mythology of Antiquity. She can be found in the works of PLINY, VIRGIL, OVID, JUVENAL, etc. and makes her appearance, together with the onocentaur, in *The Physiologus* (see, for example, Seel 1992:23-24). This combination of biblical and classical authority was indeed formidable proof and, in the words of Mia Gerhardt (1970:243), "comment l'homme médiéval aurait-il pu douter de l'existence de [ce monstre]-là?" Thus, even an examination according to the first criterion already tips the scales in favour of accepting the siren as real.

Let us now, for the sake of argument, pursue the critical evaluation of the two remaining points. Does the existence of sirens stand in opposition to the 'ratio'? Theology provided the idea of an intervening God, who could, within limits, be used to explain seemingly inexplicable phenomena.[173] The universe may look chaotic to us, and the monsters may seem to be against nature, but from a cosmic point of view, things fall into place.[174] In addition to this more transcendental argument, ancient and medieval geography alike provided rational explanations for the existence of monstrous beings. First, it was generally believed that all elements were populated by species of the 'longaevi'.[175] Secondly, the conception of the climatic zones became prominent in late Antiquity.[176] It was assumed that the climatic environment

---

[172] See C. Gerhardt (1988:159), M. Gerhardt (1970:239), and C.S. Lewis (1964:189)

[173] Flint (1988b) convincingly illustrates the fact that medieval scholars, especially the authors of the *De natura rerum* treatises, were at pains to distinguish between natural phenomena and transcendental interventions, in order to limit divine responsibility.

[174] According to ST. AUGUSTINE in *De civitate Dei* XVI, 8 (Augustinus 1965:45): "But one who cannot see the whole clearly is offended by the apparent deformity of a single part, since he does not know with what it conforms or how to classify it." See also Michel (1979:76).

[175] C.S. Lewis (1964:134) characterizes the 'longaevi' as follows: "[T]hey are a third rational species distinct from angels and men." See also JOSHUA SYLVESTER, who, in his translation of GUILLAUME DE SALUSTE SIEUR DU BARTAS' work (c. 1605), poetically expresses the belief that every element is populated by similar creatures: "Seas have (as well as Skies) Sunne, Moone and Starres:/(As well as Aire) Swallowes, and Rookes, and Stares,/[....]/And also Rammes, Calfes, Horses, Hares, and Hoggs,/Yea Men and Maydes" [emphasis added] (Sylvester 1979:232, ll. 37-45).

[176] See J.B. Friedman (1981:35) and Simek (1992:40).

would influence the phenotype of its inhabitants.[177] Thus, to be able to regard the differing climate as being responsible for the fantastic qualities of the vegetable and animal kingdoms, it was necessary to locate the habitat of the monstrous, fabulous, or at least exotic beings in those more extreme climatic zones; they usually began where the civilized world ('oikoumene') ended – or simply as far away as possible.[178] The poets of *The Old English Phoenix*, *The Old English Physiologus* (especially in *The Panther*), and *The Middle English Physiologus* (especially in *The Siren*) can be seen in this tradition. They place their strange creatures either in the inaccessible "ēastdǣlum" (*The Old English Phoenix*, Blake 1990:49, l. 2a), in "feorlondum" (the OE *Panther*, Krapp and Dobbie 1936:169, l. 10b), or in a "wankel stede ðer ðe water sinkeð" (*The Siren*, Wirtjes 1991:15, l. 396) which was not more closely specified. The same strategy can be observed on the various medieval maps of the known world, where the monstrous beings were also pushed out of the civilized countries to the very edge of the world.[179]

The 'far-awayness' of these beings brings us to the argument of 'experientia'. At a time when scholars hardly ever tried to verify the traditional assumptions about the most common and accessible facts, it is to be expected that the empirical verification of reports about exotic or fabulous creatures was even less pressing. Furthermore, they lacked the technical equipment or methods vital to the construction of empirical argumentation. From a modern point of view, the medieval scholar not only suffered from an alarming insufficiency of trustworthy and reliable encyclopaedias, but was greatly handicapped by his literary bias, caused by the very books which should have helped him to come to terms with the reality of things.[180] Thus, it is not surprising that even the so-called 'experientia' cannot be compared to modern experiments. Nature, as modern scientists are also beginning to see and as C.S. Lewis (1964:223) puts it, "gives most of her evidence in answer to the questions we ask her." To make matters even worse, the criterion of 'experientia', which may be termed the pillar of modern science, was of secondary or even tertiary importance

---

177 See M. Gerhardt (1970:242).

178 For the placing of the monstrous beings, see Cizek (1981:79) and J.B. Friedman (1981:37).

179 Simek (1992) offers illustrative pictorial material.

180 See Schmidtke (1968:144). The following selective list of references gives a representative view of the discussion of this problem in connection with fabulous beings: C. Gerhardt (1988:160), Grubmüller (1978:175), Simek (1992:75), and T.H. White (1959:257).

within the medieval model, and had not yet assumed its present crucial function.

Although we can assume with some certainty that the truthfulness of the *Physiologus* 'natura' reports was not seriously challenged, a closer look at the correlation of spiritual/moral truth and factual truth will shed some additional light on our topic. As we have seen in the earliest versions of *The Physiologus*, the original function of the 'natura' chapters is to illustrate a biblical or spiritual truth. The idea of treating the 'natura' as a means to the (transcendental) end, similar to the use of the admittedly fictitious fables and other 'exempla', had a certain appeal. Yet, as Michel (1979:83) points out, it must not be forgotten that the fact that certain things signify something else does not diminish their factuality. The question of whether or not the animal or monstrous creature was seen as a rhetorical topos largely depends on the exegete's point of view. And although the symbolic and literary value of a thing or being may well be of greater interest to the scholar than its veracity, there are, in our context, certain limits to the purely transcendental view of the world.[181] Grubmüller (1978:160) puts it in a nutshell:

> Dort aber versagen solche Lösungen [i.e. the use of literary fiction in order to illustrate moral truth], wo Wirklichkeit als Manifestation von Gottes Schöpfungs- und Gestaltungswillen behauptet werden muss: in Naturkunde und Geschichte. Geschaffenes und Veranlasstes kann nur zum Argument werden, sofern es wirklich ist oder wirklich gewesen ist[.]

The medieval clerical poets therefore had to make a choice between either regarding the 'scientific' information as merely illustrative material, in which case they would not have to worry about its veracity, or taking it at face value and seeing themselves confronted with the task of proving the veracity of the information which they wanted to allegorize. In spite of the primacy of the spiritual meaning for the exegete, there is a tradition of independent transmission of 'natura' chapters which were separated from the 'significatio'.[182] This fact suggests that the 'natura' information was accepted as true.[183] Furthermore, we have to bear in mind that a *Physiologus* 'natura' chapter is not a fable. This point is stressed by Grubmüller (1978:170): "Der Naturbericht wird sich auch im Darstellungsgestus niemals die

[181] Concerning the symbolic and literary value of things or beings, see M. Gerhardt (1970:244), Simek (1992:40), and L. White (1947:425).

[182] See Schmidtke (1968:158).

[183] See T.H. White (1959), who judges the bestiary to be "a serious work of natural history" (231) and "a serious text-book on biology" (248).

Irrealitätslizenz etwa der Fabel zu eigen machen[.]" Since the naming of an 'auctor' as the source of one's own account was sufficient proof of its veracity, we find numerous references to these authorities in all the poems examined. The outcome of this development is that, as Grubmüller (1978:164) puts it, "Wahrheit wird Verbürgtheit". As a logical consequence, all the reports which we would label 'original' and which did not trace their origin to the 'auctores' were highly suspicious and smacked of lie. Originality as we understand it was, if not non-existent, then at least very rare.[184] The critical evaluation of once 'authorized' information was limited to philological criticism (the author decided in favour of the 'better' source); this did not give rise to a new approach, but made use of the means already available, and the 'literary' quality of the debate prevailed.[185] The Middle English poet's replacement of THEOBALD's 'classical bird siren' by the 'fishtail siren', which was probably more popular by then, is an excellent example of such a philological emendation.[186] Thus, we have to assume that 'scientific' reports about even the most fantastic animals or monstrous beings were basically taken at face value, and there was especially a class of men who did not rack their brains too much about the veracity of the reports, as long as they provided illustrative material for their purpose. Here, I am talking about preachers. B. White (1954:26) observes that the bestiaries provided a profitable font of sermon material from the tenth century onwards. The scholastic movement intensified this development, so that most of the allegorical interpretations are to be found in sermons and in devotional writings.[187] Information spread by preaching had a great impact upon the public.[188] Yet, the preachers themselves often knew and used only simplified texts, since their main focus of interest was on the symbolic view of the world and on the moralistic teachings which could be derived from nature.[189] Cronin (1941:195) deals with this aspect of our problem and reaches the following conclusion:

> Unfortunately, we cannot tell precisely what they [i.e. the preachers] thought of their inherited natural history. The evidence is confusing.

---

184 C.S. Lewis (1964:210) comments: "Far from feigning originality, as a modern plagiarist would, they are apt to conceal it." See also B. White (1954:26).

185 Grubmüller (1978:172) quotes examples of such a 'philological criticism'.

186 For the possible origin of the 'fishtail siren', see Ackermann (1991:61) and Wirtjes (1991:lxxxviii).

187 See Schmidtke (1968:78-79, 134, and 182-184).

188 See Owst (1966:186).

189 See Simek (1992:34).

> [....] But many of the authors of the 'artes praedicandi' seem to adopt a very pragmatic attitude toward science.[190]

The later development of *The Physiologus* away from centring on the divine plan of salvation towards a more moralistic interpretation, which is especially conspicuous in *The Middle English Physiologus*, points in this direction, too.[191] The shift from 'sensus allegoricus' to 'sensus moralis' often weakened the former strict attitude towards the factual veracity of natural history, since the 'natura' parts within a sermon found themselves, at least functionally, on the same level as the other illustrative 'exempla'.[192] Thus, it is often impossible to tell whether a 'natura' was valued 'per se', or whether it existed solely 'propter significationem'.[193] Since the Middle Ages knew, according to Grubmüller (1978:167), "eine wenigstens partielle Wahrheit des Nicht-Wirklichen", the verification of the 'natura' information, which provided the starting point for the moralistic allegorizations of the sermons, did not enjoy the highest priority. B. White's (1954:25) words may best describe the attitude of most preachers:

> Roughly speaking, this lay somewhere between TERTULLIAN's 'Credo quia absurdum est' and ST. ANSELM's 'Credo ut intellegam', divorced from their theological contexts, and it provoked the prevailing conviction that it was the ultimate significance of things that really mattered[.]

The following graphic illustration aims to summarize the hypothetical development of a 'natura' chapter:

---

190 C.S. Lewis (1964:151-152) gives an even more pronounced judgment: "Most of those who helped either by speech or writing to keep the pseudo-zoology in circulation were not really concerned, one way or the other, with the question of fact; just as today the public speaker who warns me not to hide my head in the sand like an ostrich, is not really thinking, and does not want me to think, about ostriches. The 'moralitas' is what matters."

191 See Schmidtke (1968:94-95).

192 ODO OF CHERITON (early thirteenth century), for example, allegorizes fables and interprets them in the 'sensus moralis' (see Jacobs 1985 and Schmidtke 1968:165). Thus, at least within the greater context of sermons, the 'factual' 'natura' passages found themselves side by side with the fictitious fables.

193 Schmidtke (1968:164) draws our attention to texts which instructed preachers to make it clear that, if they used fictitious accounts to illustrate a moralistic point, "die Sache nicht in sich wahr sei, sondern nur ihrer Bedeutung wegen erzählt wird."

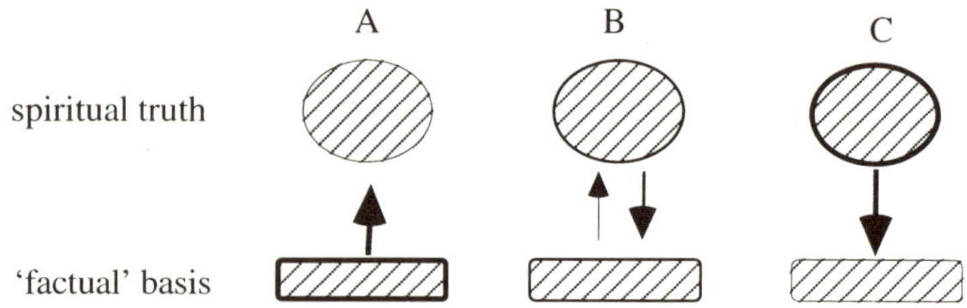

In stage A, the spiritual truth is based on a factual characteristic; the 'natura' passage has to be true. The situation becomes less clear when we reach stage B, where the veracity of the factual basis is often subordinated to the spiritual truth, and it is unclear whether the 'natura' stands 'propter significationem', or vice versa. The final phase (stage C) is reached when the importance of the spiritual truth becomes prevalent, and the function of the 'natura' passage is reduced to merely providing illustrative examples.

The Status of Monstrous Creatures

The discussion of the veracity of monstrous and fabulous beings has shown that the occurrence of the siren side by side with definitively less fantastic creatures like the spider and the elephant was probably not so much of a problem for the medieval audience. Yet in our case, the fact that the siren, obviously endowed with the ability to speak and sing, is included among creatures of otherwise clearly animal character raises the question of her status. Thus, we have to differentiate between two main 'monstrous traditions', even though they sometimes overlap.

First, there are the so-called Plinian races, mainly handed down to the Middle Ages through the works of PLINY. These Plinian races enjoyed great popularity among scholars, and they were often considered to be 'children of Adam', too – i.e. human, in the widest sense of the word. It may strike modern readers as strange that the existence of monstrous beings, once their existence was attested by the 'auctores', was not questioned any further, whereas their human or non-human status was an issue for learned discussion.[194] Mostly relying on, or taking as their starting point, the arguments of ST. AUGUSTINE, who combined the arguments of former 'auctores' and the 'ratio', medieval scholars discussed the problem of the humanity of the monstrous races with great learning and care, yet did not

[194] For an in-depth discussion of the history and status of the monstrous races, see J.B. Friedman (1981).

always reach a satisfying conclusion as to their status.[195] The possible human status of the Plinian races did not prevent the authors of bestiaries from making use of them; J.B. Friedman (1981:122-124) points out that several bestiaries included and allegorized some of the Plinian races, and at least some authors granted them human status.

Apart from the Plinian races, the Middle Ages inherited the composite and fabulous beings of classical mythology, one of which was the siren.[196] Yet, unless they made their way into the ever-growing family of the Plinian races, little scholarly attention was paid to their status.[197] C.S. Lewis (1964:150-151) considers the inclusion of the siren among the beasts of the *Theobaldi 'Physiologus'* to be rather uncommon. Yet, Lecouteux (1982:190) interprets the linking of the siren with the onocentaur (in the *Theobaldi 'Physiologus'* they share the same 'significatio'; see Eden 1972:60-63) as a sign of her animal status. Owst (1966:201), too, shares this opinion: "Among mythical beasts must be reckoned also that 'mermayde of the see'[.]" Thus, there is nothing extraordinary about the inclusion of the siren among the beasts of *The Middle English Physiologus*.

The Function of Monstrous and Fabulous Creatures

Our short discussion of the phenomenon of 'monsters' would be incomplete without a word or two about their function within the medieval model of the world. In fact, I had better speak of 'functions' in the plural, since, as Michel (1979:28) observes concerning sacred buildings, "[n]icht an jedem Ort ist jede Darstellung möglich, oder sie hat doch wenigstens an jedem Ort einen anderen Sinn." The same holds true for the monstrous and fabulous creatures in literature; the romance-dragon against which the knight has to pit his strength fulfils a different primary function from that of the 'draco' in *The Physiologus*. Lecouteux (1982:335) lists the following possible functions of 'monstra' in medieval literature:

1) In travel stories and romances which take place outside Europe: monstrous and fabulous creatures are part and parcel of the local colour.

---

[195] The following authors provide an excellent introduction to this fascinating topic: Flint (1988c), J.B. Friedman (1981), Holmes (1972), Lecouteux (1982), Michel (1979:64-79), and Simek (1992:113-117)

[196] ISIDORE obviously does not feel at ease with the inclusion of pagan mythological creatures among the 'monstra', and attempts to explain most of them rationally (see Lecouteux 1982:194).

[197] Lecouteux (1982:195) notes that many mythological creatures only leave their mythological surroundings, if at all, to live on in the medieval adaptations of the romances of Antiquity.

2) In works connected with the concept of crusade: monstrous human beings, the descendants of Cain and Japhet, are found in the rank and file of the pagan armies and are the incarnate prototypical enemies of Christendom.

3) In religious legends: they are used as antagonists of the saints to illustrate the strength of faith in overcoming them.

4) In chronicles: they are seen as omens.

5) In romances: they have an initiatory and educational function, serving as a negative example or as a means of clarifying human self-perception.

6) In scholarly writings: they are part of a tradition and testimony of God's power.

As we will see in the following discussion, *The Siren* of *The Middle English Physiologus* is an example of the sixth and last type, adapted to the poet's moralistic intentions.

The Siren
(Wirtjes 1991:15-16, ll. 391-422)

The illustration below attempts to depict the structure of the chapter. The fact that certain 'natura' traits are allegorically interpreted in the 'significatio' is indicated by the corresponding patterns of the fields in question. Those fields that are filled with an individual pattern represent the parts of the poem which stand on their own. The lines linking the different fields point to the internal coherence and mutual influencing of the parts.

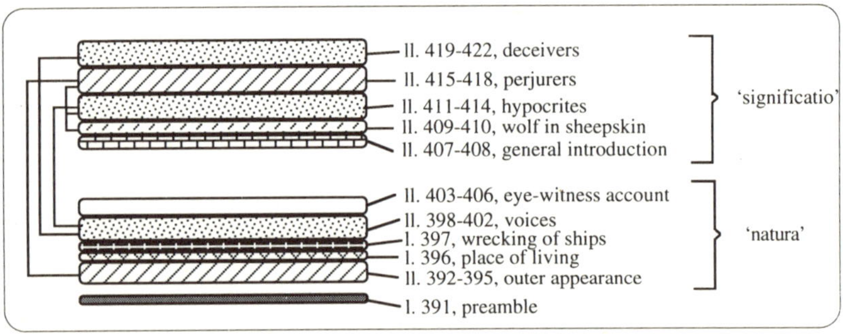

A short preamble (l. 391) refers back to the preceding chapter on the whale, and sets the tone for the following lines: "In ðe se senden selcuðes manie." Only after this introductory line do we have the subtitle, "Natura sirene" (see Wirtjes 1991:15, l. 391), which announces the 'natura' proper. The preamble has no Latin counterpart; it prepares the audience for a certain vagueness and fantastic quality in the subject, and has a function similar to that of the "[...] feor heonan/ēastdǣlum [...]" (*The Old English Phoenix*, Blake 1990:49, ll. 1b-2a), which, by referring to the fabulous lands of the East, heightens the audience's willingness to accept even the most extraordinary creatures.

'natura' (ll. 392-406)

Having begun with a general setting of the scene in the 'preamble' by means of the key-words 'se' and 'selcuðes', the poet moves on to the particular, which is, in this case, 'ðe mereman'. This procedure has the advantage of relating the familiar, yet fabulous being to the sea, which is the habitat of many a strange or even grotesque creature. Then, the Middle English poet changes the original Latin description, which gives us the classical conception of the siren as a hybrid being with a lower birdlike, and an upper maidenlike part. The Middle English siren breaks with that tradition and is described as sporting a fishtail and fins, details which accord better with its aforementioned habitat than the feathers and wings of the 'classical siren'.[198] The fact that we are given a rather detailed account of the mermaid's physiognomy is, in itself, quite remarkable. The general appearances of all other animals of *The Middle English Physiologus* are obviously taken for granted, even though animals like the panther or the elephant may not have been too well known. The detailed description of what we know today to be a purely imaginary being can thus be seen as the attempt to come to terms with the fabulous facts, at least on a verbal level, and to distinguish the Middle English siren from the one that originated in the classical tradition. The specification of the siren's place of abode adds to the overall topic of 'in the sea': she not only dwells in the sea, but within this already wondrous and mysterious realm, she is to be found "in wankel stede ðer ðe water sinkeð" (l. 396). This removes her one step further from the common world. The report of the wrecking of ships being the main characteristic action of the siren is placed before the account of how she accomplishes this by means of her voice(s), and is taken up again at the end of these allegorically relevant lines. The last four lines of the 'natura' constitute a peculiarity among the chapters of both *The Middle English Physiologus* and its Latin model. For the first time, we encounter something which comes close to a corroboration of information by means of eye-witnesses. The author usually refers to his

[198] According to Michel (1979:68), the 'fishtail siren' made its appearance for the first time in the treatise *De monstris* (see also L. Frank 1971:168); and it superseded the classical type throughout the Middle Ages. Lecouteux (1982:271) assumes the existence of a popular 'monster tradition' parallel to the classical one. The 'fishtail siren' is most probably part of this popular tradition. On the siren in general, see King (1995:143-148).

written source(s): "ðus it is on boke set/ðat man clepeð 'Fisiologet'" (Wirtjes 1991:9, ll. 190-191); or he rhetorically makes a direct appeal to his audience to verify the truth of his words: "ðat tu wuldes seien ȝet/ȝef ðu it soȝe wan it flet" (Wirtjes 1991:13, ll. 337-338.). This time, however, he presents us with 'wise and cautious men' who have been able to escape from the mortal danger posed by the siren, and who are thus able to tell the story of this 'mere'. The Latin author uses his nondescript survivors only as spokesmen to describe the outward appearance of the siren. The Middle English poet, however, also makes use of them on the allegorical level: he adds the information that these men owe their survival to their virtue and their endeavour to escape from the snares of the siren. In this way, he turns the simple eye-witnesses into paragons of virtue, while relegating their original function of corroborating the truthfulness of the report to second position.

'significatio' (ll. 407-422)

The transition from the 'natura' on to the allegorical level is explicitly marked by the last line of the 'natura' and the first two lines of the 'significatio'. Since the allegorical interpretation presupposes the idea of accepting the 'natura' as a kind of divine metaphor, we would expect a straightforward interpretation as usual. It is, therefore, all the more surprising to be confronted with yet another metaphor – this time a biblical one.[199] We can only guess at the poet's motives for inserting this new, yet apt image; it might well be that he simply preferred to give the moral interpretation in a nutshell, with the help of a better-known metaphor. The fact that the major parts of the Latin 'significatio' would have been much better expressed by means of the 'wolf in the sheepskin' metaphor might be an additional reason. The connections between the siren and the 'wolf in the sheepskin' image, however, remain vague, and the poet refrains from drawing any explicit parallels. The beautiful voices and the probably no less attractive 'maiden-part' of the siren roughly correspond to the sheepskin, whereas the 'fish-part' can be equated with the true wolfish nature of the disguised wolf. The following lines (ll. 411-418) may refer equally to the 'wolf in the sheepskin' metaphor or to the siren. The siren, the wolf, and the hypocrites/perjurers are connected by means of the 'tertium comparationis',

---

[199] See *Secundum Mattheum* 7,15: "Adtendite a falsis prophetis qui veniunt ad vos in vestimentis ovium intrinsecus autem sunt lupi rapaces[.]" The technique of explaining a metaphor or talking about metaphors by means of metaphors was, and is, not that uncommon. For a conscious use of this technique, see, for example, JEAN PAUL (1990:191).

which is, in this case, their deceitful nature.[200] The word "Twifold" (l. 415) harks back to the composite nature of the siren's physiognomy, as well as to the double nature (inside/outside) of the wolf. The ambiguous quality of the 'significatio' finally comes to an end with the reference to 'song' in line 419, which unambiguously connects this passage with the siren's 'natura'. The poet ends by recapitulating once again the double threat to the possessions and the soul of the victim.

Conclusion

Although the Latin 'significatio' is no intricate work of art or intellect and lacks any great ingenious interpretative spark, it at least doggedly keeps to interpreting the main characteristics, even if the connection between 'natura' and 'significatio' is rather tenuous. The Middle English poet, then, not only substitutes the 'fish siren' for the 'bird siren' and omits the onocentaur, which is, admittedly, not very relevant allegorically, but he also alters the line of argument of the 'significatio' section by adding a new metaphor. This corroborates the doubts mentioned earlier about the poet's allegorical versatility. Instead of interpreting the individual traits of the siren according to the different allegorical senses, he expands the central idea by means of a better-known metaphor, without referring back to the individual characteristics of the siren. The allegorical interpretation is based on the vague, associative chain of thought which starts with the siren's composite physiognomy and the deception of the seafarers through her voices, gains greater clarity in the image of the 'wolf in the sheepskin', and has its allegorical solution in the identification of the siren with hypocrites, perjurers, and deceivers. The linking, however, is poor, and the function of the siren is of no great allegorical importance: she is used to provide a 'natura' which, in itself, may capture the fancy of both the poet and the audience, yet which is not really necessary for the moral allegorization of the 'significatio'. Apart from taking up the vaguely-felt general drift of the 'natura', the allegorical interpretation establishes very few connections between the two parts, and not very convincing ones at that.

The Panther
(Wirtjes 1991:19-20, ll. 533-584)

Unlike the chapters on the siren or the spider, *The Panther* closely follows its Latin model, though there are some changes which testify to the Middle

---

200 For the differentiation of the 'evil men' in the 'significatio' part into hypocrites ('Heuchler'), perjurers ('meineidige Lügner'), and deceivers ('Betrüger'), see L. Frank (1971:173).

English poet's characteristic bend of mind. The 'natura' and 'significatio' parts are multiply linked and stand in close relation to each other, as is clearly illustrated by the following graphic analysis. The fact that certain 'natura' traits are allegorically interpreted in the 'significatio' is indicated by the pattern of the fields in question. Those fields that are filled with an individual pattern indicate the lines which stand on their own.

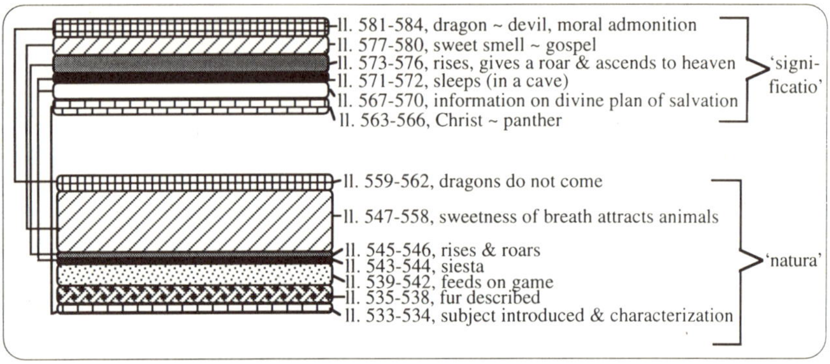

'natura' (ll. 533-562)

In accordance with the Latin model, the characterization of the panther begins with the description of its appearance. Yet, the Middle English poet cannot resist embellishing the rather prosaic Latin account and adding a few comparisons of his own (l. 535: "so bro of qual" and l. 537: "Wit & trendled als a wel"), or commenting on the beauty of the fur (l. 538: "& `itt´ bicumeð him swiðe wel"). The rest of the 'natura' is in keeping with its Latin counterpart, and only in the last line (l. 562: "Als so he weren of dede offriȝt") do we encounter an addition which is obviously intended to motivate the behaviour of the dragons.

The differences between the 'natura' of *The Old English Physiologus* chapter on the panther and that of of *The Middle English Physiologus* can be summarized briefly: the Middle English author does not seem to be disturbed by the panther's carnivorous appetite, while the *Old English Physiologus* poet omits all references to the quality of its diet; and whereas *The Old English Physiologus* first of all mentions the men who are attracted by the sweet smell, we do not find them in the 'natura' of *The Middle English Physiologus* at all. The Middle English poet exhibits a certain lack of allegorical propriety, even though he does nothing more, in this case, than to follow his Latin model. He copies characteristics which he is not able to neutralize properly on the allegorical level, be it because he has difficulty in translating the Latin verses, or be it because he is not aware of the inappropriateness of stressing predatory traits without the necessary allegorical 'antidotes' when identifying a beast of prey with Christ.

'significatio' (ll. 563-584)

The allegorical interpretation of the 'natura' part is more detailed than any of those analysed so far. In the wake of the Latin 'significatio', the Middle English poet first allegorizes the panther itself, and then, as in the 'significatio' of the siren chapter, adds a new poetic and, this time, more accurate image: Christ stands above men, as the evening star stands above the mud of the earth (l. 566). The following four lines, however, fail to render the expected allegorical explanation of the panther's predatory habit of feeding on other animals, but instead give us an appreciation of Christ's suffering with regard to the divine plan of salvation. L. Frank (1971:131) comments on these lines: "Die Tatsache, dass sich der Panther vor seinem Schlaf sättigt, legt der me. Dichter wohl deshalb nicht aus, weil er mit der unklaren Formulierung im *PT* [*Physiologus Theobaldi*] [...] nichts anzufangen weiss." "[H]ole" (l. 569) parallels the "hole" (l. 543) of the 'natura', and thus we only have a link on the level of vocabulary. The poet then reverts to following the Latin model until he comes to the point of interpreting the 'sweet smell', which THEOBALD seems to have omitted. He equates the 'swete smel' with the gospel, and thus at least partially neutralizes the panther's act of luring other animals to its den by means of the sweet odour.[201] The final lines (ll. 581-584) once again nicely illustrate the Middle English poet's moralistic turn of mind: not being satisfied with identifying the dragon with the devil that flees from God, he turns it into an admonition 'in nuce': man is protected from the wiles of the devil as long as he listens to the word of God, obeys the commandments, and loves his neighbour.

Conclusion

The overall impression given by the chapter on *The Panther* is one of textual fidelity to its Latin model, and the few additions are of little consequence for the whole. The description of the panther is a close copy of the Latin

201 The original purpose of the 'swete smel', as mentioned by ARISTOTLE, AELIAN, PLUTARCH, and PLINY, was to attract other animals in order to prey on them (see L. Frank 1971:128, fn. 5). This technique is also used by the *Physiologus* whale. The poet's reinterpretation of the originally negative odour as the positive 'swete smel' is probably due to the influence of the exegesis of the *Song of Songs* (*Canticum Canticorum* 1,2-3: "fraglantia unguentis optimis oleum effusum nomen tuum [...] trahe me post te"). See also L. Frank (1971:133, fn. 10).

‘natura’, and the Middle English poet did not adapt it to the changes in the ‘significatio’ part, which are mainly due to his failure to understand the meaning of the Latin lines. On the one hand, the ‘significatio’ part does not just use the general idea, but refers to individual traits; on the other hand, we have the description of an animal with some characteristics that are not allegorically resolved. Because of this, the ‘natura’ part here plays a much more important role than those we have analysed up to now. The Middle English poet’s typical moralistic disposition makes itself felt in the last four lines. The allegorical interpretation of the chapter on the panther is usually restricted to the ‘sensus allegoricus’ (see *The Old English Physiologus*); the Middle English poet, however, shifts the focus on to a more moralistic level.

The Dove
(Wirtjes 1991:21, ll. 585-602)

The last and, at the same time, shortest chapter of *The Middle English Physiologus* is of special interest to us, since it does not have a counterpart in the Latin *Theobaldi ‘Physiologus’*. Although it is not a genuinely original poem by the Middle English poet, it nevertheless gives us a deeper insight into the workings of the poet’s mind than yet another translation of a *Theobaldi ‘Physiologus’* chapter. The main source of *The Dove* can be found in ALEXANDER NECKAM’s *De naturis rerum*, where NECKAM lists eight characteristics, five of which make their appearance in *The Dove*.[202] NECKAM also provides the alternating structure which is copied in the Middle English poem: each ‘natura’ trait is immediately followed by its allegorization. Thus, *The Dove* conspicuously differs in its structure from the ‘norm’ chapter taken from the *Theobaldi ‘Physiologus’*, a fact which is easily verified by comparing the following graphically illustrated structure of *The Dove* with the structure of any of the other chapters.

[202] A discussion of the exact relationship between NECKAM’s account and the Middle English chapter on the dove can be found in Wirtjes (1991:xc-xci).

Preamble (ll.585-588)

I use the term 'preamble', since the first four lines do not yet belong to the 'natura' and 'significatio' parts proper, even though they share their structural peculiarity. The poet announces the enumeration of the seven 'costes' of the dove and admonishes the audience to meditate on these examples (ll. 586 and 588).[203]

'natura' and 'significatio' parts (ll. 589-602)

All of the seven 'natura' lines are immediately followed by an interpretation in the 'sensus moralis'; i.e., the 'significatio' lines instruct the audience how to lead a virtuous life, be it by admonishing us to imitate the action of the dove (for example l. 596: "So oȝ ur (ilk) to don wið oðer"), by urging us to be like the dove (for example l. 590: "Simple & softe be we alle"), or by contrasting the dove's virtuous character with our own imperfect one (for example l. 592: "Ilc robbinge do we of hac"). In contrast to the chapters modelled upon the *Theobaldi 'Physiologus'*, the structural unity of the 'natura' and 'significatio' parts have been sacrificed to the functional aspect; the allegorical interpretation of the individual traits occupies such a dominant position that the 'natura', which was formerly independent, at least structurally, becomes fragmented and reduced to a mere chain of cues which finds its fulfilment in the 'sensus moralis'.

Conclusion

Although the chapter on the dove is a relatively short one, its inclusion is of some importance, since the poet has finished the translation of the *Theobaldi 'Physiologus'* and is no longer following a given set of chapters. He is free to do as he wishes, so to speak. Therefore, it is very likely that the quality of the 'extra' chapter tells us a great deal more about the poet's spiritual and literary disposition than an individual chapter based on the *Theobaldi 'Physiologus'*, where, once the model for his version has been chosen, he is more or less obliged to adhere to the sequence outlined in the Latin original. There are several points to be considered. First, the poet chooses not to compose a poem of his own; this decision is in keeping with the medieval obsession with basing almost everything on the writings of an 'auctor'. Secondly, he selects a poem which is written in a similar spirit to the rest of his translation (allegorical interpretation of an animal). However, he does

203 The reduction from the original eight to the present seven characteristics may be due to the poet's intention of making use of the symbolic value of the number seven (for example the seven gifts of the Holy Ghost, or the seven cardinal virtues). However, I have not been able conclusively to establish such a correlation.

not adapt an available chapter on the dove from another Latin *Physiologus*, but opts for the structurally different one by NECKAM. Thirdly, he makes some minor alterations, yet leaves the basic structure of the poem untouched. Fourthly, the structure of the poem differs conspicuously from that of the other chapters and renders explicit the almost omnipresent strong moralistic tone to an even greater extent.

General Conclusion

Slightly modified, my observations on *The Dove* can also be applied to *The Middle English Physiologus* as a whole. To sum up, we can say the following about *The Middle English Physiologus*: first, the poet based the bulk of his poem on a Latin model, namely the *Theobaldi 'Physiologus'*; secondly, he did not produce a slavish translation of his model, but felt free to improve on his source or alter it, whilst at the same time taking care to preserve the basic structure; thirdly, whenever the opportunity arose, he additionally strengthened the already strong moralistic tone of the original.

These points, together with the numerous lines in which the poet directly addresses the audience and his efforts to enliven the often rather dull descriptions with allegorically irrelevant details, add to the overall impression that his main interest lies in using the poems on animals as a means of capturing the audience's attention and putting across moral instructions. Therefore, most of the 'natura' parts are designed to sweeten the otherwise bitter moral medicine, and the main focus of the poem is not on the animals themselves, even though the structural division applicable to the chapters based on the *Theobaldi 'Physiologus'* guarantees a certain independence, which is lost only in the final chapter on the dove.

The 'Bird Poems'

III. The 'Bird Poems'

"[F]or a bird of the air shall carry the voice, and that which hath wings shall tell the matter."
Ecclesiastes 10,20

1. Introduction

The following chapter will deal with four Middle English poems which have birds as their main protagonists. Apart from this common element, three of those poems, namely *The Owl and the Nightingale, The Thrush and the Nightingale*, and *The Cuckoo and the Nightingale*, belong to the genre of debate poetry. Therefore, they will be treated together, even though this means that we cannot always strictly adhere to the chronological order. Thus, *The Parlement of Foulys*, which, chronologically, comes before *The Cuckoo and the Nightingale*, will be discussed last. CHAUCER's poem contains a considerable debate element, which links it to the other works, yet at the same time its overall structure differs conspicuously from that of a standard debate, and thus justifies the decision to treat it separately.

2. *The Owl and the Nightingale*[204]

Introduction

The Middle English poem of the owl and the nightingale is the first of the four 'bird poems' dealt with in this section. Its name derives from the superscription INCIPIT ALTERCACIO INTER FILOMENAM & BUBONEM found in MS. J.[205] *The Owl and the Nightingale* takes precedence over the other poems, not only because of its early date (end of the twelfth/beginning of the thirteenth century), but also because of its

204 All quotations are taken from, and all references are to, the edition by Stanley (1972).

205 The expression 'altercatio' is a clear indication that it is a debate poem. See Walther (1920:3). For a discussion of the history and development of the debate form, see page 108ff. of this study.

artistic merit and the enormous critical attention it has attracted for more than a century.[206]

Author, Date, Manuscripts, and Sources

Of unknown, or at least uncertain authorship, the poem is extant in two manuscripts, namely MS. C (London: British Library, Cotton Caligula A. IX) and MS. J (Oxford: Jesus College 29), both of which have been dated in recent examinations as belonging to the second half of the thirteenth century.[207] Both manuscripts seem to stem from a common predecessor, now lost, which is, in turn, believed to be a copy of the lost original manuscript which Stone (1988:155) assumes to have been "written about one hundred and sixty years before CHAUCER was in his prime as a poet."[208]

Although the efforts of scholars over the last century have unearthed a host of allusions, links, and connections which place *The Owl and the Nightingale* within the literary framework of the second half of the twelfth and the first half of the thirteenth century, there has been no trace of evidence of an exclusive source upon which the whole poem might be based.[209] These facts leave us alone with the poem itself, in spite of the

---

206 Perryman (1984:97), like Klingender (1971:365), calls it "the first of a number of bird debates in English[.]" Sauer (1983:143) praises the poem as being "einer der ersten Höhepunkte mittelenglischer Dichtung." The earliest critical evaluation of *The Owl and the Nightingale* which has been taken into account is ten Brink's (1877), and the most recent one Conlee's (1991). The great amount of critical attention paid to *The Owl and the Nightingale* is reflected in the fact that the selective bibliography of books and articles that deal with this poem contains c. 50 entries.

207 See Sauer (1983:137). Atkins (1922:xxii), however, dates MS. C to the first half of the thirteenth century, and MS. J to the fifteenth century.

208 A discussion of the manuscripts and their tradition can be found, for example, in Atkins (1922:xxi-xxxiv), Gadow (1909:3-6), Grattan and Sykes (1935:xv-xviii), Huganir (1931:67-69), Ker (1963:ix-xx), Sauer (1983:137-139), and Stanley (1972:3-5). Opinions concerning a possible date for the composition of the poem range from 1174 (Baldwin 1967:207) up to the 1230s (Gadow 1909:13), with the majority of critics favouring 1176 as the 'terminus a quo' and 1216 as the 'terminus ante quo'. See Atkins (1922:xxxv), Breier (1910:160), Cawley (1951:174), Hilgers (1973:2), Hinckley (1919:250), Holtei (1990:10), Huganir (1931:96 and 184), Lumiansky (1953a:417), Perryman (1984:97), Russell (1969:185), Stanley (1972:19), Torre Bueno (1934:130), and Tupper (1934:418).

209 For a discussion of the literary environment of *The Owl and the Nightingale*, see Mertens-Fonck (1987:186-192), Stone (1988:156-159), and Williams (1981). Murphy (1978a:199) draws our attention to the fact that "the monastic library at Titchfield records a French work with the same title." Yet, apart from this, nothing points to a French or Latin model, so that Sauer (1983:135-136), after listing the most important parallels

various attempts by the critics, who obviously do not feel quite at ease with the 'sourcelessness' of such an eminent poem.[210] It is, indeed, one of the major challenges – if not the major one today – to come to terms with the poem as it is, a challenge which has been taken up by Hume (1975) and, more recently, by Holtei (1990), who attempts what is, in my opinion, a successful coherent interpretation of the poem as a whole.

The Critics

As already mentioned above, the body of scholarly research into *The Owl and the Nightingale* has grown to such dimensions that in 1975, Kathryn Hume published a detailed critical overview of available publications, together with her own contribution towards an interpretation of the poem. The scholarly attention devoted to the poem since then has yielded some new and innovative approaches, and has added new titles to the already long list of articles and books on this topic. Thus, to use the introductory words of James J. Murphy (1978a:198), "[i]t requires some temerity to add another analysis of a very famous Middle English poem which has already been examined by so very many famous modern English [and here I may add: German] scholars." The host of well-argued investigations into the identity of the author, as well as the allegorical, historical, linguistic, structural, rhetorical, and scientific-philosophical aspects of the poem might easily discourage the student from taking a new look at the poem, which is in danger of becoming lost in the thicket of secondary literature.[211] However,

---

and/or sources, concludes (1983:145): "Eine unmittelbare (lat. oder afrz.) Quelle hat *O&N* als Ganzes aber nicht; lediglich für einzelne, relativ kurze Passagen lassen sich literarische Parallelen beibringen[.]" Atkins (1922:lxi), Baugh (1948a:156), Gadow (1909:14), and Hilgers (1973:88) agree with this statement. Hässler (1939:33-34) tries to trace the poem, at least formally, to a "bestimmten Tenzonenform" and the "Joc-partit", and Hinckley (1929:348), not very convincingly, tries to establish a parallel between this poem and the fable of *The Bee and the Fly* by MARIE DE FRANCE.

210 For a discussion of (partial) sources and/or literary or topical parallels, see Atkins (1922:lxii), Conlee (1991:xxii), Gellinek-Schellekens (1984:107), Gottschalk (1966:660), Hässler (1939:7-36), Hinckley (1919:257, fn. 3; 1929:343-359, and 1932), Huganir (1931:8-62), Hume (1975:15-23), Sauer (1983:135-136), and Swanton (1987:263), to name just a few.

211 The following list gives a select overview of the major contributions to each of the aspects mentioned above:
I) Author: Valuable information concerning the author is provided by Atkins (1922:xxxviii-xlvi), Eadie (1986), Gadow (1909:12), Grattan and Sykes (1935:xxii), Huganir (1931:144 and 164-176), Lumiansky (1953a:416), Murphy (1978a:230), Sauer (1983:142), Stanley (1972:19-22), and Tupper (1934:423).

the reader still has the possibility to enjoy the "plait" which was "stif & starc & strong" (l. 5) without having to pay too much attention to the particulars of secondary literature.

Approaching the Poem

In considering the present scholarly evaluation of the poem, I will not attempt to sum up the state of research to create an up-to-date comprehensive overview. Nor will it be my task to provide an entirely new interpretation of the poem as a whole, but the scope of my investigation will be limited to the function(s) of the birds in this poem. We will contrast this later on with the use of birds in the poems *The Thrush and the Nightingale*, *The Cuckoo and the Nightingale*, and *The Parlement of Foulys*, thus highlighting the features peculiar to *The Owl and the Nightingale* as well as those which are characteristic for the other poems.

II) Allegorical aspects: Critics more or less in favour of an allegorical interpretation are R.E. Allen (1970; with reservations), Atkins (1922:xii, lvii, lxxix, and lxxxi), Baldwin (1967; historical allegory), Burrow (1982:98), Cawley (1951), Colgrave (1966; historical allegory), Gadow (1909:9-10), Hässler (1939:18, 49, 94-95, 145, and 164), Harrison (1956:28), Klingender (1971:365), Lumiansky (1953a:414; overview of critical research into the allegorical aspect), Moran (1978), Olsson (1977:351), Peterson (1956:14, 22, and 26), Russell (1969; historical allegory), Sauer (1983:152-153), Stanley (1972:22), Stone (1988:155), and ten Brink (1877:270-271). Arguments against an overall allegorical interpretation are given by Baugh (1948a:155), Hieatt (1968:156), Holtei (1990:99 and 128), Hume (1975:77 and 82), and Schleusener (1973:186).
III) Historical apects have been examined by Atkins (1940), Baldwin (1967), Colgrave (1966), Hinckley (1919 and 1929), Huganir (1931:70-123 and 1937), Russell (1969), Stone (1988:160-162), Torre Bueno (1934), and Tupper (1934). Holtei (1990:33), however, refutes the validity of a historical approach for an overall interpretation of the poem.
IV) Linguistic and philological questions are treated by Breier (1910), Hinckley (1937), Kenyon (1913), Noelle (1870), and Sundby (1950).
V) Structural characteristics are considered by Carson (1967:96), Hieatt (1968:157), Holtei (1990:42, 48, and 147), Hume (1975:99), Mehl (1988:82), Sauer (1983:147), Stanley (1972:33), Stone (1988:162-163), and Swanton (1987:267).
VI) Rhetorical features, often linked with structural considerations, are discussed by Carson (1967), Hässler (1939:37-89), Hanford (1911:143), Higuchi (1987), Holtei (1990:124), Mehl (1988:79 and 82), Murphy (1978a), and Reale (1984).
VII) Scientific-philosophical aspects in connection with the literary background of the twelfth and thirteenth centuries are analysed by Atkins (1922:xiv-xxi, xlviii, and lxxxviii-xc), Cawley (1951:161-162), Ferruolo (1984), Finkelstein (1970), Hässler (1939:90-161), Holtei (1990:112 and 199-201), Iser (1959:316 and 323), Metlitzki (1977:56-73), Murphy (1978a:200-201 and 230), Reiss (1969:870-871), Rossiaud (1989:76), and Swanton (1987:266-267 and 280).

On first perusal of *The Owl and the Nightingale*, the modern reader will be struck by the medieval poet's 'realism', especially in the description and characterization of the two main protagonists; this feature is stressed by numerous early critics.[212] However, it would be wrong to consider the author to be a very early example of a birdwatcher. A closer reading and an examination of the footnotes and annotations found in most editions reveal the numerous well-known sources of many of the seemingly first-hand experiences, and thus soon destroy the reader's initial impression. Thus, it is no wonder that several more recent critics have shifted the emphasis on to the 'bookish' quality of the author's lore.[213] Yet, book-lore and the accurate observation of nature, even in the Middle Ages, need not always be mutually exclusive. Traditional book-lore may very well be valuable, even by modern standards – but the opposite was true more often than not, too. Especially because of the allusions to the traditional bird-lore which was familiar from the writings of contemporary and classical authorities, the overall impact on the original audience must have been one of great realism, and thus have been comparable to the modern reader's initial impression. It will be our task to have a closer look at the way in which the author takes advantage of the various possibilities which were opened up by generally choosing two birds – and in particular, an owl and a nightingale – as the main protagonists of his work.[214]

Tapping the Resources

In writing a debate with two birds as the main disputants, the author is able to fall back upon three resources; these are the possibilities offered by the form of debate itself, the many layers of meaning provided by the symbolic and allegorical dimensions of the two birds, and finally, the potential

---

212 Stanley (1972:3), too, observes that the poem, for several reasons, "makes an immediate appeal to the modern reader."

213 See, for example, Huganir (1931:17): "The fact that the poet makes them [i.e. the birds] seem very real indeed does not mean in the least that they are drawn from nature. Examine the poem for unquestionable naturalistic detail, derived from personal observation, and one will find himself at a loss." See also Hinckley (1932:303 and 314), Huganir (1931:183), Sauer (1983:142, fn. 6), and Stanley (1972:31-32).

214 I refer to 'the author' in the masculine form, since the chances that a woman might have written the poem are very slim indeed. For what is, up to now, a unique proposal of a female authorship, see Eadie (1986).

inherent in the beast fable.[215] Let us now examine these three components in detail.

The Debate Form[216]

The Owl and the Nightingale is the very first Middle English example of the debate form, which had enjoyed varying popularity in Middle Latin literature since the Carolingian era and eventually found its way into the vernacular literatures.[217] Although the debate poetry is, as Conlee (1991:xii) puts it, "primarily a medieval literary phenomenon" with France as its recognized home, the literary form and the basic concept obviously go back to the classical pastoral eclogues of THEOCRITUS and VIRGIL.[218] Conlee

---

215 Iser (1959:311) distinguishes between three components, which partially coincide with my own categories. The first one is derived from the animal fable and the beast epic tradition; a second element originates in the debate tradition; and the third has its source in proverbial wisdom. Holtei (1990:106) uses the same categories as Iser (1959). Perryman (1984:99) classifies the sources which provide the basis of the birds' characters "roughly as bestiaries, beast fables, encyclopaedic works on natural history, together with ISIDORE OF SEVILLE's book of etymologies, and certain classical writings, in particular OVID's *Metamorphoses*."

216 The oldest 'debate poems' known are Babylonian literary fables, which Blackham (1985:3) describes as follows: "A mythological introduction leads to a meeting of the contestants, who dispute superiority, mainly in terms of their usefulness to man; a judgement scene settles the affair." Thus, he (1985:58) comments on *The Owl and the Nightingale*: "This is not a fable; it is of a type that may be one, [and belongs to] a tradition that goes back to Akkadian literature, although of course not maintaining the strict stylization of their convention."

217 Hanford (1911), and to a lesser extent, Stone (1988:159-160) examine the origins and development of medieval debate poetry. Conlee (1991:xii), Sauer (1983:144), and ten Brink (1877:269) list *The Owl and the Nightingale* as the first debate poem in Middle English. Walther (1920:3) defines the 'Streitgedicht' as follows: "Ich nenne hier Streitgedichte im eigentlichen Sinne Gedichte, in denen zwei oder seltener mehrere Personen, personifizierte Gegenstände oder Abstraktionen zu irgend einem Zweck Streitreden führen, sei es um den eigenen Vorzug darzutun und die Eigenschaften des Gegners herabzusetzen oder um eine aufgeworfene Frage zu entscheiden." For the difference between dialogue and debate, see Hilgers (1973:8). Furthermore, she (1973:26) defines the poem more narrowly as belonging to the 'conflictus' class, since "[t]he owl and the nightingale undoubtedly are personifications involved in a contest for supremacy. Their strife is not so much a difference over outside issues which are being discussed, but rather it is caused by the differences which are theirs by nature."

218 See Atkins (1922:xlvii), Hume (1975:35-36), Jantzen (1896:1-3), and Walther (1920). The 'pastoral origin' is most obvious in the setting of the debates, which often take place in springtime (see Hilgers 1973:22). For France as the home of the medieval debate poem, see Hilgers (1973:10).

(1991:xiii) regards the eighth-century poem *Conflictus Veris et Hiemis*, which is the earliest extant example of a debate poem, "as the probable point of origin of medieval debate poetry[.]"[219] This poem, together with SEDULIUS SCOTTUS' *Rosae Liliique Certamen* (mid ninth century), sets the initial pattern for subsequent medieval debate poems. Atkins (1922:l) describes the general structure of a debate as comprising:[220]

> (1) a short introduction descriptive of the scene and circumstances of the dispute,
> (2) a spirited discussion with some amount of dramatic incident, and
> (3) a brief judgment pronounced by an appointed judge, though the judgment was not by any means always given.[221]

It may be added that, to quote Hilgers (1973:16), "[t]he framework of any debate is by its nature related to courtroom procedure. It is also natural that a debate would borrow legal terminology."[222]

The increasing popularity of Latin debate poems reaches its climax in the latter half of the twelfth century, and they subsequently flourish in most European vernacular literatures between 1200 and 1500.[223] This can be attributed, according to Bossy (1987:xvi), to "the growth of literacy and textuality, the ethos of polemics in education, and the focalizing of group consciousness in cities and courts."[224] Moreover, as Hanford (1911:134) observed, since "the debate, as a combination of allegory and dialectic, was perfectly in accord with mediæval tendencies and tastes[, it] became enormously popular." Conlee (1991:xii) agrees with Hanford but circumscribes the 'tendencies and tastes' more exactly as the medieval propensity for observing contrasts and dualities, so that "this habit of mind became the generating principle underlying the entire literary enterprise."[225]

---

[219] See also Hanford (1911:19) and Jantzen (1896:5). For a more detailed discussion of the classical precedents, see Walther (1920).

[220] For a discussion of the differences between the 'Germanic' and the 'Romance' debate traditions, see Gadow (1909:18)

[221] See also Hilgers (1973:25).

[222] See also Stone (1988:155).

[223] See Hanford (1911:137), as well as Bossy (1987:xi) and Conlee (1991:xii). For a comprehensive discussion of medieval Latin debate poetry, see Walther (1920).

[224] See also Sauer (1983:145).

[225] Baugh (1948a:154) sees the popularity of the debate in a more negative light: "The literary debate, very popular in the Middle Ages, is a form that is likely to flourish in a period of intellectual immaturity. It represents argument for the sake of argument[.]" This statement is echoed even as late as Stanley (1972:25).

By the thirteenth century, according to Conlee (1991:xv), the Latin and vernacular debate poems share "a set of conventions which suggest that debate poetry had come to be accepted, however tacitly, as a discrete literary genre."[226] This 'new genre' can be divided into four broad categories, according to what sort of protagonists are debating with each other:[227]

1) Personified abstractions (for example Justice and Mercy)
2) Inanimate objects or substances (for example Water and Wine)
3) Living things (for example Violet and Rose, Chicken and Pigeon)
4) Rival aspects or parts of a single entity (for example Body and Soul)

Although the technique of limiting the debate to two specific birds seems to be, according to Hilgers (1973:1-2) and Utley (1944:42), a peculiarity of the English debates, *The Owl and the Nightingale* must be, first and foremost, considered to belong to the genre of debate poetry which was popular at the time.[228] All other traits are subordinated to this overall characteristic. A contemporary audience would have had little difficulty in categorizing the poem after the first dozen lines, especially since the key-words "tale" (l. 3) and "plait" (l. 5) point the direction. The textual signs at the beginning are so unambiguous that the audience's expectations related to debate poetry must necessarily have come to mind.[229] Thus, the audience expects the treatment of one or several weighty questions concerning philosophy, theology, or love, in the form of alternating speeches, possibly with a judgment at the end. Though we will indeed encounter such topics later on in the poem, the poet at first baffles his audience by announcing that the argument is not about a topic imposed from the 'outside', but that it has its origin in the very nature of the antagonists, namely in their respective "custe" (l. 9) and "songe" (l. 11).[230] Confronted with these admittedly rather irrelevant themes (on a human level), the readers or listeners find

[226] Burrow (1982:57 and 84) discusses the difficulty of applying modern 'genre' definitions to medieval texts, yet he (1982:85) also stresses the important function of these genres as "an indispensable condition of understanding".

[227] See Conlee (1991:xv). Hume (1975:36) divides the poems into two subgroups, depending on whether they have human or non-human protagonists.

[228] Hilgers (1973:27) thinks it "quite natural that this poetic form commonly employed for singing contests among the poets of nature be expanded to include contests among nature's prime singers, the birds."

[229] See also Holtei (1990:20).

[230] See Holtei (1990:27): "Die Vögel streiten sich nicht über ein von aussen vorgegebenes Thema, wie das in vielen der lateinischen Streitgedichten des 12. Jahrhunderts der Fall ist."

themselves forced to look for an additional dimension to the seemingly trivial protagonists and themes, if the traditional concept of the debate is to be kept up. To an audience which is acquainted with contemporary works of both natural and unnatural history, this would pose no great difficulty at all.

The Symbolic and Allegorical Dimensions

The host of critics who argue in favour of an overall allegorical interpretation of the poem, and who base their point of view on the symbolic values ascribed to each of the birds, are reacting exactly like an 'average medieval audience'. It is now our task to gather the various symbolic and allegorical traditions connected with the two birds. These diverse traditions which use the birds as their focus are primarily responsible for the multiplicity of meanings read into the poem. The problems which any interpreter faces when trying to establish the precise and definitive allegorical value of each bird are legion.[231] Thus, the following discussion of the symbolic and allegorical values of the two birds must be seen as a kind of stocktaking, with the aim of giving an approximate idea of the shifting quality of each bird's allegorical potential.[232]

The Owl

The two main attitudes towards the owl can be traced back to – or are at least corroborated by – the three 'species' of owls which are mentioned in the Bible. Thus, we have the *Vulgate* 'nycticorax' in *Psalmi Iuxta Hebraicum* 101,7 ("factus sum sicut nycticorax in domicilio"), which is interpreted by ST. AUGUSTINE as the Christian who does not abandon those who dwell in the night of sin, yet who can still be saved.[233] CASSIODORUS and BEDE similarly see it as the sensitive Christian.[234] HUGH OF ST. VICTOR, in the

---

[231] See Holtei (1990:28): "[Es] gibt [k]eine eindeutig festlegende Tradition der symbolischen Verwendung der Tiere in mittelalterlichen Kunstwerken[.]" See also Hume (1975:15) and Hume (1975:23), where she points to a related problem: "We simply cannot demonstrate the presence or absence of lore not explicitly mentioned, and very few religious traditions are alluded to directly." Concerning the relationship between the allegorical and literal levels, R.E. Allen (1970:53) makes the interesting observation that "the literal details tend to overshadow the allegorical intention[.]"

[232] In a manner of speaking, we are going to render explicit Baugh's (1948a:157) general statement that "each [bird reveals] the characteristics which are associated with its species in the popular mind." See also a similar statement by Higuchi (1987:78).

[233] Medieval traditions are, unfortunately, not always consistent even within this basic division. Thus, the *Physiologus Y* sees the 'nycticorax' as a negative bird (Hilgers 1973:49).

[234] See Donovan (1956:208) and also Conlee (1991:xxiii-xxiv).

same vein, believes the 'nycticorax' to signify, in mystical terms, Christ, and in moral terms, the just man.[235] The identification of the owl with the monk is just another offshoot of this tradition.[236] Although of no great importance during the Middle Ages, there still existed the literary tradition of the 'wise owl', the bird connected with Athena, the goddess of wisdom.[237] However, the more or less parallel Germanic tradition may be of greater importance for our poem. Hinckley (1932:308) points out that "the prophetic character of the Owl in our poem is drawn from Germanic, that is to say English, popular belief, and is not derived from Roman poetry."

The negative interpretation of the owl goes back to *Liber Levitici* 11,16-17 ("strutionem et noctuam et larum [...] bubonem et mergulum et ibin"), where 'noctua' and 'bubo' are listed among the unclean birds.[238] This, together with its widely-known filthy habits and the belief that it shunned the light of the sun, led to the interpretation of the 'bubo' as the sinner who flees from the light of truth.[239] Sometimes, the 'sinner' was more clearly identified as the Jew.[240] In allegorical interpretations (for example by RHABANUS MAURUS), the 'noctua' shared the fate of the 'bubo'.[241] From classical Antiquity, we have the association of the owl with Nyctimene, who was transformed into an owl after committing incest with her father. Thus, as Hirsh (1974:146) states, "the owl was by no means a necessarily respected bird in late classical times."[242]

---

235 See Donovan (1956:209), Hilgers (1973:50), Iser (1959:313), and also Hume (1975:18).

236 See Huganir (1931:19). Hume (1975:18) reports on EADMER OF CANTERBURY, who likens the monks to owls. B.K. Martin (1971:408) draws our attention to ST. ANSELM, who refers to himself as the 'pietatis avis' (i.e. owl) who is harassed by smaller birds (allegorically, politicians and the nobility).

237 See Hume (1975:17) and Stone (1988:174), as well as Hirsh (1974:151-152), who points out that "the bird did not widely enjoy [the reputation of being wise] during the medieval period." Perryman (1984:100) mentions that the Christian fathers interpreted the owl, because of its association with the pagan goddess Minerva/Athena, "as a symbol of idolatry representing the useless wisdom of the heathen faith."

238 See Conlee (1991:xxiii-xxiv).

239 See Donovan (1956:213). For the negative characteristics attributed to the owl and the popular belief that it was a prophet of evil, see Atkins (1922:lxviii), Huganir (1931:19), Hume (1975:15), Iser (1959:312), and Sauer (1983:124, note to ll. 1145-1330).

240 See Huganir (1931:19), Hume (1975:19), and Stone (1988:174).

241 See Donovan (1956:212).

242 For a more detailed discussion of the 'bubo' in the works of the Latin poets, predominantly as a bird of woe and ill omen, see E.W. Martin (1914:43-46). For the 'noctua', see E.W. Martin (1914:153-157).

The Nightingale[243]

The nightingale, in Latin 'philomela' or 'luscinia', which was associated in Antiquity with heavy sadness, sorrow, tragedy, and death, came to replace the cuckoo as the herald of spring.[244] According to Gellinek-Schellekens (1984:5), the 'leta' or 'joyous philomela' tradition became dominant in the field of lyric love poetry. Thus, the nightingale soon turned into the minstrel of love, and advanced one step further to become the songstress of divine praise and love (for example in ALCUIN's *De Luscinia*).[245]

So much for the individual traditions. The pairing of these two birds can be traced back to literary models, too, though the explicitness and skill of the Middle English poet's exploitation of the juxtaposition of the owl and the nightingale is new and original.[246] Before proceeding with our discussion of

---

[243] Gellinek-Schellekens (1984) discusses the different functions of the nightingale in Middle English poetry at length.

[244] For the significance of the nightingale in Antiquity (associated mostly with sorrow, sadness, etc., but also used as a metaphor for a human singer or poet) and the (non-) influence of this tradition upon the poets of the Middle Ages, see Gellinek-Schellekens (1984:1-4), Hilgers (1973:46), and also E.W. Martin (1914:125-142). For its new function as the herald of spring, see Atkins (1922:lxix), Conlee (1991:xxiii), Huganir (1931:18 and 36), Hume (1975:16), Iser (1959:313), and Swanton (1987:241). ISIDORE, in his *Etymologiae*, reports that its song brings about the rising of the sun, hence its Latin name 'luscinia' (see Hilgers 1973:45).

[245] See Atkins (1922:lxix), Huganir (1931:18, 35, and 40), and Iser (1959:313-314). Not only is the nightingale believed to be the minstrel of love, but its song is even said to win love (Gellinek-Schellekens 1984:18). For its function as the singer of divine love, see also Conlee (1991:xxiii), Donovan (1956:212), Gellinek-Schellekens (1984:8), Hilgers (1973:45), Hinckley (1932:309), Huganir (1931:18), Perryman (1984:100), and Swanton (1987:261 and 271).

[246] Basing his argument on the juxtaposing of owl and nightingale in WALTER MAP's *Epistle of Valerius to Rufus*, Hinckley (1919:257, fn. 3) assumes the proverbial character of this antithesis. He (1929:343) later tries to corroborate his earlier assumption with German proverbs linking the owl and the nightingale, and refers (1929:344) to "examples of the contrast in Anglo-Latin of the twelfth century, one by WALTER MAP, another by ALEXANDER NECKAM[.]" He (1929:344) mentions Persian poets who contrast the nightingale with the owl, and sees another parallel in VIRGIL's eighth eclogue (Hinckley 1929:353, fn. 74: "Certent et cycnis ululae sit Tityrus Orpheus"). Hirsh (1974:145), apart from referring to VIRGIL's eclogue and WALTER MAP's epistle, quotes THEOCRITUS: "'let the owls cry to the nightingales'[.]" Huganir (1931:30) finds evidence of a tradition of the opposition between the nightingale's and the owl's songs in fable literature. Swanton (1987:263) thinks it "natural that the owl and nightingale should be found together; both are creatures of the night, and both favour woodland haunts." Yet at the same time, he (Swanton 1987:263) refers to ALANUS' *Anticlaudianus*, where "the pleasant song of the nightingale is heard side by side with the ominous cry of the

the (possible) consequences of the combination of the traditions mentioned above, let us now have a look at the third component of the poem: the animal fable element.

The Animal Fable Element[247]

The beast fable element, which is of importance to us, must not be confused with the occurrence of two animal fables within the poem itself (the young owl in the falcon's nest, ll. 101-138, and the tricks of the cat and the fox, ll. 809-834), which may be seen in the context of the popularity of works like the different Latin and French versions of AESOP in England in the Middle Ages.[248] We will concentrate on examining the implications of the choice of two talking birds as the main protagonists. Thus, after classifying the poem as a debate, Gottschalk (1966:659) adds: "Because the main figures are birds, the poem is also considered a fable."[249] Holtei (1990:29), however, stresses the fact that the author succeeds in having the birds act like birds, and that the beast fable dimension is only alluded to.[250] Thus, we have a situation in which the birds, as talking animals, are bound to the conventions of the literary genre of the beast fable, yet at the same time they resist such a clear-cut classification.[251] The birds rely on verbal action and, in contrast to the fable animals, they are not characterized by their deeds.[252] Without trying to solve the problem of genre classification, Hume (1975:25) names the depersonalizing and generalizing effect and the incidental humour as the

---

owl." Even though we have such minor parallels with the protagonists' antagonism, Holtei (1990:93), in my opinion correctly, considers the combination of these two birds to be something new, "denn eine konventionalisierte Kombination dieser beiden Vögel ist nicht bekannt."

247 On the beast fable element, see also Stone (1988:169-170).

248 For a discussion of the fable tradition in England, see Atkins (1922:xx), Hässler (1939:13 and 15-16), Huganir (1931:15-16), and page 173ff. of this study. The following critics have commented on the two beast fables mentioned in *The Owl and the Nightingale*: Atkins (1922:lxiii), Huganir (1931:22 and 24), and Murphy (1978a:228). Huganir (1931:58) stresses the fact that "so much of the poem can be [...] connected with fable literature" that this cannot be considered accidental. See also Huganir (1931:183).

249 See also Hinckley (1929:343), who makes a distinction between the form ('Streitgedicht') and the content (animal fable).

250 Huganir (1931:15), too, points to the fact that, whilst the birds are, on the one hand, humanized and made to talk, on the other hand they "remain birds, retain their personalities, their natural characteristics as birds."

251 See Holtei (1990:95).

252 See Holtei (1990:98), who contrasts 'sprachliches vs. tätiges Handeln'.

major advantages of using animal protagonists – as evident in beast fables and beast epics. As a result, we have the comic distancing of serious issues and the opportunity for satire and parody of human institutions.

Let us now sum up the most important points established so far: by using the form of a debate as the basic structural device, the author makes the audience expect a discussion of theologically or philosophically relevant questions pertaining to human life; moreover, the fact that he chooses talking birds as the main protagonists of his poem creates the link with beast fables. Yet, since his protagonists do not talk about issues relevant to men – at least at first – the allegorical and symbolic dimensions are necessarily activated. We will now have a closer look at the consequences of the author's decisions in general, and especially of those which can be seen in connection with his choice of avian contestants.

Consequences

The consequences of the author's choices have found their general expression in critics' interpretations of *The Owl and the Nightingale*, and according to their judgment on the poem, we can assign those critics to two categories. Those belonging to the first group find sufficient meaning within the debate itself, and accordingly emphasize one particular issue as containing the main message of the whole poem.[253] The second category embraces those critics who cannot ignore the multiplicity of the often contradictory statements and issues in favour of one overall topic. To them, the meaning of the poem only becomes apparent if one leaves the textual level of the debate and enters the sphere of a metadiscussion.[254] Although the

[253] Among those of the first group are Baldwin (1967:226): the poem "is not a plea for preferment, but rather is a clever way of pointing up the evils of pluralism and of royal intervention in Church matters."; Bossy (1987:xviii): "The Owl articulates a serious, even dour outlook on human life, while the Nightingale voices more youthful and pleasure-seeking concerns."; Peterson (1956:26): "Pedagogically, it is a dialectical exercise in which two irreconcilable attitudes toward human experience – the one, essentially traditional and Christian, and the other, sensual and heretical – are represented respectively by a logician in quest of truth and a rhetorician in quest of sophistical victory."; and ten Brink (1877:269-270): "Es ist der alte Streit zwischen Schönheit, Glanz, Jugend, Heiterkeit und einem ernsten, finstern, mürrischen Alter, zwischen Lebenslust und Ascese."

[254] This second category embraces a variety of widely differing critics: Atkins (1922:xlii): The main object of the poem is to commend the case of Nicholas. Yet at the same time he (1922:lxxxix-xc) sees it as the "simple sincere handling of one of the great problems – the age-long contest between asceticism and pleasure."; Baugh (1948a:155): "[T]he poem [is nothing] more than a lively altercation between two birds[.]"; L. Boone (1985:161):

critics of the first group make use of the possibilities offered by the allegorical and symbolic dimensions of the birds, it is not possible to assign a definite and consistent allegorical value to each of the avian protagonists. This fact has, in the end, caused most critics to conclude that the very allegorical and symbolic ambiguity of the birds precludes any consistent overall allegorical interpretation.

The Function of the Birds

There is a danger that one may take the avian identity of the protagonists for granted, without further questioning. The poet has exhibited considerable skill in endowing the owl and the nightingale with realistic characters, so that Atkins (1922:lxxviii) remarks: "The birds, as drawn by the poet, are [...] taken directly from life [and] reveal the hand of the naturalist[.]" Even though we must reject the idea of an 'ornithologist author' in this form, as our research into sources and parallels has shown, Atkins' statement nevertheless contains some truth. If we replace the two birds by, for example, the personifications Water and Wine for a moment, the relative naturalism of the avian protagonists becomes apparent. Indeed,

---

"It is much more likely that Nicholas used this poem to advertise his qualifications as an itinerant judge."; Gellinek-Schellekens (1984:128): "The poem is still a better poem for the complexity it contains."; Gottschalk (1966:657): "[T]his debate-fable offers advice on right living in the world. The advice is offered indirectly through the comedy of its subject matter and directly through its dialogue and proverbs."; Hieatt (1968:159): "A debate about nothing in particular which gets nowhere at a furious rate, the poem can certainly be called a mock-debate."; Holtei (1990:115): "Der Dichter propagiert keine leicht identifizierbare, direkt applikable Norm, sondern lädt seine Rezipienten in ein Spiel widerstreitender normativer Bezüge ein[.]"; Huganir (1931:152): "The primary object of the poem was not to present an engaging fable – that was incidental, however important. Its object was to present a certain Nicholas for preferment."; Hume (1975:100): she favours the burlesque-satiric interpretation of the poem; Kohl (1988:137): he favours the idea that the poem's contradictory elements force the audience to find its own point of view; LeSaux (1987:8): the poem is a lesson on the nature of harmony and love; Lumiansky (1953a:412): the poem is used to display the legal acumen and the knowledge of the poet, and thus the plea for preferment for Master Nicholas "is undeniably the reason for the poem's existence."; Olsson (1977:365): the audience is called to reason and to find the truth without authoritative help, by looking at the issues from both sides; Reale (1984:424-425): the main object of the poem is not to be found in the issues raised in the debate, but in the power of rhetoric with which the audience sees itself confronted; Schleusener (1973:189): "The debate is not merely an exercise in dialectics; it is also the real confrontation of real characters in a real world."; and Swanton (1987:277): "[W]e must recognize the voices for what they actually are – merely chattering, quarrelsome birds."

personifications of abstract principles or, to a lesser degree, conventional human protagonists would more or less confine the poet to their strictly circumscribed traditional sphere of action. Yet, by choosing two not yet conventionalized birds, he gains considerable freedom with regard to the contents of his debate.[255] The additional fact that the two birds do not stand in any clear hierarchical relation to each other is the fundamental presupposition for the real openness of the outcome of the debate. If we had a conventional antagonistic pair, their very cultural value would most likely make it clear from the outset who would be the winner.[256] In *The Owl and the Nightingale*, however, we have two participants of more or less equal standing.[257] Yet at the same time, the link with the allegorical and symbolic tradition remains vital.[258] A simple substitution test will again illustrate this point. If the poet had taken the woodpecker, which was completely unknown to the allegorical tradition, and as its antagonist the likewise allegorically nondescript duck instead of an owl and a nightingale, we would possibly have an amusing and lively debate poem, but it would nevertheless most likely lack the depth of our poem and evoke far less critical response. The same would be true in the case of the replacement of just one of the contestants by an allegorical nonentity.[259] Thus, it is evident that the disturbingly controversial allusions to the various traditions are of such importance that the selection of the avian antagonists must have been undertaken with the utmost care and consideration, and in full awareness of their implications for the interpretation of the poem.

The beast fable element also contributes to the understanding of the function of the birds. Atkins (1922:lxxix) characterizes them as "birds with the minds that human beings would possess, could we imagine them transformed, for the time being, into birds: and it is in this dual character that their fascination lies." At the same time, they "act in conformity with

---

[255] The selection of a pair of birds with, as yet, no definitely fixed allegorical values may be said to be a precondition for the unconventional handling of the debate, but it is no guarantee of originality – as we can see in the later bird debate poems, where the protagonists assume conventional roles.

[256] See Burrow (1982:98), who notes this point in his comparison of *Winner and Waster* with *The Owl and the Nightingale*.

[257] See Holtei (1990:93-94).

[258] See Perryman (1984:99): "In presenting this theme through talking creatures the poet had not only the natural qualities of these two familiar birds to call on to provide the basis of the characters but also the traditional lore explaining the habits and significance of each."

[259] See Gellinek-Schellekens (1984:176-177), who correctly notes that the interpretation of the nightingale and its song depends on the character of the opponent – which is, in our case, also true of the owl.

their nature" as birds (Atkins 1922:lxxx).[260] Yet, the birds never turn into the 'stock characters' which are so typical of the beast fable.[261] They do exhibit human traits, but because of the narrative frame, the narrator's comments, and the numerous references to explicitly avian issues like their song or their breeding habits, the audience is constantly reminded of the fact that the two protagonists are birds. Thus, we may assume that Hume's (1975:25) definiton of the advantages to be gained from using animals holds true for our poem, too; these are, for us, first and foremost, the generalizing function of animal protagonists, secondly, the incidental humour, and thirdly, a distancing effect.

After having collected the most important and for us most relevant information on the birds, let us now proceed to examine the poem itself.

Literary Birdwatching

In addition to a pair of binoculars (of the type 'allegoria et symbolum'), a wide-angle lens will most likely produce good results and ensure that we do not share the fate of many a birdwatcher who relied exclusively on the binoculars, and thus disregarded the overall setting of the debate. Since critics like Reale (1984) and Holtei (1990) pay close attention to the structure of the poem and integrate their findings into their overall interpretation of the debate, we will take a shortcut and forego a step-by-step analysis of the entire work. Nevertheless, we have to start at the beginning.

Voilà les Oiseaux

The debate proper, i.e. the alternating exchange of arguments according to certain rules, does not start until line 217. Yet, it would definitely be wrong to neglect what look like preliminary skirmishes and tactical testing of the opponent's strength. It is within these c. 12 per cent of the poem that basic notions and ideas are shaped, notions which will be questioned, confirmed, rejected, and modified within the remaining 88 per cent of the text, and which thus constitute the starting point for the interpretation of what follows. Moreover, it is the presence of the birds and the traditional lore attached to them which is vital to the 'mise en scène', and which allows the poet – via the voice of the narrator – gently to goad the audience in the desired direction. Although the very first lines start unobtrusively and conventionally enough, with a short description of the natural setting of the

---

[260] See also Cawley (1951:166) and Perryman (1984:105).

[261] On this point, see page 173ff.

action, the first problems already appear in line 4, with the naming of the two antagonists, "An Hule and one Niȝtingale". Indeed, the further the poem proceeds, the greater the necessity for an allegorical interpretation, in order to satisfy the literary conventions conjured up by the key-words "plait" (l. 5) and "plaiding" (l. 12). Instead of choosing a topic of obvious relevance and importance to the human audience, the poet tries the listener's patience by insisting on treating avian themes like the song (for example l. 40, ll. 46-54, and ll. 81-82), the relation of the owl to small birds (ll. 61-70), its appearance (ll. 71-80), its feeding habits (ll. 85-88), and the filthy nesting habits of the young owls (ll. 91-138). The reader or listener, in trying to place this poem within the framework of debate poetry, will naturally consider the allegorical and symbolic qualities of the two birds, very likely with satisfactory results.[262] Indeed, were we intent on finding clues to an allegorical reading of the poem, a careful sifting of the first 217 lines would yield enough points of reference to back up a reading in the allegorical sense. Thus, the placing of the nightingale on a blossoming bough (ll. 15-16), and the corresponding positioning of the owl "on old stoc" (l. 25) which is overgrown with ivy, literally force the audience at least to consider the possibility of an allegorical reading of the poem. The narrator's comments on the two birds often serve to reinforce the likelihood of a more than literal meaning. By referring to the owl's hooting as "tide" (l. 26), he implicitly compares the bird to the monk who sings the hours (ME 'tide').[263] Consequently, the two birds can be seen as having a function similar to that of the *Physiologus* animals: they are the visible proponents of an allegorical truth.[264] The idea of equating the owl with the monk, or at least with a cleric, is a familiar one. Thus, as we have seen above (page 112), some interpretations of the passage from *Psalmi Iuxta Hebraicum* 101,7 connect the owl with the monk, and also ST. ANSELM compares himself with the owl being mobbed by smaller birds. The nightingale's account of the same incident (the mobbing of the owl) in lines 65-68 alludes to this, even though the nightingale certainly does not intend to link the owl with such a positive tradition.[265] Yet, while on the one hand dropping hints towards a possible

---

262 See the findings of those critics who favour an allegorical interpretation (footnote 211).

263 See Sauer (1983:115).

264 See Hässler (1939:49): "So wie in diesen Werken [der *Physiologus* Literatur] zum Teil die kreatürlichen Dinge und Wesen mit einem tieferen weltanschaulichen Gehalt erfüllt sind, so hat auch unser Dichter die beiden Vögel als Verkörperung zweier Welthaltungen dargestellt." However, in this context Hinckley (1932:314) and Perryman (1984:105) stress the difference between the often grotesquely distorted *Physiologus* animals and the relatively realistic depiction of the two birds.

interpretation of the owl (here obviously identified with the 'nycticorax') as a monk, thus representing the ascetic way of life, on the other hand the narrator explicitly alludes to the tradition of the owl ('bubo' or 'noctua') as an 'unclean' and filthy bird (ll. 31-32). This notion, based on *Liber Levitici* 11,16-17 (see page 112), was, most probably, also well-known in folk lore. It is very important not to forget that our initial impression of the two birds is based on the narrator's often biased comments, rather than on our own observations.[266]

To sum up, we can say that the first 32 lines of the 'proem' (which comprises the lines 1-216) evoke certain expectations by means of the narrator's comments, and at the same time also raise questions with regard to the mode of reading the poem.[267] To an open and critical reader, the following 184 lines increase the uncertainty as to interpret the main protagonists, and consequently the poem itself. The only absolutely reliable

---

[265] This point supports Holtei's (1990:88-89) observation that, depending on the situation, the traditional allusions fulfil different functions.

[266] Several critics comment on the narrator's function. Atkins (1922:lxxvi) regards the narrator's comments as serving "a dramatic purpose by throwing light on the personalities of the two disputants; and at the same time, they supply a running commentary, chorus-fashion[.]" Carson (1967:101) finds the narrator's comments helpful in reaching a judgment, whereas Higuchi (1987:86) thinks that "the narrator does not side with the Owl or the Nightingale[.]" Holtei (1990:75-76) sees the narrator as a kind of sometimes unreliable intermediary between the protagonists and the audience, a "Proto-Rezipient" (1990:76). For Huganir (1931:142), the narrator's comments are "wholly colorless as regards personality, absolutely without dramatic significance or connection, so far as making the hearer a participant in the fable is concerned, while of utmost value as stage-directions indicating the passing states of mind and forensic address of disputants." Although I agree with Hume's (1975:89) interpretation of the facts, her conclusions are at variance with my own: "Though we lose awareness of the narrator once we get involved in the exchanges, he is responsible for our strong inital impression that the contestants are only birds engaged in a silly fight, not debaters deserving serious concern. So firmly are they established as birds, in fact, that we may very early begin to think that they are meant to be comparable to men only in a very general sense." Peterson (1956:20), discussing lines 659-668, equates the narrator with the poet himself. Reale (1984:418-420), like Holtei (1990), looks upon the narrator as being an intermediary between the avian contestants and the reader, and notes (1984:419) that the "narrator's comments subtly shape the reader's reactions to the birds and their arguments. [....] The presence of the 'persona', then, serves a double function; it both shapes the reader's response to the 'conflictus' and presents a detailed interpretation of it."
Conlee (1991:xiv), Burrow (1982:61), and Kohl (1988:134-135) discuss the more general literary-historical aspects of the narrator's function in medieval poetry.

[267] The poem can be divided into a central 'debate section' (ll. 217-1652) and two 'frame sections' (ll. 1-216, also called 'proem', and ll. 1653-1794).

point of reference which is not called into question either by the birds or by the narrator's comments is the authority of Nicholas of Guildford, who is invoked to sit in judgment on the debaters.[268] As soon as we leave the first frame section of the poem (i.e. lines 1-216), we find ourselves in the deep waters of a debate which seems to raise more questions and doubts than it can answer. The judicial authority (Nicholas of Guildford) and the referential human framework – the poem starts with a human narrator (ll. 1-216) and ends with the birds turning towards a human judge (ll. 1717-1794) – are more or less the only two pieces of safe ground which can be found at the beginning and at the end of our journey through the 'swamp of the debate', into which the will-o'-the-wisp-like narrator and the birds lure the unwary reader. It is now our task to guardedly follow the avian protagonists into the debate proper, and to keep a watchful eye on how the fact that they are birds affects the poem.

The Importance of Being Avian

The reader probably soon discovers that the protagonists are not willing to deny their 'birdliness', even after the debate proper has started; the dispute still centres around avian topics like song, the nocturnal habits of the owl, or the contestants' appearance. Thus, up to the introduction of the theme of man's destiny on this earth (l. 716) and the 'predestination-theme' (l. 1145), which organically develops out of the quality of the two birds' songs and the symbolism of the owl as a bird of ill omen, the debate is not only carried on by birds, but it is primarily about birds.[269] Instead of gradually disappearing behind relevant human themes, the avian antagonists persistently remind the audience of their non-human nature, even though – or is it because? – stray references to the human level in the form of proverbs, similes, or sayings sneak in, and in spite of the fact that the owl finally succeeds in establishing usefulness to man as the main criterion.[270] If not opting for an allegorical reading of the poem, therefore, the audience thus has to bear with primarily

---

[268] Holtei (1990:178) lists three categories of normative elements: a) absolutely binding norms which are not questioned (Nicholas' qualifications as a judge belong to this group), b) the indefinite norms which allow a wide range of interpretation, and c) stereotypical value judgments which are questioned.

[269] See Hilgers (1973:98): "The Nightingale and the Owl are the subject, theme and contestants."

[270] The owl's first attempt in this direction takes place in ll. 329-330, yet the nightingale does not accept the criterion of usefulness to man before l. 707; usefulness to man was a common criterion to be found in many a debate. See Jantzen (1896:7).

'avian trivialities' for more than two fifths of the poem.[271] Actually, the further the poem proceeds, the harder it becomes to do so, so that this 'tolerance' finally takes on the character of active resistance against the 'lure' of an at least partially allegorical interpretation, which tantalizingly dangles in front of the reader. This is mainly due to the fact that many of the potentially allegorical interpretations of the two birds are either implicitly or explicitly alluded to. The following table illustrates the frequency of these references to the main allegorical traditions.[272]

Typeface: normal: statement by the narrator
italic: statement by the owl
bold: statement by the nightingale

[271] Mehl (1988:83) comments on the evaluation of 'avian details' and the weightier themes: "Tierische Eigenschaften und Lebensgewohnheiten werden mit gleicher Emphase diskutiert wie moralische und religiöse Fragen aus dem Menschenleben. Ständig wird der Leser an die Lebenswelt der Tiere erinnert und damit vieles von dem Ernst der moralischen und theologischen Auseinandersetzung in eine komisch-satirische Distanz gerückt[.]" See also LeSaux (1987:4).

[272] Both here and in general, we have to bear in mind that, as Hume (1975:23) puts it, "[w]e simply cannot demonstrate the presence or absence of lore not explicitly mentioned, and very few religious traditions are alluded to directly."

OWL			**NIGHTINGALE**		
(wise) prophetic bird	'nycticorax'	'bubo'/ 'noctua'	herald of spring	singer of love or lust	singer of divine praise
			15-16 (sits on blossoming bough)		
	26 ('tide')				
		32 ('fule')			
		33-40 ('fule unwiȝht')			
	(65-68) (hated by other birds)	**65-138** (hated by other birds, general foulness)			
		163-168 (conceils its evil in the dark)			
				203-205 (Nicholas' former pre-dilections)	
		217-252 (sings at night)			
	275-308 (mobbed owl: loves peace and quiet)				
	323-328 (sings hours)				
	329-330 (warner)				
	355-362 (vs. earthly joys)				

(wise) prophetic bird	'nycticorax'	'bubo'/ 'noctua'	herald of spring	singer of love or lust	singer of divine praise
	(417-432) (mis-anthropist)				
			433-466 (herald of spring)		
	473-486 (Xmas helper)				
				489-522 (singer of lust)	
	523-540 (altruist)				
	(603-612) (useful to man)				
					716-742 (sings of the joys of heaven)
	854-932 (admonishes man to repent)			*894-902* (singer of lust)	
				955-970 (noble love)	
	(971-1042) (negative: only laments)				**971-1042** (singer of joyful praise)
				1045-1066 ('Laustic': singer of adultery and lust)	
				1075-1110 (positive: love, not lust)	

(wise) prophetic bird	'nycticorax'	'bubo'/ 'noctua'	herald of spring	singer of love or lust	singer of divine praise
		1111-1144 (hated by all)			
		1145-1174 (bird of ill omen)			
1189-1280 (fore-knowledge seen positively)					
	1209-1212 (orthodoxy of fore-nowledge)				
	1219-1232 (sympathetic altruist)				
	1261-1264 (warner)				
	1279-1280 (stresses transitori-ness of the world)				
1298-1330 (negative: prophetic power = witchcraft)					
		1315-1316 (hated by all)			
				1331-1510 (singer of decent and natural love, not lust)	
	1563-1570 (sympathizes with harrassed wives)				
	1585-1602 (consoles lonely wives)				
	1615-1617 (sheds its blood for man's sake)				

The preceding table shows that the owl is persistently concerned with linking itself with the 'nycticorax' tradition, rather than with attacking the nightingale, which can be interpreted as a reaction to the nightingale's repeated attempts to force the owl into the 'bubo'/'noctua' tradition. The nightingale itself spends less time and energy on creating a positive image of itself, which may reflect the fact that it is able to profit from being predominantly associated with pleasant things. The owl, on the other hand, has to fight the very strong tradition of the 'unclean bird', which not only goes back to the biblical text, but which obviously also finds considerable backing in the folk lore of the times.[273] It is telling that the narrator's first statement on the one hand depicts the nightingale as the herald of spring and relates the owl to the 'nycticorax', yet on the other hand we simultaneously find a placing of the owl within the unfavourable 'bubo'/'noctua' tradition.[274] The fact that the author has chosen two beings with a rich allegorical background has its effect from the very beginning, and may even be responsible for the inconclusive ending. Even though the two protagonists are related to several allegorical traditions, they are, nevertheless, not allegorical beings, but in the first place live animals – a fact which is reflected in the variety of associations and the ease with which they switch from one tradition to another.[275] Considering our evidence concerning the characters of the birds, we are compelled to conclude that no single one of the possible traditions already found in the 'proem' (ll. 1-216) has been successful in clearly defining the character of either protagonist.[276] In contrast to the characters of such popular fable animals as the wolf or the fox, the owl's and the nightingale's personalities are not automatically

[273] See Perryman (1984:99): "The traditions of the nightingale were predominantly favourable; those of the owl on the whole unfavourable[.]" See also Hilgers (1973:53). Hilgers (1973:103) gives an illuminating comment on the respective tactics of the two birds in relation to these traditions.

[274] Hilgers (1973:53) comments: "The owl as a debate contestant is not an easily defined character. [....] Also, there is some question as to whether the owl of the debate is actually a 'nicticorax' (the manuscript calls it a 'bubo')."

[275] See also Hilgers (1973:41), who notes that "the characters of the poem are birds and remain true to their bird nature. [....] [Thus, an] allegorical reading of the debate must be rooted in the natural opposition of the birds."

[276] See Perryman (1984:102): "So the reader comes to the poem with expectations based on the bird lore which at the very start have to be adjusted, and throughout the poem reassessed." See also the ambiguity of the setting in a 'sumere dale' as discussed by Williams (1981:172-174). Hilgers' (1973:59) general comment on the bird debates is especially appropriate here: "For each of the bird contestants one cannot point to natural history, to folklore, or to literature as the one influential factor in the formation of the bird as contestant. In most instances all three factors have combined in the bird."

defined: even though they remain within the framework of the traditions and lore surrounding them, they are free to define their respective roles 'ad bonam' or 'ad malam partem'. This means that both opponents have an equal right to draw upon the wide and often contradictory potential of roles ascribed to either bird as a storehouse from which they take the information needed for their positive self portrayal, as well as for the denigration of their antagonist's character. Thus, the owl stresses those characteristics which link it with the 'nycticorax' tradition, whereas the nightingale tries to place its opponent on a par with the 'noctua'/'bubo' owl. The nightingale's self-identification with the coming of spring and with the season of joy is attacked by the owl, who emphasizes the lustful and sensual qualities of that season. In response to this, the nightingale shifts its stance and adopts the role of the 'singer of heavenly praise'.

It would be irresponsible to accept the self-representation of either of the protagonists without paying any attention to the counter-arguments. Yet at the same time, we must not be too easily taken in by the accusations and insinuations of the opposing party. After all, this is a debate in which each opponent tries to get the better of the other. Thus, we have to accept that the initial ambiguity is not only still around, but has even been reinforced by the protagonists' contradictory statements.[277] Those who turn to a non-avian authority in order to clarify what is – on a logical level – a rather unsatisfactory situation may feel tempted to rely on the narrator's comments; and indeed, at first sight this seems to be a good idea. It is the narrator who introduces the two contestants in the 'proem' section, and who creates the first impression the audience receives, by referring to the owl's song as "tide" (l. 26) and by comparing the nightingale's singing to the sound of "harpe & pipe" (l. 22). His running commentary on the reaction of each protagonist to the verbal attacks provides welcome additional information and, at least at the beginning, reinforces the initial impression of the nightingale as being a versatile rhetorician that is contrasted to the ponderous and, in the narrator's description, slightly ridiculous owl.[278] However, we have a fundamental change in the narrator's attitude as early as lines 391-400: after the owl's impressive rebuttal of the nightingale's arguments and its counter-attack, the narrator describes the nightingale as being at a momentary loss for a reply. Thus, the primary notion transmitted by the narrator's earlier comments has proved wrong: the 'ponderous' owl

[277] The fact that each bird's line of argument is "riddled with flaws" (Perryman 1984:103) adds even further to this. Perryman (1984:103-105) lists the logical mistakes made by the contestants. On this point, see also Hilgers (1973:78 and 80-81).

[278] See, for example, ll. 41-45, ll. 143-149, and ll. 215-216. The element of ridicule can be clearly seen in ll. 42-44 and l. 146.

has turned out to be a skilful debater that drives its opponent to take the bull by the horns, without – according to the comment – caring too much about the factual truth of its arguments.[279] It is now the previously defensive owl that sets the pace of the debate, and it is the nightingale's turn to swallow 'one frogge' and ponder the reply.[280] The debate reaches its climax in the heated exchange of arguments, delivered by both sides with great zest (ll. 1043ff.), then reverts to a more normal pace, with the nightingale again shown as being hard pressed for a valid counter-argument, until a minor formal mistake by the owl provides the opportunity to claim victory and close the debate.[281]

The Importance of Being Human

Even though the avian characteristics of the two protagonists must be given precedence over their human traits, there are still these undeniably human elements which contrast, mix, or fuse with the basic avian quality of the protagonists.[282] The most central and obvious human element is the language used by both birds during their debate; yet, even though each opponent displays outstanding rhetorical skill, the poet does not forget to contrast their linguistic qualities with their singing and hooting. He also takes care not to allow the reader to forget that his protagonists are not human beings. Thus, after the owl has told the tale of the equine quartering of the nightingale (ll. 1049-1066) – a punishment which seems odd for a bird and therefore suggests transfer to a human level – the narrator's comment "ȝif ho mon were" (l. 1069) stops all such speculation dead in its tracks. Even when weighty human issues like predestination, love, or the correct attitude towards life are at stake, the contestants never ignore their avian roots. All in all, it is only after having laid a sound animal foundation that the poet moves on to the discussion of human topics, which themselves grow organically out of the avian ground and remain closely linked to the

---

279 See also ll. 659-706. Holtei (1990:56) believes the poet to use the narrator "zielgerichtet und mit der Absicht [...], das Rezeptionsverhalten seines Publikums auf die strategisch-technischen Implikationen des Disputationsverfahrens zu fokussieren[.]" He (1990:63) warns the reader not to accept the narrator as a judge, but to evaluate his comments in the same way as he does the birds' speeches.

280 See, for example, ll. 933-954.

281 See ll. 1291-1297 and ll. 1638-1666.

282 The anthropomorphical qualities of the birds are, for individual critics, of equal importance to the avian ones. See, for example, Gottschalk (1966:662): "One is constantly aware that the Owl and the Nightingale seem to be women as well as birds[.]" See also Munsterberg (1980:34) and Stanley (1972:30).

characteristics of the birds.[283] The allegorical ambiguity connected with the avian identity of the protagonists has its continuation in their stance in the discussion of human issues: on the one hand, the owl does not live up to the stereotype of the misogynistic, moralistic, and fanatical orthodox cleric, even when the discussion is about women and love; on the other hand, the nightingale rather surprisingly fails to style itself as the uncompromising defender of love.

The Wren

Even though the narrator introduces the 'hule' and the 'niȝhtingale' as the main protagonists of the poem, we should not forget at least to have a look at the third bird which is given a 'speaking part'. The wren is first introduced by name in line 1717 and is said to have arrived in the morning to help the nightingale. Thus, it most likely arrived together with the other birds mentioned in lines 1659-1660; they came to celebrate the alleged victory of the nightingale, and at the same time announced dawn and thus the end of the nocturnal debate. The wren is traditionally believed to be the king of birds and the rival of the eagle.[284] Furthermore, in spite of having only a "steuene smale" (l. 1720), it is characterized as a bird that can sing well and that enjoys a reputation of wisdom due to being "itoȝen among man*k*enne" (l. 1725). It is, therefore, the ideal mediator between the avian and the human levels in the poem – and this is indeed its function; the wren initiates the gradual movement from the world of birds back to the world of man.[285]

Conclusion

Having examined the two main protagonists and the other birds, we may now try to reach a more or less accurate assessment of the birds' role within the complex and multilayered structure of the poem.

First, by choosing two birds as his protagonists, the poet clearly signals the fictitiousness of the action.[286] Secondly, avian protagonists allow him to treat weighty topics with a certain lightness situated somewhere between the farcical and the serious.[287] Thirdly, far from being mere mouthpieces or

---

[283] See Hume (1975:89-90 and 92). Perryman (1984:106) sees adultery and prophecy as the two main themes of the poem, both of which draw on the bird lore connected with the owl and the nightingale.

[284] See Hinckley (1932:310).

[285] See Holtei (1990:85-86).

[286] See Holtei (1990:92) and Hume (1975:28).

[287] See Hume (1975:29 and 103).

one-dimensional representatives of a strictly-defined view of the world, the protagonists draw upon a wide variety of multiple meanings and display an astonishingly human(e) attitude in the discussion of love and marriage.[288] The poet has succeeded in skilfully blending the components of the debate form, the allegorical tradition, and the beast fable. The fact that the debate is set within a human framework by the introduction of the narrator and the judge increases the likelihood of anthropological relevance, yet by omitting the final judgment, the author forces his readers and listeners to reach a conclusion of their own.[289] The poem can thus be seen in the tradition of ABELARD's *Sic et non*, though of course the means of prompting the audience to think and doubt are somewhat different.[290] The choice of two allegorically relevant, yet at the same time not exactly defined birds is at the core of the poem's resistance to any rash and superficial categorizing, and is thus responsible for the fact that the poem has cast its spell over several generations of critics and scholars.

---

[288] Holtei (1990:87) comes to the conclusion "dass der Autor von *The Owl and the Nightingale* seinen beiden Protagonisten nicht von vornherein eindeutig identifizierbare und den Verstehensmodus des Textes festlegende Konzepte zugeordnet hat." He (1990:128) continues: "Die Vögel bleiben von Anfang bis Ende Vögel und werden nicht zu verlängerten Metaphern ausgestaltet, und folglich bleibt das von ihnen und über sie Gesagte auch kohärent nur auf der literalen Ebene verständlich."

[289] Holtei (1990:49-50) notes that, by establishing a human framework, "es dem Verfasser [gelingt], einerseits das folgende Geschehen auf die menschlichen Verstehensnormen zu fokussieren, und andererseits eine deutliche Distanz zu den handelnden Tieren zu schaffen." Thus, he also prevents too rash an identification with the protagonists.
Only a few modern critics, probably uncomfortable with the idea of leaving the debate open, have decided in favour of one of the contestants; with some, however, one gains the impression that their judgment tells us more about their own moral attitudes than about the poet's intentions. Thus, Atkins (1922:lviii) favours the nightingale, while Carson (1967:98) and Peterson (1956:26) see the owl as the winner. The great majority of modern critics, however, stress the importance of the fact that no conclusion is reached in the poem, or emphasize the equal worth or worthlessness of both attitudes. See Conlee (1991:xix), Donovan (1956:214), Gadow (1909:11), Gellinek-Schellekens (1984:113 and 126), Gottschalk (1966:663), Hässler (1939:164), Hirsh (1974:150), Hume (1975:45), Kinneavy (1967:664), Lumiansky (1953a:414-415), Olsson (1977:364), and Reale (1984:426).

[290] See Holtei (1990:112-113) and Reiss (1969:870-871).

3. *The Thrush and the Nightingale*[291]

Introduction

Like its predecessor and probable model, *The Owl and the Nightingale*, *The Thrush and the Nightingale* takes its name from the heading in the manuscript. In MS. Digby 86, the poem is introduced by the French superscription "Ci commence la cuntent parente le Mauuis & la russinole". Yet unlike *The Owl and the Nightingale*, it has not attracted much critical attention: most scholars have thought it sufficient to present a more or less incidental discussion in connection with other bird debate poems. However, even though *The Thrush and the Nightingale* cannot compete with the much longer and more complex poem of *The Owl and the Nightingale*, it nevertheless deserves more than the superficial attention it has received up to this day.[292]

Date, Author, Manuscripts, and Sources

The 192 lines of the anonymous poem have been completely preserved in Bodleian Library MS. Digby 86. Conlee (1991:237-238) assigns the poem to the second half of the thirteenth century.[293] A second, but fragmentary text which contains seventy-five verses is found in the Auchinleck manuscript, though, as Conlee (1991:238) notes, "with considerable departures from the Digby text."

Although it is generally assumed that the (slightly?) earlier and much more famous *The Owl and the Nightingale* gave rise to the composition of *The Thrush and the Nightingale*, Conlee (1991:237) observes that the two poems have, "aside from their use of birds as disputants [...] little in common." Concerning its form and content, *The Thrush and the Nightingale* fits the definition of a debate poem to a far greater extent than its model, and it is also a much more conventional poem in other respects.[294]

---

[291] I use the edition by Conlee (1991:237-248).

[292] Hilgers (1973:119) reaches a similar conclusion: "The discussion [of the poem] indicates that this debate has more complexity than a number of editors have allowed it."

[293] Dickins and Wilson (1951:71) assign it more precisely to the last quarter of the thirteenth century.

[294] Iser (1959:317) notes that both *The Thrush and the Nightingale* and *The Cuckoo and the Nightingale* "deutlich die kontinentale Struktur [zeigen]." This means that the debate sets off from a narrowly-confined issue and ends with a choice between two alternatives. See also Dickins and Wilson (1951:71), who comment that *The Thrush and the Nightingale*

The opening verses of *The Thrush and the Nightingale* have an almost word-for-word parallel in the opening lines of the slightly later, well-known Harley lyric *Lenten is come with love to toune* (Luria and Hoffman 1974:6-7). Thus, the mentioning of the thrush's song as a response to the nightingale's in the selfsame lyric (Luria and Hoffman 1974:6, ll. 5-7) leads Conlee (1991:239, fn. to ll. 1-8) to assume that "[i]t is possible that the notion of a debate between birds stems from lines 5-7 of the Harley lyric," which presupposes the existence of the Harley poem some time before it was recorded in the Harley manuscript.[295]

Approaching the Poem

In contrast to *The Owl and the Nightingale*, we can approach the present poem without having to fear the quicksand of contradictory allegorical values and the misleading comments of an unreliable narrator, though there are, at least at the beginning, some potential pitfalls.[296] After he has been mentioned once in line 7 and has introduced the topic, the contestants, and their respective positions, the I-narrator disappears and leaves the stage entirely to the two avian antagonists. Thanks to the narrator's introductory lines, we know that it is (very early) summer, that the blossom is out, and that the birds are singing happily.[297] Furthermore, we are informed that the 'strif', a word which indicates the poem's affiliation to the debate tradition, is between "on of wele, þat oþer of wo" (l. 8), namely between the nightingale, which we find here in the role of the singer of love and defender of women (l. 10 and ll. 13-15), and the thrush, which assumes the position of the misogynist (l. 11 and ll. 16-18).

"is much closer to the conventional French and Latin models than is *The Owl and the Nightingale*."

295 Hilgers (1973:54), too, sees the idea of a 'thrush vs. nightingale' debate as stemming from the Harley lyric *Lenten is come with love to toune*. A parallel with the thrush vs. nightingale opposition in this poem can also be found in the Anglo-Norman poem, *Melior et Ydoine* (Windeatt 1982:100-102).

296 L.J. Owen (1969:3) points out that the narrator's summary of the thrush's position (ll. 16-24) possesses a syntax that "obscures the indirect discourse, so that we gradually become unsure about whether we are listening to the narrator's report or to the Thrush himself[.]" Lines 25-26 exhibit a similar ambiguity, and it is not quite clear who is speaking until line 27, where the nightingale is identified as the speaker.

297 The description of the season points towards spring. Thus, in the Harley lyric, it is indeed 'lenten', and not 'somer'. For a discussion of the naming of the seasons, see A. Fischer (1994) and A.K. Moore (1949).

The Debate

The beginning of the debate proper has been located by Conlee (1991:240, fn. to ll. 19-24) in line 19, when the thrush starts to speak. L.J. Owen (1969:3), however, previously argued that these lines should still be ascribed to the narrator: in this way, the regularity of the individual speeches is retained, whereas Conlee's arrangement breaks the uniform pattern visible throughout the rest of the poem. After the narrator's initial summing up of the two contestants' positions (ll. 10-24), each of the birds' alternating turns comprises a dozen verses. Thus, we have an extremely regular, uniform, and almost ritualistic pattern, which stands in contrast to the varied and irregular length of speeches in *The Owl and the Nightingale*;[298] and whereas we found a wide variety of (mostly avian) topics in that poem, the author of *The Thrush and the Nightingale* limits himself to a single one, namely the (non-)worth of women.

Arguments

What is a debate without arguments? Probably it is mere emotional gibberish – which is, at least in some parts of the poem, the impression an audience gains at first sight or hearing. Yet, a closer examination yields some arguments of the 'exemplum' type, mostly found in the speeches of the thrush. The nightingale seems to be content to contradict the thrush and to try to assert, rather unconvincingly, the courteousness of women, relying more on the force of repetition than on proof by means of 'exempla'.[299] Even though the debate proper contains 162 lines (ll. 19-180) – or, if we accept L.J. Owen's (1969:3) arguments, 156 lines (ll. 25-180) – we cannot speak of a noticeable development either of character or of argument. Once taken up, the positions of the two contestants remain fixed throughout the debate, and only the thrush's defeat and subsequent surrender at the very end brings about a change. Before turning to the function of the birds within the poem, let us now have a closer look at how the author structures the exchange of arguments.

---

[298] Dickins and Wilson (1951:71) note that "nearly all the speeches are complete within the stanza[.]" They ascribe lines 94-96 to the nightingale, whereas L.J. Owen (1969) convincingly argues in favour of the thrush as the speaker of these lines, thus restoring the regular pattern of the debate. For a comparative table of the length of speeches in the different debates, see Hilgers (1973:143, Appendix I).

[299] See Hilgers (1973:81): "In its argument, the Nightingale repeats without example the qualities associated with the courtly lady for its defense."

We can differentiate three categories of arguments:

1) General assertions (for example the thrush's initial statement in ll. 19-24).

2) 'Exempla': Here we have to distinguish between
   a) biblical 'exempla' (for example ll. 139-140) and
   b) 'exempla' from secular literature (for example ll. 43-45).

3) Personal experiences (for example ll. 62-66).

The debate starts with the presentation of general assertions in the first two speeches (ll. 19-36). After this preliminary skirmish, the thrush sets out to prove its point by referring to "Alisaundre þe king" (l. 43). Yet, instead of parrying the blow and striking back with a counter-example, the nightingale lamely insists on the general worthiness of women. The thrush, however, pursues its line of reasoning, adding its personal experience with women (ll. 62-66) and the biblical 'exemplum' of Adam (ll. 70-72).[300] The nightingale's rejoinder again lacks persuasive power, and it tries its luck by threatening the thrush with banishment. The thrush counters with the 'exemplum' of "Sire Wawain" (l. 88), while the nightingale resorts to relating its positive and entirely lawful personal experiences with women (ll. 100-102). Then the thrush cites another secular 'exemplum' which illustrates the moral depravity of women (ll. 115-119);[301] this draws from the nightingale the threat of punishment by imprisonment. Unimpressed by such empty threats, the thrush falls back upon the authoritative "holibok" (l. 136) for the 'exemplum' of "Saumsum þe stronge" (l. 139) and calls women the "worste hord of pris/þat Jesu makede in Parais" (ll. 142-143), thus referring to Eve and indirectly preparing the ground for its own defeat. Yet, its opponent trudges on in its set way for another twelve lines, duly reinforcing the impression we have gained so far of a rather slow-witted and rhetorically unskilled contestant. It takes the thrush's insistence on being given a valid counter-example to jolt the nightingale into realizing that Mary is not only the most obvious, but also the most persuasive and authoritative 'exemplum' far and wide.[302] The debate then ends with the thrush's acceptance of its defeat.

---

300 The idea of a thrush having intimate knowledge of women, of course, necessitates the anthropomorphization of the bird.

301 In the thrush's 'exempla', Hilgers (1973:115) recognizes "some of the stock examples used by the medieval misogynists."

302 Hilgers (1973:116) interprets the nightingale's rather slow rebuttal more positively: "The character who appeared to be ignorant and ineffectual in the contest has proved to be the cleverest by saving its strongest argument until the end." Yet, it may be added that the very same argument has lost its power of winning the debate in the later poem *The Clerk and the Nightingale* (Conlee 1991:269-270, ll. 45-56). See also Hilgers (1973:84).

As can be gathered from an examination of the debate, it would be wrong to ascribe the nightingale's final victory to any lack of rhetorical skills on the part of the thrush. The sudden defeat of the thrush, who is not unskilled rhetorically, must rather be seen as a stroke of luck on the part of the nightingale – or, if one believes in such things, as a literally Godsent idea. So far so good and, as the spoilt reader of *The Owl and the Nightingale* may add, so boring. Yet, even though I do not want to put *The Thrush and the Nightingale* on a par with the much more sophisticated *The Owl and the Nightingale*, there are two aspects which deserve closer inspection.

The Typological Twist

Going over the poem once more, but this time armed with the knowledge of how the thrush comes to fall, we suddenly notice that the poet contrives the final twist very early in the argument: his mentioning of Adam (l. 70) immediately calls to mind Eve. From Eve, the 'typus' in the Old Testament, it is only a short and very obvious step to Mary, who is commonly known as Eve's 'antitypus' in the New Testament;[303] and it is telling that the thrush's other biblical 'exemplum' ('Saumsum', ll. 139-140) is also taken from the Old Testament (*Liber Iudicum* 16,1-22), as is its allusion to the creation of Eve in paradise. Thus, the nightingale had only to sidestep the attacking thrush and either render all the preceding examples powerless by means of the typological inversion, or relegate them to a subordinate role, since secular examples cannot compete with the authority of the Scriptures. Yet in order to do so, the nightingale would have had to abandon its position on courtly love and make a new and more successful stand on the theological battlefield.

---

303 Man fell through Eve, but was redeemed through Christ, the son of Mary. The salutory words of the angel announcing the conception and birth of Christ to Mary (*Secundum Lucam* 1,28: "[...] have [sic] gratia plena Dominus tecum") have been interpreted as additional evidence of the typological relationship between Eve and Mary ('Eva' ~ 'Ave'). See the fourteenth century poem *Heyl, Levedy, See-Sterre Bright* (Luria and Hoffman 1974:174), where we find the line "[Godes moder] That turnst abakward Eves nome". Hilgers (1973:72) sums it up as follows: "The medieval Church [...] had an answer for misogyny. As the exegetes regarded Adam as a type of Christ, so they saw Eve as a type of Mary." For a more detailed discussion of the typological method in general, see page 31f.

The Unvanquished Misogynist

The poem may be interpreted as a simple and straightforward contest between a clerical misogynist – as we can assume from the erudition displayed – and a courtly defender of women and love, who wins in the end thanks to his selecting Mary as the champion of the women's cause. Although most readers would be happy with this interpretation and would accept the superior persuasive power of the implicitly typological argument, there are some slight dissonances which may hint at a hidden meaning that renders the poem more ambiguous. First of all, the general impression of women's depravity and falsehood which the thrush successfully imparts is not completely obliterated by the nightingale's solitary argument. Mary may, indeed, have undone Eve's misdeed, and we have to accept the persuasiveness of the argument on a theological level, but at the same time we still have to contend with the minor, but nevertheless still valid secular examples from courtly literature.[304] Even though it often happened, before and during the spread of the courtly literature ('Minnesang'), that Mary was addressed as the venerated courtly lady, we cannot easily shake off the feeling that there is something amiss in putting a courtly lady on a par with the mother of God.[305] After all, Mary's virtues and assistance have little to do with the kind of merits and solace which the nightingale's ladies seem to offer, so that, as Hilgers (1973:86) puts it, "what appears to be a defense of the courtly lady is proven to be a defense of the Christian woman whose virtue is derived from the Virgin."[306] Consequently, some of the criticism voiced by the thrush remains and although it has finally been defeated, we cannot simply forget its previously superior performance on the battlefield

---

304 Hilgers (1973:116) correctly observes that "[i]f the Nightingale as the proponent of courtly love cannot win the debate, it can succeed if it assumes its religious role. Before this final point the Thrush believed itself to be the moralist." However, she does not draw any explicit conclusions from this regarding the validity or invalidity of the thrush's former arguments.

305 Hilgers (1973:74) states: "Mary is not only 'mater', but she is also 'domina' and 'regina'. In her role as sovereign lady, Mary received courtly attentions from her devotees before the practices of 'fin amour' came into vogue in Western Europe."

306 Conlee's statement (1991:237-238) that "the poet – although exonerating women from the criticisms of misogynists – probably intends to venerate the Blessed Virgin more than to praise the goodness of women in general[,]" points in the same direction. Hilgers (1973:76), however, states that "[t]he medieval writers of lyrics did not limit the qualities of purity, beauty, and motherliness to Mary alone, but, using her as the prime example, they ascribed these qualities to other women as well."

of rhetoric – which leaves the members of the audience with the problem of rethinking the issue for themselves once more.[307]

The Function of the Birds

From the very beginning to the very end, we are left in no doubt that the two birds are little more than mere mouthpieces for two human attitudes towards women.[308] Avian elements, if they occur, are of no importance and often have to give way to an implicit yet cogent anthropomorphisation.[309] The symbolic and allegorical values of the two birds also play a rather limited role: the nightingale's allegorical potential is limited to the conventional role of the songstress of courtly love, followed by a sudden and rhetorically motivated impromptu shift towards the role of the songstress of divine praise in the last stanza. The thrush is probably chosen because of its reputation as a quarrelsome bird.[310] If, instead of the two birds, we had the abstractions 'the Misogynist' and 'the Courtly Lover' contending with each other, the poem would neither lose nor gain very much – with the proviso that the 'typological twist' would be more difficult to motivate.

Conclusion

Even though *The Thrush and the Nightingale* as a whole is not quite the simplistic poem which it has often been assumed to be, the function of the birds remains within the narrow limits of providing stage-props, and thus contrasts unfavourably with the varied and complex use made of the avian identity of the protagonists in *The Owl and the Nightingale*.

---

[307] Hilgers (1973:118) sees the reason for the nightingale's victory in the fact that it "can appeal to a womanly ideal higher than the courtly[.]"

[308] Hilgers (1973:60) differentiates three medieval attitudes towards women: "[C]ourtly love, misogyny, and the cult of the Virgin."

[309] See, for example, lines 62-66.

[310] Hilgers (1973:53) writes of the thrush: "The thrush [...] is not mentioned by the writers of the bestiaries. Its reputation is established by literature rather than by natural history. Even folklore has little to say about this bird, noted for its sweet song. [....] [It] appears to have no distinctive character other than its sweet song and its association with springtime." In the Harley lyric *Lenten is come with love to toune* (Luria and Hoffman 1974:6, l. 7: "The threstelcok him threteth o;"), however, it has also a cantankerous streak, which may have influenced the characterization of our thrush.

4. *The Cuckoo and the Nightingale*[311]

Introduction

Like *The Thrush and the Nightingale* before, *The Cuckoo and the Nightingale*, also known as *The Book of Cupid, God of Love*, deals with one major human problem. This time, it is the value of love and its effect on lovers.

Date, Author, Manuscripts, and Sources

For a long time, the poem was attributed to CHAUCER, with whose works it shows many parallels. Modern critics now ascribe it to Sir JOHN CLANVOWE, who knew CHAUCER personally and who died in 1391. The basis for this correction is provided, as Conlee (1991:249) reports, by manuscript "Camb. Univ. Lib. MS Ff.1.6, which concludes with the phrase 'Explicit Clanvowe'[.]" Other critics, however, have spoken in favour of Sir THOMAS CLANVOWE as the author.[312] He was probably Sir JOHN CLANVOWE's son, and if he did indeed write the poem, we would have to move the date of composition to the early fifteenth century.[313] Yet, as Conlee (1991:249) writes: "[I]t seems more likely that the poem was written by Sir JOHN CLANVOWE during the late 1380s[.]"

The poem can look back upon something of a tradition which started in the English vernacular with *The Owl and the Nightingale*, was continued in *The Thrush and the Nightingale*, and was most recently represented by CHAUCER's *The Parlement of Foulys*, which must have been written only few years before the assumed date of composition of *The Cuckoo and the Nightingale*. Indeed, it is easy to detect allusions to each of the poems named.[314]

The text of *The Cuckoo and the Nightingale* is preserved in five manuscripts, namely Bodl. Library MS. Tanner 346, Bodl. Library MS. Fairfax 16, Bodl. Library MS. Arch Selden B 24, Bodl. Library MS. Bodley 638, and Cambridge Univ. Library MS. Ff. 1.6.[315]

---

[311] I use the newest edition available, which is Conlee's (1991:249-265); he bases his edition on MS. Tanner 346.

[312] See, for example, Ward (1929).

[313] Ward (1929:226), however, assumes the year 1392 to be the date of composition – even with THOMAS CLANVOWE as the author.

[314] See the edition by Conlee (1991:249-265).

[315] See Conlee (1991:250).

Approaching the Poem

The poem is best divided into three connected parts, namely the introduction, the debate proper, and the conclusion.

The Introduction (ll. 1-111)

Before reaching the debate proper, which does not start until line 112, the audience is subjected to a lengthy introduction which foreshadows and anticipates many of the issues which will be treated later in the debate.[316] It provides information on the theme of love and on the narrator, which will later serve to contrast the statements voiced in the debate part. Thus, the introductory part begins with a eulogy on the god and the power of love, and hints at the dual nature of love, i.e. that it "can make of lowe hertis heiȝe,/And of hie lowe" (ll. 3-4). The theme of the dual effects of love is further enlarged upon in the following lines, and then gradually gives way to a conventional description of May as the time during which the power of love is most strongly felt (ll. 20-35). It is in this part that birds, belonging to the stock paraphernalia of spring, are first mentioned in connection with their song (l. 26).

The theme of the power of love gains an additional dimension through the personal experiences of the narrator, which are related in lines 36-45: he, too, suffered from the agonies of love sickness in his youth.[317] Now, however, he is cast in the role of the old and unsuccessful lover.[318] It is also the narrator who explicitly mentions the belief among lovers that the nightingale's song is a good omen, whereas the cuckoo's call is thought to bode ill (ll. 46-50). Next, the narrator leads us in search of the nightingale's song to the 'locus amoenus', where the debate is going to take place.[319] This time, the birds are introduced as part of the concrete 'locus amoenus' (ll. 66-85), and in connection with them St. Valentine's Day is mentioned (l. 80). The I-narrator sits down and is lulled by the sound of the brook and the

[316] *The Cuckoo and the Nightingale* is, in this respect, similar to *The Parlement of Foulys*. In addition, both share the element of the 'dream vision'. For a more detailed discussion of the dream vision genre, see Spearing (1976a).

[317] Thus, as Hilgers (1973:123) mentions, "[t]he sorrow, heaviness, illness, and care described by the Cuckoo have already been seen in the narrator."

[318] See Conlee (1991:252, fn. to ll. 37-42): "In *Lenvoy de Chaucer a Scogan* CHAUCER portrays also himself as an old and unsuccessful lover (ll. 29-36), as does GOWER in the *Confessio Amantis* (VIII, 2403)."

[319] For a discussion of the 'locus amoenus' tradition, see Curtius (1961:202-206).

birdsong. He falls into a state between sleep and wakening (l. 88).[320] Soon, he hears the voice of the cuckoo (ll. 89-90), followed by the song of the nightingale (ll. 98-99); his cursing of the cuckoo and his joyous greeting of the nightingale leave no doubt as to his position in the forthcoming debate. Up to this point, the poem has not required the suspension of disbelief; everything so far has been perfectly possible in the real world, although the move to the 'locus amoenus' did have a somewhat distancing effect. Now, the following five lines (ll. 106-110) provide the means of bridging the gap between the 'real world' and the world of the bird debate, by simply placing this part of the poem within the tradition of dream poetry.[321] Yet, in addition to this, the dream is a structural and thematic unit of fundamental significance: the central disputation, in which matters responsible for the narrator's anxiety are examined, is surrounded by the framework of the dream vision.[322]

The Debate (ll. 112- 215)

Formally akin to the regular and equally-spaced exchange of arguments in *The Thrush and the Nightingale*, the debate does not open directly with the central theme of the effects of love. As in *The Owl and the Nightingale*, the nightingale begins with an attack on the quality of its antagonist's song and receives a rejoinder which shows a strong resemblance to the owl's defense; it is also the song which provides the cue for the contestants to start discussing love and defining their respective positions.[323] Thus, the nightingale assumes the role of the uncompromising defender of courtly love (ll. 131-135), whereas the cuckoo takes up the position of the cynic who defies love and stresses its negative effects (ll. 141-144). The debate continues with each of the antagonists trying to persuade its opponent of its

---

320 According to Spearing (1976c:176), *The Cuckoo and the Nightingale* thus belongs to the class of 'day-dream' poems. Hilgers (1973:28) rather prosaically observes that it "show[s] the influence of the dream vision poem." Conlee (1991:xxix) draws our attention to the fact that "[b]y the twelfth century it was not uncommon for Latin debate poems to be set within dream-visions. The fusion of dream-vision and debate became even more commonplace in vernacular poetry of the later Middle Ages."

321 See Spearing (1976c:178): "One function of the dream, then, is to mark off the element of fantasy or fiction in this courtly poem; the birds in the dream are singing in the same meadow as in real life, but only in the dream can the narrator understand what they are saying." Both *The Owl and the Nightingale* and *The Thrush and the Nightingale*, not being dream poems, do without this device.

322 See Conlee (1991:xxx).

323 Thus, lines 117-120 of *The Cuckoo and the Nightingale* roughly correspond to lines 46-48 and 313-320 of *The Owl and the Nightingale*.

own point of view. The line of argumentation only uses general statements, without reinforcing them by means of 'exempla', with the exception of the cuckoo's rather improper personal attack in lines 181-185.[324] The debate closes with the nightingale's nervous breakdown (ll. 206-210) and its desperate plea for help from the god of love (ll. 214-215). Formally speaking, the nightingale has thus proven to be the less skilled rhetorician of the two and has therefore lost the debate.

The Conclusion (ll. 216-290)

The poem now takes a rather unexpected turn. Having been more or less forgotten during the exchange of arguments, the narrator reminds the audience of his existence by passing a comment in the debate proper (ll. 206-207), and now steps in, in response to the nightingale's plea, to replace the god of love, who is probably otherwise engaged, and chases the cuckoo away (ll. 216-225).[325] In view of what we know about the narrator's own experience with lovesickness, we may feel inclined to agree with the cuckoo, which calls him a "popingay" (l. 222), implying that he is a lecherous old fool.[326] The grateful nightingale, however, offers the narrator its help and advice and calls together an assembly of birds to condemn the cuckoo's improper behaviour.[327] The birds, in turn, agree on a parliament to be held on the morning after St. Valentine's Day.[328] The poem ends with the narrator being awakened by the loud song of the nightingale.

---

[324] Hilgers' (1973:122) characterization of the cuckoo is quite to the point: "[It] does behave like a churl. The bird is loud, rude, and insistent upon its own point[.]" However, this should not prejudice us against the value of its arguments.

[325] Hilgers (1973:83) neatly sums up the action: "The Cuckoo is defeated, not by a winning argument, but by force. This Nightingale has no clinching statement, as did its predecessor in the previous debate [i.e. *The Thrush and the Nightingale*]. Courtly love in opposition to the representative of reason and experience, as the Cuckoo is, can only appeal to the irrational for defense."

[326] See Conlee (1991:262, fn. to l. 222). In *Florence et Blancheflour* (Windeatt 1982:92-95), the parrot or popinjay is the representative of courtly love. See also Hilgers (1973:123, fn. 12).

[327] Whereas in French love poems we often have an interdependence between the debate and a visit to the court of love, Middle English poetry offers no such instances. Yet, as Hilgers (1973:20) remarks, "[w]e approach a combination of love debate and court in *The Cuckoo and the Nightingale* at the conclusion[.]"

[328] The date of the parliament is, interestingly, fixed for the morning after the mating, when the heat of love may have cooled down a little. See also Spearing (1976a:180).

The Function of the Birds[329]

The role of the two avian protagonists in *The Cuckoo and the Nightingale* can best be described as a compromise between the functions of the birds in the two poems discussed previously. Thus, in *The Owl and the Nightingale* the antagonists' avian individuality and their allegorical values were of prime importance, whereas the contestants in *The Thrush and the Nightingale* were without personality: they were mere mouthpieces of two opposing concepts. In *The Cuckoo and the Nightingale*, we find both of these elements, along with other aspects. Even though the two birds are, for most of the time, used as mouthpieces for contrasting human attitudes, they begin their debate by discussing the merits of each other's song, which then leads to the relevant human topic of love. The other 'avian' element of importance is in line 185, where the cuckoo, being the bird itself and not an abstraction, is able to make a pun on its own name.[330]

The symbolic value of both the cuckoo and the nightingale is explicitly defined and limited by the narrator himself (ll. 49-50). The nightingale, as the songstress of courtly love and as a bird of good omen for lovers, advocates the refining influence of 'fin amour' and even considers this to be the origin of all other virtues (ll. 151-160). The cuckoo, on the other hand, brings bad luck to all who hear its cry in May.[331] It is cast in the role of the disillusioned ('cuckolded') lover who has adopted a cynical attitude towards love. In this way, the cuckoo is contrasted with the equally frustrated, yet

---

329 Hume (1975:26-27) states: "A more important advantage offered by the use of birds is the particular lore associated with each species which can be used to reinforce the human traits being considered under animal guise. Bird lore functions thus in *The Cuckoo and the Nightingale* and *The Parliament of Fowls*."

330 Hilgers (1973:125) assesses the function of the birds as follows: "[W]e see that the characters of the two contestants are based upon their bestiary and natural lore depictions, but that the poet develops them and gives them individuating traits. A nightingale by reputation is known to be the advocate of courtly love, but the combination of this characteristic with the trait of cowardice is the poet's own special contribution. Likewise, the cuckoo by reputation is a rude bird; the cynical wisdom and experience manifested by the cuckoo of this poem is a further development of this essential characteristic. If the characters of the birds lacked development beyond their basic traits, the poem would have neither its complexity nor its irony."

331 The definition of the protagonists' specific symbolic value is important, especially in the case of the cuckoo, since it was, from Anglo-Saxon times onwards, welcomed as the herald of spring, as can still be seen in the Harley lyric *Sumer is icumen in* (Luria and Hoffman 1974:4-6). See also Grimm (1875-78:563 and 636), Hilgers (1973:55), and Jantzen (1896:5-6). Hilgers (1973:56) notes: "The poet of *The Cuckoo and the Nightingale* in depicting the cuckoo combined the bird's less favourable associations, which originated in the writers of natural history, with the superstitions of folklore."

still besotted old fool of a narrator. Indeed, the stones thrown at the cuckoo may be the expression of the narrator's unwillingness to acknowledge that the cuckoo's statements are true not only in general, but even more so for him personally. Were we looking for a psychological interpretation of the poem, we could see the nightingale's position as representing the restrictive norms of society and the superego, whereas the cuckoo's rebellious attitude would express the narrator's unsuccessfully-suppressed realization that he cannot live up to these ideals. The pelting, chasing away, and thus silencing of the unwanted bird is just another attempt to suppress these doubts.

Conclusion

As in *The Owl and the Nightingale*, the issue at stake here is left undecided. Yet in *The Cuckoo and the Nightingale*, it is not a human judge to whom the birds turn for a decision but a parliament of birds, which is to debate the question and either reconcile the two opponents or pronounce a judgment. Like *The Thrush and the Nightingale*, the poem is characterized by a certain ambiguity, and the lack of a resolution on the level of the debate makes matters even worse. The nightingale is obviously rhetorically inferior to the cuckoo, yet it continues to insist on the benefits of love, while ignoring the unpleasant side-effects. This makes it hard – at least for an unbiased audience – to identify wholeheartedly with the nightingale: one does not like to identify with mere impersonal attitudes. The same holds true for the cuckoo's position: it is also far too extreme to be accepted by a courtly audience – even though it voices truths which have already been asserted by the introductory praise of the power of the god of love, and which would not normally be denied, even by the servants of love.[332] Do we have, then, a figure to identify with at all? I do not think so – at least, not within the poem itself. Even the narrator, normally the most likely figure for us to identify with, is depicted in such a way that we feel very little motivation to share his point of view.[333] In fact, the author himself is the most attractive person to identify with: he displays urbane wit and gentle irony by casting himself in the role of the old, unsuccessful, and foolish lover, and he cloaks the two extreme attitudes towards love in the amusing antics of the two birds.

Using animals instead of human beings also has here the distancing effect which we normally encounter in the beast fable. Thus, as Hilgers (1973:87)

---

332 Spearing (1976c:181), however, obviously suspects the author of harbouring an attitude towards courtly love which is similar to the cuckoo's – which would make the cuckoo the logical figure of identification.

333 Hilgers (1973:120) characterizes him as "old, somewhat simple and blundering, luckless and lovelorn – which gives the poem its humor and contributes to its ultimate satire."

states, the arguments are placed "at one remove from the world where they are issues and into the mouths of less biased proponents." The humour connected with the use of talking birds additionally helps to soften the otherwise harsh truths, without completely taking away their sting. By means of his gentle irony, the author holds a mirror before us, and we are asked to look beyond the figures of the poem to see ourselves in the protagonists and to laugh about their limitations, as well as our own. Therefore, it is important to realize that, as Hilgers (1973:125) puts it,

> [i]t is on the ground of reason alone that the Cuckoo attacks the courtly code and it is on that ground that the Nightingale falters in response. The debate as a whole is not a condemnation of courtly love, but a gentle mockery of it.

5. *The Parlement of Foulys*

Introduction

Even though *The Parlement of Foulys* cannot be considered a debate proper, i.e. an alternating exchange of arguments between two contestants, it has nevertheless been included in this section of the study together with the bird debates.[334] By comparing it with the debates proper, we will be better able to appreciate their specific traits.

Author, Date, and Manuscripts

GEOFFREY CHAUCER is unanimously accepted to be the author of the poem; the exact date of composition, however, is subject to dispute. Those critics who favour the assumption that the poem was written more or less at one time have variously placed the date of writing in the years 1377, 1380, and 1382, based either on the internal evidence of the astronomical reference in line 117, or on their interpretation of the poem as depicting historical

[334] In this, I follow Conlee (1991), who included *The Parlement of Foulys* in his anthology of Middle English debate poetry. He (1991:xxi) justifies his decision with the fact that *The Parlement of Foulys*, "even if it cannot be characterized as being principally a debate poem, possesses a substantial debate element."

events.[335] Those scholars who assume a composite genesis of the poem remain silent, for understandable reasons, on matters of dating.[336]

We are in the fortunate position of having fourteen manuscripts and CAXTON's 1477-78 edition of *The Parlement of Foulys* at our disposal.[337] I will use Brewer's edition (1972, first edition 1960), which is based on Cambridge University Library MS. Gg. IV. 27.

Sources, Literary Influences, and Parallels

A medieval poem without a host of very likely, or at least possible, sources and connections with other works is about as rare as a white elephant. Bennett (1957), in his book-length analysis of the poem, gives the most extensive in-depth discussion of the various direct and indirect sources, influences, and parallels. *The Parlement of Foulys* is a courtly poem and abounds with allusions to other courtly literary works, as well as to more scholarly philosophical treatises. Verbatim translations rub shoulders with mere associations, as well as the most general ideas taken from different works. Thus, we find more or less explicit allusions and parallels to the folk tale of the 'contending lovers', to ALAN OF LILLE's *Anticlaudianus* and *De Planctu Naturae*, to BOCCACCIO's *Teseida*, to the works of DANTE, GOWER, MACHAUT, DESCHAMPS, and OTON DE GRAUNSON, to the *Roman de la Rose*, French dream visions and love debates, to MACROBIUS' commentary on the *Somnium Scipionis*, and to the ideas of ST. THOMAS AQUINAS on the principle of plentitude – to name only the most important.[338] Yet, it would be wrong to think that CHAUCER makes indiscriminate use of his source

---

335 Baker (1968:362) writes that most critics agree on 1381-82. Braddy (1931:1019) favours 1377, Lange (1940:204) 1380, and both Brewer (1972:2-3) and Manly (1913:288), the year 1382.

336 For example Bronson (1948) and Emerson (1911:111).

337 For a list and the grouping of the manuscripts, see Brewer (1972:57-58).

338 For a more detailed discussion of the works mentioned above and their relation to *The Parlement of Foulys*, see Bennett (1957). The connection of our poem with the folk tale of the 'contending lovers' has been examined in detail by Farnham (1917 and 1920). The following authors give either a general or a detailed analysis of sources and parallels, and may be consulted if the necessity arises: Baker (1968:358), Brewer (1958 and 1972), Bronson (1948:257-258), Clemen (1938:190-193), Conlee (1991:xxii), Damon (1952), Donaldson (1980), Economou (1972:125-150), Emerson (1923), Everett (1955:100), Hammond (1916), Hilgers (1973:30 and 112), Koch (1877), Kreisler (1971), Lowes (1927:43-44), Manly (1913:284-285), Pratt (1947), Rickert (1920:3-4), Seelmann (1888), and Stillwell (1950:470-472). The most important source and parallel texts can be found in Windeatt (1982:73-124).

material; he admittedly feels free to adapt whatever he deems appropriate to his own poetic aims, but, to quote Bennett (1957:17), "the total effect in CHAUCER is far from that of a pastiche or a poetic exercise."[339]

The Genre of *The Parlement of Foulys*

Both *The Parlement of Foulys* and the later poem of *The Cuckoo and the Nightingale* share the elaborate frame of the dream vision.[340] After discussing the problem of genre at length, Brewer (1958:326) comes to the following conclusion: "The genre of the *Parlement* may therefore be described as a love-vision containing a 'demande d'amour'."[341] Most critics who voice an opinion on that issue agree with this classification.[342]

Yet, even though we are able to place *The Parlement of Foulys* within the system of medieval genres, we have to be aware that the given conventions merely form CHAUCER's point of departure; being a medieval poet, he

---

[339] For an illustration of CHAUCER's use of source material, see the discussion of his adaptation of parts of the *Teseida* by Economou (1972:134), McDonald (1955:448), and Pratt (1947).

[340] On the medieval scientific basis of CHAUCER's dream vision frame, see Curry (1960:234-240). Hieatt (1967) provides an illuminating discussion on the use of the dream vision by CHAUCER and his contemporaries. Concerning *The Parlement of Foulys*, she (1967:84) writes: "He [CHAUCER] uses the dream for whatever it can give him, but does not let it dictate the content of the poem. He needs dream logic as a sort of glue to hold together the many facets of his poem."

[341] A short outline of a love vision can be found in Brewer (1972:9): the lovesick poet, after initial sleeplessness, falls asleep and dreams that he enters a beautiful garden. There, he listens to the birdsong and overhears the birds debating about love. The hawk, the noblest of the birds, is usually the first to speak. Then, the poet is guided to the god of love, or to Venus. For a comparison between the Old French love vision *Fableau dou Dieu d'Amors* and CHAUCER's poem, see Pelen (1979).
The 'demande d'amour', as set forth in Brewer (1972:10 and 11), is a poem in which ladies ask and answer questions pertaining to love in general and/or in specific. Brewer (1972:11) sums up the essence of the 'demande d'amour' as presenting "a dilemma, in which choice must be made between different but apparently equal values."

[342] See Baker (1968:362), Brewer (1972:12), Emerson (1914:566), Manly (1913:282), Oruch (1983:23), and Tatlock (1966:65), who all see it primarily as a conventional love vision. Stillwell (1950:495) modifies this: "The *Parlement* is a comedy of medieval manners and ideas adapted to the framework of the love-vision." Only Jordan (1977:384) tries an entirely new approach and defines it as a 'manifesto': "Crowding all these diverse elements and more within its brief compass, the *Parlement* subordinates narrative continuity to the essentially expository and dilatory impulses which are associated with 'manifesto'." The significance of the date on which the parliament takes place (St. Valentine's Day) is discussed by Oruch (1981).

makes use of the conventional devices and formally stays within the limits of the genres.[343] However, the way in which he applies these devices is highly original – as we will see later, when discussing the parliamentary debate section.[344]

The Structure of the Poem[345]

As one may have guessed from the discussion of the genre and the great variety of sources, the structure of the poem is rather complex;[346] so complex, indeed, that some critics think the poem to have been composed piecemeal over a long period of time.[347] Nevertheless, most critics see the poem as a unified whole, conceived in this way by CHAUCER; and even if it is the product of a revision during which he joined two previously independent parts – or expanded an already existing poem – it still has to be regarded as an artistic unity, since the final product in its current form obviously met with CHAUCER's approval and, as Everett (1955:106) remarks, "in the composition of such a poem nothing is likely to be unconsidered."

There are various possible ways of structuring the poem, and different critics favour differing approaches.[348] I myself prefer a primary division

---

343 For a discussion of conventions and originality in CHAUCER's early poems, see Clemen (1938:3-4).

344 For an appreciation of CHAUCER's original use of conventional elements in *The Parlement of Foulys*, see Bennett (1957:17) and Everett (1955:102).

345 For a discussion of the inconclusive form of the poem, see Sklute (1981).

346 Baker (1968:357) notes that CHAUCER "employs the common vision device of development by link and parallel rather than by straight narrative."

347 Bronson (1948), Dubs and Malarkey (1978), and Emerson (1911:111) believe the poem to have been composed over a period of several years. Clemen (1938:166), even though never explicitly doubting the poetical unity, finds no "Einheitspunkt [...], auf den die verschiedenen Teile des Gedichtes hinweisen würden." He (1938:167) thus favours the theory of a retrograde writing of the poem, taking the parliament section as the starting point.

348 Thus, Bennett (1957:6) favours a structure consisting of 1) preliminary statement, 2) thesis, 3) antithesis, and 4) synthesis. Similarly, Brewer (1972:47) distinguishes: 1) prologue (ll. 1-14), 2) thesis (ll. 15-112), 3) prelude to antithesis (ll. 113-119), 4) antithesis (ll. 120-692), and 5) epilogue (ll. 693-699). Conlee (1991:xxx) recognizes a central disputation section and an elaborate surrounding dream vision framework as the two major structural elements. R.W. Frank (1956:530) argues in favour of a tripartite division, which he links with different modes: 1) prelude before the dream (expository mode), 2) scene in the garden of love (descriptive mode), and 3) debate among birds (dramatic mode). Jordan (1977) puts forward an interesting re-examination of our notion

into framework (ll. 1-91 and ll. 693-699) and dream vision (ll. 92-692), with a subsequent division of the latter into the 'Africanus-cum-garden' section (ll. 92-294) and the parliament of birds part (ll. 295-692).

Meaning

The question of meaning, of 'What is it about?' is closely connected with the problem of structuring the poem. The representatives of the first decades of modern criticism, one of the most influential of whom is Koch (1877), regarded *The Parlement of Foulys* as a conventional love vision, containing a 'demande d'amour', and concentrated on the historio-allegorical interpretation of the parliamentary debate section. Much ingenuity, knowledge, and energy was spent on the attempt to identify historical persons with the formel eagle and the three tercel eagles.[349] The passage of

---

of literary unity and assigns an acentric structure to the poem. Kelley (1979) sees the antithesis on the stylistic and contentual levels as the major principle of design. Lumiansky (1948:81) speaks of two major divisions, namely the 'envelope' (ll. 1-91 and ll. 693-699), and the middle part (ll. 92-692). Rothschild (1984), finally, advocates a sequential structure with three distinct movements: 1) book dream, 2) experienced dream, and 3) state of wakefulness. She finds clues to a structural mirroring of the recurrent themes of order and accord, annual customs, and the idea of time in general.

349 The following scholars interpret the poem in a narrowly-defined allegorical way, and try to identify the main protagonists with various historical persons: Braddy (1931, 1935, and 1953) sees Marie, daughter of Charles V of France, in the role of the formel eagle, and Richard II, William of Bavaria, and an unknown third suitor as the three tercel eagles. Emerson (1910, 1911, and 1914), emending Koch's original proposal of 1877, equates the formel eagle with Anna of Bohemia, the three suitors with Richard II, Friedrich of Meissen, and Charles, son of Charles V of France. This interpretation is still to be found in Howard (1987:311-315). Koch (1877:288-289) was the first to identify the formel as Anna of Bohemia and the three tercels as Richard II, an unidentified Bavarian princeling, and a margrave of Meissen. S. Moore (1911:12) shares Emerson's point of view. Rickert (1920) was the last to put forward a new historio-allegorical interpretation; she discards the Koch/Emerson theory and presents Philippa of Lancaster as the formel eagle, and Richard II, William of Hainaut, and John of Blois as the three tercels. Critics who are opposed to, or at least sceptical of, this sort of interpretation are: Clemen (1938:164-165), Macdonald (1955:1), and, above all, Manly (1913, 1934, and 1935).
Other critics are content to propose more general allegorical analogies; for example, Brewer (1972:21) notes a rough correspondence between the four classes of birds and the comparable, yet not exactly matching hierarchy of worth in fourteenth century society. Cowgill (1975:332-333) interprets it as a philosophical-political allegory, with the birds mirroring human society. Gardner (1977:61) detects parallels with the 'Good Parliament' of 1376. McDonald (1955:456) takes the birds as representatives of the different classes. Selvin (1965:156) and Tupper (1921:197 and 199) argue for the

time, however, brought new insight into the poetic qualities of the work, so that, referring to *The Parlement of Foulys*, Bennett (1957:2-3) wrote: "[T]he more sure and satisfying the imaginative work, the less important will become the topical references, or autobiographical scaffolding." Brewer (1972:33) sums up decades of historio-allegorical criticism as follows: "No convincing case has ever been made for an allegorical application in his [i.e. CHAUCER's] poems where there is no such specific reference."

After the initial controversy over the interpretation of the poem had been fought over to the point of exhaustion, a new generation of critics tentatively stepped on to the battlefield. While still paying obeisance to the hoary veterans of the historio-allegorical period, they nevertheless 'let them lye' where they had found them and turned their attention to other aspects of the poem. The previously almost monolithic block of criticism which had at its core the issue of the allegorical interpretation gave way to a wide variety of new approaches and interpretations, and the question of the theme of the poem was put anew and with fresh vigour.[350] Even though we must not

identification of at least some of the birds with human society (birds of prey ~ the nobles).

350 Aers (1981) believes the poem to be an attack upon dogmatic knowledge and an exhortation to continuous self-reflection. Baker (1968) sees the question of love and common profit at its centre. Bennett (1957:12) regards *The Parlement of Foulys* as an attempt at evaluating human love. Bethurum (1959:229) sees "the contrast between books and experience, between the stable world of learning and the fragile world of love" at the heart of the work. For Brewer (1958:326 and 1972:22), the different attitudes towards love are the central issues. The same is true for E. Brown (1975) and Clemen (1938:200). Cowgill (1975:315) considers the "contrast between the ordered state wisely governed according to natural law and the chaos of a state whose leadership is selfish and irresponsible" to be the unifying theme. Dubs and Malarkey (1978) focus on the craft of poetry, by means of which CHAUCER wanted to fuse all the different elements into a harmonious poem. For Entzminger (1975), the cyclic structure of the poem and the topic of love and procreation relate it to human life and the universe. Everett (1955:113) believes it to be a "delicately ironical fantasy on the theme of love and not merely of Courtly Love presented through a series of contrasts, variously achieved." R.W. Frank (1956:535) sees the crux of the poem in the contrast between the certainty and order of the moral universe and the uncertainty and anarchy of the universe of love. To Gardner (1977:62-64), it is a poem about poetry and the question of (courtly) love. Goffin (1936:499) perceives the antithesis between the heavenly paradise of the *Somnium* and the earthly paradise of the *Roman de la Rose* (as seen in the garden) to be at the centre of the poem. Hilgers (1973:137) sees the confrontation of courtly love and nature as the theme. Huppé and Robertson (1963:101-148) consider the futility of earthly love to be of prime importance. According to Hutchinson (1977), the poem is a sophisticated literary entertainment that plays with the expectations of the audience. Lumiansky (1948:88) identifies CHAUCER's dilemma of how to reconcile true and false felicity as the most important question. Macdonald (1955:9) states: "[The] main theme is the association of

completely ignore the question of the poem's subject, we will discuss only those aspects of the problem which are relevant to our main purpose, i.e. the role of the birds and their function within the framework of the poem.

Birds

For the time being, therefore, let us focus our sole and undivided attention on the birds. If we tried to spot any birds in the first part of the poem (ll. 1-189), we would be wasting our time. Indeed, the first explicit mention of birds is in connection with the 'locus amoenus'-like description of the garden in lines 190 and 191: "On euery bow the bryddis herde I synge/With voys of aungel in here armonye[.]" First of all, together with the other "bestis smale of gentil kynde" (l. 196), they belong to the stock paraphernalia of the paradisical garden.[351] At the same time, however, we may here have the first link back to the *Somnium*. MACROBIUS, in his commentary on the *Somnium Scipionis*, mentions birds and birdsong. Bennett (1957:51) suggests that

> [f]rom them [i.e. these lines in MACROBIUS's commentary] may have been born the first suggestion that, as Scipio's heavenly dream had been to the accompaniment of the music of the spheres, the consolatory dream of an earthly paradise that now follows should be accompanied by birdsong[.]

Moreover, it may be noted that this is not merely plain, normal birdsong: the birds sing with "voys of aungel" (l. 191) – which is about as far as a

---

certain codes of behaviour with certain classes." For McDonald (1955:444), the subject matter is love and the idea of 'commune profyt' and Nature. McGall (1970) finds no single linear theme, but a dynamic harmony which keeps the different parts in balance. Olson (1980) reads the poem as an example of how to overcome the urge for private profit in favour of the common good. Patrick (1930:61-62) assumes the poem to be an ironic portrayal of the love code of the upper classes. Pelen (1979) considers the discussion of two contrasting kinds of love, namely celestial and earthly love, to be at the centre of the poem. Polzella (1975:281-282) focusses on the topic of love and the artistic process as parallel experiences. Rothschild (1984:175) contradicts Patrick (1930): "The allegory of the *Parliament* is not one of social satire, but rather one which shows the difference [...] between rational, 'immortal', and self-conscious man, and irrational unthinking beasts." Selvin (1965) interprets the poem as an evaluation of love which embraces the extremes of 'caritas' and 'cupiditas'. Spearing (1976b:100) writes: "The subject of the poem [...] is that central subject of anthropological study, the relation between nature and culture." Finally, Stillwell (1950:473) ascertains that "comedy is the real point of the poem[.]"

[351] See Bennett (1957:70-75).

courtly author can go in approaching heavenly paradise, without crossing the borderline into religious poetry.

The second encounter with birds, which takes place in lines 306-315, contrasts vividly with the passage discussed above, and it brings the narrator into much closer contact with the 'bryddis'. This time, they not only prove to be much livelier, but their musical abilities also seem to have deteriorated, so that the narrator complains about the "noyse" (l. 312) they make. However, Nature tries to bring some kind of order into this avian pandemonium, and every bird sits down in "his owene place" (l. 320), i.e. the birds of prey at the highest point, the worm-eating fowls below them, then the water-fowls, and finally the seed-eating fowls "on the grene" (l. 328) in fourth place. This division of birds into four classes has its origin in a similar classification by ARISTOTLE and is primarily a scientific one.[352] Parallels with the division of medieval society into social classes are certainly discernible – and also, to some extent, certainly intended – yet we cannot simply equate birds with human beings on a one-to-one basis.[353]

After the dust has settled and the air is clear again, the narrator presents us with a description of some thirty-five birds in the form of a conventional catalogue.[354] This rather bookish and learned list relies more on allusions to *The Physiologus*, the bestiaries, and other learned sources than on the poetic description of nature itself.[355] At first sight, it seems to reflect the re-established harmony and order of the avian world which we encountered in the garden scene, where the birds sat on the trees and filled the air with the "armonye" (l. 191) of their song. On closer inspection, however, we notice

---

352 See Bennett (1957:149).

353 For a more detailed discussion of the allegorical value of the birds, see page 156f.

354 For a discussion of the relationship of the arboreal and the avian catalogues, see Bennett (1957:73 and 1979:139).

355 See Bennett (1979:139-141). Brewer (1972:35-36) observes: "CHAUCER's knowledge of birds was as much due to reading as to observation, though there are more observed characteristics in his list of birds than usual." Hilgers (1973:131) writes: "Included in this list of fowl is a distinguishing characteristic for each, drawn from bestiary and natural lore." Klingender (1971:374) calls the list "an entrancing summary of medieval bird-lore in which fragments from ARISTOTLE, PLINY and the *Physiologus*, are mingled with native superstition and observation[.]" Lawton (1985:43) writes: "Instead of bird-characterizations drawn from nature, we have bird-caricatures which owe their elements to a ready wit and bestiary lore." Munsterberg (1980:37) sees the list as an example of the learned tradition. She (1980:38) adds: "Since the material was so familiar, CHAUCER could reduce his descriptions to the briefest statements, mere tags which identify the traditions." Rowland (1962:381) observes that few of CHAUCER's descriptions are based on personal observation. Spearing (1976b:96) sees the tag for each bird as serving "to humanize it or to align it with some aspect of human life[.]"

that the disturbingly large number of birds prevents an easy return to the paradisical and harmonious setting encountered in the garden. Too many of them represent, as R.W. Frank (1956:536) puts it, "nature red in tooth and claw" and make the reader realize that this is not the celestial garden any more, but a sublunar place with all its dangers and insufficiencies.[356] Yet, by presenting all the birds within the framework of the all-embracing hierarchical order under the auspices of Nature, CHAUCER makes it clear that they are not 'let loose', but that – to use YEATS' words slightly differently – the 'falcon can still hear the falconer' (here: Nature). The details may be cruel and gory, but the overall impression is one of order and of sublunar harmony.[357]

Up to now, we have experienced the birds first as paradisical paraphernalia, then as a noisy and unruly crowd, and finally, in the catalogue, as part of a diversified sublunar harmony. Our fourth and most important encounter with the birds now takes us into the realm of the bird parliament, where the otherwise anonymous denizens of the air step out of the uniformity of the mass or species and are given a voice and an individual character.[358] Much of what has been said concerning the interpretation of *The Parlement of Foulys* has its inspiration and its justification in this part of the poem, so that Clemen (1938:167) is quite correct to locate the point of origin as well as the centre of the poem in this section.[359] Thus, a closer look

---

[356] See also Bennett (1957:152).

[357] Bennett (1957:148) talks about an "all-inclusive pattern, the sense of glorious richness in diversity" and says that (1957:180) "all of them [i.e. the birds] have a place and function in God's multifold scheme of harmonious creation." Brewer (1972:36) takes a different, though not altogether contradictory view: "The variety of birds is significant. It symbolises the fulness of nature, and more particularly the structure and diversity of human society. At the same time the birds are closer to nature, have a stronger actuality, than those in the lists of other medieval poets." In Cowgill's (1975:323) opinion, "the catalogue represents the cooperative social order as it exists in the terrestrial paradise." McGall (1970:26) comes to the conclusion that "[l]ooked at narrowly, in detail, the gathering fowls are marked by tensions, contrasts and strife. [....] And yet overall the crowded scene has its edenic side: every bird is in its place[.]" Selvin (1965:155), however, sees things less idyllically. For her, sin dominates in the temple as well as in the list of birds and "the evil ones mingle with the good and outnumber them."

[358] See Hume (1975:26), whose more general observation on the development of bird poetry holds true for our special case, too: "From mere background details, the birds became songsters with a definite role[.]" Jordan (1977:382) notes that "these courting birds bear no relationship at all to the birds that fill the trees in the garden section[.]"

[359] Both Luminasky (1948:87) and Stillwell (1950:477) appreciate this sequence as the most original section of the poem.

at the parliamentary debate will yield valuable insights into the way in which CHAUCER makes use of the avian protagonists.

The Parliamentary Debate

The parliamentary debate differs from a traditional debate insofar as there are more than two contestants involved. However, the section discussed here starts as a 'demande d'amour' and only incidentally turns into a parliamentary debate. At the beginning of the assembly, all seems to be in good and accustomed order: every bird is in "his owene place" (l. 320), and Nature is in charge of the entire proceedings. She opens the assembly with a short speech (ll. 383-404) and reminds the no doubt eagerly waiting birds of the basic rules which have to be adhered to. In order to guarantee an orderly and smooth completion of the business in hand, she starts with the hierarchically highest bird, the royal eagle. Yet, from the very moment when the royal tercel opens his mouth, or rather beak, things go wrong. Instead of complying with Nature's mandate and choosing a 'fere' and having done with it, he casts himself, in keeping with his elevated status, in the role of the courtly lover and proclaims: "Vnto myn souereyn lady & not myn fere/I chese, & shes with wil & herte & thought" (ll. 416-417).[360] Thus, by relinquishing the privileges which Nature has given him in favour of the ideals of courtly love, he is directly responsible for the ensuing conflict.[361] It is only now, on the field of courtly love, that the other, lower-ranking eagles are able to compete with the hierarchically higher bird: if the royal eagle had chosen the formel eagle in accordance with the custom of Nature, there would have been no dispute.[362] Each of the two other suitors then applies for the hand (or rather claw) of the formel, using different arguments. The second eagle stresses the length of his service, while the third tries to counterbalance the newness of his devotion by means of its intensity. The basic setup is thus that of a conventional 'demande d'amour', with a lady who has to choose between three competing suitors. Since the eagles' speeches mark the transition from the conception of birds as an ordered, yet unindividuated mass – as we encountered them in the catalogue – to the realization of them as individuals, they are of special importance for

---

360 Hilgers (1973:62) sees this statement as being in accordance with courtly love, since it "places man in an inferior and woman in a superior position, thus reversing the traditional position of the sexes." Stillwell (1950:490), however, thinks that "[t]o choose one's sovereign lady is a contradiction in terms."

361 See Chamberlain (1970:38), Cowgill (1975:328), Huppé and Robertson (1963:130), Macdonald (1955:6), and Pelen (1979:302-303).

362 See Cowgill (1975:328).

the subsequent interpretation of the poem. First of all, it must be remembered that talking birds 'per se' are nothing new; and apart from the notion that birds of prey are allegorically connected with the nobility, courtly poetry has a tradition of depicting lovers as birds.[363] It is, therefore, quite appropriate that an eagle should start to utter courtly words, if he is to speak at all. However, the fact that the courtly pleas of the eagles neither quite live up to the lofty standards of the 'real' courtly code of behaviour, nor succeed in letting the audience completely forget their basic 'birdliness', has led many critics to undertake a closer examination of this passage.[364] The tone of these speeches has proven to be especially elusive.[365] The only conclusion we can draw with any certainty is that the basic elements are those of courtly speech; and even within this general framework, we note differences of degree.[366] Thus, it is obvious that the speech of the second eagle is to be placed, in comparison to the royal eagle's, a notch or two further down on the scale of courtliness, and neither is the third eagle's long-winded plea on a par with that of the royal eagle.[367] Yet, even in this epitome of courtly conduct, we find passages which slightly, but nevertheless

---

[363] Clemen (1938:192) draws our attention to the fact that birds as servants and retainers of the goddess of love were already known in Antiquity. This idea was elaborated in the *Roman de la Rose* and its successors. Moreover, in *Florence et Blancheflor*, we have a court of birds that has to decide the question of who should be given priority in matters of love, the cleric or the knight. See also Munsterberg (1980:33).
For the correlation between birds of prey and the nobility, see Tupper (1921:197), who refers to *The Book of St. Albans*. Brewer (1972:6) notes that "[t]he 'lovers' seem to have been often 'allegorized', or represented, in poetry, according to a common medieval device, as birds." See also Munsterberg (1980:34).

[364] See, however, Bennett (1957:162): "That the royal tercel who first speaks pleads as a complete courtly lover engaged in a 'débat d'amour' is obvious enough[.]" See also Clemen (1938:195), who considers the speech of the royal tercel to be a "Musterbeispiel für ein 'gentil ple'[.]"

[365] Stillwell (1950:494) makes the following comment on the tone of the speeches: "Tone is very hard to achieve – especially if one is a bird arguing one's case in a Valentine's Day parliament, which is altogether too public a place."

[366] Or, as Macdonald (1955:8) writes: "All the eagles [...] acknowledge and behave according to something very like [my emphasis] the courtly love code."

[367] Clemen (1938:196), however, writes: "[D]ie Reden aller drei Adler liegen noch auf derselben Ebene des feinen höfischen Tons und spiegeln die ritterliche Liebeskonvention wider." Yet R.W. Frank (1956:537) characterizes the language of the second eagle as curt and uncourtly, and that of the third as being of pussyfooting long-windedness. Even Patrick (1930:63) already comments on the third eagle as being an "impossible bore." Stillwell (1950:493) observes a lack of humility in the second eagle's speech and identifies him with some rough-hewn lord from the provinces.

noticeably, jar with the ideal aspired to.[368] Line 417 may serve as an illustration of this point: "I chese, & shes with wil & herte & thought[.]"[369] At first sight, these words seem courtly enough – and indeed, they would be perfectly acceptable, if only their sequence were inverted. As it is, however, we can interpret them as 'I choose (you) with desire, emotion, and thought', thus putting undue emphasis on the libidinous aspect of the choice.[370] Thus, CHAUCER on the one hand presents conventional courtly pleas; yet on the other hand, he partially undercuts the courtly stance with minor deviations which are certainly not lost on an audience interested in such matters.

Such fine details are lost, however, on the lower birds present. Even though the assembly bears a general resemblance to a parliament, we must not forget that its explicitly-stated purpose is the business of finding a mate, and not debating questions of love. It is, therefore, quite understandable that the other birds grow restless and insist on a speedy conclusion of the gathering. Indeed, were it not for the rather rude "Cum of!" (l. 494) of the lower birds, the eagles would probably continue with their 'demande d'amour' for ever. It is this noisy and chaotic intervention which marks the transition from the 'demande d'amour' to the orderliness of parliamentary debate. As a matter of fact, the parliamentary debate proper does not start until line 521ff., where we finally have the necessary elements; these are: 1) an issue to be discussed ('Whom should the formel choose?'), 2) the appointment of a spokesperson for each faction or class, 3) a regulated taking of turns, and 4) a limit of one turn per speaker. This is the setting in which the courtly attitude of the birds of prey is to be contrasted with the 'common sense' of the lower fowls. All the birds that are to give their judgment on the issue at stake have been introduced by the catalogue (l. 337: "The gentyl facoun"; l. 355: "The wedded turtil, with hire herte trewe"; l. 358: "The wakyr goos" and "the cokkow *euere* onkynde"; and l. 360: "The drake [i.e. male duck], stroyere of his owene kynde"). The fact that we can trace the basis of the characterization of all the avian speakers back to traditional lore has implications for the examination of their allegorical value.

---

368 See Stillwell (1954:546), who notes that "even First Eagle, the most successful of the three, does not consistently maintain the true courtly tone."

369 On the subject of choice, see also Stillwell (1954).

370 See Chamberlain (1970:40): "In this case, the order in which the royal eagle declares his love suggests an inversion of that 'symphonia' in which reason should rule, heart execute, and appetite obey[.]"

Some Observations on the Allegorical Value

Even the first modern critics already noticed the general correspondence between the parliament of birds and human society. First of all, the assembly of birds under the presidency of Nature displays many parallels with a fourteenth century English parliament, and the birds of prey are unanimously seen as the representatives of the courtly aristocracy.[371] Concerning the identification of the other birds, however, no generally accepted solution has been found. Thus, the worm-eating birds are interpreted as either the luxury-loving clergy, the haute bourgeoisie, or the citizenry. The water-fowls are believed to stand for either the rich (sea)merchants or the petite bourgeoisie, and the fowls of seed are seen as either the peasants or the simple country gentry.[372] In this context, it might be added that only members of the aristocracy were allowed, at that time, to take a seat in Parliament.[373] The identification of the non-predatory birds as representatives of the lower classes of fourteenth century society in Parliament would thus place an allegorical interpretation in contradiction to the historical facts. Also, the interpretation which identifies them with the lower social classes in general is questionable insofar as it does not strictly agree with medieval social theory, which divided society only into three classes: knights, clergy, and ploughmen.[374] A third possibility tries to avoid these contradictions by identifying the individual groups of birds as representing the different factions within the aristocracy. These differing interpretations have led Bennett (1957:169) to the conclusion that "[i]n any

371 See Bennett (1957:140): "The birds that crowd into Nature's presence behave for all the world like the lords, burgesses, knights of the shire that thronged Westminster Hall during the session of a fourteenth-century parliament[.]"

372 Clemen (1938:198) remains vague in his identification of corresponding classes, but notes: "Dass die einzelnen Vogelarten Stände repräsentieren, finden wir vereinzelt in der an politischen Satire so reichen Dichtung des 14. Jahrhunderts." For a discussion of a classification, see McDonald (1955:456), Olson (1980:62-63), Rickert (1920:27-28), and Stillwell (1950:483-484).

373 See Clemen (1938:197, fn. 77), who refers to Willi Pieper's article «Das Parlament in der mittelenglischen Literatur.» (*Herrigs Archiv* 146) and points out that "die Dichter und auch die Verfasser der Reimchroniken bis ins 14. Jhdt. hinein bei 'parlament' nur an eine blosse Adelsversammlung denken."

374 See Brewer (1972:35). Nevertheless, he (1972:21) sees the birds as composing "a hierarchy of worth comparable to, though not exactly matching, that of fourteenth-century society, with the hawks and eagles highest, representing the highest, knightly class, and the other groups of birds lower in the scale." Huppé and Robertson (1963:125, fn. 39) state that in "the English parliament a fourfold grouping prevailed: lords spiritual, lords temporal, court officials, and commons."

case, CHAUCER is aiming at 'vraisemblance' rather than complete exactitude."

Even though these interpretations do offer explanations for some aspects of the poem, we must consider two points. First, it is a fact that, by dividing the avian population into the four groups mentioned, CHAUCER was following VINCENT DE BEAUVAIS' classification, which bears close similarities to that of ALBERTUS MAGNUS and ARISTOTLE.[375] Therefore, we have an independent scientific classification as the model, and it is not only unnecessary, but also unlikely, to assume an inspiration from medieval socio-political theory. This does, of course, not rule out the possibility that CHAUCER was aware of certain analogies between the human and the avian realms, and that he felt free to allude to these parallels from time to time. Yet, these admittedly very handy analogies are side-effects, and any attempt to construct a consistent and systematic allegorical interpretation on the basis of these corresponding elements means stretching the quite elastic limit of allegory too far. Secondly, and this may be an even weightier objection, we may ask how far the allegorical interpretation contributes to our understanding of the poem as a whole. The answer is: it hardly does so. An allegorical interpretation which centres on the equation of the classes of birds with similar classes of human society is able to illuminate some aspects of the parliamentary debate proper, yet it does not take into account the other parts of the poem. Therefore, its importance for the poem as a whole must not be overestimated. None of the various overall interpretations stands or falls with the allegorical argument alone. What, then, is the function of the birds within the overall framework of the poem – if we try to provide a more comprehensive alternative interpretation to the historio-allegorical approach?

The Function of the Birds

Rather than representing any recognisable historical personalities or exactly corresponding social classes, I see the main function of the birds in their ability to express various human attitudes towards love – though, of course, such an approach does not necessarily rule out an allegorical interpretation.[376] The philosophical and moralistic discussion of Scipio's 'comoun profyt', obviously equated by the author with the Christian virtue of

---

[375] See Bennett (1957:149), Brewer (1972:35), and Huppé and Robertson (1963:125).

[376] See also Cowgill (1975:333). Tatlock (1966:67) notes: "The vehicles here of sex-love, birds, are fitting for their conspicuous love-making every spring-time, as well as their inexhaustible charm and conspicuousness in the poetry with which the *Parliament* belongs."

'caritas', provides the background for the contrasting of the medieval courtly ideal of love, as found in the speeches of the three eagles, with the differing non-courtly attitudes of the other birds.[377] Thus, CHAUCER offers his audience a panoramic view of the central theme of love, stretching from the austere and highly idealistic 'comoun profyt' to barren and frustrated sexual love, as found in the temple of brass, with various gradations in-between.

The overall theme of *The Parlement of Foulys*, as I take it, is the complex question of love. CHAUCER makes no attempt to simplify or limit this, but takes on the challenge of treating the topic in its entire complexity.[378] The only limitations which he has had to take into account are those in connection with the overall mode of the poem; he obviously does not want to write a scientific treatise for scholars, but targets an educated and courtly audience.[379] Thus, at the centre of the poem we find the problem of courtly love, with the other aspects used to question and contrast with the notions set forth in the eagles' speeches. The summary of the *Somnium Scipionis* can, therefore, be regarded as the philosophical prelude to the theme of love. CHAUCER does not directly launch a full-scale attack on the central question, but prefers to approach the subject cautiously, under the protection of a universally-recognized authority – which he has found in MACROBIUS' commentary on CICERO's work.[380] Not unlike a skilled coach, he takes his readers or listeners by the hand and slowly leads them from the well-known and safely-charted realms of classical Antiquity into the equally familiar, yet somewhat less safe garden, finally confronting them with the parliament,

---

377 On the interpretation of 'comoun profyt' as 'caritas', see Selvin (1965:146).

378 Thus, Bennett (1957:28) does not dismiss the narrator's "For al be that I knowe nat Loue in dede" (l. 8) as an empty cliché or trick, since "it helps to prepare us for a full, impersonal treatment of an ancient theme." Bethurum (1959:218) writes: "This withdrawal of the narrator from love constitutes not merely the only possible position for a bourgeois poet writing for a courtly and largely feminine audience, but it allows him increasingly his own ironic and realistic comment on the fashionable subject." Similarly, Dubs and Malarkey (1978:20) observe: "In *The Parlement of Foules* [...] he has begun the process of removing himself from any direct involvement." The narrator of OTON DE GRANDSON's *Le songe Saint Valentin* similarly denies all first-hand knowledge of love (Windeatt 1982:124), and the narrator of *The Cuckoo and the Nightingale* also describes himself as "oold & vnlusti" (Conlee 1991:252, l. 37), thus distancing himself from the immediate love experience.

379 See Clemen (1938:15), who characterizes the audience as being "nicht mehr gelehrt, sondern gebildet[.]"

380 Brewer (1972:19) puts it this way: "So CHAUCER in 'the logic of the imagination' connects the new material of experience with the old material of authority, and the old authority shelters the new experience[.]" See also Clemen (1938:168).

where all binding and authoritative values seem to be lacking, and everything is questioned. It is no accident that the narrator's dream-guide, Scipio, leaves him at the gates of the garden. It is as if CHAUCER wants to tell us: 'Well, this is how far the ancient 'auctor' gets us; from now on, we cannot rely on any 'auctores'. For the last part of our journey, we are on our own.' The encounter with the allegorical figures inside the park and the description of the temple and its inhabitants are merely additional steps to bring us closer to the 'real thing'.[381] They demonstrate the treatment of love by means of allegorical personifications, and at the same time make it clear why CHAUCER does not employ this lifeless and formalistic mode for the central discussion of love. In spite of all their allegorical splendour, they are nothing more than props, and their lack of vitality stands in stark contrast to the abundance of it in the birds of the parliament. This switch from the lifeless allegorical mode to the noisy clamour of the bird parliament is too great to happen without at least some moments of surprise; and indeed, there are some rather nice twists in the course of the poem which often catch the audience unawares. Thus, the 'Natura-cum-birds' sequence begins conventionally enough, even though the fact that CHAUCER omits the description of the figure of Nature 'per se' and simply refers to ALAN OF LILLE should arouse our suspicion.[382] In retrospect, even at this point we already observe the change of mode from allegorism to a realism of sorts, and it is also in this sequence that the audience experiences its first shock when witnessing the narrator's sudden immersion in the avian pandemonium. Allegorical static order is suddenly pushed aside by disturbingly non-allegorical birds. From now on, it becomes increasingly clear that CHAUCER is neither writing a conventional allegory of love nor taking up the old *Physiologus* tradition of interpreting each animal in an allegorical sense. True, he makes use of the *Physiologus* and the bestiary traditions during his temporary return to the allegorical order in the catalogue of birds; but CHAUCER is not really interested in exploiting the allegorical potential. He is a courtly poet who, together with his courtly audience, delights in learning and would not want to miss the chance of showing off a little, especially when he can fit this into the master-plan of

---

381 McDonald (1955:449) notes that the elements of courtly love allegory are generally described in a rather unattractive way. Their sterility is emphasized by the lack of qualifying adjectives, which stands in contrast to the descriptions of the arboreal and avian catalogues.

382 Knowlton's (1920:243) explanation that CHAUCER omits the description of Nature "for the reason that ALAIN had performed the task once for all" fails to convince me. Clemen (1938:186) more convincingly argues that the lack of a systematic portrayal of Nature is due to CHAUCER's allusive style.

his poem. Thus, the poet leads us, step by step, away from the philosophical and allegorical aspects and closer to the centre of this genuinely courtly poem. The allegorical garden scenes are one possible way of giving the topic of courtly love a full-scale treatment. CHAUCER, however, opts for the combination of the likewise courtly forms of the 'demande d'amour' and the parliament. It is in this dramatic mode that he shows his mastery. The descriptive mode employed by the narrator up to this point, which creates a certain distance between the audience and the action, is replaced by the much more immediate form of directly related speech. This is only the final stage in a development which starts at the very beginning of the poem, where the narrator reads and tries to understand the *Somnium Scipionis* – which is quite an intellectual challenge. Next, the dream vision of the garden is perceived and described, a process which involves less intellectual effort than the summarizing of the *Somnium Scipionis*, yet more than the mere relating of the direct speeches in the last section. Thus, the gradual dissolution of the narrator as the intermediary between the audience and the action has reached its climax, and he does not really remind us of his presence again until the very end.[383] We are, so to speak, left alone with Nature and her avian retinue. The following graphic depiction attempts to represent the roles of the birds within the parliament section in particular, as well as within the poem as a whole.

---

[383] Howard (1987:321) sees the narrator in this section "as an amused nonpartisan casting a detached eye." The fact that CHAUCER originally came from a bourgeois background may partly account for his ability to see courtly matters from a more distanced point of view. On the role of the narrator specifically in this poem, see Gardner (1977:42-64), Lawton (1985:38-48), and Sklute (1981:120). Valuable observations on the function of the narrator in general can be found in Bethurum (1959:220), Manzalaoui (1962), and Polzella (1975).

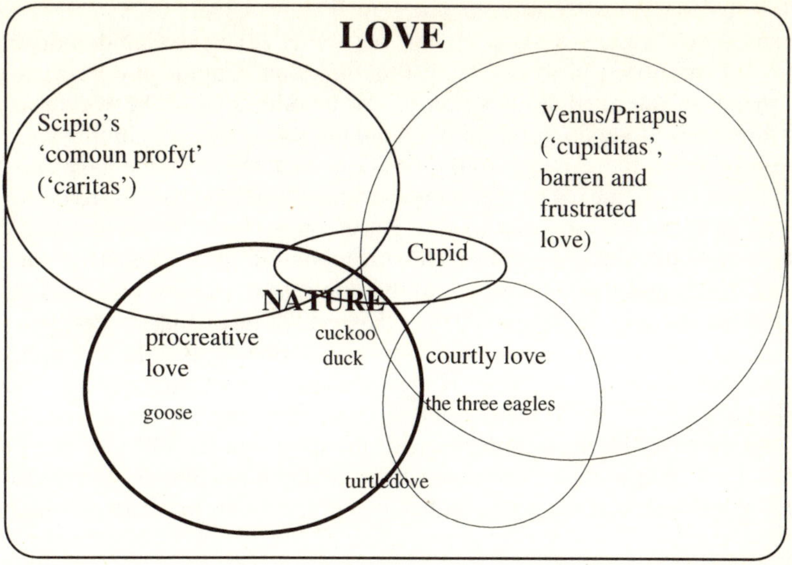

The all-embracing frame is provided by the subject of love. At the centre, and also at the intersection of the various and often contradictory aspects of love, we do not find the god or goddess of love, but Nature.[384] It is she who, as the 'viceregent of God', acts as the overlord over the sublunar spheres.[385] This is of importance insofar, as Venus and Priapus are thus not really opponents situated outside her sphere of influence, but rather perversions of the natural 'status quo', who nevertheless find their place within the all-

[384] For a discussion of the symbolism of Nature, see Bennett (1957:141), who sees her as representing not only fecundity, but also harmony, decent order, and hierarchy. Brewer (1972:30) and Selvin (1965:154) come to similar conclusions. Macdonald (1955:4), however, stresses the contrast between the formal order and artificial splendour of the temple, and the clamorous and unruly mob which constitutes the court of Nature. McDonald (1955:456-457) considers the figure of Nature "the greatest single unifying factor [who] is capable of embracing 'courtly love', 'the love between perfect mates', and 'sexual love' within her understanding and within the compass of the garden in which she rules." Oruch (1983:25) sees her as an "ironically comic figure when she tries to cope with the demands of a 'demande', a function quite outside her province." Stillwell (1950:474-475) connects Nature with the central message of the *Somnium Scipionis* and has her take up where Africanus leaves off.

[385] Bethurum (1959:213) points out that, in ALAN OF LILLE's *De Planctu Naturae*, which is CHAUCER's most immediate source, Nature is divine, and Eros (~Cupid) is a sacred power. See also Knowlton (1920:242).

embracing concept of Nature.[386] The formel eagle's reply to Nature's wish that she should choose a mate, "I wele nat serue Venus ne Cupide/Forsothe as ȝit" (ll. 652-653), also points in this direction. Cupid may be seen as occupying an intermediate position.[387] At the other end of the scale stands the Christianized version of Scipio's 'comoun profyt'.[388] It is in this area of tension between these two extreme positions that the parliamentary debate takes place.[389] By means of their courtly competition, the eagles are the first ones to raise the question of where to place courtly love.[390] The description of the temple obviously suggests a classification of unfulfilled courtly love as 'barren love', and thus moves it into the unpleasant vicinity of 'cupiditas'; and indeed, there is the serious danger that, on the one hand, at least two of the suitors will end up as new additions to the collection of the 'Temple of Brass'. The successful courting of the remaining eagle, on the other hand, would very likely lead to mating and thus, by fulfilling the requirements of procreative love, be in accordance with the divine order and the 'comoun profyt'.[391] The importance of having avian protagonists already shows itself at this point, since it would be rather inappropriate to have noble knights

---

[386] See Brewer (1972:21), who points out that the natural and legitimate pleasure of procreation is perverted in the temple of Venus. Furthermore, it is interesting that CHAUCER distinguishes between the benevolent planetary Cytherea-Venus (see l. 113) and the allegorical and libidinous Venus of the temple. Bennett (1957:98) regards this duality in the references to Venus as an indication of real uncertainty in medieval thought about love. Everett (1955:112), however, thinks that "in the goddesses [i.e. Nature and Venus] we have a contrast between artificial Courtly Love and the neutral love of creature for creature[.]" For an in-depth analysis of the figure of Nature and her relation to Venus, Priapus, and Cupid, see Economou (1972:125-149).

[387] See Selvin (1965:151): "[Cupid] stands between the innocent, productive sexuality that the landscape itself symbolizes and the lustful sexuality symbolized by the Temple of Venus." Gardner (1977:58) sees Cupid even more positively: "Cupid represents the noble, potentially uplifting side of love[.]"

[388] On the importance of Scipio as the model statesman and embodiment of the classical virtues, see Cowgill (1975:317-318).

[389] E. Brown (1975:272) prefers a different setup: "Perhaps we should see the noble suitors and Priapus as the foolish and unproductive extremes of an unstated central position." Rothschild (1984:176), too, defines the area of tension differently: "But between this mere temporal succession and the eternity of divine love is the realm of rational love, exhibited by the eagles, in which change is transformed to permanence, and the movement of time partially transcended through ceremonial enactment."

[390] For Hilgers (1973:137), it is the placing of courtly love in the world of nature which causes confusion and disharmony.

[391] Macdonald (1955:5) thinks that "[i]t is thus with the eagles that the two varieties of love, those of Nature and of Venus, overlap."

pleading for their chosen lady's favour with the notions of procreative and barren love in the background: if we had human protagonists, it would simply not do to connect the procreative aspect with a courtly plea for love. Birds, to whatever degree anthropomorphized, need not suppress their more basic instincts; indeed, it is rather the other way round. It is not their mating which is subject to discussion but their presumptuousness, which leads them to ape the rituals of courtly love. True, the eagles could, possibly, pass for mere mouthpieces and create the illusion that there are really some noble knights speaking.[392] Yet, as soon as the lower birds interrupt their lofty courtship, the illusion breaks down: they are undeniably birds who voice their own point of view and, with the exception of the rather unnatural-looking turtledove, they are all obviously eager to get on with the business of choosing a mate. A similar setup with human beings would have been rather difficult to realize and, in front of a courtly audience, very daring indeed. The attempt to contrast the notion of courtly love with other modes of love demands special feeling, and the dual quality of the birds enables the poet to subject the concept of courtly love to radical questioning. Since the protagonists are birds, it is possible to ask the most daring questions, to confront the representatives of courtly love with the futility of their endeavour, to suggest connections with 'cupiditas', barren and frustrated desire, and to attempt to place courtly love within the all-embracing notion of love itself. It is in the parliamentary section that CHAUCER makes use of the allegorical potential of the birds, while at the same time endowing them with such liveliness and vivacity that they leave the limitations of allegory behind.[393] In order to do so, he selects most of the still anonymous protagonists from the list (ll. 330-364) which provides the conventional characteristics of each bird in greatly abbreviated form, and by means of his craftsmanship he creates unmistakably unique birds whose characters are, nevertheless, mostly based on the characteristics given in the catalogue.[394]

Thus, the "gentyl facoun" (l. 337) sums up the position of the nobility in a dignified and reasonable manner, and respects the conventions of courtly

---

[392] Economou (1972:144) objects to a complete identification of the eagles with courtly lovers: "If the tersels were in fact 'courtly lovers', they would not be in this place where marriages are made and where they have to speak of their love in full view of the lower classes."

[393] See Hilgers (1973:130): "CHAUCER's birds are more than mere mouthpieces for giving information and conveying moral instruction. They are first and foremost themselves, individual birds, speaking and thinking as individuals."

[394] See Rowland (1963:367): "[T]he simple conventional ideas which he uses about animals were already part of popular tradition."

love.[395] The "cokkow *euere* onkynde" (l. 358), on the other hand, gives the impression of being a rather unruly and impatient bird, which appeals to the ideal of the 'comoun profyt' only as long as it serves its aims.[396] Both its conspicuous desire to go on with the business of choosing a mate and the fact that the catalogue characterizes it as being 'onkynde' place it dangerously close to the notion of 'cupiditas'.[397] The male duck, the "stroyere of his owene kynde" (l. 360), finds itself in a similar position. The catalogue-characterization undercuts its robust, no-nonsense attitude in the parliamentary section (ll. 589-595) and bestows an unintended ambiguity on its "There been mo sterris, God wot, than a payre!" (l. 595).[398] The turtledove, "with hire herte trewe" (l. 355), also lives up to its bestiary reputation: advocating a life of chaste devotion to their unobtainable lady for the unsuccessful suitors, it aspires (unknowingly?) to the lofty ideals of courtly love. Even though this ambition has some backing in the allegorical foundation of the turtledove's character, it is still inappropriate: a turtledove is no royal eagle, and even the noblest of birds does not always manage not to look slightly ridiculous when uttering words of courtly love.[399] Thus, it is no wonder that the turtledove looks more than somewhat silly. The "wakyr goos" (l. 358) is down-to-earth and practically-minded, and would be glad if the whole assembly were over.[400]

---

395 Selvin (1965:156) thinks that the tercelet "airs the views of the practical, uncourtly noblemen [and thus] represents the way marriages were actually arranged in the fourteenth century."

396 See Selvin (1965:158) and Stillwell (1950:486).

397 Even though the cuckoo does mate and procreate, its unnatural habit of placing its eggs in other birds' nests makes it an avian representative of barren 'cupiditas'. On the cuckoo, see also Bennett (1957:173) and Munsterberg (1980:39).

398 The catalogue-characterization "stroyere of his owene kynde" probably goes back to VINCENT OF BEAUVAIS' report "that drakes sometimes kill the female in the fury of their wantonness" (Brewer 1972:117).

399 See Selvin (1965:157): "[The turtledove] does not see the tremendous difference between loyalty in marriage and loyalty in a completely nonproductive relationship." Stillwell sees the turtledove's attitude in a more positive light. According to him (1950:484), it agrees with the ideals of courtly love "by virtue of [its] instincts, not [by] a literary training in love[.]" At the same time, however, he points out that courtly love does not demand that the lover should remain forever true after the death of his lady – which the turtledove is said to do.

400 Macdonald (1955:15) assumes a basic division into birds that follow the code of courtly love (eagles and falcons) and those that are ignorant of its notions (cuckoo, goose, and duck), with an intermediate class of birds that know about the code of courtly love, yet that do not necessarily follow it (sparrowhawk), or whose attempts to live up to it are not appropriate to their class (turtledove).

It is this highly artistic characterization, with its delicately balanced mixture of human and avian traits, which raises the birds above the sphere of mere allegorical figures and mouthpieces. Thus, the formel is able to blush (ll. 442-445), and the duck swears "By myn hat!" (l. 589).[401] But we are never allowed to forget completely that they are merely birds.[402] Their avian nature is the foundation upon which CHAUCER can build his complex and intricate discussion of love, without fear of the slings and traps which could prove fatal in a setting with human protagonists. Selvin (1965:160) comments on this difference: "Without immortal souls to concern them, they [i.e. the birds] do not have to worry about 'caritas' and 'cupiditas'. For the birds worldly love may well be pure joy." Thus, being neither solely birds nor allegorical props or mere mouthpieces, they are, as Hilgers (1973:138) observes, "as characters [...] the dynamic principle behind *The Parlement of Foules*."

Conclusion

Within the scope of this poem, we have the entire variety of the different functions of birds 'in nuce'. First, the birds are introduced as poetic paraphernalia pertaining to the 'locus amoenus' (ll. 190-192). Secondly, in the avian catalogue (ll. 330-364), CHAUCER alludes to their allegorical values; and last but certainly not least, he uses his avian protagonists to unrestrictedly explore the subject of love in general, and of courtly love in particular.[403] Neither human protagonists nor 'per definitionem' limited allegorical personifications would suit his purpose half as well.[404] Of all the animal species known to medieval man, birds display the greatest 'unified

401 At least the anthropomorphical behaviour of the formel is not completely unexpected: the description of the formel eagle in courtly terms (ll. 372-378), as pointed out by Clemen (1938:195), should have prepared the audience.

402 See Hilgers (1973:133), who stresses the fact that, in spite of the mixture of human and birdlike qualities, "the reader is reminded frequently that the parliament members are birds."

403 The dream-vision setting is another important device which allows CHAUCER great freedom. See Bethurum (1959:214) and C.S. Lewis (1938:167-168).

404 See Bennett (1957:21-22): "The bird motif allows CHAUCER both to distance and to isolate the particular conditions of human love with which the poem is concerned – to free himself of the complications attending a human story while making capital out of the minor incongruities in giving the birds human attitudes and anxieties." The choice of birds was also, to some extent, conventional. See Hume (1975:26): "[B]irds were inevitable denizens of the courtly love garden landscape, and authors with love-question 'plots' evidently felt that birds were suitable actors."

variety' and therefore resemble human race to the greatest extent;[405] and even though many of CHAUCER's birds do have an allegorical value of their own, they are not used as mere symbols, as so often in the *Physiologus* tradition, or as mouthpieces for certain human positions, as in *The Thrush and the Nightingale*, but they are characterized by a delicately balanced combination of serious allegory, comic vivacity, and anthropomorphical traits, the result of which is the creation of undeniable individuality.[406] Even the open ending of the poem would not be possible if CHAUCER did not endow the birds with autonomous characters.

CHAUCER's birds, in contrast to allegorical personifications whose main function is representation, do not primarily represent, but 'live'. When shaping the characters of his debating birds, CHAUCER makes use of only the most general ideas from the *Physiologus* and the bestiary traditions and exploits them for his discussion of love, without going into an allegorical interpretation of these traditions. They remain representatives of their classes, which is, to some extent, reflected in their attitudes towards love, but CHAUCER endows them with so much verve, vivacity, and lovingly-drawn detail that it is hardly possible to reduce them to mere allegorical figures or props. It is this composite aspect of their being which makes them so dear to modern readers.[407]

---

405 Spearing (1976b:96) talks of "the longstanding human tendency to think of birds as constituting a society parallel to human society."

406 Stillwell (1950:487) especially stresses the comic aspect of the birds. C.S. Lewis (1938:172-173) makes some important observations concerning the comic treatment of the avian protagonists.

407 Bennett (1957:15) thinks that the "pleasure of the *Parlement* comes, at least in part, from the embodying of 'doctrine' in birds whom we recognize as our fellow creatures under their feathers."

The Beast Fable and the Beast Epic Traditions

IV. The Beast Fable and the Beast Epic Traditions

"Take us the foxes, the little foxes"
Song of Songs 2,15

1. Introduction

The usual habitat of the 'vulpes communis Anglicus' and its companions are the realms of the English beast tales, the Latin – and also French – fables, and *The Physiologus* and its successors, the bestiaries.[408] Yet, sometime during the Middle Ages, the Middle English fox took the evolutionary step towards becoming, at least momentarily, 'Reneuard the Fox', only to disappear once more into relative anonymity until the time of CAXTON.[409] The problems of when, where, and to what extent the Middle English fox acquired the characteristics of his Continental cousin 'Renart' have been the subject of discussion for quite some time. In the following chapter, I therefore wish to reconsider the function of the fox and the other animal protagonists by analysing the Middle English *The Vox and the Wolf* and *The Nun's Priest's Tale*. *The Vox and the Wolf* is not only the first English vernacular poem that uses an episode from the *Roman de Renart* as its central section, but it is also the first to mention the beast epic names of the protagonists – though, as Blake (1975:54) notes, in their Anglicized forms, 'Sigrim' and 'Reneuard' (vs. 'Ysengrin' and 'Renart' in the *Roman de*

408 I use the term 'beast tale' to denote an often non-literary and otherwise undefined type of tale which is about animals or whose protagonists are animals. A detailed discussion of the genre problem can be found in Harkort (1970) and also in Grubmüller (1977:16). Concerning the German term 'Tiermärchen', see also Grubmüller (1977:41).

409 The history of the *Roman de Renart* in England has been discussed by Flinn (1963:672-688).

Renart).[410] In *The Nun's Priest's Tale*, however, the fox is not known by the name of 'Reynard', but as "daun Russelle" (Pearsall 1983:235, l. 4524).[411]

A word of warning before we descend into the 'puteum analysis'; up to now, we have dealt with literary forms that are basically foreign to a modern audience, and the range of potential protagonists of those genres has not been limited only to animals. This basic unfamiliarity, in combination with the fact that animals are not a necessary requirement of the literary genres analysed, has prevented us so far from taking them for granted. The beast fable and the beast epic, however, are two relatively well-known genres. Thus, there might be a risk of accepting the admittedly conventionalized use of animals, without inquiring further into the function(s) of the animal protagonists. In order to sharpen our critical awareness, we therefore have to consider the literary background from which *The Vox and the Wolf* and *The Nun's Priest's Tale* originated, namely the traditions of the beast fable and the beast epic, and, to some extent, from that of *The Physiologus* and the bestiary.

The *Physiologus* and Bestiary, Beast Fable, and Beast Epic Traditions

It would be slightly preposterous to speak, without further restriction, of a 'beast fable' or 'beast epic tradition' in vernacular Middle English literature. For, just as it normally takes at least two to make a crowd, it also takes more than one poem to make a tradition. Unfortunately, Middle English animal poems are rather few and far between. Wilson (1970:124) comments on the dearth of Middle English animal literature:

> [N]o English work comparable with the continental Reynard cycle has survived. Before CAXTON's translation of it only three isolated episodes are known in English, in *Vox and the Wolf*, CHAUCER's *Nun's Priest's Tale*, and the 26-line rhyme of the *Fox and the Goose*, written in a fifteenth-century hand on a fly-leaf of MS. Royal 19 B.iv[.]

If fate had also cast these last three remaining poems into oblivion, we would now only be able to write an obituary for what was probably once a

---

410 The cock's name, 'Chauntecler', however, is directly taken over from the *Roman de Renart*, though not from Branch IV, where we find no cock at all.

411 The name of the hen, 'Pertelote', also differs from the one found in the *Roman de Renart* ('Pinte'). The cock's name, 'Chauntecleer', however, has a parallel in the French "Chantecler" (Hulbert 1941:648, l. 81).

flourishing genre;[412] and with the disappearance of *The Nun's Priest's Tale*, we would have lost one of the most entertaining tales in Middle English literature. Luckily, CHAUCER's masterpiece has survived into our times and, together with *The Vox and the Wolf*, *The Fox and the Goose*[413], and *The Fals Fox*[414], gives us a hint of what probably once existed and is now lost. However, *The Fox and the Goose* and *The Fals Fox* will not be taken into consideration here, since they fall outside the chronological scope of our study.

Yet, these few extant works and those vernacular poems whose existence can be inferred from circumstantial evidence tell only half the story – or even less. Parallel to them, we have a relative abundance of works belonging to the Latin and (Anglo-)French branches of beast literature, which include poems that were also (widely) known in Britain; these can be categorized into *Physiologus* and bestiary literature, beast fables, and beast epics.[415]

In the following discussion, we will briefly examine the genres of the *Physiologus* and the bestiary traditions, the beast fable, and the beast epic.[416]

---

[412] Iconographical evidence of the widespread popularity of animal poems and tales is discussed in Blake (1975:62) and Varty (1964, 1967, and 1975). Wilson (1970:126) comes to the following conclusion: "Altogether it seems clear that the lack of extant written works on the subject in Middle English is due more to accident than to lack of contemporary interest." He (1970:124-125) adduces further evidence of the former existence of other episodes from the *Renart* cycle: thus, a catalogue entry in the library of Dover Priory, compiled in 1389, mentions a *Fabula de Wlpe medici in angl.*, ODO OF CHERITON quotes English proverbs in his Latin fable collection, and in BARBOUR's *Bruce*, the story of the fox and the fisherman is mentioned. Bergner (1973:284), however, has his doubts, at least with regard to the widespread popularity of the beast epic genre itself (in contrast to the isolated episodes): "Insgesamt entfallen also die Anlässe, den ohnehin kaum existenten höfischen Roman zu parodieren [which is the main function of the *Roman de Renart* and its successors]. Folglich besteht in mittelenglischer Zeit kein Bedarf an einer grösseren Produktion von Tierepen." He (1973:285) comes to the conclusion that: "Es ist zweifelhaft, ob es im Mittelenglischen überhaupt mehr als diese beiden Tierepen-Episoden [namely *The Vox and the Wolf* and *The Nun's Priest's Tale*] je gegeben hat."

[413] For a discussion of *The Fox and the Goose*, see Bowers (1952).

[414] On *The Fals Fox* see also footnote 484.

[415] Or, as McKnight (1908:497) puts it: "There were the bestiaries, in which the medieval symbolists attempted to give a moral interpretation to the habits of beasts; there were the fables, in which beast tales were told for the sake of the lesson they taught; and third, there was the distinctively medieval set of stories, told because of their own intrinsic power of affording amusement, to which is generally given the name 'beast epic'."

[416] There is, of course, always the possibility that an item which originated in one tradition is transferred into another. See Blackham (1985:35-36): "Although Bestiaries were so

The *Physiologus* and the Bestiary Traditions[417]

The Physiologus and the bestiaries, roughly speaking, contain individual chapters on animals, mythological beings, plants, and stones. In the first part of a chapter (the so-called 'natura', here A) information is given on the characteristics of the animals, plants, etc. (elements of A). In *The Physiologus* and in most bestiaries, some of these (animal) characteristics are then allegorically interpreted, so that the second part of that chapter (the so-called 'significatio', here A') provides the 'sensus moralis', the 'sensus allegoricus', and/or the 'sensus anagogicus' of the report. Thus, the fox is described in the *Physiologus* and the bestiary traditions as a wily animal which feigns death in order to lure scavenger birds.[418] This behaviour is then allegorically interpreted as the devil's (= fox's) attempt to ensnare the unwary souls (= birds) of those who believe him to be dead.[419] The illustration below schematically shows this process.

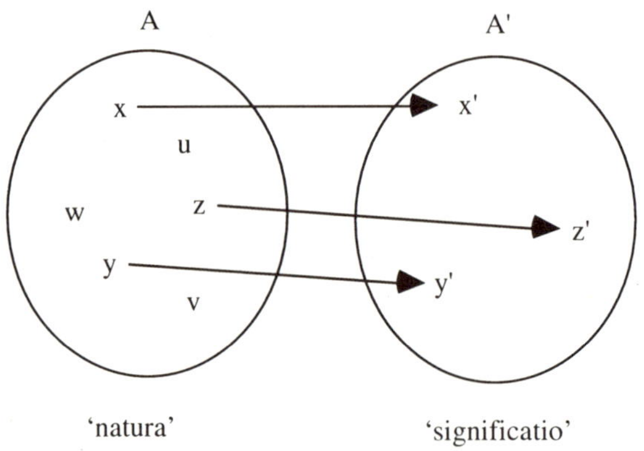

different from fables in structure and function, what is obviously the same material does occur in both." On the 'adaptability' of the fable, see also Grubmüller (1977:7).

417 For a detailed discussion of the *Physiologus* and the bestiary traditions, see page 17ff.

418 See, for example, Seel (1992:26-27) or T.H. White (1959:53-54).

419 The devils themselves, too, can assume the shape of animals and haunt the realms of man as wolves and foxes. See, for example, *An Old English Martyrology* (Herzfeld 1900:192, ll. 15-16).

The Beast Fable Tradition[420]

Most critics and scholars who deal with the question of what elements constitute a beast fable agree on at least five characteristics.[421] The first is that its main protagonists are (mostly familiar) animals who act and speak like human beings.[422] Secondly, however, they retain their basic animal characteristics, even though they are in many respects like human beings.[423]

---

[420] Plessow (1906:xxvi), in his overview of the history of the English fable up to 1726, believes the (Indian and other) beast fables to have developed out of the beast epics. Blackham (1985:33), at least for the *Roman de Renart*, contradicts this point of view: "[The *Roman de Renart*] originated as a clerical creation out of the fables."

[421] An in-depth discussion of the characteristics of the fable genre can be found in Leibfried (1976). Jauss (1977:89) contrasts the fable with the beast epic and thus gains an additional characteristic: "Die Beispielhaftigkeit der Fabelsituation überdeckt die typischen Charaktere der Tiere, so dass ihr vorgeprägtes Wesen nur noch in eine mögliche, nicht aber in eine notwendige Relation zu der Bedeutung ihrer Erscheinung tritt. [....] [I]m Bereich der Fabel erscheinen die Tiere als Beispielfiguren, die ihre Deutung aus der Situation erhalten." This has a parallel in *The Physiologus*, where, out of a number of natural characteristics, those which suit the purpose of the author are chosen for interpretation. The difference between *The Physiologus* and the fable has been commented on by Grubmüller (1977:22): "Die Differenz zur Fabel ist im Bildteil deutlich: Die Enthüllung des Sinnes von Geschaffenem setzt voraus, dass Reales berichtet wird." Dithmar (1971:97) contrasts the fable with the parable, and Grubmüller (1977:9-47) undertakes a contrastive comparison with those genres which have an affinity with the fable.

[422] See A. Clark (1975:113-114): "What distinguishes the fable from other literary forms is that it relates incidents in the lives of animals who speak and act like human beings." The apparent unreality of this characteristic has already been commented on by Lessing (1759:147 and 149), and especially Grimm (1834:vi): "Sobald wir eingelassen sind in das innere gebiet der fabel, beginnt der zweifel an dem wirklichen geschehnsein ihrer ereignisse zu schwinden[.]" In more recent times, Grubmüller (1981:120) has reached a similar conclusion: "Die Tierfabel konstituiert sich aus dem Verstoss gegen Solidaritätsregeln, die aus unserer Erfahrung über Eigenschaften und Verhaltensmöglichkeiten von Tieren einerseits und von Menschen andererseits folgen." See also Grubmüller (1977:13). Blackham (1985:177) characterizes the function of animals in fables as follows: "The Aesopic use of animals is the primal and simplest form of [the] freedom of representation." They allow a distanced and more objective assessment of a situation or problem (see Dithmar 1971:144).
The use of animals which are familiar to an average medieval audience, namely fox, ass, wolf, cock, etc. (see Leibfried 1976:21-22) stands in contrast to the exoticism of the *Physiologus* and the bestiary traditions.

[423] This point is stressed by Lessing (1759:151). Furthermore, he (1759:154) observes: "[Die] allgemein bekannten und unveränderlichen Charaktere der Thiere [sind] die eigentliche Ursache [...], warum sie der Fabulist zu moralischen Wesen erhebt[.]" See also Grimm's (1834:viii) comment: "Wer geschichten ersinnen wollte, in denen die thiere

Thirdly, the Aesopic fable, unlike a *Physiologus* or bestiary 'natura', needs no exegesis; or, to use Blackham's (1985:240) formulation, it "is immediately recognizable and applicable, and is explicit and practical in this sense."[424] Fourthly, the fable relates a fictitious event.[425] And finally, a beast fable does not only instruct, but it also delights.[426]

Very often, we notice a tendency to emphasize one single characteristic to the exclusion of the others, so that in the end we do have 'types' rather than fully-developed characters.[427] The character of the fable fox, then, is, more often than not, limited to being 'the flatterer' or 'the hypocrite'. Thus, we find a reduction of the formerly multiple nature of an animal to one typical trait.[428]

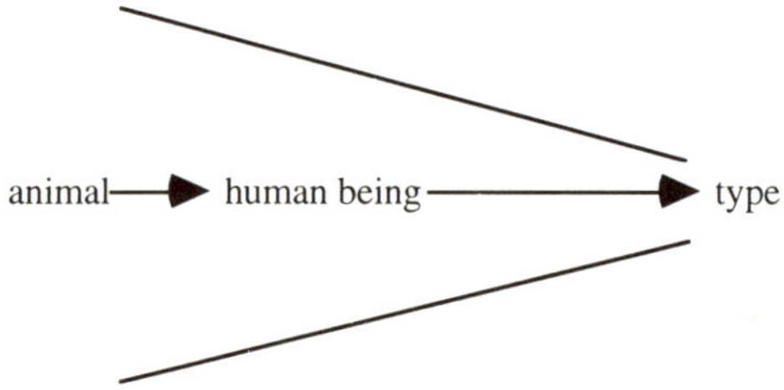

sich bloss wie menschen gebährdeten, nur zufällig mit thiernamen und gestalt begabt wären, hätte den geist der fabel ebenso verfehlt, wie wer darin thiere getreu nach der natur aufzufassen suchte, ohne menschliches geschick und ohne den menschen abgesehne handlung. fehlte den thieren der fabel der menschliche beigeschmack, so würden sie albern, fehlte ihnen der thierische, langweilig sein."

424 See also Dithmar (1971:82).

425 See A. Clark (1975:114), who comments on the difference between the *Physiologus* and the bestiary traditions and the fable: "One essential difference between the fable and the bestiary is that the former, though presented as fact, was not expected to be believed but merely to prove both entertaining and instructive, whereas the bestiary accounts were offered as simple truth[.]" Similarly Schmidtke (1968:165): "[Die] bewusstseinsmässige [...] Faktizität des Berichts im Bereich der Tierauslegung steht der bewussten Fiktivität des Fabelberichtes [...] gegenüber." See also Grubmüller (1977:14).

426 Yet, 'prodesse' remains the main function of the fable. See Dithmar (1971:100): "Zweck der Fabel ist die Belehrung und nicht die Unterhaltung."

427 The use of 'typical' animals meets the requirement of brevity essential to the fable. See Dithmar (1971:111): "Fabeltiere sind bevorzugte Akteure, weil man ihre Eigenschaften nicht mehr zu beschreiben braucht. [....] Es gibt bestimmte Eigenschaften und Verhaltensweisen, die den Fabeltieren eigen sind und die man auch in Sprichwörtern, Redensarten und in der Heraldik findet."

428 Leibfried (1976:23) calls this process "Typisierung der Figuren".

Grubmüller (1977:6) characterizes the situation of the fable in the Middle Ages as follows:

> Fabeltradition ist im Mittelalter primär lateinische Tradition – trotz der prinzipiell vorhandenen, aber auf die Randbereiche der Tiererzählung konzentrierten und nur im Tierepos zur Schriftlichkeit vorstossenden Möglichkeit volkstümlich-mündlicher Überlieferung und trotz der Verbreitung in der bildenden Kunst: volkssprachige Fabeldichtung variiert lateinische Muster. Das heisst freilich nicht, dass sie an schriftlich fixierte Vorlagen gebunden wäre. Durch Schule und Predigt ist die lateinische Fabel zu allgemeiner Kenntnis gebracht und verbreitet eingeübt worden, ohne deshalb ihren angestammten Bildungsbereich schon verlassen zu haben.

Those medieval beast fables which were current in England and which have been handed down to us have to be primarily divided into two groups. Thus we have, on the one hand, the (Anglo-)French 'courtly' beast fables by MARIE DE FRANCE, and on the other hand, the 'exempla' beast fables found in sermons and handbooks for preachers.[429] Most of the medieval beast fables go back to the collections of Antiquity, namely the fables of AESOP and their adaptations by PHAEDRUS (first century A.D.), AVIANUS (fourth century A.D.), and the legendary ROMULUS.[430]

MARIE DE FRANCE's *Ysopet* (end of the twelfth century) goes back – according to the author's epilogue – to an English version of AESOP's fables ascribed to a certain "[...] reis Alvrez, ki mult l'ama,/le translata [from Latin] puis en Engleis,/e jeo l'ai rimé en Franceis" (Gumbrecht 1973:274, ll. 16-18).[431] It contains probably the best-known collection of fables written

---

429 Henderson (1981:164) comments on MARIE's fables: "She has [...] adapted fable to her audience and made it courtly entertainment." Jauss (1959:24-56) argues in a similar way. Concerning the use of Aesopic fables in medieval sermons, see Henderson (1981:160) and Owst (1966:206-209).

430 Blackham (1985:1-84), Dithmar (1971:13-26), and Grubmüller (1977:48-85) provide detailed introductions to the history and development of the fable. Some of the most important medieval Latin fable collections in England are the *Anonymus Neveleti* (twelfth century), the *Novus Aesopus* by ALEXANDER NECKAM (†1217), and the *Liber Parabolarum* (c.1219) by ODO OF CHERITON (see Grubmüller 1977:77-104).

431 Plessow (1906:xxix) assumes that there was an English model composed by a man called ALFRED, whose fable collection in turn went back to the *Romulus Nilantii*, the "gewöhnliche *Romulus*", other oriental sources, and animal tales in general. See also Wilson (1970:68): "There is no reason to doubt that MARIE was translating from an English original, and it is possible enough that the author of it may have been called ALFRED, but it is unlikely that he is to be identified with the king." A similar point of view is held by Grubmüller (1977:72). Owst (1966:204), however, thinks that "[t]he

on English soil before CAXTON's edition and translation of AESOP's fables in 1484. Not surprisingly, her fable of *Du goupil et du cok* is most likely a major source with regard to the structure of *The Nun's Priest's Tale*.

MARIE DE FRANCE's fable collection may be of great importance to the subsequent literary development of the genre in England, but it is neither the first nor the only one. Thanks to their combination of entertainment and moral instruction, the (beast) fables were adapted by preachers quite early.[432] Thus, the first vernacular English beast fable – that of the young crab which, when asked by its mother to swim forward and not backwards, answered by asking the old crab to do so first – is to be found in a twelfth or thirteenth century sermon.[433] Owst (1966:204) summarizes the relevant points concerning the 'exempla' beast fables as follows:

> When the wisdom and solemn fantasy of Bestiary-lore have been exhausted, there remains yet a further contribution to preaching from the animal world in the shape, not of instruction in natural history, but of entertainment once again by means of semi-humorous fiction, namely, the animal fable. [....] Whether or not the appetite for such fables was strong and indigenous, at all events the comparative rarity of this animal fiction in English sermons suggests that it remained, with few exceptions, as it had begun, the particular entertainment of the Anglo-Norman aristocracy. Nevertheless, England produced at least one leading moral fabulist of the Middle Ages in the person of ODO OF CHERITON[.][434]

Indeed, ODO OF CHERITON's (c. 1185-1247) Latin fables are good examples of the international character of the 'exempla' beast fables.[435] Educated in Paris, he eventually returned to his native England and

---

animal fable proper, [...] so far as England is concerned seems to have been an importation from France along with the other Norman influences upon our language and literature, following the Conquest."

432 See Grubmüller (1977:97): "Die Verwendung von Fabeln in der Predigt liegt in der Konsequenz ihrer von altersher bezeugten Einstufung als ein Überzeugungsmittel der Rede."

433 See the edition by Morris (1869:51-53).

434 Whitesell (1947:350) critically comments on this passage: "Owst's statement [...] is hard to reconcile with the collections of JOHN OF BROMYARD, ODO OF CHERITON and NICOLE BOZON in England, not to mention the numerous others on the continent."

435 Blake (1975:56) and Flinn (1963:672) comment only briefly on ODO OF CHERITON, whereas Henderson (1981:166-168) and Plessow (1906:xxxi-xxxii) give a slightly more detailed evaluation of his fables. A valuable translation of ODO's fables was published by Jacobs (1985).

compiled a collection of 81 fables (c. 1219-1221).[436] Even though the fables themselves are in Latin, ODO quotes three Middle English proverbs, two of which may be interpreted as proof of a vernacular (oral?) beast fable tradition;[437] and it is in ODO OF CHERITON's work that we find the first evidence (apart from the fables of BERECHJA HA-NAKDAN[438]; end of the 12th century) of familiarity with the beast epic in England, since he mentions 'Ysengrimo' and 'Reinardus'.[439] More fables, with the *Romulus* (Latin prose fables, c. A.D. 400) as their main source, can be found in other writings of his which he compiled as collections of material for sermons.[440] In the fourteenth century, JEAN OF BROMYARD uses several of ODO's fables in his *Summa predicantium*. He also quotes the proper names of 'Reynard' and 'Tebert' and thus gives us another hint concerning knowledge of the beast epic tradition, which obviously influenced the fable tradition.[441] JOHN OF SHEPPEY, Bishop of Oxford from 1352 to 1360, uses several of ODO's fables, too.[442] Finally, we must mention NICOLE BOZON (c. 1320-1350), who also included some fables in his Anglo-Norman story collection.

---

[436] See Blackham (1985:51), Jacobs (1985:10-28), Owst (1966:204), and Plessow (1906:xxxi).

[437] See Plessow (1906:xxxi). The Middle English proverbs can be found in Fable 6, *An Abbot, Food, and Some Monks* (Jacobs 1985:73): "Selde cumet se betere"; Fable 10, *The Buzzard and the Hawk's Nest* (Jacobs 1985:75): "Of on egge y the brouzgyt bytt of thy kynde y maye nouzght"; and Fable 34, *The Wolf Who Longed to Be a Monk* (Jacobs 1985:93): "Thai thu Wolf hore hodi te preste tho thu hym sette Salmes to lere, evere beth his geres to the groue-ward". Whereas "Selde cumet se betere" is a general truth not even here connected to a beast fable, the two other proverbs can be seen as pointing towards an oral vernacular beast tale tradition. On the (assumed) oral tradition of beast tales, especially in connection with *The Vox and the Wolf*, see Flinn (1963:677).

[438] For more information see the article on BERECHJA HA-NAKDAN by Scheiber (1979).

[439] See Plessow (1906:xxxii). ODO further mentions "Chantecler, scilicet Gallus" (Plessow 1906:xxxii; see Jacobs 1985:96: "Chanticleer, the cock"), "Tebergo, id est Cato" (Plessow 1906:xxxii; see Jacobs 1985:113: "Tib the Cat"), and "Berengarius, scilicet Ursus" (Plessow 1906:xxxii; see Jacobs 1985:119: "Berengarius, the bear"). It is interesting to note that ODO hardly ever mentions the names of beast epic protagonists other than 'Reinardus' without adding a tag like '..., id est/scilicet ...'. He obviously could not yet count on any general and widespread familiarity with Reynard and his fellows.

[440] See Plessow (1906:xxxii).

[441] See Flinn (1963:673) and Whitesell (1947:357): "[T]he motifs of the beast epic occur with relatively high frequency among the 'exemplum'-fables."

[442] See Blackham (1985:52).

The Beast Epic Tradition[443]

The beast epic, in contrast to the moralistic fable, has no ambitions to instruct its audience. This distinguishes it, in connection with its now individualized protagonists, who bear proper names, as well as its epic length, from the related beast fable.[444] As in the beast fable, the element of the supernatural is limited to the animals' ability to speak.[445] In contrast to, and sometimes also in accordance with, the animals of the beast fables, the protagonists of the medieval stories about Reynard the fox

> have human names and ranks, [yet] they nevertheless retain their animal individuality and behave in accordance with their animal nature. [....] The animals never become mere personifications of human vices and virtues, for they continue to live in a non-human world.
> (Blake 1970:xi)

Thus, they do not fully participate in the interpretative and limiting metamorphosis from animal to man and then to type:[446] they not only retain most of their animal characteristics, but they also exhibit strongly individualistic traits and a greater range of features, which distinguish them from the mostly limited fable animals.[447] A graphic depiction of this development might look as follows:

---

[443] Jauss (1959:56-113) provides an excellent introduction to the beginnings of the medieval beast epic. Blackham (1985:40) characterizes the *Roman de Renart* as follows: "Inspired by the Aesopic fables, and using these fables freely in its making, *Le Roman de Renart* is obviously not itself an Aesopic fable. Described as a 'beast-epic', whether it is itself a kind of fable, or is a parody of heroic poetry, or an allegory, or something else is hardly a profitable question, since in the long run it is all these and not consistently anything."

[444] See Harkort (1970:20): "Das Tierepos hat im Gegensatz zur Fabel – der lehrhafte Charakter der Fabel fehlt ihm vollkommen – und vor allen Dingen zur Tiervolkserzählung eine epische Breite und ist daher in Komposition und Stil (Versform) zu einem eigenen Genre, zu einer literarischen Gattung geworden."

[445] See Jauss (1959:66).

[446] Also compare Jauss (1977:60): "Auf die neue Tierdichtung des 12. Jahrhunderts [i.e. the beast epic and the 'courtly' beast fable] hat die typologische Allegorese der Bestiarien so gut wie gar nicht eingewirkt. Die Charaktere der Tierfiguren im *Esope* und im *RdR* [i.e. the *Roman de Renart*] haben mit der typologischen Bedeutung der Tiere, die im *Bestiaire* PHILIPPS VON THAUN und seiner Nachfolger die heilsgeschichtliche Situation des Menschen zwischen Gott und Teufel auslegen, nichts gemein. Der Fuchs, der im Tierepos zum Gegenspieler des Wolfes wird, hat damit aufgehört, 'figura diaboli' zu sein[.]" See also E. Martin (1908).

[447] Shallers (1975:331) puts it thus: "All in all, the *Renart* world is free-wheeling and iconoclastic; it gains force and verve as it touches on the contemporary human scene, but

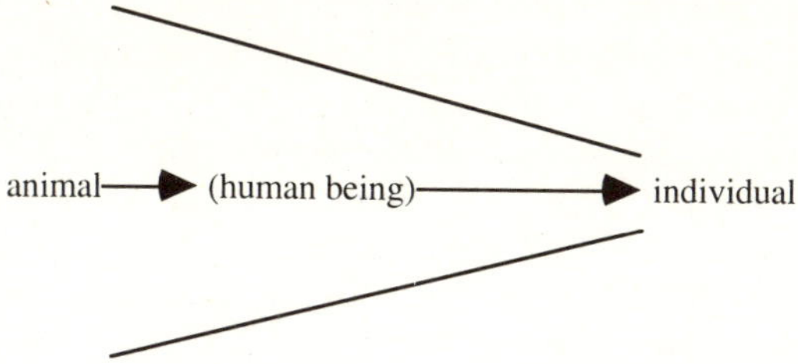

The fox is not simply 'the flatterer' or 'the hypocrite', but a likeable, though admittedly rather roguish and, to some extent anthropomorphic, animal character, who takes advantage of the credulity and naivety of his fellow beings.

The origins of the beast epic are somewhat obscure. Ganzenmüller (1914:102) traces its beginnings to the fables of PAULUS DIACONUS (A.D. 782), yet we do not have a 'real' beast epic until about 260 years later.[448] The first prototype of the beast epic is the Latin *Ecbasis Cuiusdam Captivi Per Tropologiam* (1043-1046, hereafter referred to as *Ecbasis*), written by a Cistercian monk of Germanic stock.[449] Part of the action springs from the antagonism between fox and wolf, and it is here in the *Ecbasis* that an attempt is made to link certain beast fables into a coherent poem.[450] In the

it never really rises from its naturalistic base to point out the vices and follies of that human scene."

448 Blackham (1985:41) writes: "How it all began has been a matter of controversy, in the main between those who wanted to find the roots in folklore and oral tradition, whether immemorial or contemporary, and those who found it evident that the source is bookish and clerkly, in the Latin collections of fables derived from Greece and Rome that were in the schools and in clerical hands." Ganzenmüller (1914:157) speaks in favour of a learned and scholarly origin of the beast epic. See also Gupta (1975:242). Jauss (1959:70 and 1977:55) finds no sufficient reason to assume a pre-literary development of the beast epic before the twelfth century, and thus concludes that there is no continuity in animal poetry from the Latin poems to the early medieval ones. For a discussion of the Latin beast poems in early Carolingian times, see Schaller (1970). The possible connection between popular beast tales and beast epics has been discussed by Suchier (1922).

449 See the edition by Trillitzsch (1964:25), who writes: "Auf jeden Fall aber tritt uns in der *Ecbasis* das mittelalterliche Tierepos zum ersten Mal selbständig entgegen[.]" Jauss (1959:84-92) and Ross (1954) discuss some of the most important characteristics of the *Ecbasis*.

450 See Blake (1970:xiv-xv). Grimm (1834:xix) already comments on the traditional antagonism: "Die classischen thiere der fabel sind der fuchs und der wolf. es wäre

Latin *Ysengrimus* (1148), formerly attributed to MASTER NIVARDUS OF GENT[451], then, the animals are given names for the first time.[452] Many episodes taken from earlier fables or beast stories are, as Blake (1970:xv) puts it, fashioned "into a unified whole by subordinating them to the general theme of the enmity of the fox and wolf."[453] The prime examples of the medieval beast epic genre are the French *Roman de Renart* (composed between 1174 and 1250), its shorter Middle High German counterpart, *Reinhart Fuchs* (1180), attributed to HEINRICH DER GLICHEZAERE, and the anonymous Middle Dutch *Reinaert de Vos* (between 1200 and 1250).[454] The French stories about Reynard the fox are, most probably, the (partial) sources for both *The Vox and the Wolf* and *The Nun's Priest's Tale*, though we have only indirect evidence that the *Roman de Renart* was available and known in England before the time of CAXTON.[455] As we will see, the first of

---

geradezu unmöglich zwei andere an ihre stelle zu setzen, die gleich vortrefflich alle erfordernisse der fabel erfüllen könnten." Blackham (1985:43) also notes the rivalry and enmity between fox and wolf in the Latin fables of BABRIUS and PHAEDRUS, and Brinkmann (1970:166) writes that the two are "in der Tierfabel die satirischen Entsprechungen zu den beiden Grundtugenden des eigentlichen Helden, nämlich der 'fortitudo' und der 'prudentia'. Der Fuchs ist in seiner List das satirische Widerspiel der 'prudentia' und der Wolf in seiner Gewalttätigkeit das satirische Widerspiel der 'fortitudo'." Ganzenmüller (1914:153) relates an interesting variation on this antagonism: "So schützt den hl. Odo ein Wolf gegen die vom Teufel gesandten Füchse[.]" Stoob (1991:192-196) discusses the zoological basis of the fox vs. wolf antagonism.

451 For a comprehensive discussion of the question of authorship, see Mann (1987:156-181).

452 Jauss (1977:27) comments on this development: "Zwischen den Gattungsnamen der antiken Figuren der Fabel und den Eigennamen des mittelalterlichen Tierepos liegt eine Schwelle der Individuation." On the *Ysengrimus* in general, see also Jauss (1959:93-113). P. Lehmann (1963:70-71) interprets it as a satire on monastic life.

453 Jauss (1959:75-77) observes that the fox vs. wolf antagonism, which was missing in the Latin 'Tierschwank', is an important element for the development of the individual episodes into an epic cycle. He (1959:79-81) also comments on the older antagonism of fox vs. (she-)bear, which can be seen as a forerunner of the fox vs. wolf antagonism. See also Schaller (1970:94).

454 Gupta (1975) comments on the Indian parallels to the fox story.

455 See Blackham (1985:53): "English churchmen educated in Paris, like ODO and JOHN OF SHEPPEY, might easily have known *Le Roman de Renart*, but there is little evidence that it was available in circulation in England." Also Blake (1975:56): "No manuscripts of it [i.e. the *Roman de Renart*] were either written or found in England by 1250. On the other hand, collections of fables and other animal stories were common." Only recently, however, Varty has conclusively proven that the French *Roman de Renart* was available in manuscript form (and therefore known) in England in 1359 and draws attention to a reference to Branch II of the *Roman de Renart* in GUILLEAUME LE CLERC DE

the two Middle English poems in question displays important characteristics of the beast epic, yet at the same time there are also influences from the beast fable, and even from the *Physiologus* and the bestiary traditions.

2. *The Vox and the Wolf*[456]

Author, Date, and Manuscript

The Vox and the Wolf was written by an unknown author during the second half of the thirteenth century, and is handed down in one single manuscript, namely MS. Digby 86 of the Bodleian Library.[457]

Sources and Parallels

The basic plot of *The Vox and the Wolf* probably goes back to the corresponding episode in Branch IV of the *Roman de Renart* (c. 1178), which is in turn assumed to be an elaboration of a story found in the *Disciplina Clericalis*, an 'exempla' collection by PETRUS ALFONSUS (written between 1109 and 1114).[458] With PETRUS ALFONSUS, however, the wolf is

NORMANDIE's *Bestiaire divin* (1210/1211) (paper given at the 11th International Colloquy of the Reynard Society, Düsseldorf 17th – 20th July 1995).

456 All references are to the edition by Bennett and Smithers (1968:65-76). A slightly altered version of this chapter is going to be published in *Reinardus* 9 (1996) under the title «A Fox is a Fox is a Fox: *The Vox and the Wolf* Reconsidered.».

457 The only critic who hazards a vague guess at the author's identity seems to be Plessow (1906:xxxii), who thinks that the poem was "von einem Südengländer verfasst, offenbar von einem Kleriker[.]"
Concerning the date of composition, see Flinn (1963:Appendix II) who dates it to c. 1250, and Plessow (1906:xxxii), who assumes 1272 to be the 'terminus ante quo'.Concerning the manuscript, see Bennett and Smithers (1968:297).

458 All references to Branch IV of the *Roman de Renart* are to the edition by Jauss-Meyer (1965:150-173). The connection between *The Vox and the Wolf* and Branch IV of the *Roman de Renart* is discussed by Blake (1975:53-54), Flinn (1963:674-678), and Kreisler (1970:652-653). On the so-called 'short version' of Branch IV (MS H), which has its first 148 lines in common with the longer version, see Kenneth Varty, «'Renart et Ysengrin dans le puits': la version courte, la version longue, et la version plus longue de la branche IV du 'Roman de Renart'.», (unpublished manuscript); and also Varty (1991:330-343).
Hermes (1977) offers a modern English translation of the *Disciplina Clericalis*. On the *Disciplina Clericalis*, see Bennett and Smithers (1968:65-66), Flinn (1963:677), Jauss (1959:126), and McKnight (1908:501). The important deviations from the *Roman de*

lured to the bottom of the well by the reflection of the moon in the water, which he thinks to be a whole cheese.[459] The version related by RABBI RASCHI in the eleventh century seems to be the oldest one.[460] The basic pattern of the fable may go back to AESOP's fable of *The Fox and the Goat*.[461] In the Middle Ages, as Bennett and Smithers (1968:65) observe, the episode of the fox and the wolf in the well

> was also available to Englishmen in summary form in the Latin prose fables of ODO OF CHERITON (c. 1219) and JOHN OF SHEPPEY (ob. 1360), and in the AN *Contes moralisées* of NICHOLAS BOZON (first half of the fourteenth century).[462]

Renart are treated in Blake (1975:54) and Kreisler (1970:651-652). The relationship between Branch IV of the *Roman de Renart* and the 'exemplum XXIII' of the *Disciplina Clericalis* is discussed in Jauss (1959:128-141), who reaches the conclusion that the origin of the vernacular tale must be located somewhere between the 'exemplum XXIII' and the episode from the *Roman de Renart*.

459 See the edition by Hermes (1977:143-144). On PETRUS ALFONSUS' 'exemplum', see also McKnight (1908:501). For a more detailed comparison of the differences, see Jauss (1959:128-141).

460 See McKnight (1908:502).

461 See Plessow (1906:xxxii) and ten Brink (1877:322). The fable of *The Fox and the Goat* can be found in Ogilby (1668:144-146).

462 ODO, however, interprets his version of the tale, the XIXth 'exemplum' of his *Liber Parabolarum*, according to the rules of allegory, and thus presents the anonymous fox as a 'figura diaboli'. Since ODO OF CHERITON's account can be considered a near contemporary of *The Vox and the Wolf*, it is quoted in full (Grubmüller 1977:105):

> De vulpe et lupo et situla putei
>
> Vulpes casu cecidit per unam situlam in puteum. Venit Lupus et querebat quid faceret ibi. Que ait: Bone compater, hic habeo multos pisces et magnos; utinam mecum partem haberes! Et ait Ysemgrimus: Quomodo possem illuc descendere? Ait Vulpecula: Supra est una situla; pone te intus, et venies deorsum. Et erant ibi due situle; quando una ascendit, alia descendit. Lupus posuit se in situlam, que erat supra et descendit insum; Vulpecula in alia situla ascendit sursum. Et quando obviaverunt sibi, ait Lupus: Bone compater, quo uadis? Et ait Vulpes: Satis comedi et ascendo. Tu descende et inuenies mirabilia. Descendit miser Lupus nec inuenit aliquid nisi aquam. Venerunt mane rustici et extraxerunt Lupum, et usque ad mortem uerberauerunt.
>
> Vulpecula significat Diabolum qui dicit homini: Descende ad me in puteum peccati et inuenies delicias et multa bona. Stultus adquiescit et descendit in puteum culpe, et ibi nullam inuenit refeccionem. Tandem ueniunt inimici et extrahunt impium, percuciunt et perimunt. Diabolus multa bona Ade promisit; sed multa mala persoluit.

An English translation can be found in Jacobs (1985:89). Blackham (1985:44) comments on ODO's fable: "[W]hen *Renart* offers a later fabulist material for his purpose, it is stripped for that purpose of its narrative complications and circumstantial detail – as ODO

Let us now descend into the 'puteum analysis', in order to contrast *The Vox and the Wolf* with the near-contemporary fable by ODO (c. 1219) and with the older Branch IV of the *Roman de Renart*.[463]

Analysis

In order to facilitate the analysis, we will divide the poem into four parts, namely: 1) the initial entry of the fox into human territory (ll. 1-26); 2) the hen-coop incident (ll. 27-64); 3) the 'Fox and Wolf in the Well' story proper (ll. 65-260); and 4) the discovery of the wolf in the well by brother Ailmer (ll. 261-295).

The Initial Entry (ll. 1-26)

Even though the first section of the poem does not contain any events indispensable to the subsequent development of the narrative, it is nevertheless of central importance to our understanding of the poem itself and of its main protagonist and his motives. First, the fact that *The Vox and the Wolf* is written in verse separates it from its less direct sources (PETRUS ALFONSUS' 'exemplum XXIII' and ODO's 'exemplum' fable) and links it with the *Roman de Renart*. Furthermore, the first two lines imply more than first meets the eye: "A VOX gon out of þe wode go,/Afingret so þat him wes wo –" (ll. 1-2).[464] First of all, our hero is not introduced by his personal name – which is in accordance with PETRUS ALFONSUS' 'exemplum XXIII' and ODO's 'exemplum' fable, but stands in contrast to Branch IV of the *Roman de Renart* (ll. 21-22). Only in line 133, after all the other protagonists have been given a name, do we learn that our fox is the (in)famous 'Reneuard'.[465] Up to this point, he remains merely an anonymous fox who comes into our field of vision because he wanders out of his natural habitat into the world of men, represented by the "strete" (l. 5), which he avoids, the "wal" (l. 10), and, finally, the "hous" (l. 11).[466] Secondly, it is

OF CHERITON simplifies the *Renart* story of Renart and Isengrim in the well." BROMYARD makes a passing allusion to "lupus et vulpes in situla" (Owst 1966:207) in his *Summa Predicantium*, and thus, as Owst (1966:207) observes, "shows clearly enough how familiar these fables must have been to clerical readers of the period."

463 The 'short version' (in MS H) will also be taken into account.

464 On the importance of hunger and thirst in motivating the action of the poem, see also Bergner (1973:270-273) and LeSaux (1990: 69).

465 Thus, the cock is called "Sire Chauntecler" (l. 37) and the wolf "Sigrim" (l. 128).

466 Borst (1991:207-210) discusses the historical reality and poetic importance of the human backdrop in the beast epic.

also within the very first lines that we become acquainted with the prime motivation of all the protagonist's subsequent actions: he was "[a]fingret so þat him wes wo –" (l. 2). The repeated and stressed reference to the state of hunger parallels that found in Branch IV of the *Roman de Renart* (see, for example, ll. 37-38 and ll. 48-56). Thus, the first part of *The Vox and the Wolf* shows great similarity to lines 35-120 of Branch IV of the *Roman de Renart*. Yet, there is one crucial difference: in spite of the verse-form, and in spite of the fact that the poet relates a story and not merely characteristic behaviour, he nevertheless fails to identify his poem unambiguously as a beast epic, since he introduces the main protagonist as a 'generic fox'; and also, the anthropomorphism of the beast epic is not yet evident.[467] We may well wonder what kind of fox this is. The naturalistic and rather long description of the fox's search for food speaks against a hasty identification of the fox with that of the Aesopic fable, even though we cannot yet rule out this possibility completely; and since the traditional bestiary does not deal in stories but in characteristic behaviour, and would thus rather open with 'the fox' than 'a fox', a classification of our poem within the *Physiologus* and bestiary traditions seems rather unlikely.[468] However, since even clearly 'non-bestiary foxes' are sometimes allegorised, we cannot rule out this possibility 'a priori'.[469]

The Chicken-Coop Raid (ll. 27-64)

It is not clear whether the event which must have taken place between lines 30 and 31, namely the raid on the chicken-coop by the fox, has been deliberately omitted by the poet or the scribe.[470] Yet, if we consider lines 31-32 ("þe kok him wes flowen on hey,/And two hennen him seten ney"), 39-40 (fox: "I nabbe don her nout bote goed –/I have leten þine hennen

---

[467] On the fable elements, see Blake (1975:55). The only anthropomorphic detail can be found in line 23, and is connected to the theme of 'trespassing', which is treated in detail by LeSaux (1990). Thus, the fox actually laughs derisively (l. 23) and "hadde gome inou" (l. 24) after illegally making his way into the settlement ("he com in wiþouten leue/Boþen of haiward and of reue!" ll. 25-26).

[468] I thus use the genres which Henderson postulates (1981:162): "Beast literature at the end of the twelfth century includes three prominent genres: bestiary, beast epic, and fable." At the same time, I am aware of the fact that these genres are more or less modern categories and that medieval authors often had no explicit 'genre-consciousness'.

[469] Thus, the fox-protagonist of ODO OF CHERITON's 'exemp!um' fable is allegorically interpreted as a 'figura diaboli'. In the related fable *The Taill of the Foxe, that begylit the Wolf, in the schadow of the Mone* (MacDiarmid 1973:55-63), HENRYSON (second half of the fifteenth century), also gives an allegorical interpretation.

[470] The first to notice that some lines are probably missing was ten Brink (1877:322).

blod"), 55 (cock: "Go mid þan þat þou hauest nouþe"), and the parallel passage in Branch IV of the *Roman de Renart* (ll. 133-141), it is obvious that the fox must have killed and (at least partially) eaten three of the five hens.[471] The poem in its present form, however, only implies the killing. Thus, the attention of the audience is focused upon the ensuing dialogue between the cock and the fox, which is, most importantly, not found in Branch IV of the *Roman de Renart.* The dialogue foreshadows the conversation between the fox and the wolf in the third section of *The Vox and the Wolf.* Up to now, the action has managed with a minimum of anthropomorphic elements. The first 30 lines give a detailed and naturalistic report of the fox's approach towards the hen-coop and show no obvious signs of anthropomorphism. The dialogue between the cock and the fox (ll. 33-64) and the naming of the rooster ("Sire Chauntecler" l. 37) can therefore be seen as the elements which mark the explicit beginning of the beast epic dimension in *The Vox and the Wolf.* This is in spite of the fox's anonymity, which links it to the beast fable, and also in spite of the fact that it is written in verse form and the very first part is already most likely to have been modelled upon lines 35-120 of Branch IV of the *Roman de Renart*, which connects it with the beast epic tradition.

The conversation between the two animals offers the opportunity to characterize the fox further and to make us realize that he is – especially since he has now dined – more than the hunger-driven animal of the opening part of the poem. In the French poem, we do not have the conversation between the fox and the cock, nor are any of the bird protagonists named – in contrast to our 'Chauntecler'. In the *Roman de Renart*, the mention of the name suffices to introduce the main protagonist: Renart is well known from previous adventures. In *The Vox and the Wolf*, however, the fox protagonist is usefully characterized by means of the contrasting figure of the cock.[472] Thus, our still anonymous fox develops into a wily and sly character, who tries to deceive his potential victim by pulling the wool over his eyes. Yet, the cock is – in contrast to his namesake in *The Nun's Priest's Tale* – alert, sees through the fox's web of lies, and cannot be lured down from the safety of his perch.

'The Fox and the Wolf in the Well' Story (ll. 65-260):

The two sections which precede this part of the poem are more than mere narrative embellishments, even though it is here, in the third part, that the

---

[471] See also Bennett and Smithers (1968:299).

[472] This concurs with Dithmar's (1971:113) observation that the protagonist of the fable is characterized – among other things – by means of a contrasting figure.

main action takes place.[473] On a superficial level, the raid on the chicken-coop provides the motivation for the fox's second urgent need. He has eaten too much (three hens, to be exact) and now wants to quench his thirst. The thematic parallel with the first two sections is obvious. Both then and now, the fox is driven by his desire to satisfy a basic physical urge which blots out all other considerations, dims his otherwise sharp wit, and makes him jump into the bucket. The parallel event in Branch IV of the *Roman de Renart* (ll. 157-174) gives a different account of the fox's motivation for entering the well: Renart wants to drink, but when he looks into the well, he is misled by his reflection in the water[474] and the echo of his voice, so that he believes his beloved lady to be down there. His immediate motivation for getting into the well is thus love (or lust), and not thirst. The 'short version' of Branch IV (MS H), however, likewise does without the 'mirror & lust motif' and similarly mentions neither Renart's wife nor Ysengrins' wife Hersent.[475] Furthermore, it also establishes a connection between the chicken-coop raid and the well-adventure. There, Renart shows Ysengrins the third hen (taken along for later consumption) in order to lure him down.[476] The 'short version' is, in this respect, a more self-contained poem than even *The Vox and the Wolf*, which is, by means of the wolf's 'confession', linked to events outside the scope of this tale and thus, at least to some degree, embedded in the 'beast epic' frame. Concerning the fox, we can say that the poet of *The Vox and the Wolf* remains true to the central motif of the need-driven animal and does without unnecessary additional motivation. He is, therefore, closer to the 'short version' than to the 'long version' of Branch IV of the *Roman de Renart*. The Middle English poet makes it very clear that the 'hero' of his poem is not a clever fox who is hungry or thirsty – or amorous, as Renart of the 'long version' is – but that he is, first and foremost, a hungry or thirsty fox who eventually sets his brains to work in order to extract himself from a difficult situation.[477] It is, therefore, in keeping with the general character of the fox that he is not able to figure out the mechanism of the two buckets over the pulley, while he suffers thirst and

473 It is this section which has its (partial) parallels in the 'exemplum XXIII' by PETRUS ALFONSUS and the 'exemplum' fable by ODO OF CHERITON.

474 The motif of the reflection in the water is also found in PETRUS ALFONSUS' 'exemplum', though there it is the moon that is reflected.

475 See reprint of the 'short version' in Varty (1991:332-33, lines 9ff.).

476 See Varty (1991:336, lines 166ff.).

477 Kreisler (1970:655-656) comments on this: "He [the author] has combined Reneuard's two most prominent characteristics, insatiable hunger (or thirst) and slick intellect, to give a significant new twist to the tale: he has subordinated the Fox's wiles to his greed[.]" See also LeSaux (1990:70).

thus gets himself trapped at the bottom of the well.[478] Having been able to quench his thirst beyond expectation in the well, the fox finds himself in a situation similar to that in the hen-coop. Indeed, the pattern of the action roughly parallels that of the chicken-coop raid: the following table gives a schematic overview.

The Chicken-Coop Raid	**The Fox in the Well**
The fox satisfies his hunger.	The fox quenches his thirst.
The fox wants to eat the cock.	The fox wants to escape from the well.
The fox wants the cock to fly down from the perch.	The fox wants the wolf to jump into the other bucket and come down to the bottom of the well.
The fox pretends to be a physician.	The fox pretends to be in paradise.
The fox offers to treat the cock.	The fox lets himself be persuaded to shrive the wolf.
The *cock rejects* the offer.	The *wolf accepts* the offer.
The *fox fails* to delude the cock.	The *fox succeeds* in deluding the wolf.

The parallelism between the two events becomes especially clear when we consider how the *Roman de Renart* reports them.[479] There, Renart also kills three chickens, but no cock is mentioned at all. Also, Renart seems to be more than satisfied with the success of his raid – he even takes along some of the leftovers (the third hen) for later consumption – and thus has no reason to plot further mischief. Furthermore, we have the additional motif of both the wolf and the fox being deceived by their reflections in the water.[480] Finally, the wolf does not confess his sins to Renart.

The fox in *The Vox and the Wolf* is obviously still lusting for more food, even after devouring three hens, and the poet sustains the central motif of need by means of the variant 'greed'; this leads us to the well adventure. After having satisfied his basic need, the fox finds himself, in both cases, in

---

478 In PETRUS ALFONSUS' 'exemplum', however, the fox sees through the mechanism of the pulley and, before he descends into the well, already knows very well how then to trick the wolf. ODO's account of the same event limits itself to a simple statement of facts, namely "Vulpes casu cecidit per unam situlam in puteum" (Grubmüller 1977:105), and thus does not characterize his 'exemplum' fable fox any further.

479 I concentrate on the *Roman de Renart*, since neither the 'exemplum' by PETRUS ALFONSUS nor that by ODO OF CHERITON contains a 'chicken-coop raid' episode.

480 However, as mentioned before, the 'short version' does without this additional motif.

an 'inferior' position, spatially as well as hierarchically. He is 'down there', and, to a certain extent, dependent on the goodwill, or rather credulity, of the person opposite him. In both the first and the second instance, the fox tries to invert the actual positions of the protagonists. At this point, the anthropomorphical elements and, thus, the beast-epic quality start to take over. In order to gull the person opposite him, the fox adopts the strategy of pretending to be something or someone else.[481] He also starts to reinterpret the facts according to his will.[482] As a fox, of course, he is the born enemy of the cock; but as a fox physician, he would find himself in a position of power towards the cock patient.[483] The potential victim, however, rejects his attempt to redefine their roles and remains in his spatially as well as hierarchically superior position; and by mentioning real human beings (see ll. 59-64), he sabotages the fox's attempt to arrogate a human identity as a physician. It was a fox driven by need that entered the barn, and it is still a need-driven fox that takes its leave: its transformation into an anthropomorphic fox was very short-lived.

With the wolf, however, the same strategy is more successful. He not only believes the fox's tale of paradise, but also accepts the slyly and indirectly proposed distribution of roles, with the fox as the priest/confessor and the wolf as the sinner:[484] the wolf's use of "Maister" (l. 206) for addressing the fox priest shows this clearly. Yet, even though he is manipulated into humbling himself before the fox, the primary dimension of the real situation (the fox trapped in the well, the wolf in the position of power) is not completely faded out. At the beginning of his retelling of the adultery scene, the wolf changes the form of address: the fox is no longer the 'maister', but his 'gossip' (l. 209 and l. 220). This new form of address, together with the story of the fox's adulterous behaviour, not only relegates Reneuard to a humbler position than before, but it also contains a hidden, yet discernible element of threat, which makes the fox priest forego any further probing

---

[481] This strategy can be observed in many of the adventures related in the *Roman de Renart* and its successors, *Renart le Bestourné* (1261), *Le Couronnement de Renart* (1263-70), and *Renart le Nouvel* (1289).

[482] LeSaux (1990:72-73) sees this inversion of language and facts as part of the more general theme of transgression.

[483] Even though the fox as a physician is a popular theme (see Varty 1967:68-75), there exist no exact parallels with this episode in *The Vox and the Wolf*.

[484] In *Renart le Contrefait* (first half of the fourteenth century) we have a parallel event when Renart asks Chantecler to confess his sins. The fox also shrives and absolves geese in the fifteenth century poem *The Fals Fox* (Luria and Hoffman 1974:126-127). For a general discussion of the tradition of the 'fox religious', see Varty (1967:51-59).

into the wolf's catalogue of misdeeds.[485] We are now, as the attentive reader may already have noticed, well into the beast epic dimension: the previously anonymous, instinct-driven fox has become the sly and roguish "Reneuard" (l. 133), and the hungry wolf is now "Sigrim" (l. 128), the duped and cuckolded husband. Thus, the author's decision to have the tale start with 'a vox' and later change temporarily to 'Reneuard' is worth a closer look.

The Different Levels of Interpretation

All the animal protagonists are first introduced by means of their generic terms: "A Vox" (l. 1) opens the tale and is then followed by "on kok" (l. 30) and "a wolf" (l. 108). Throughout the entire length of the tale, the narrator uses only these generic terms: he himself never uses a proper name. It is the animals themselves that start to call each other, or themselves, by their individual names. Thus, the fox twice uses the cock's personal name in the space of their short conversation ("Sire Chauntecler" l. 37 and "Chauntecler" l. 46), yet he himself remains anonymous until he reveals his identity to the wolf: "Ich am Reneuard, þi frend" (l. 133). Up to this point, the function of the fox remains ambiguous, and the narrative theoretically remains open to allegorical and moral interpretation, not least since PETRUS ALFONSUS' well-known 'exemplum' gives a moral, too.[486] Indeed, the longer the fox's anonymity lasts, the greater becomes the temptation to search for an allegorical or moral subtext hidden beneath the folds of satire – even though the verse-form and the fact that it relates a 'story' and not only characteristic behaviour speak against this. The allegorical and moral residues linger on even after the beast epic dimension has been fully established by the revelation of the beast epic identity of each protagonist (fox ~ Reneuard; wolf ~ Sigrim; cock ~ Chauntecler). Thus, we can postulate a three-fold structure for the interpretation of the central episode of the fox and wolf in the well. First, there is the obvious beast epic dimension – the scurrilous, individually-named hero tricks his stronger, yet less clever opponent. Secondly, we have the moralistic beast fable dimension, with the implied moral: 'Beware of greed!' Thirdly and finally, there are – more than once removed – the *Physiologus* and the bestiary

[485] On this point, see also Bergner (1973:274).

[486] The protagonists of the beast epics have had names at least since the writing of the *Ysengrimus* (1148; see Mossé 1951:71), in contrast to the usually anonymous fable animals (see Blake 1970:xvi, Mossé 1951:71, and Sisam 1927:xv). Thus, to begin with an anonymous fox makes a categorization as 'beast fable' at least theoretically possible. Blake (1975:55) writes: "*The Fox and Wolf* may best be explained as a fable illustrating deceit and how one should guard against it[.]"

traditions, which see the fox as a 'figura diaboli'. Let us now interpret the tale according to each of these three possibilities.

1) The beast epic dimension

Regarding *The Vox and the Wolf* as a beast epic, we could say that it is nothing more than a variant of the well-known episode from Branch IV of the *Roman de Renart*. The added conversation between the fox and the cock, as well as the introductory lines, help to preserve some of the 'epic' quality of the original.

2) The moral beast fable dimension

Even though there is no explicit 'moralitas' to be found – which is due to the fact that, by the time such a moral could be drawn, the beast epic elements have taken over – we can still easily recognize the fable elements of the tale. Moreover, we may recall that the central episode has its parallel, or even its partial source, in the Aesopic fable of *The Fox and the Goat*. The fable element may be obscured by the humour and bawdiness of the beast epic, but its moral potential is still intact. Thus, the audience is free to extract a fitting moral – be it 'Do not trust flatterers!' or 'Do not let greed be your guide!'[487]

3) The allegorical *Physiologus*/bestiary dimension

Being one of the animals that are allegorically interpreted in *The Physiologus* and its successors, the bestiaries, the fox is commonly used as a 'figura diaboli', representing the arch-tempter and arch-seducer. This is the most widespread use of the fox in ecclesiastical writings[488], and, as we saw earlier, ODO OF CHERITON uses exactly this tradition for the allegorical interpretation of his 'exemplum' fable.[489] The cock, then, can be seen as representing the watchful cleric who does not succumb to the wiles of the

---

487 In *The Nun's Priest's Tale*, CHAUCER makes fun of the possibility of extracting a moral from an entertaining tale.

488 For a more detailed discussion of the allegorical value of the fox, see Rowland (1974:76-80) or page 221ff. of this study.

489 As mentioned before, HENRYSON (second half of the fifteenth century) provides another excellent, though later example of the allegorical interpretation of the same story (i.e. PETRUS ALFONSUS' 'exemplum XXIII') in his fable *The Taill of the Foxe, that begylit the Wolf, in the schadow of the Mone* (MacDiarmid 1973:55-63).

devil.[490] The wolf, finally, stands for the man dominated by unrestrained greed.[491]

An allegorical reading of the chicken-coop episode would roughly look like this: the devil (fox), hungering for the souls of men, manages to seduce and thus spiritually kill several men (the hens). His attempt to beguile the morally alert cleric (cock), however, fails owing to his watchfulness. The allegorical interpretation of the central second episode, however, is not so straightforward.[492] True, the two protagonists, fox and wolf, fit into the allegorical pattern – the greedy man gets seduced by the devil. Yet, apart from this basic constellation, there are too many elements which are left unaccounted for: why does the fox/devil fall into the well in the first place? What is the symbolism of the two buckets? How does the wolf's confession fit in? Even though medieval allegorists had no scruples and selected those parts of a tale which suited their purpose, we have no right to do so with this tale.[493] There is no sly and probably slightly malicious narrator who tells us (Pearsall 1984:255, l. 4630): "Taketh the moralitee, goode men."

Furthermore, it must be remembered that the *Physiologus*/bestiary tradition deals in the characteristic behaviour of its subjects and not primarily in story. Thus, the *Physiologus* fox is more than once removed from our protagonist, and there is no clear link between the characterising *Physiologus* tradition and the 'story' of *The Vox and the Wolf.* Our reluctance to reject an allegorical interpretation right from the beginning, and thus at least to consider the possibility of an allegorical dimension, is mainly due to the fact that allegorical interpretation did not remain limited to the *Physiologus* and bestiary traditions. ODO OF CHERITON's 'exemplum' fable is an excellent 'contemporary' example of the ability of the allegorical 'mode' to cross (genre) borders. Weighing the evidence in our case,

---

490 Evidence of the medieval interpretation of the cock as a cleric/preacher is given by J.B. Allen (1969:28), Bishop (1979:258), Dahlberg (1954:282), Donovan (1953:501-503), Friedmann (1980:203), Myers (1972:218), Rowland (1981:345), Steadman (1959:243 and 244, fn. 39), and Yates (1983:116).

491 ODO OF CHERITON's fable, *The Wolf Who Longed to Be a Monk* (Jacobs 1985:92-93) excellently illustrates this aspect. The allegorical dimensions of the wolf in general are discussed by Rowland (1974:161-167).

492 Bergner (1973:276) doubts the appropriateness of a medieval allegorical interpretation. Bercovitch (1966), however, finds sufficient clues to interpret the poem as a satirical allegory on the clergy.

493 ODO OF CHERITON's fable 'exemplum' (see Grubmüller 1977:105 or Jacobs 1985:89) omits all the details which do not contribute to the allegorical interpretation. HENRYSON, in his fable *The Taill of the Foxe, that begylit the Wolf, in the schadow of the Mone* (MacDiarmid 1973:55-63), preserves all the ornamental details and allegorically interprets quite a few of them.

however, I feel that it would be rather unwise to force an overall allegorical interpretation, especially since it raises more questions in our case than it can answer.[494]

The Discovery of the Wolf (ll. 261-295)

After the fox has regained his freedom, the narrator focuses on the world of man, which, while the monks were fast asleep, provided the playground for the animal protagonists. The beginning of the fourth and final part of the narrative is marked by yet another parallel with the fox's initial search for food and drink. The thirsty monk, Ailmer, leaves the church (~ the forest sheltering the fox and the wolf) during the "houssonge" (l. 274) – which continues the theme of transgression on the human level – and approaches the well in order to quench his thirst. Upon seeing the wolf inside the well, he exclaims: "þe deuel is in þe putte!" (l. 282). Besides being a natural yet, for the audience, comical reaction to something as unexpected as finding oneself face-to-face with a wolf when pulling up a bucket, this can be seen as either questioning an allegorical reading – the one who has been and normally is presented as 'þe deuel' in the allegorical dimension is the fox, and not his victim, the wolf – or the poet is poking fun at the allegorical ignorance of Ailmer, who mixes up the allegorical dimensions.[495] The ensuing beating of the wolf, besides having a close parallel in Branch IV of the *Roman de Renart*[496], is a common enough beast epic conclusion, and therefore fits the main episode.

From Beast Tale[497] and Beast Fable to Beast Epic

The development of the tale goes from (potential) beast tale and beast fable to beast epic. The first section of the tale (ll. 1-26) consists almost exclusively of a longish, naturalistic account of the anonymous fox's approach. The relative length, as well as the inclusion of subsidiary action later on, stand in contradiction to the required shortness and tight structure

---

494 In their interpretation of *The Nun's Priest's Tale*, Levy and Adams (1967) unintentionally provide an excellent example of the dangers of allegorical over-interpretation.

495 The wolf, however, could also be equated with the devil. See T.H. White (1959:56-61).

496 However, in the 'short version', the wolf escapes unscathed.

497 The term 'beast tale' (German 'Tiervolkserzählung') is used to denote an often non-literary and otherwise undefined type of tale which is about animals or whose protagonists are animals. A detailed discussion of the genre problem can be found in Harkort (1970) and also in Grubmüller (1977:16).

of a fable[498], and point towards the beast epic. Yet, since the poet does not introduce the anonymous fox as 'Reneuard' in this section, the tale cannot be unambiguously identified as a beast epic – which leaves the beast tale as the obvious choice. The second part (ll. 27-64) sees the increase of the beast epic character (the anthropomorphic behaviour of the animals; the cock with an individual name), which finally takes over in the third part (ll. 65-260; both animal protagonists possess a proper name; another beast epic episode is mentioned; there is more explicit anthropomorphism) and likewise dominates the fourth and final part (ll. 261-295).

Taking into account our analysis of the tale, we may classify *The Vox and the Wolf* as a beast epic 'en miniature', interspersed with beast fable elements and some vague hints at the allegorical level.[499] Yet, even though I have been able to demonstrate that all three levels are found in *The Vox and the Wolf*, it would be wrong to assume that they are of equal importance. The great bulk of the tale is made up of, and dominated by, elements belonging to the beast epic level. The beast fable elements and the allegorical qualities are only perceptible because the author chooses to begin his narrative on a level different from the beast epic.

From 'a Vox' to 'Reneuard'

We may well ask why the poet does not begin his poem as a beast epic. The answer must be sought in the fact that the *Roman de Renart* in its entirety was, to an English vernacular audience at least, probably not very well known at the time of the composition of *The Vox and the Wolf*.[500] It seems that this poem is the first Middle English literary evidence of the fact that 'Renart' had crossed the 'linguistic channel' which separated the Anglo-

498 See Dithmar (1971:104-106). ODO's 'exemplum' fable, in contrast to *The Vox and the Wolf*, lives up to these demands.

499 I thus disagree with Blackham (1985:58), who calls *The Vox and the Wolf* a fable. Bergner (1973:278), like McKnight (1908:499) before him, detects links with the fabliau, yet finds it impossible to fit the poem properly into any of the existing genres.

500 Blake (1975:57) thinks it "reasonable to assume that our poet both used as his source and modelled his poem upon fables then current in England. [....] [Furthermore, it is likely] that the *Roman* itself was not known in England and was not used as a direct source by poets writing in English." Iconographical evidence of the widespread popularity of animal poems and tales is discussed in Blake (1975:62) and Varty (1967). Only recently, however, Varty has conclusively proven that the French *Roman de Renart* was available in manuscript form (and therefore known) in England in 1359 (paper given at the 11th International Colloquy of the Reynard Society, Düsseldorf 17th – 20th July 1995; see also footnote 455).

Norman nobility from their English subjects.[501] The likely unfamiliarity of an English-speaking audience with the crafty beast epic hero would also provide the explanation for the narrator's consistent use of generic names for the animals; he has to take into consideration the fact that his listeners most probably do not make any associations with the beast epic names famous elsewhere. Thus, he first uses the cock and the wolf to characterize the main protagonist, and didactically skilfully introduces the names by having the animals call each other and themselves by their proper names.[502] The initial openness of the tale and the ambiguity of the function of the fox might, therefore, be due to the poet's endeavour to link his poem with the already familiar traditions of the beast tale, the beast fable, and the *Physiologus* and the bestiary. This enables the various possible dimensions to come into being and to coexist, even after the beast epic elements have started to dominate. The development of the main animal protagonist, the fox, is closely connected with the gradual shift from beast tale to beast epic. In the audience's perception, the fox of the first section is not the same as the 'Reneuard' of the central episode: our fox first has to establish his individual character – in contrast to the protagonist of the *Roman de Renart*. The anonymous fox who opens the action is only vaguely defined by means of the characteristics ascribed to his species by popular belief and by allegorical and moral interpretations, i.e. cleverness and cunning.[503] The metamorphosis from anonymous animal to named individual is gradual and does not quite reach Renart's level of individuality. The French 'Renart' and its German and Dutch counterparts, 'Reinhart' and 'Reinaerde', are part of a broader tradition, and the mentioning of their names immediately triggers a host of associations and memories, thus making, for a continental audience, any further characterization redundant.[504] The English poet, however, cannot or does not want to make use of this possibility: his fox's role is not fixed from the very beginning, but undergoes a development which leads to his new identity as the 'beast epic fox':

---

[501] It is of interest to note that the 'second coming' of the fox, this time as 'Reneuard', coincides temporally with the beginning of the greatest influx of Anglo-Norman/French words into the vocabulary of Middle English.

[502] ODO OF CHERITON, when using personal names, also deems it necessary to introduce most of the animals of his fables as, for example, "Chantecler, scilicet Gallus" (Plessow 1906:xxxii; see Jacobs 1985:96: "Chanticleer, the cock", my emphasis). On the problem of the beast epic names, see also Bergner (1973:281).

[503] See Borst (1991:209-210), E.P. Evans (1906:56-57), and Rowland (1974:76-80).

[504] See, for example, the introductory lines of Branch IV (ll. 21-22): "C'est de Renart, bien le savez,/Et bien oï dire l'avez."

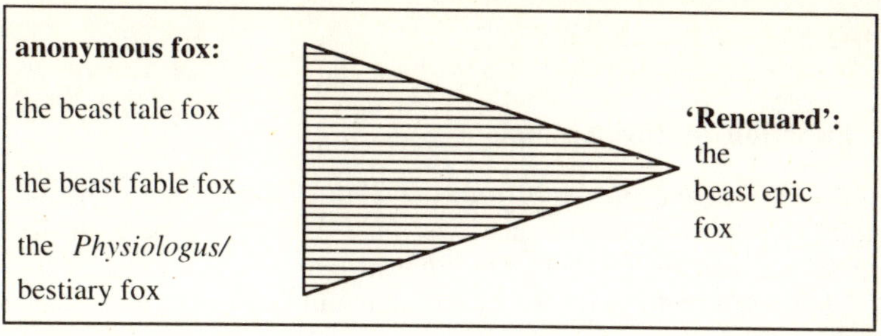

Thus, the belief that the fox is a cunning and wily animal provides the basis for the characterization of the literary offspring of the natural 'vulpes'.[505] Its cunning and slyness are stressed in most beast tales and find their way into common folk traditions. The development of the fox into the archetype of the deceitful or, at least, cunning and clever character becomes fully visible in the literary genre of the beast fable, and later on in the beast epics. The allegorical interpretation of the fox's character reinforces its negative tendencies in the secular estimation, and even leads, via the allegorically interpreted 'exempla' and fables, to the identification of the fable fox with the *Physiologus*/bestiary fox (see ODO OF CHERITON's 'exemplum' fable). The fox of *The Vox and the Wolf* at least partially inherits the accumulated symbolic potential, and simultaneously participates in several literary traditions.

If we assume that the *Roman de Renart* was not (very well) known as such to a potential English audience, then the development described acquires additional importance. The poet introduces the animal protagonist by linking his story of the fox and the wolf with the (only vaguely documented) beast tale tradition, takes advantage of the popularity of the beast fables, and selects events and episodes which highlight those characteristics of the fox which were ascribed to him by the *Physiologus* and the bestiary traditions. Thus, the author of *The Vox and the Wolf*, assuming he takes Branch IV of the *Roman de Renart* as his source, changes the material and adds to it so that the tale will fit his purpose. He subordinates every action to the central motif of hunger and thirst, and fashions the encounters with other animals so that they contribute to the characterization of the fox. Thus, we can say that the beast epic fox, true to his nature, makes his way into vernacular English literature, together with his companions, hidden within the Trojan horse of material that is mainly taken from the traditions of the beast tale, the beast

505 E.P. Evans (1906:56-57) reports that the fox is generally seen as a malicious and wily beast. The possible zoological foundations of the fox's reputation as a clever animal and its influence on the beast epic fox are discussed by Stoob (1991:196-198).

fable, and, marginally, also from the traditions of *The Physiologus* and the bestiary.

The Function of the Animals

Seeing *The Vox and the Wolf* from our 20th-century point of view, we are liable to overlook its importance; we must thus try to see it in the line of succession which begins with *The Physiologus* and continues first with the bird debates, and later with the beast fable and beast epic traditions. All the animals encountered so far have had, more or less, just one function, namely to illustrate (at least partially) a spiritual, philosophical, or moral truth. The 'prodesse' stood in the foreground, though the 'delectare' did not completely get lost.[506] In *The Vox and the Wolf*, however, it is primarily the 'delectare' which is stressed.[507] Indeed, the narrator does not even pretend to tell a tale with a somewhat hidden allegorical truth, even though the tale chosen would easily lend itself to allegorical interpretation. We can say that, for the first time, the main function of the animal protagonists is to contribute to the entertainment of the audience by means of the comic contrast between their basic animal nature and their attempt to assume anthropomorphic roles. The two central comic scenes, namely the dialogues between the fox and the cock and between the fox and the wolf, clearly show this. The animals' basic anthropomorphic trait – their ability to speak – is tacitly accepted: it is not seen as standing in contrast to the animal nature of the fox, the cock, or the wolf. However, the comic dimension becomes obvious when the fox tries (not always successfully) to arrogate the roles of physician and priest. We may accept a talking fox, yet we cannot help but laugh at the incongruity of the fox's unchanged basic animal nature and his pretensions to being something different from what he is. A further function of the animals is to help the audience to maintain a certain distance, and to prevent unreflected identification. Even this general function is here made to serve the endeavour to delight. In this way, the human audience remains aloof and eyes the antics of the animals – which would look cruel with human protagonists – with amused detachment. In contrast to the Nun's Priest, our narrator does not seem to be at all worried about the aspect of 'prodesse'. There are elements of allegorical teaching and satire, yet these remain vague and can be seen as adding to the overall delight of the reader or listener. The

---

[506] Thus, *The Owl and the Nightingale*, *The Cuckoo and the Nightingale*, and *The Parlement of Foulys* contain a considerable portion of 'delectare' elements.

[507] See McKnight (1908:509): "[I]n Middle English it [the story of *The Vox and the Wolf*] is told merely as an entertaining tale, and in general it may be said that its associations more than in the case of most other beast stories are with tales designed solely to amuse."

basic orientation is not backwards to the *Physiologus* and the bestiary traditions, but forwards, pointing to a more secular and lighthearted notion of literature.

3. *The Nun's Priest's Tale*[508]

Introduction

Derek Pearsall (1980:165) once characterized the fate of CHAUCER in general as being too much held "up to the mirror of our own civilization and culture rather than [being recognized as] a window through which we can look into the civilization and culture of another age." This is true of *The Nun's Priest's Tale* in particular, which is one of the most popular tales with critics. Hardly any other of CHAUCER's *Canterbury Tales* has been given so much critical attention as this tale of "the Cok and Hen" (Pearsall 1983:139). Yet, even though there is general agreement concerning the high quality of the tale – some critics consider it to be one of the best, if not the best, of CHAUCER's works - we have, up to the present day, no commonly accepted interpretation of the tale proper.[509] The reason for this unusually pronounced critical disagreement regarding the 'sententia' of the tale may be traced back to the discussion of the sources of *The Nun's Priest's Tale*.

Sources[510]

The tracing of the sources of any medieval poem has its justification in the fact that the medieval poets themselves stressed their being part of an older and, in their eyes, therefore nobler literary tradition. To take up time-honoured topics and themes, to retell ancient tales in polished and skilful language was of greater importance than to be original.[511] Indeed,

---

508 All references are to the Variorum Edition by Pearsall (1983).

509 Concerning the appreciation of the tale, see, for example, Ruggiers (1965:222), who thinks that it "constitutes a complex of most that is happy in CHAUCER's artistic and intellectual equipment [...]. It is, in short, 'sui generis'."

510 Despite some new insights, the almost one-hundred-year-old study by Petersen (1898) is still the most comprehensive and detailed work on the sources of *The Nun's Priest's Tale*. For a more recent overview of the research, see Pearsall (1983:14-29).

511 On 'originality' in the Middle Ages, see, for example, Kelley (1979:70): "In an age when poetic composition is predominately viewed as the art of re-telling, re-arranging, re-disposing one's sources, rather than the creation of entirely new material to be arranged,

originality without at least some sanctioning from tradition was unwelcome. Yet, even the retelling of a familiar plot offered – to the gifted author, at least – various possibilities of enhancing his or her version. This holds especially true for CHAUCER: his tale of the Nun's Priest is only superficially the old story of the cock who nearly lost his life in the fangs of the fox, and even the heading "Here bigynneth the Nonnes preestes tale/of the Cok and Hen, Chauntecler and Pertelote" (Pearsall 1983:139), which can be found in some of the manuscripts, points the way to some of the more fundamental changes.

The basic pattern of the story-line derives from one of the many versions of the well-known fable of *The Cock and the Fox*.[512] The specific relationship between the extant versions of this and other fables, the *Roman de Renart* and its descendants, and CHAUCER's *The Nun's Priest's Tale*, is the subject of several studies.[513] Not only the basic structure of *The Nun's Priest's Tale*, but also many of the ornamental and digressive elements are borrowed. A host of literary critics, in alliance with philologists and scholars from different areas, have tried more or less successfully to establish the provenance of nearly every line the Nun's Priest utters.[514] Thanks to their

---

design and structure are more likely to emerge as focal areas of a poet's virtuosity and creativity."

512 On the different pre-Chaucerian versions and variants of this fable, see Schaller (1970:96-98).

513 The following authors deal (at least partially) with this question: Blake (1975:57-59 and 65) comments on the function of the fables as sources; Bloomfield (1979:75) sees the *Roman de Renart* as a source; Coote (1985:21-26) gives an overview of the various possible sources; Dargan (1906) writes on the origins of the 'Cock and Fox' fable; Flinn (1963:679-688) analyses the differences between CHAUCER's poem and Branch II of the *Roman de Renart*; Lecompte (1917) considers Branch II of the *Roman de Renart* to be the original source; Mossé (1951:84) sees CHAUCER as the heir to an English 'Renart' tradition; Muscatine (1957:238) believes that CHAUCER's source is the *Roman de Renart*; Petersen (1898:87-89) assumes a common source for Branch II of the *Roman de Renart* and *The Nun's Priest's Tale*. This common source, however, is derived from an intermediary link, which is the source of the Middle High German *Reinhart Fuchs*, and Petersen attempts to reconstruct the story-line of the ultimate original; Pratt (1972:443) believes that CHAUCER closely follows MARIE DE FRANCE's *Del cok e del gupil*; Severs (1946) discusses the 'originality' of the tale; Shallers (1975:325) assumes the existence of a popular, didactic, and moralistic source; Sisam (1927:vii-xxiii) discusses fable and beast epic influences; Varty (1967:33 and 37) treats the development of the *Chauntecler and the Fox* fable in England; and Yates (1983) discusses the Latin parallels and roots of our tale. The pictorial evidence related to *The Nun's Priest's Tale* and its possible sources is treated by Tatlock (1914), by Varty (1964 and 1975), and, most extensively, by Varty (1967).

studies, we know today that CHAUCER incorporated allusions to, or even wholesale sections from, authors like DANTE, BOCCACCIO, VINCENT DE BEAUVAIS, and a multitude of other poets and scholars. Some critics, however, in their efforts to give the possible source of nearly every single line or motif, show the rather unhealthy tendency to reduce *The Nun's Priest's Tale* to a kind of patchwork. In particular, they often forget that the skilfully-composed whole is more than the sum of its parts, and that CHAUCER did more than just stitch together random bits and pieces. Apart from the fact that these results once more confirm the truth, already sufficiently well-established, that CHAUCER was a very well-read poet, they contribute little to our discussion of the role of the animals in *The Nun's Priest's Tale*.[515] We will therefore consider the analysis of the sources – if the need arises – within the discussion of the tale itself.

Manuscripts

Pearsall (1983:82-104) discusses the textual tradition in detail and, furthermore, provides an extensive description of the most important

---

[514] The more general studies which analyse the relationship between *The Nun's Priest's Tale* and beast epic and fable literature are mentioned above. I will here list only the more specialized ones. The provenance of the 'exempla' in the discussion of dreams is dealt with by Coote (1985:65), Petersen (1898:98-103 and 117), Pratt (1977), and Sakanishi (1932). CHAUCER's sources for Pertelote's medical diagnosis are treated in Aiken (1935), Curry (1960:221-228), Hoy (1969:146), Paffard (1957), and Pratt (1977:546). The medieval dream lore which provides the background for Chauntecleer and Pertelote's discussion of dreams is the subject of Bishop (1979:265), Coote (1985:61), Curry (1960:xxi-xxii and 195-234), Hamm (1954), Hieatt (1967:40-42 and 1970:6), Lindahl (1987:42), and Pratt (1977). Parallels and sources of individual lines are given by the following critics: Cook (1924) writes that CHAUCER's comparison of Chauntecleer to an organum may come from the Easter poem by VENANTIUS FORTUNATUS; R.W. Elliott (1965:31) states that the way of describing someone from head to foot is most likely from GEOFFREY OF VINSAUF's *Nova poetria*; J.B. Friedman (1972:258) also comments on the 'effictio', the description of a person from top to bottom; Henning (1965) writes on the connection between the astronomical constellation of 'Taurus' and Chauntecleer's fate; P. Meredith (1970) comments on the "Mermayde in the see" (l. 4460); Pratt (1949) sees GEOFFREY OF VINSAUF's *Nova poetria* as the main source for the lamentations of the hens; Rowland (1965) provides information on the 'owles and apes' of l. 4282; and Shaver (1943) also writes on 'owles and apes'.

[515] Bryan and Dempster (1941), Miller (1977), and Windeatt (1982) provide most of the relevant texts which CHAUCER knew, or which are otherwise of importance for the understanding of his work.

manuscripts which contain *The Nun's Priest's Tale* in its full length.[516] All references are to the Variorum Edition (Pearsall 1983), which is based on the Hengwrt manuscript.

Date of Composition[517]

Even though the tale does not contain any reference which enables us to determine its date of composition accurately, we can at least establish a 'terminus a quo', since CHAUCER mentions "Jakke Straw and his meynee" in line 4584, and this obviously refers to the Peasants' Revolt of 1381. Therefore, we have a theoretical 20-year range for the date of composition (from 1381 to 1400, when CHAUCER died). Hinckley (Pearsall 1983:29) favours 1381 as the year of writing, based on astrological references in the tale. At the other end of the scale, we find Hotson (1924), who has to assume a date after 1398, in order to keep up the historical parallelism (see page 203), and C.A. Owen (Pearsall 1983:29), who places the date (of the last revision) as late as 1398 or 1399.

The Critics

Hardly any other poem of CHAUCER's *Canterbury Tales* has attracted so much attention over the centuries; Pearsall (1983:30-81), as editor of the Variorum Edition of *The Nun's Priest's Tale*, takes on the heroic task of surveying and summarizing the 'state of the art' in the introduction to his edition. Thus, I can limit myself to briefly sketching the main critical approaches, and otherwise refer the reader to Pearsall's excellent and comprehensive survey.[518]

Among the interpretative studies, we can, roughly speaking, distinguish between contextual and non-contextual approaches to the tale.

---

[516] The tale appears complete in a total of fifty manuscripts (see Pearsall 1983:91). The most important ones are: Hengwrt, Ellesmere, Additional 35286, Corpus 198, Cambridge Dd.4.24, Cambridge Gg.4.27, Harley 7334, Helmingham, Landsdowne 851, and Petworth.

[517] See Pearsall (1983:29-30).

[518] Articles and books on *The Nun's Priest's Tale* which were published after 1983 or which somehow escaped Pearsall's searching eye will be referred to only if they make a valuable contribution to the argument. The articles and books listed under each heading represent a selection; for a more comprehensive list, see Pearsall (1983).

Contextual Approaches

The problem of the 'dramatic reading', i.e. the appropriateness or inappropriateness of the tale to the teller, is central to most of the works which belong to this category.[519] The articles and books which analyse the connection between *The Nun's Priest's Tale* and the other tales and tellers of *The Canterbury Tales*, especially the preceding *The Monk's Tale*, the so-called 'Marriage Group', and the other tales of Fragment B^2, must be included here, too.[520]

Non-contextual Approaches

The scholars who contribute to this second, and larger, category focus rather on the tale itself than on the narrator, though they also, of course, sometimes touch upon questions connected with the contextual category. The great variety of critical contributions within this group makes a subdivision necessary.

---

519 The following works deal wholly or partially with the question of the 'dramatic reading': Boyd (1978:69), Broes (1963), Coote (1985:19-20, 32, and 89-90), R.W. Elliott (1965:3), J.B. Friedman (1972), Gallick (1977:237), Hemingway (1916), Howard (1976:282-283), Lumiansky (1953b and 1955:105-116), Myers (1972), C.A. Owen (1953:308-309), Pearcy (1968), Petersen (1898:118), Pichaske (1969), Ruggiers (1965), Sherbo (1949), and Watkins (1969). Pearsall (1980:172), Sisam (1927:xlii), and Standop (1980:420) acknowledge a basic correspondence between the teller and the tale, yet remain critical towards a dramatic interpretation. Lawton (1985:1-13) discusses the development of the narrator in general at the time of CHAUCER. On the narrator and fictitious orality in Middle English literature, see also Kohl (1988).

520 The relationship with the Monk and/or *The Monk's Tale* is explored by Coote (1985:10), Donovan (1953:508), R.W. Elliott (1965:8-9 and 23), Hatton (1967), Hemingway (1916), Kaylor (1989), Ruggiers (1965:223-225), Watson (1964), and Wentersdorf (1982:40-42). The connection with the 'Marriage Group' is discussed by Hemingway (1916:482), Kenyon (1916), and Ruggiers (1965:222), and that with the other tales of Fragment B^2 by Howard (1976:283 and 288). Pearsall (1983:85-93) gives a comprehensive discussion of the textual problems concerning *The Nun's Priest's Prologue* and *Epilogue*, and the position of *The Nun's Priest's Tale* within the framework of *The Canterbury Tales*.

1) Moral Interpretations

a) General Moral Interpretations[521]

The implicit or explicit aim of these studies is to 'take the moralitee' (see l. 4630), or at least attempt to define the tale's 'morality'.[522]

b) Allegorical Interpretations[523]

The main focus of these studies is on the unlocking of the text by means of the exegetical tool of allegorical interpretation.[524] Thus, the 'Fall of Chauntecleer' is seen as a parallel to the Fall of Adam. The fox is equated with the devil, Pertelote with Eve, and Chauntecleer with the 'old Adam', who gains redemption through the 'new Adam' of Christ (alluded to by the fact that the saved rooster sits on a tree).

c) Scepticism Concerning Moral and Allegorical Interpretations[525]

The results of the exegetes' endeavours are not unanimously appreciated; the subjection of *The Nun's Priest's Tale* to thorough allegorical interpretation also yielded some rather strange fruits, so that several critics, appealing to the biblical authority of "ex fructu arbor agnoscitur" (*Secundum Mattheum* 12,33), began to question the appropriateness of the exegetical and moral interpretative methods in the case of *The Nun's Priest's Tale*.[526] Bloomfield (1958:79), though not speaking of *The Nun's Priest's Tale* in particular, sums this up as follows:

---

521 See Pearsall (1983:50-57). The fact that Blackham (1985:60) considers *The Nun's Priest's Tale* to be a fable backs general moral interpretations.

522 Studies like those by R.W. Elliott (1965:27-28), Hieatt (1970), Johnson (1985), C.A. Owen (1953:306-311), Pratt (1972:660 and 667), and Ruggiers (1965) deal (partially) with this question.

523 See Pearsall (1983:57-62).

524 Representatives of this school of thought are Dahlberg (1954), Donovan (1953), J.B. Friedman (1972), Levy and Adams (1967), and, to some extent, also Coote (1985:11, 39-46, 59, 70, and 76-77), Gallacher (1976), Gardner (1977:313), Hatton (1967:35), Muscatine (1957:242), Myers (1972:218), C.A. Owen (1953:307), Varty (1967:102), and Wentersdorf (1982). Two 'freak studies' which interpret the tale astrologically are North (1969) and North (1988:456-468 and 541-542).
Nearly a century later, HENRYSON's *Morall Fabillis* (c. 1480, MacDiarmid 1973) often show an explicit point-for-point moral interpretation of the narrative (see Henderson 1981:170-171).

525 See Pearsall (1983:62-64).

526 The studies of J.B. Allen (1969), Boyd (1978:68), Donaldson (1960:19), Manning (1960), Muscatine (1957), A.F. Payne (1975:211), Pearsall (1980), and Standop (1980) deal (at least partially) with this point.

In view of the fact that the historical trend was moving away from the heavy symbolic interpretation of Scripture and that a secular tradition of entertainment and literature was very much alive in the Middle Ages, it seems to me that to believe that the medieval author would presume to write as God wrote through his chosen servants in Holy Scripture is the height of folly.

2) Historio-Political Interpretation[527]

The first full-scale interpretative study of the tale (Hotson 1924) extracts a 'sensus politicus', so to speak, and is of special interest insofar as it is, to quote Pearsall (1983:64), "an example of the misapplication of historical evidence to the interpretation of literature." Frese (1981), though on a lesser scale, provides historical parallels, but explicitly refrains from an overall historical interpretation. Standop (1980:411-412), like Dahlberg (1954:277) before him, refutes Hotson's (1924) identification of the 'col-fox' with historical persons.

3) Non-interpretative Evaluation[528]

There remain about half-a-dozen articles or books which Pearsall unites under this heading, and which mostly deal with such topics as the mock-heroic mood of the poem, rhetorics, the multiple perspective of the tale, its sermon characteristics, the relevant literary conventions, theological questions, the illumination of dark allusions, and style in general.[529]

---

527 See Pearsall (1983:64-65).

528 See Pearsall (1983:65-81).

529 The following authors discuss one or more of these aspects of *The Nun's Priest's Tale*: J.B. Allen (1969) writes that the tale is poking fun at 'moralists'; Bishop (1979) discusses the function of the liberal arts; Bloomfield (1979:75-78) comments on the mock-heroic tone, the epic devices, and the question of foreknowledge; Boyd (1978) writes on the theme of free will and predestination; Coote (1985:12) comments on rhetorics, (1985:13/83) on how the language relates to the ear/oral tradition, (1985:51) on the sermon style, and (1985:93) on the application of 'high' rhetorics to low subject matter; Dieckmann (1938) discusses the lines 4483-4484 ("[...] moore feelynge/Than hadde Boece [...]"); Donovan (1953:498) believes the tale to be a sermon; J.B. Friedman (1972) comments on the preaching background in the Middle Ages; Gallick (1975) deals with the preaching elements; Gallick (1977) sees *The Nun's Priest's Tale* as a parody of the theory of the three levels of style; Gardner (1977:314-315) comments on the 'marriage' of two styles; Guerin (1973) writes on the allusion to 'Launcelot de Lake' in line 4402; Hotson (1924:763) discusses the homiletic form of the fable; Hoy (1969:136) treats the sermon elements, (1969:140) the dual focus, (1969:156-159) the preaching and rhetorics, and (1969:161) the sermon form; Lenaghan (1963) looks at the rhetorical background; Manly (1926) also writes on the rhetorical background; Muscatine

The Tale

The Narrator

Nowadays, the importance of the character of the teller of the tale is undisputed (its degree of importance, however, is still open to question). Nevertheless, I shall start with the tale proper. This is justified, not only because the prologue offers little or no direct information on the 'sweete preest Sir John', but also because there is considerable disagreement among critics concerning the appearance and character of this 'preest'. Most of what we know about the Nun's Priest is either based on the epilogue, whose authenticity is still a matter of dispute, or it is inferred from the tale itself.[530] Thus, it seems wiser to me to start out with a rather nondescript clerical storyteller, who begins his tale of "the Cok and Hen, Chauntecler and Pertelote" (Pearsall 1983:139) after the wearisome and tedious tragedies related by the Monk.

Yet, before we proceed to the discussion of the animal characters, we have to pay close attention to the 'setting of the scene', which greatly influences our perception of the non-human protagonists.

The Introduction (ll. 4011-4036)

The Nun's Priest's tale begins inconspicuously enough: as Lindahl (1987:40) remarks, the opening description of the widow's farmhouse is a sight familiar to all travellers and typical of a folk tale, and the 'narwe cotage' and the widow's meagre diet acquire greater importance in hindsight than at the time they are related. Nothing so far suggests that the tale will be a version of the well-known story of *The Fox and the Cock*:[531] all the other extant versions introduce a rich farmer as the owner of the henyard which is

---

(1957:241) discusses the multiple point of view; Myers (1972) comments on the overlapping structure of three centres of attention; A.F. Payne (1975) discusses the theological question of foreknowledge and free will; Petersen (1898:95) comments on the sermon form; Shallers (1975:335) analyses the shifting focus; Steadman (1959:236) deals with the exaggerated discrepancy between 'high' style and 'low' subject matter; and Watson (1964:284) considers *The Nun's Priest's Tale* to be a good, vital sermon.

[530] The epilogue to *The Nun's Priest's Tale* is discussed by Brosnahan (1961), Gibbons (1954), Kenyon (1916), Lumiansky (1955:110-112), Pearcy (1968), Pearsall (1980:172), and Sherbo (1949).

[531] On the popularity of this tale, see Coote (1985:27). Varty (1964, 1966, 1967, and 1975) provides more general evidence of the widespread popularity of the fox in the Middle Ages.

to be the setting for most of the action of the tale.[532] Thus, unless one accepts the assumption that CHAUCER's tale goes back to an otherwise unknown and now lost version that already exhibited the changes, we have to account for the most significant peculiarities of *The Nun's Priest's Tale* and try to explain them by means of their function within the narrative proper or the framework of *The Canterbury Tales*.[533]

The description of the poor widow's cottage and her frugal meals is open to several interpretations. Some critics detect an attitude which is critical of society in general, while others note the critical contrast with the Prioress' way of eating her meals (Benson 1987:25, *GP* ll. 127-136) and her habit of feeding her pet dogs with such luxurious food as "rosted flessh, or milk and wastel-breed" (Benson 1987:25, *GP* l. 147).[534] A third group of critics see the widow's humble way of life as providing the moral standards for the 'fable section' of the tale, and still others stress the contrastive function of the introductory lines, which furnish the backdrop for the 'royal splendour' of the henyard.[535]

This wide variety of complementary or even contradictory interpretations is typical of the critical response to *The Nun's Priest's Tale*. One of the main reasons for this critical dissent is the tricky problem of the tone of the poem. A lot has been written in the attempt to throw some light on Chaucerian irony;[536] yet, even though we know that CHAUCER made use of both structural and verbal irony, we must still analyse each passage in question anew. To reach an overall verdict on the basis of individual cases of irony

532 This change was already noticed by Petersen (1898:67-68).

533 The differences between CHAUCER's probable source, namely Branch II of the *Roman de Renart*, and *The Nun's Priest's Tale* are discussed in detail by Severs (1946).

534 See J.B. Friedman (1972:257): "CHAUCER's portrait of her [the Prioress] at table provides another marked contrast with the widow." See also Broes (1963:159-160), who sees Pertelote as the galline alter ego of the Prioress, and the description of the widow's dire circumstances as the foil to the Prioress-hen.

535 Coote (1985:53) first contrasts the spry widow with the comically proud Chauntecleer, and later on (1985:81) the chaste widow with the abundantly fleshly cock. Hoy (1969:137-139, 151-152, and 165) comments on the contrast between the widow in her narrow cottage and Chauntecleer in his 'court'. Petersen (1898:68) draws the reader's attention to the function of the introductory description of the widow's life "as a foil to the high breeding and elegant manners and conversation of Chantecler and Pertelote." Watkins (1969:459) sees the poor widow as "the moral norm that allows the Priest's audience to take the moral measure of Chauntecleer."

536 See Bloomfield (1979:78) and especially Birney (1985) and Rowland (1985). Birney (1985:29) reaches the following conclusion: "The more jovial Burlesque draws laughter not from the form it affects but from the material which it pretends to consider worthy of that form. This is the spirit of the mock-heroic *Nun's Priest's Tale*."

and to read CHAUCER solely through the 'glasses of irony' implies an unjustifiable reduction of the complexity of his poems, and an undue limitation of our interpretatory freedom. With these 'caveats' in mind, we may approach the realm of 'royal Chauntecleer'.

Chauntecleer[537]

The change from the anonymous world of human beings (the widow and her two nameless daughters) to the individualized henyard universe of Chauntecleer and his paramours is gradual.[538] From the "dale" (l. 4013) and the "narwe cotage" (l. 4012), the narrator zooms in on the "yeerd [...], enclosed al aboute/With stikkes and a drye dych withoute" (ll. 4037-4038), slowly fades out the widow – she will make her comeback at the very end of the tale (l. 4565) – and focusses on Chauntecleer ("In which she hadde a cok heet Chauntecler", l. 4039). However, the rooster that enters our field of vision is not yet the almost completely anthropomorphized cock of the animal fable or the partially humanized one of the beast epic. Apart from his name, we have no real clues to his fable or beast epic character. The next nine lines accomplish the shift from the human world to the henyard universe, but not quite to the 'storyland' proper: by praising Chauntecleer's unique prowess in crowing ("In al the land of crowyng nas his peer", l. 4040), the Nun's Priest reverses the process of zooming in. Thus, the formerly small chicken world is established as the point of departure for future actions and placed in relation to the 'wide world' by means of the comparisons of Chauntecleer's voice with "the myrie orgon" (l. 4041), and of his timekeeping ability with that of "a clokke or any abbey orlogge" (l. 4044).[539] These galline qualities, however, are only remarkable insofar as they are present in Chauntecleer to such a degree of perfection: crowing and marking the passage of time 'per se' is, according to medieval lore, natural

---

537 The 'speaking' name of our hero is found in the parallel texts as well.

538 Frese (1981:331) mentions the juxtaposition of the anonymous humans (with the exception of "Malkyn" in l. 4574) to the named, and thus individualized, animals (the sheep 'Malle', the hen 'Pertelote', the rooster 'Chauntecleer', the fox 'daun Russelle', and the dogs 'Cogge', 'Talbot', and 'Gerland'). Rowland (1968) comments on the name of the sheep, 'Malle', which has a plebeian ring, and thus contrasts with the French-sounding 'Pertelote'. She (1968:86-87) reaches the conclusion that "[t]he sheep's name has a three-fold function: it tells us of the widow's simplicity, her poverty, and one of the ways in which she was 'a maner deye' (l. 4036)." The also rather 'plebeian' names of the dogs can be seen as linking the 'courtly world' of Chauntecleer and Pertelote with the wider world of the farm, which includes human beings.

539 On the telling of time in CHAUCER's day, see Mooney (1993).

to the cock, and the border to the 'storyland' proper has thus not been crossed.[540]

The ensuing description of the cock 'from coxcomb to claw' fulfills two purposes at once. On the surface, it provides a rather realistic and detailed picture of a cock's splendid and colourful appearance – so detailed, indeed, that L.P. Boone (1949:79) was able to identify Chauntecleer as a "Golden Spangled Hamburg".[541] The way in which this information is imparted, however, is quite special. The narrator uses the rhetorical model description found in GEOFFREY OF VINSAUF's *Nova poetria*, normally used to describe a noble lady or any other member of the (human) aristocracy, and thus announces the introduction of the level of courtly language and behaviour which will provide the contrasting background to the henyard trivialities of the galline universe.[542] This deliberate 'misapplication' of a typically courtly form in order to describe a barnyard fowl is only the mock-heroic precursor of what is to follow, and its overall effect on the audience is slightly ambiguous.[543] On the one hand, we are able, or indeed compelled, to imagine a rather magnificent rooster. On the other hand, the very rhetorical technique which paints such a convincingly noble image undercuts this achievement because of the incongruity of the rhetorical machinery (fit to describe a king) and the subject (a cock).[544] If the animal fable or beast epic

---

540 The question of the 'scientific' basis of CHAUCER's description of Chauntecleer is the topic of Steadman's (1959) article.

541 Even though it may well be that CHAUCER based his description upon nature, he might equally have followed a literary model or convention. See *I have a gentil cok* (Luria and Hoffman 1974:77), which provides a similar description.

542 R.W. Elliott (1965:31) and J.B. Friedman (1972:258) comment on CHAUCER's use of the *Nova poetria*. The relevant passage can be found in Gallo (1971:44 and 46) where GEOFFREY OF VINSAUF gives the following advice to his readers (ll. 603-604): "A summo capitis descendat splendor ad ipsam/Radicem, totumque simul poliatur ad unguem."

543 Bäuml (1980) comments on the underlying developments which make such a 'misapplication' possible, and concludes (Bäuml 1980:250): "The increased distance between author/scribe and text, and between text and reciting reader, leads to an increase in the distance between text and content: the content [...] can now be subjected to alienating functions of a text which, while relying on tradition to arouse traditional expectations, counteracts that tradition[.]" On medieval satire and parody in general, see P. Lehmann (1963).

544 Jauss (1959:63) finds a similar technique already used in the ninth century poem *Epitaphium Multonis* by SEDULIUS SCOTTUS: "Er [the narrator] kleidet sein Bedauern in den erhabensten Stil, der ständig mit der Geringfügigkeit des Gegenstandes kontrastiert, und bauscht dabei das Alltagsereignis derart zur epischen Handlung auf, dass er das

dimension had been unambiguously established right from the beginning, many of the now incongruous-looking elements would have passed unnoticed. Within the fable world – and, to a lesser degree, also in that of the beast epic – animals do act like men and are therefore also treated like human beings.[545] An 'effictio' of a cock according to the rules and precepts of rhetoric would be appropriate. In *The Nun's Priest's Tale*, however, we note a pronounced tendency to keep the audience from entering the unambiguous and clearly circumscribed realms of either the animal fable or the beast epic, and the narrator prevents the shutting of the gates to the trivial reality of this world. We are allowed to venture into these realms, but never so far as to lose sight of the other side. Thus, the gradual approach to the henyard universe and its ruler has prepared us to respond with ambiguity to the 'effictio' of Chauntecleer.

The initial descriptive approach to the rooster is soon supplemented by a characterization by means of his actions and his relationship with Pertelote. The narrator animates the splendid yet, up to that moment, rather static picture of Chauntecleer by letting us share in the henyard life of our hero, which comes into view "in a dawenynge/As Chauntecler among his wyves alle/Sat on his perche that was in the halle" (ll. 4072-4074). The rooster, obviously a noisy sleeper, is haunted by a nightmare in which he sees himself abducted by "a beest/[...] lyk an hound" (ll. 4089-4090). Pertelote, to whom he confides his frightening dream, scolds him and attributes his bad dream to the "humours [that] ben to habundant in a wight" (l. 4115). The ensuing argument about the value of dreams displays a learnedness in medical matters on Pertelote's side, and an even greater scholarly knowledge on the part of Chauntecleer, who brilliantly defends the notion that "dremes ben signyficaciouns" (l. 4169).[546] Yet, even though he summarily refutes his wife's arguments, he himself falls prey to his amorous inclinations and thus disregards the obvious consequences of his line of reasoning. For him, "Mulier est hominis confusio" (l. 4354) as well as his "joye and al his blys" (l. 4356).[547] By this point, the story has taken us a great deal further into the

---

Schicksal seines 'Helden' [i.e. the wether] als Leidensweg eines Märtyrers parodieren kann."

545 See Scheps (1970:1): "The convention which underlies all fables is that animals behave as people do, that, in fact, they are the people of the fable." See also Coote (1985:38) and R.W. Elliott (1965:15).

546 On medieval dream lore and its use by CHAUCER, see Curry (1960:195-240), Hieatt (1967), and Windeatt (1982).

547 This (in)famous line and its 'translation' is discussed by the following critics: Aiken (1935:286) notes that the Latin line is also found in VINCENT DE BEAUVAIS' *Speculum Naturale* and *Speculum Doctrinale*; Broes (1963:162) thinks that it is a deliberate

realm of the animal fable, and it is now time to consider in greater detail some of the characteristics of the cock that are often only alluded to. Modern critical analysis has unearthed a wealth of possible exegetical interpretations for the cock, as well as some rather secular ones. The following digression is intended to give a brief overview of the most important symbolic traditions which provide the background to CHAUCER's use of the rooster; however, it must never be forgotten that the tale is, in spite of its symbolic dimensions, primarily the comic account of a cock who nearly lost his life in the fangs of a fox.

Digression on the Allegorical and Symbolic Value of the Cock

We can divide the various traditions into five groups.

1) The Cock as Virtuous Man[548]

a) The Cock as 'Wise Man'

The exegetical tradition that interprets the cock 'ad bonam partem' goes back to the Old Testament, namely *Liber Iob* 38,36 ("quis dedit gallo intellegentiam"). Apart from simply endowing the bird with a reputation for possessing wisdom, this verse caused the exegetes to take a closer look at the

---

mistranslation by Chauntecleer; C. Brown (1920) discusses the origin of the Latin phrase and its misogynistic environment; Coote (1985:90) writes that Chauntecleer is so overcome by female charm that he mistranslates the phrase; Frese (1981:331) notes that these lines at once evoke centuries of clerical antifeminism and the 'felix culpa' interpretation of the Fall; J.B. Friedman (1972:261-263) sees the fate of the cock as an illustration of the Latin gnomic tag; Kenyon (1916:286) believes that "[h]is quotation of the proverb expresses his inner sense of fate, while his humorously gallant interpretation of it shows his wife's power over him"; Law (1922:214) discusses the sources of the phrase; C.A. Owen (1953:310) detects in it the covert expression of the Nun's Priest's antifeminism; Ruggiers (1965:228) sees it as a joke at Pertelote's expense; Scheps (1970:5) considers the mistranslation to be an ironic gloss; Sisam (1927:xxix) writes that Chauntecleer turns the Latin sentence into a jest; and Steadman (1965) provides another source/parallel.

548 Dahlberg (1954:282) mentions that, in JEAN DE CONDÉ's *Li Dis de Trois Estas dou Monde* or *Dit du Koc*, the cock "represents the ideal knight, priest, and husband." For the idea of the warrior cock, see Rowland (1981:341-342). The general virtues of the cock are also implicit in PLINY's comparison of the rooster with the lion (see Donovan 1953:503). Steadman (1959:241) notes that BARTHOLOMEW describes the cock as a great fighter and that NECKAM relates cockfights "in terms appropriate for loftier conflicts[.]" He (1959:241) comes to the conclusion that "CHAUCER's mock-heroic treatment of Chauntecleer and his household was rooted not merely in the traditional beast-epic, but also in a conventional picture of the domestic cock as a prince and warrior."

rooster in general, and to subject its characteristics, whether actually observed or merely reported, to exegetical interpretation. Thus, the cock soon denoted not only the 'wise man', but also more specifically the wise and virtuous cleric.

b) The Cock as a Preacher/Cleric

Based upon the general equation of the rooster with the 'wise man', we then encounter the more specific interpretation of the cock as the morally attentive preacher or cleric. Details taken from the natural cock's behaviour and/or appearance, such as the beating of its wings, its announcement of dawn, and the colours of its feathers, were allegorically interpreted and led to an identification of the rooster with the preacher or cleric.[549]

c) The Cock as a Good Christian

The rooster was also interpreted as the virtuous Christian 'per se', especially in works which did not focus primarily on the preacher or cleric, but which took a larger section of mankind into consideration. Thus, in PHILIPPE DE THAUN's Anglo-Norman *Le Livre des Creatures* (twelfth century), "[t]he white cock [...] signifies the man of holy life" (Collins 1913:118), and in BERCHORIUS' *Reductorium Morale*, the rooster allegorically represents "religiosus vel etiam omnis qui est fidelis & catholicus christianus" (Steadman 1959:244, fn. 39).[550]

2) The Cock as Sinful Man

a) The Cock as Uxorious Man[551]

Even though the biblical and exegetical tradition stresses the 'interpretatio ad bonam partem', the real and also proverbial sexual prowess of the rooster is too obvious to remain without influence on the development of the symbolic value of the cock. Thus, Steadman (1959:236) writes: "Chauntecleer's <u>uxoriousness</u> [my emphasis], regal pride, and choleric temperament are characteristic traits of 'gallus domesticus'."[552] This trait makes it possible to

[549] The following authors provide evidence of the medieval interpretation of the cock as a cleric/preacher: J.B. Allen (1969:28), Bishop (1979:258), Dahlberg (1954:282), Donovan (1953:501-503), Friedmann (1980:203), Myers (1972:218), Rowland (1981:345), Steadman (1959:243 and 244, fn. 39), and Yates (1983:116).

[550] See also Donovan (1953:498).

[551] The various symbolic references to Chauntecleer's carnal nature are analysed by Wentersdorf (1982).

[552] For further information on the medieval natural historical background of CHAUCER's cock, see Steadman (1959). Coote (1985:39) thinks that Chauntecleer "personifies the

link him with Adam, who ate of the forbidden fruit because he placed marital love before obedience to God.

b) The Cock as Vain Man

Bishop (1979:258) relates that "the strutting cock was a symbol of vanity and, as in all ages, was regarded as one of the stupidest creatures", and Steadman (1959:240) notes that "[a]ccording to PLINY, the vanity of 'gallus domesticus' nearly equalled that of the peacock."

3) The *Physiologus*/Bestiary Cock[553]

The crowing of the cock seems to be its most outstanding characteristic. The compilers obviously took St. Peter's denial of Christ and his subsequent penance after hearing the cock crow (for example *Secundum Mattheum* 26,69-75) as their point of departure for the interpretation of the cock crow as a sign of repentance, of having the ability to drive away evil influences, and to imbue sinful man with renewed hope.[554]

4) The Fable Cock[555]

Unlike his allegorical brothers, the cock of the fable is not primarily characterized by outstanding wisdom. His natural ability to announce the new day at dawn and his quick-wittedness are reflected in some Aesopic fables, yet at the same time, as Rowland (1981:348) reports, a misinterpretation of a line in PHAEDRUS "resulted in the cock acquiring a reputation for stupidity rather than wisdom." Thus, we have no homogeneous picture of the fable cock.

5) The Beast Epic Cock

Not unlike his elder brother the fable cock, the beast epic cock has an ambiguous reputation: on the one hand, he is the vain and gullible fool, but on the other hand, his quick wits save his neck.

Summary

What, then, is the relevance of the aforementioned traditions to *The Nun's Priest's Tale*? Does any of those allegorical and symbolic traditions provide

---

chief of the vices, Pride, and the primal sin that led to man's fall, uxoriousness, the placing of married love before reason and faith."

553 See T.H. White (1959:150-151).

554 See Donovan (1953:502) and Rowland (1981:340 and 343).

555 See Rowland (1981:347-350).

the key to a hitherto unseen dimension of the tale? As we saw in the chapter on the critics, many of them do think so and, following the Nun's Priest's cue to take the "moralitee" (l. 4630), many attempt to separate the moral wheat from the narrative chaff. Thus, the animal 'natura' of the rooster provides the starting point. On a second, intermediary level ('allegoria' I), we have the interpretation of the animal as man in general. This is specified on the third level ('allegoria' II), where the cock is, according to one's point of view, equated either with 'virtuous man', with the cleric in general (who can shift to either of the other two extremes), or with 'sinful man', and specifically Adam, who was the first man to sin. On the contextual level, Chauntecleer has been variously identified with either the narrator himself – when the cock's positive sides are stressed – or with the rather secular-minded Monk in the other case.[556]

The following graphic depiction attempts to illustrate the various dimensions of the cock.[557]

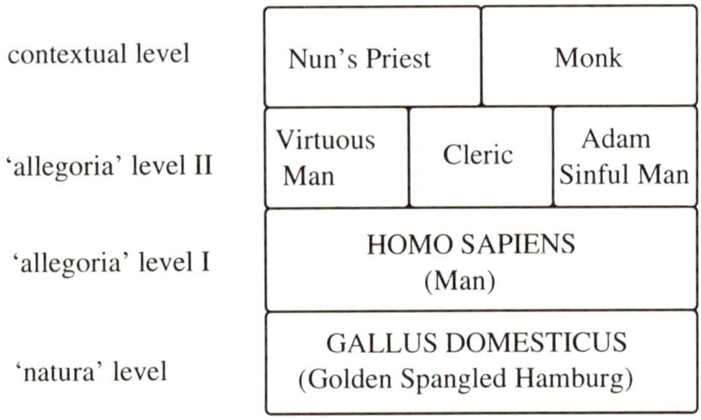

Chauntecleer's animal nature provides the basis for this complex multiple structure.[558] Yet, its relationship to the subsequent levels is by no means a monolateral affair. Within the textual frame of the beast fable, we have the interpretation of the animals as human beings; in the 'normal' beast fable, this process is irreversible, and there are no such blatantly contrasted and

556 See Hatton (1967:32): "Chauntecleer's character reflects not only the victims in the Monk's tragedies but the Monk himself."

557 The 'Cleric' here takes up a morally neutral position between the two extremes, towards either of which he can move.

558 As was the rule in the Middle Ages, not only the observable characteristics of an animal, but also – or even more so – the auctorial accounts of the beast or bird in question were of great influence.

highlighted relapses into the animal world as we have in *The Nun's Priest's Tale*.[559] With CHAUCER, however, one is never quite sure whether the next line will not bring a return to the animal level.[560] As R.W. Elliott (1965:16) observes: "In this continuing game of dressing up the animals in human costume and then letting us peep through the disguise lies much of the humour and fun of the Tale." Yet, it is not only fun that is achieved by this switching between levels. J.B. Friedman (1972:258) comments: "The Priest, therefore, by presenting his cock and hen simultaneously as people and as chickens, is building both the moral impact and the humor of his tale." However, this building of the 'moral impact' is questioned by Mann (1975:275): "[The tale] presents us with the problem both of applying moral analysis to animals, and of bringing the comic style of the Tale into relation with a serious meaning." Lines 4055-4057 illustrate this dilemma: "This gentil cok hadde in his governaunce/Sevene hennes for to doon al his plesaunce/Whiche were hise sustres and his paramours". If we applied human moral standards, as we might feel free to, since we are given leave to do so by both the fable conventions and the narrator – by anthropomorphizing the cock and the hens ('gentil', 'sustres', 'paramours') – we would have to severely condemn his polygamous incest; and yet, our response is not dominated by moralistic indignation, but rather by good-natured laughter.[561] The sudden changes of perspective keep the audience in a state of continuous suspense and uncertainty, and do not allow the hearer or reader ever to relax in a smug position of righteousness.[562]

---

559 Bloomfield (1979:75) assumes that the beast epic influence is responsible for the mock-heroic tone. Shallers (1975:330) observes that, in the *Roman de Renart*, the cock sometimes talks like a nobleman, but "the trouvère never lets us forget that he is speaking of animals[.]"

560 See Bloomfield (1979:76): "These animals with their human problems, human interests and human failures bring us close; but we are never allowed to forget that they are animals." See also R.W. Elliott (1965:15), C.A. Owen (1953:307), A.F. Payne (1975:208), and Pratt (1972:660). Shallers (1975:333) thinks that "CHAUCER blurs the distinction and gives us characters that are animals and men simultaneously." See also Scheps (1970:4) and Standop (1980:415).

561 R.W. Elliott (1965:18) notes this effect with regard to the person of Chauntecleer: "[A]s a man we probably would not care for him very much, but as a cock in human guise he is thoroughly likeable. It is in order to achieve this sympathy, this liking for him, that the story-teller switches again and again from one level to the other."

562 Hoy (1969:152) gives the following interpretation: "The dual focus created by the presence of the human and the animal in Chauntecleer and Pertelote demands a complex response from the listeners to the Tale. We are invited to laugh not at the subject of dreams itself, but at the incongruity of such a debate carried on between two birds." Pratt (1972:660) thinks that oscillating between the gallinaceous and the human serves another purpose: "By means of subtle flattery based on implications of superiority, he entices

Pertelote[563]

After having introduced Chauntecleer, the Nun's Priest again widens our field of view for a moment, to draw our attention to the other inhabitants of the henyard, namely the seven hens, Chauntecleer's "sustres and his paramours" (l. 4057). Yet, it soon becomes clear that the lines mentioning the hens merely serve to prepare the ground for the next protagonist, i.e. Pertelote. It is towards her that the attention of both the audience and Chauntecleer is directed. She is Chauntecleer's feminine counterpart, his noble lady in the mock-heroic universe of the henyard: "Curteys she was, discret and debonaire/And compaignable, and bar hirself so faire" (ll. 4061-4062). Our royal hero lost his heart to her when she was "seven nyght oold" (l. 4063), and ever since then, she has been his favourite paramour.[564] Yet, besides being Chauntecleer's courtly lady, she has two other roles: firstly, she is the down-to-earth, no-nonsense housewife who debates with her husband about the value of dreams and prescribes a variety of medicinal herbs for him. Secondly, she is, at the same time, also the 'seductress' and

members of his audience – whether ordinary people, lords, princes, or learned clerks – to laugh at the pompous cock; then without warning he lowers the boom by making them suddenly realize that they laugh at themselves. The butt of his satire is man." Scheps (1970:7) believes that "[i]n opposition to the perilously easy identification of men and beasts which the beast fable ordinarily requires us to make, the Nun's Priest demonstrates a profound understanding of the grave inadequacy of such an identification, and thus he refuses to make it complete. By involving his animal characters in learned disputation, he anthropomorphizes them; but, by making their arguments irrelevant to the central action of the fable, he in effect returns them to the level of beasts." Shallers (1975:335) finds that "[t]he elusiveness of these conflicting themes [the 'exemplum' exhortation to eschew pride and over-confidence, and the questioning of our ability to do so by the Reynardian story] could only have been maintained by means of an unusual kind of beast allegory in which the characters are neither allegorical representatives of human beings (as they are in 'exempla') nor literal animals (as they are in the *Renart*), but animals and humans simultaneously."

563 Dahlberg (1954:286) interprets the name as being derived from Old French, meaning 'loss of a portion in a heritage' or 'loss of birthright' (i.e. theologically speaking, the kingdom of heaven). See also Pratt (1972:655), who gives the following etymology: 'perte' ~ 'to destroy, to confuse' and 'lote' ~ 'lot, fate'. He (1972:655) concludes: "In other words, she is 'hominis confusio'." Since we have no indication as to the literary provenance of the name 'Pertelote', we may assume that it is a genuine Chaucerian creation (vs. 'Pinte' in the parallel texts). Its French origin and its length help to stress the hen's courteous qualities, whereas the 'Pinte' of the *Roman de Renart* distinguishes herself only as the one who lays the big eggs – "qui les gros hues ponnoit" (Hulbert 1941:648, l. 90; see also Petersen 1898:91).

564 CHAUCER obviously alludes to *The Romance of the Rose* (Horgan 1994:14): "[Joy] had given him [i.e. Pleasure] her love when she was no more than seven years old."

main focus of Chauntecleer's libidinous desires.[565] Thus, on the second allegorical level, where we have Chauntecleer equated with uxorius man, and more precisely with Adam, she also is the equivalent to Eve, the 'arch-seductress'; and on the contextual level, her courtly qualities make it possible to connect her with the Prioress. We can thus draw up the following schematic illustration:

contextual level	Prioress		
'allegoria' level II	Lady	Wife	Eve Seductress
'allegoria' level I	HOMO SAPIENS (Woman)		
'natura' level	GALLINA DOMESTICA (Golden Spangled Hamburg)		

For the narrator, Pertelote is the perfect tool with which to manipulate the audience's responses to Chauntecleer. Instead of being allowed to identify completely with the anthropomorphized fable rooster, we are now and then reminded of the basic 'cockishness' of Chauntecleer by his feminine galline counterpart (as well as by the notorious shifts of perspective). Chauntecleer's "Ye ben so scarlet reed aboute youre eyen/It maketh al my drede for to dyen" (ll. 4351-4352) and his subsequent, repeated 'feathering' of Pertelote should jolt even the least involved reader to attention.[566] It

---

565 Coote (1985:73) finds in Pertelote the combination of "two medieval conventions in the literary presentation of women – the courtly lady of romance and elements of the middle-class spouse of 'fabliaux', or stories of low life." Ruggiers (1965:227) remarks on Pertelote: "Her wisdom is for the most part the wisdom of the home dispenser." Standop (1980:415) sees her as the "Vertreterin einer fortschrittlichen Naturheilkunde." Bishop (1979:266), however, remarks: "The whole pharmacopoeia, swallowed at once, would have killed the wretched bird."

566 A.F. Payne (1975:208) comments on this: "[CHAUCER] fails to regard the animals' right to a human role consistently and turns them back into animals. [....] [This] is a part of the technique of intentional violation of the conditional necessity governing literary genre."
Chauntecleer's "Ye ben so scarlet reed [...]" echoes and pokes fun at a similar line from ODO DE GRANDSON's *Le Songe Saint Valentin* (Windeatt 1982:120-124), where we have a peregrine falcon praising his beloved noble falcon (Windeatt 1982:123): "I am in

makes him or her realize that, in spite of the learned discourse on the truthfulness of dreams, we are still in the ambiguous no-man's-land between animal fable, beast epic, and folk tale. On the one hand, the anthropomorphized animals aspire to human status; on the other hand, their typical animal characteristics are retained. This makes the evocation of a homogeneous and stable picture impossible, since we have no guarantee whatsoever that the narrator will not suddenly change the direction of the narrative and shatter, or at least disturb, our illusion of either genre affiliation.

The Debate on Dreams (ll. 4078-4361)

Pertelote plays a crucial role in preparing the audience for what is (in terms of the narrative structure) the climactic encounter between the cock and the fox. It is thanks to her reproach and her medical advice that we are able to glimpse more of Chauntecleer's character.[567] It is the debate section of the tale that provides the most striking deviations from its parallel versions. In the *Roman de Renart*, it is Pinte the hen who not only speaks in favour of the truthfulness of dreams, but who also gives the correct interpretation of Chauntecleer's (allegorical) dream.[568] In *The Nun's Priest's Tale*, however, we have a change of roles.[569] Chauntecleer, about whose galline qualities we were already informed in the course of the introductory description, now has the opportunity to distinguish himself as a highly learned and widely-read cock.[570] He realizes that his very realistic dream is a warning. Yet, his inability to recognize the 'beest' – of which he gives a very accurate description (see ll. 4089-4095) – as a fox highlights the discrepancy between instinctive and acquired knowledge.[571]

---

perfect delight while looking at her face. [....] I am so happy when this happens that I no longer remember my woe."

567 Thus, we can say that, with regard to structure, the conversation between Pertelote and Chauntecleer has the same function as the dialogue between Chantecler and the fox in *The Vox and the Wolf*: both dialogues contribute to the characterization of the (main) protagonist.

568 See Hulbert (1941:652, ll. 218-258).

569 Severs (1946) comments in detail on the consequences of this change of roles.

570 Pratt (1977:570) comments on Chauntecleer's learning: "The magnificence of his learning – clearly that of a great university – was matched only by his uxoriousness."

571 Scheps (1970:2, 4, and 8) bases his interpretation of the tale on this discrepancy. Coote (1985:49) thinks that Chauntecleer's delight in reason corrupts him and makes him susceptible to the fox's seduction. It is interesting to note that 'daun Russelle' employs the same strategy to deceive Chauntecleer as 'Reneuard' uses to trick the wolf in *The Vox and the Wolf*. 'Russelle' calms the cock with the rhetorical question "Be ye affrayd of me that am youre freend?" (l. 4475), and thus partially regains his trust. Similarly,

It is interesting to watch how CHAUCER, after thus departing from the original storyline, gets back on to the track again. Chauntecleer ends his impressive and extensive argument in favour of the truthfulness of his dream with an affirmative, yet logically somewhat unsound "Shortly I seye as for conclusioun/That I shal han of this avysioun/Adversitee [...]" (ll. 4341-4343) and, having thus re-established his authority, leaves the level of the 'learned cock' in order to revert, with greater self-confidence, to his role of the courtly lover: "Now lat us speke of myrthe and stynte al this./Madame Pertelote, so have I blys,/Of o thyng God hath sent me large grace/For whan I se the beautee of youre face" (ll. 4347-4350). The following lines bring the mock-heroic climax of the whole argument, and mark the re-entrance of the 'deviant' Chaucerian version into the main storyline: "Ye ben so scarlet reed aboute youre eyen/It maketh al my drede for to dyen" (ll. 4351-4352). The illusion of the 'learned man', created and kept up by the scholarly discourse on dreams, is shattered, and the audience again finds itself face to face with a cock whose ideas of beauty are somewhat different from the corresponding human notions; and it is nonsense to expect a cock, whose carnal instincts are rather pronounced, to take action based on the logical conclusion of that elaborate discourse.[572] CHAUCER thus skilfully guides his audience from one level to another ('learned man', 'courtly lover', and 'cock') and, by a stylistic sleight of hand, he succeeds in leading us back to his point of departure.

Having now seen how CHAUCER manages to incorporate this deviant digression into the main storyline, we may ask why he changed it in the first place. Some critics see the reason in the Nun's Priest's general, as well as particular, anti-feminism.[573] In the guise of the scholarly Chauntecleer, he establishes his intellectual superiority over the Prioress whose tale of the child martyr is parodied.[574] R.W. Elliott (1965:10) assumes that CHAUCER

that am youre freend?" (l. 4475), and thus partially regains his trust. Similarly, 'Reneuard' disguises his deceitful intentions towards the wolf behind his assertion "Ich am Reneuard, þi frend" (Bennett and Smithers 1968:71, l. 133).

572 R.W. Elliott (1965:12) sees the true motivation for Chauntecleer's learned digression on dreams in his unwillingness to take any of Pertelote's laxatives.

573 We may assume the existence of a certain general anti-feminism in the Nun's Priest, which can be blamed on his clerical training. This general misogynistic attitude takes the Prioress as its specific target. See also C.A. Owen (1953:309), and on medieval anti-feminism in general, see Blamires (1992).

574 See the reference to St. Kenelm (ll. 4300-4309) and his "Mordre wol out, that se we day by day./[....]/Though it abyde a yeer or two or thre" (ll. 4242-4246), which makes fun of the Prioress' "Mordre wol out, certeyn, it wol nat faille" (Benson 1987:211, *Prioress' Tale* l. 576).

wants "to make the familiar story fresh for his listeners" by means of the digression on dreams, with its shift of focus from Chauntecleer to his dream. The wish to postpone the chaotic climax of the chase scene may also have caused CHAUCER to let his digression grow beyond normal proportions. Most important, however, is the fact that the digression contributes to the characterization of Chauntecleer. Indeed, if we had to base our assessment of Chauntecleer solely on the limited amount of information which the narrative voice provides, we would be ill-prepared for the events to come. The narrator's account of the cock stresses his natural abilities, namely accurate timekeeping, the outstanding quality of his crowing, and his abundant sexual prowess. These instinctive qualities should, and indeed do, warn the cock when he sees the fox that he is facing trouble.[575] A 'normal' cock would seek the safety of the perch – as is the first instinctive impulse of Chauntecleer.[576] However, from to the learned dispute between our hero and Pertelote, we know that Chauntecleer is not only a model rooster with an unmatchable 'natural', i.e. instinctive, knowledge of things, but also something of a scholar, who takes pride in his extensive 'unnatural' knowledge, i.e. knowledge acquired through reading. Moreover, it is the same pride that causes him to be taken in by the fox's trick – in contrast to the less learned, but practical-thinking cock in *The Vox and the Wolf.* The stressing of Chauntecleer's learnedness is made necessary by the fact that the narrator denies us a clear-cut categorization of the animals as either 'fable animals' or 'natural animals'. Within a fable, an animal's susceptibility to flattery needs no further explanation; men are susceptible to it, and so the fable animals may exhibit the same faults. Yet, in such an ambiguous narrative as *The Nun's Priest's Tale*, where we have no clear division between the fable universe and reality, it is necessary to provide a motivation for the cock's susceptibility to flattery, in spite of his instinctive dislike of the fox.

'Daun Russelle' the Fox

The pre-eminence of our two avian protagonists is, to a large extent, due to the fact that the tale is not, like all other parallel versions, part of a greater epic cycle centred around the figure of the fox. Even though, on various levels and to different degrees, the tale 'per se' is related to and connected with the other *Canterbury Tales* (especially *The Prioress' Tale*, *The Monk's*

---

575 See "For naturelly a beest desireth flee/Fro his contrarie if he may it see/Though he nevere erst hadde seye it with his eye./This Chauntecler whan he gan hym espye/He wolde han fled but that the fox anon/Seyde [...]" (ll. 4469-4474).

576 See Scheps (1970:2): "Chauntecleer's initial reaction is the correct one."

Tale, *The Knight's Tale*, and *The Tale of Melibee*), it is an independent and self-contained narrative. After first lifting the story from its original frame, CHAUCER uses the newly-won freedom to shift the focus of attention towards the cock and the hen. This is mainly achieved by providing additional characterization of the cock and, to a lesser degree, also of the hen Pertelote. The extensive description of Chauntecleer's virtues, his relationship with Pertelote, and the disproportionately long debate on the value of dreams all contribute to focussing the greatest part of our attention on to the cock. The fox, then, is relegated to the position of an intruder into the galline universe. The audience's view of the action is, for most of the time, from within the henyard, and thus they are able to share the chicken perspective, whereas access to the fox's point of view remains denied.

In contrast to the cock, who is not only introduced by the narrator's voice but also characterized by means of his dispute with Pertelote, our knowledge of the fox remains limited to the narrator's description.[577] The Nun's Priest is obviously trying to avoid any identification of the fox with Renart/Reynard, since such an identification would utterly destroy the balance of the tale and shift the focus of attention on to the well-known hero of the beast epics.[578] It is not the fox, then, that stands at the centre of attention, but the cock Chauntecleer and his relationship with Pertelote. Indeed, the fox is not introduced until about half of the tale has been told, nor is he the famous 'Reynard':[579] he remains anonymous for most of the

---

577 R.W. Elliott (1965:13-14) puts it thus: "[The discussion of dreams] is a means of developing these characters [Pertelote and Chauntecleer], especially Chauntecleer's, further. [.....] Beside Chauntecleer even Pertelote pales into insignificance, [... a]nd Russell the col-fox plays a smaller part still." Gallick (1975:475) places the emphasis slightly differently: "[I]t is the cock as preacher that CHAUCER was most interested in developing." Ruggiers (1965:226) comments: "It is Chauntecleer's character and his virtues or absence of virtues, his self-assurance and 'bragga docio', his pride, his sensuality, his susceptibility to flattery, and his sly intelligence that engage our minds." By using other figures in order to characterize the main protagonist, CHAUCER employs a technique similar to that used by the author of *The Vox and the Wolf* – but there it is the fox who stands at the centre of attention.

578 Petersen (1898:65) already noticed this important change: "[T]he lateness of the appearance of the fox [...] may easily be ascribed to CHAUCER's own authorship, on artistic grounds. He was writing a tale of a cock and a hen who were personages of heroic importance." See also Coote (1985:26), Lumiansky (1955:113), Pratt (1972:652-653), Shallers (1975:332), and Sisam (1927:xxviii).

579 The name 'Renart' (also 'Renaud', 'Reynarde', etc.) was known in medieval England at least from the second half of the thirteenth century, as is shown by the use of 'Reneuard' in *The Vox and the Wolf* (Bennett and Smithers 1968:71, l. 133). Further (later) vernacular examples are to be found in *Sir Gawain and the Green Knight* (Tolkien and Gordon 1967:52-53, ll. 1898, 1916, and 1920) and in CHAUCER's *Legend of Good*

tale, and when he is finally given a name, it is 'daun Russelle' (l. 4524).[580] Pratt (1972:652-653), like Kenyon (1916:283) and Petersen (1898:65) before him, draws the following conclusion: "And as 'daun Russell', the fox does not disturb the centrality of Chauntecleer and Pertelote, whereas with the name 'Renart' he might have tended to upstage them."[581] Thus, it is primarily an anonymous 'col-fox' living in the neighbouring woods that enters our field of vision (ll. 4405-4406). Together with the accurate description of the 'beest' given by Chauntecleer when relating his dream, we are provided with a number of naturalistic details which are of great importance, since they help to distinguish this 'concrete' fox from his famous cousin Renart. As with the cock before, CHAUCER cannot cut off the exegetical and allegorical associations connected with the figure of the fox, even if he wanted to; parallel to the cock's various levels of allegorical and symbolic meanings, we have also to consider the various potential roles ascribed to the fox.

Women (Benson 1987:627, l. 2448). The question of the familiarity of medieval English authors and audiences with the *Roman de Renart* is discussed by Blake (1975) and Varty (paper given at the 11th International Colloquy of the Reynard Society, Düsseldorf 17th – 20th July 1995; see footnote 455 of this study).

[580] Hotson (1924:765-766) believes the change of name and description ('colfox' instead of the normal 'fox', 'Russelle' instead of 'Renart') to be due to CHAUCER's intention to create parallels with historical personalities. Concerning the probable provenance of the name 'Russelle', Dahlberg (1954:277) observes that "[i]n the French vernacular literature of the century before CHAUCER, the fox [...] appears [...] in two cases [in *Renart le Nouvel* and *Li Dis d'Entendement* by JEAN DE CONDÉ] with the same name, Russell, that CHAUCER uses[.]" 'Roussiau', which is the French version of 'Russelle', is one of Renart's sons. This, of course, considerably weakens Hotson's (1924) claim that 'Russelle' denotes one of Richard II's minions. Weighing the extant evidence, Pratt (1972:651-652) reaches the conclusion that CHAUCER deliberately gave his fox a different name "from that of the eponymous hero of such poems as the *Roman de Renart*, *Renart le Bestourné* of RUTEBEUF, the *Couronnement de Renart*, etc. Yet, in contrast to the (in)famous 'Renart', we have no clue concerning the popularity of 'Russelle'.

[581] Lumiansky (1955:113), too, notes that the role of the fox has been diminished. Sisam (1927:xxiv), however, traces the name 'Russelle' back to the obscure red squirrel in the *Roman de Renart* and ignores the fact that 'Russelle', or 'Roussiaus', is actually the name of Renart's younger son in *Renart le Nouvel* (see Dahlberg 1954:278). Sisam (1927:xxiv) comes to the conclusion that the relegation of the fox protagonist to second, or rather third place as "just a wily fox" may not be due to a conscious change on CHAUCER's part, but that this might have been a 'natural' development, since "the Reynard cycle had gone out of fashion in England, as it had in France, by the latter half of the fourteenth century."

Digression on the Allegorical and Symbolic Value of the Fox

1) The *Physiologus*/Bestiary Fox

In the *Physiologus* and the bestiary traditions, the deceitful fox that feigns death in order to lure the scavenger birds is allegorized as the devil who tries to ensnare unwary souls.[582]

2) The Fox as a Heretic

Dahlberg (1954:280) notes that GREGORY THE GREAT, in his commentary on *Canticum Canticorum* 2,15 ("capite nobis vulpes vulpes parvulas quae demoliuntur vineas nam vinea nostra floruit"), equates the 'vulpes' "with heretics, the vines with the churches, and those who are to catch the foxes with the priests, represented by dogs."[583]

3) The Fox as a Friar

One step further away from the original identification of the fox with the heretic in general, we often find him, in the French vernacular literature of the century before CHAUCER, depicted as a friar.[584] Dahlberg (1954:280) comments on this new development: "The writers who made of the fox a symbol for the friars drew upon a tradition of long standing which equated the fox with corrupting influences in the church."[585]

4) The Fable Fox

The characterization of the fable fox draws, on the one hand, on the *Physiologus* and the bestiary traditions, and on the other hand, it makes use of the fox's popular reputation of being a clever and cunning animal that tries to deceive others. Thus, in the fables influenced by the *Physiologus* and the bestiary traditions, we have, according to Blake (1975:55), "the fox playing the role of a devil or arch-tempter[.]" The Latin fable *Gallus et Vulpes*, for example, explicitly equates the 'vulpecula' with 'Sathanas'.[586]

---

582 See, for example, Seel (1992:26-27).

583 See also Donovan (1953:498-501).

584 See Dahlberg (1954:277, 279, and 281).

585 The pictorial evidence for the 'fox friar' is discussed by Varty (1967:51 and 56)

586 See Dahlberg (1954:280), and also Coote (1985:76-77) and Donovan (1953:498). See, later on, HENRYSON who, in his *The Taill of the Foxe, that begylit the Wolf, in the schadow of the Mone* (MacDiarmid 1973:55-63), explicitly says: "The Foxe the Feind I call in to this cais" (MacDiarmid 1973:62).

Shallers (1975:324) comments on the alternative tradition: "[T]he fabulist's fox generally stood for either a man who ironically outwits himself with excessive cleverness (fox and stork) or a man who knows how to win by capitalizing on others' weaknesses (fox and crow)[.]"[587]

5) The Beast Epic Fox

In contrast to the allegorical and moralizing interpretations of the fox as the embodiment of hypocrisy, deceit, evil, and sin, the fox in the early beast epics first starts out as the villainous hero, and only afterwards develops into the epitome of falsehood.[588] Varty (1967:94) summarizes this development as follows: "Just as Reynard enlivened the *Physiologus*' fox, so the sinful defects of that fox were to weigh heavily on Reynard in his later adventures."

Summary

In whichever form the fox made his appearance, he was, to quote Varty (1967:102),

> a popular figure with sculptors in the late Middle Ages, partly because he was a very common nuisance with certain admirable qualities, partly because he came to symbolize the Devil himself and many of his characteristics in an age which was much concerned about spiritual values, and partly because he was the villainous hero of a beast epic with an international reputation.

---

[587] Thus, HENRYSON, in his fable *The Taill of Schir Chantecleir and the Foxe* (C. Elliott 1963:13-19), writes concerning the fox: "This fenyeit foxe may weill be figurate/To flatteraris with plesand wordis quhyte" (C. Elliott 1963:19, ll. 600-601). With regard to the connection between the fable fox and the more recent beast epic fox, Varty (1967:97) observes: "Many of the fox fables were, however, drawn into the mainstream of the *Roman de Renart* right from the beginning and in this way lived a double life."

[588] See Jauss (1977:60) and Varty (1967:21-22).

For our purpose, we can summarize the findings as follows:

contextual level	Temptations			
'allegoria' level II	Devil	Heretic	Friar	Hypo-crite
'allegoria' level I	HOMO SAPIENS (Man)			
'natura' level	VULPES (Colfox/'Brandfuchs')			

Of especial interest here are the two highest levels ('allegoria' II and the contextual level). Depending on the interpretatory approach, we may equate the fox with either the devil, the heretic, the friar or, more generally, with the hypocrite. On the contextual level, he symbolizes all the various temptations which either the Monk or the Nun's Priest himself face. The following paragraph will provide a more detailed and comprehensive analysis of the interconnections between the different levels of the cock and the fox.

The Function of the Animals

All the above-mentioned allegorical, symbolic, and otherwise important traits of the cock and the fox must be borne in mind when discussing the role of the animals in *The Nun's Priest's Tale*.[589] CHAUCER finds himself the heir to a rich and still vigorous tradition of the allegorical interpretation of nature. Contemporary sermons abound with the allegorical 'reading' of birds and beasts, and their allegorical traits make their way, via the great encyclopaedias of the time, into the slowly emerging genre of scientific literature. Yet, CHAUCER does not present us with a simplistic and straightforward one-to-one allegory like the ones found in *The Physiologus*. On the contrary, in his literary quest for truth he ventures into uncharted territory. The fable of *The Cock and the Fox* provides the stem on to which he grafts the branches of allegorical interpretation and sermonizing, and the

589 See J.B. Friedman (1972:250): "The very fact that the *Nun's Priest's Tale* is a beast fable seems to invite interpretations in which the animal characters stand for something other than themselves."

resulting hybrid growth defies easy classification.[590] On the one hand, it is an 'anti-fable', since it explodes the traditional concept of 'fable'; on the other hand, it is also an 'anti-allegory', owing to its failure, or even refusal, to sustain an overall allegorical approach.[591] CHAUCER plays (in the best sense of the word) with literary and allegorical conventions; the result is a poem which opens up new vistas, surprises the hearers with the unexpected, and probably delights them more than any other tale told on the pilgrimage – it certainly did so with the critics.

The specific functions of the animal protagonists within this framework can be seen as follows. First, Chauntecleer and his ilk share the animal protagonists' general literary function of, at least initially, creating a certain distance between themselves on the one side and the human narrator and audience on the other. Even though they are anthropomorphized, it is not as easy to identify with them as with human heroes. Secondly, they provide a

---

590 See Shallers (1975:335): "CHAUCER effects the 'shifting focus' of the *Nun's Priest's Tale* by crossing Reynardian irony with the solemnity of English fable-'exempla' and creating a hybridized variety of beast tale clearly unlike either parent stock." Bloomfield (1979:70), however, thinks that *The Nun's Priest's Tale* "belongs to the genre of beast fable and its related beast epic", and Coote (1985:7) believes it to be "a beast fable", or to be precise (1985:51), "an exemplary sermon in the form of a beast fable." Hotson (1924:764) sees it as "CHAUCER's first and only fable". Hoy (1969:135) gives the following assessments: "Although CHAUCER's narrative takes the basic form of a conventional beast fable, he refuses to be bound by the formal restrictions of the genre"; and (1969:155): "The *Nun's Priest's Tale* as a whole is an 'exemplum'[.]" Lenaghan (1963:305) writes: "By the introduction of Fortune and high style into the Aesopic fable the Nun's Priest has created a hybrid genre, the merry tragedy." Lumiansky (1955:105) categorizes it as "an 'exemplum' and as a mock-heroic beast-fable making use of learned material[.]" Mann (1975:282, fn. 17) notes: "It is in applying the moral directly to the cock, and thus exploiting the opportunities offered by this one fable where disastrous effect doesn't irrevocably follow on its practical cause, that CHAUCER lifts the Tale out of the beast-fable type." A.F. Payne (1975:208) discusses the rules governing the literary genres and observes: "But this particular writer is already violating the form by writing simultaneously with the fable a romance, a mock-epic, and several other things which lend themselves less easily to being named." Petersen (1898:46) reaches the conclusion that "the *Nun's Priest's Tale* belongs to the epic type of the Cock and Fox narrative." For Scheps (1970:1), it is "CHAUCER's Anti-Fable", in which he renders the traditional fable conventions 'ad absurdum'. Watkins (1969:463) thinks that the Nun's Priest "offers a beast fable that will also be an 'exemplum'."

591 Scheps (1970) calls *The Nun's Priest's Tale* CHAUCER's anti-fable. Bloomfield (1979:78), however, thinks it "is a fable devoted to the teaching of wisdom being undercut and destroyed by its mock quality [...] but finally leading us back, but on a higher level, to its original didactic purpose." Concerning the failure to sustain an allegorical interpretation, see Boyd's (1978:68) criticism: "[T]he fox, who is only following his natural instincts, is not a very convincing devil-figure."

cover for criticism.[592] By choosing the fable of *The Cock and the Fox* as the foundation of the Nun's Priest's narrative, CHAUCER not only inherited the animal protagonists, but also their allegorical background. It is, in my opinion, a fruitless task to try to reconstruct a hypothetical 'original' from which CHAUCER might have started.[593] The extant text of Branch II of the French *Roman de Renart* (Hulbert 1941:646-658) and that of the twelfth century Middle High German *Reinhart Fuchs* (Hulbert 1941:658-662) provide us with an accurate enough starting point for our analysis of CHAUCER's use of animals.

We can sum up the major deviations which directly concern the animals as follows:[594]

1) The names of the hen and the fox are changed.
2) The independent position of *The Nun's Priest's Tale* stands in contrast to the fact that the parallel episodes are part of a larger cycle, which is centred around the figure of Renart/Reinhart.
3) The mock-heroic treatment of the animal protagonists is peculiar to *The Nun's Priest's Tale*.
4) In *The Nun's Priest's Tale*, Chauntecleer and Pertelote occupy a pre-eminent position, and the fox plays a subsidiary role.
5) CHAUCER considerably extends the debate on the truthfulness of dreams.
6) The positions of the cock and the hen in the debate are reversed.
7) Chauntecleer displays great erudition.

The seven points listed above are crucial to the function of the animals, irrespective of whether CHAUCER himself is responsible for the changes or whether he took them over from an unknown 'original'.

However, even the most original deviations from the source text and even the longest digressions have to come to an end, and thus we find ourselves back in the mainstream of the old storyline. Yet, to use HERAKLITUS' words, one cannot enter the same stream twice: even though the subsequent encounter between the cock and the fox follows the sequence of events outlined in the parallel versions, our perception of this encounter has been radically changed, and it is no longer the straightforward and one-

---

592 See also Watkins (1969:464): "The farmyard scene allows the Priest to hold the human world at a distance, to display for it a proper contempt."

593 Petersen (1898:87-89) attempts such a reconstruction.

594 A detailed overall comparison of *The Nun's Priest's Tale* and its parallels can be found in Petersen (1898).

dimensional event of the beast fable. The following illustration attempts to render more explicit some of the implied multiple references.

<table>
<tr><td>4</td><td colspan="3">Nun's Priest</td><td colspan="3">Monk</td><td colspan="4">Temptations</td></tr>
<tr><td>3</td><td colspan="2">Virtuous Man</td><td colspan="2">Cleric</td><td colspan="2">Adam
Sinful Man</td><td>Devil</td><td>Heretic</td><td>Friar</td><td>Hypo-
crite</td></tr>
<tr><td>2</td><td colspan="6">HOMO SAPIENS
(Man)</td><td colspan="4">HOMO SAPIENS
(Man)</td></tr>
<tr><td>1</td><td colspan="6">GALLUS DOMESTICUS
(Golden Spangled Hamburg)</td><td colspan="4">VULPES
(Colfox/'Brandfuchs')</td></tr>
</table>

Both the cock and its opponent have, in the meantime, become something more complex and meaningful. On the 'natura' level (1), we still witness the encounter between a fox and a cock, and on the general intermediate allegorical level (2), we also still have the interpretation of the event as an interaction between two human beings ('beast fable level'). Levels (3) and (4), however, are peculiar to *The Nun's Priest's Tale*: it is here that the specific allegorical values of the two animal protagonists are activated, so that at least a partial allegorical interpretation becomes possible. Thus, on a more general allegorical level (3), the cock can be identified with the cleric who succumbs to the wiles of the devil/heretic/friar/hypocrite. Depending on one's point of view, he is either the 'sinful man' who falls prey to the devil because of his sins – as Adam did – or he symbolizes the 'virtuous man' who is able to escape from the snares of Satan. The application of these interpretations within the context of *The Canterbury Tales* (level 4) leads, on the one hand, to the identification of the 'sinful' and proud cock with the Monk, and thus to the reading of the tale as a warning addressed to the Nun's Priest's fellow cleric. Or, on the other hand, we have the view that the regal and erudite rooster, who is able to extricate himself from a difficult situation, is no-one but the narrator himself, thus compensating for his subordinate position under the petticoat rule of the Prioress.[595]

[595] See Lumiansky (1955:105): "[The] subtle antifeminist theme makes it [i.e. the tale] appropriate for a cleric under the 'petticoat rule' of the Prioress."

Conclusion

In order adequately to appreciate CHAUCER's innovative artistic achievement in his use of elements from the traditions of *The Physiologus* and the bestiary, the beast epic, and the beast fable, we must contrast it with the interpretative patterns and literary qualities of each of these traditions. The illustration depicted above (page 226) gives a systematic and orderly view of the different levels inherent in two of the Nun's Priest's central animal protagonists. Yet, the very static quality and orderliness which help us to gain an insight into the complex structure of the interactional relations of the protagonists are, at the same time, an illusion which has tempted numerous critics to take a very limited reading of the tale. It is possible to interpret *The Nun's Priest's Tale* meaningfully on any one of the four levels, but in order to do so successfully, one has to close one's eyes to all the facts that do not fit this specific interpretation – and the author explicitly warns us against this 'wynken with eye'.

As a consequence, the role of the animals in *The Nun's Priest's Tale* cannot be satisfactorily described by means of any of the schemes discussed above. True, the fox, for example, is a hypocrite and exhibits parallels with the fable fox. Yet at the same time, we detect traits and characteristics which link him to the allegorizing *Physiologus* and bestiary traditions, as well as to the individualizing one of the beast epic. CHAUCER inherits and makes use of all of these traditions. All the levels coexist side by side, and CHAUCER delights in the exploitation of the various possibilities which such a combination offers to a gifted storyteller. He runs the whole gamut of the various levels, jumping from one dimension to the other, juxtaposing the most exalted with the basest, and in general keeping his listeners on their interpretative toes.[596] We thus have to accept and enjoy the multiple valency of Chauntecleer and his ilk, since it is not only *The Nun's Priest's Tale* itself which is, as Ruggiers (1965:222) puts it, "'sui generis'", but also its animal protagonists.[597]

---

[596] See also Muscatine (1957:239): "The difference between this and animal fables is that this cannot long be taken more seriously in one direction than in the other. Fable respects the boundary between animal fiction and the human truth it illustrates. But the whole spirit of this poem is to erase or at least to overleap the boundaries: animal and human, fiction and truth severally join and separate, change partners and flirt here."

[597] See also Hoy (1969:135): "[CHAUCER's] animals [...] take on personalities of their own, and this is something quite new. Even *The Owl and the Nightingale*, one of the most delightful of the longer medieval beast fables, lacks the human quality of CHAUCER's fable."

CONCLUSION

V. Conclusion

> [Rat]: "But I tell you, I'd take any trouble on earth for you, if only you'd be a sensible animal."
> Kenneth Grahame (1991:130), *The Wind in the Willows*

In this chapter, I first want to present an in-depth summary of the findings of this study, highlighting the poems' typical traits, considering their dependency on models or sources, as well as their relevant European literary background and thus evaluating their originality. Secondly, a brief look at later centuries not covered by this study will show how the various traditions lived on. Lastly, I will provide an assessment of the status of the individual poems in relation to the other extant vernacular English 'animal' texts, and thus give an integrated view of medieval vernacular English animal literature.

1. The Three Traditions: a Summary

The *Physiologus* Tradition

CHAUCER's entertaining masterpiece of the cock and the fox can be considered the culmination of our literary journey through the menagerie of animal protagonists, from our starting point far back in the monastic scriptoria of the early Middle Ages.

In contrast to the highly ambiguous Chauntecleer, the *Physiologus* animals are definitely 'moral animals'. At the same time, however, they are all-rounders, which is also reflected in the range of their literary transmission. They are not restricted to one single poetic habitat, but are encountered in almost every literary genre. The original *Physiologus* can be seen as a kind of blueprint; it is thus not so much a work of poetry, but rather an illustration of the almost universal allegorical view of the world, which also includes the spiritual interpretation of plants and stones. The universal concept of allegory is of greater importance than the interpretation of individual animals, and this makes it possible to apply the allegorical technique to any creature – whether mentioned in *The Physiologus* or not – and within any literary genre. The *Physiologus* animals are a means of exemplarily illustrating this new idea; at the same time, in spite of the basic openness of the concept, they mark the beginning of the predominance of animals within works attempting an allegorical interpretation of nature. As a consequence, *The Physiologus* casts its long shadow on to the animal protagonists of heroic poetry (*The Old English Phoenix*), of the beast fable, of the bird debate, and of the beast epic, to mention just those genres dealt with in this study. Like an undercurrent, it is discernible throughout the centuries and extends even into modern times; and it is thanks to *The Physiologus*' allegorical concept that animals do not remain mere ornamental trappings, but become the subjects of vernacular literary texts other than the traditional beast fable.

Firstly, the behaviour and the typical characteristics of an animal are of allegorical importance, and thus force the author to pay closer attention to those characteristics and to make them the subject of his poetic description. This is the case in *The Old English Physiologus* and *The Middle English Physiologus*. Each poem shows a close linking of the animals' characteristics with the allegorical interpretations, and in so doing follows the beaten track of its Latin model. *The Middle English Physiologus* in particular is mostly a close translation of the very popular *Physiologus Theobaldi*. Both vernacular English poems are thus lacking in originality, and they suitably represent a genre that flourished all over Europe.

Secondly, the discovery of the allegorical dimension makes it possible once again to see the animal as something more than just a part of the human environment – as was the case earlier, in pagan Germanic poetry, where the animal was often seen in connection with the Germanic gods.[598] Re-establishing the link with the divine lifts the animal on to a higher level; it achieves general human relevance and becomes a subject (almost) in its own right. This new development allows the poet to explore possibilities beyond the structurally rather simplistic model of *The Physiologus*, as can be seen in the heroic poem, *The Old English Phoenix*. In its artistic complexity, this poem is not only worlds apart from the limited horizon of its relatives within the vernacular *Physiologus* tradition, but it is also unique in the vernacular European animal literature of its time and age. Even though the first half of the poem is based on LACTANTIUS' *Carmen de ave phoenice*, it presents an approach that is at least partially original. Thus, by transferring the basic interpretatory structure ('natura' followed by the 'significatio') on to an epic heroic poem, the anonymous poet goes beyond the limits of the *Physiologus* model. Though reintegrated allegorically later on, the 'natura' part acquires a limited autonomy for the first time in English vernacular literature. In exchange for the epic length and narrative autonomy of the

598 See Beck (1965 and 1970) and Hatto (1957).

'natura' part, the poet is prepared to accept a loss of structural clarity in the 'significatio' part. The comparatively lengthy 'natura' part mitigates the anthropocentrism of the 'significatio', so that the bird Phoenix 'per se' gains an importance which exceeds that of its allegorical function. Nevertheless, it does not proceed to become an interacting, lively character like its cousin (more than once removed), Chauntecleer. Two factors can be held responsible for this: first, the genre of the epic heroic poem, with its lofty diction, is not the ideal poetic means for the creation of individualized characters; second, even though the auctorial information available on the bird Phoenix vouches for its 'real' existence, it remains a 'literary' bird, for the simple reason that – in contrast to the cock – it is not to be encountered anywhere in the known world. Thus, the only sources of information on this bird are the literary accounts – which is not very helpful to the creation of a realistic character.

The fact that the most original product of this tradition takes on the form of a heroic poem confirms our observation that many of the later poets use *The Physiologus* as a source of inspiration for their own creations rather than spending their poetic energy on the development of the original text itself. This is in accordance with *The Physiologus*' overall orientation towards instruction. The texts of the *Physiologus* tradition are intended for practical clerical use – be it to illustrate a dogmatic truth or to reinforce a point of moral adhortation. They place special emphasis on the aspect of 'prodesse', and relegate aesthetic concerns to second position. The presentation of the animals, which are mostly exotic ones, is basically anthropocentric, as the main function of the texts remains limited to conveying a religious or moralistic message to mankind. With the passing of the centuries, however, the predominantly exotic offspring of *The Physiologus* start to mix with the animals of western Europe, increasing in number, and beginning to populate, or at least influence, literary genres that lay outside their former scope (for example the beast fables and the later beast epics). Yet, even though the area of activity or even the animal subjects themselves change, the basic pattern of the division into a descriptive 'natura' and its interpretation in the 'significatio' part remains the same, well into the late Middle Ages and even into the first centuries of the modern era.[599] Within *The Physiologus*, the animals are used to illustrate the

599 See, for example, TOPSELL's *The Historie of the Foure-Footed Beastes* (London 1607), which contains some of the traditional *Physiologus* lore together with its allegorical interpretation. However, for most of the time TOPSELL strives to critically evaluate this rather fantastic heritage. See, for example, his discussion of the belief that beavers castrate themselves in order to escape the hunter, who is after their precious testicles (in the chapter «Of the Beauer», Topsell 1607:46-47). See also the works of the sixteenth

underlying allegorical dimension; yet, the use of the *Physiologus* animals is not restricted to a specific literary genre or style. Accordingly, the poet on the one hand enjoys great freedom and flexibility with regard to style and form, while on the other hand, this very freedom makes a sustained development of the basic text very difficult.[600] Thus, *The Physiologus* and its successor, the bestiary, can be seen as the nourishing soil out of which the various poetic seeds grow and flower: the soil provides the necessary conditions for the flower to bloom, yet it neither receives any praise for the flower's beauty, nor does it participate in the flowering itself.

The Bird Debates

Although debate poetry can look back upon a long and international tradition, the fully-fledged bird debate seems to be an English speciality and bears witness to the early enthusiasm of the English for birds.[601] With regard to their view of life and their philosophical outlook, these poems of the second group take us into a world utterly different from the one where the *Physiologus* beasts roam. The monastic sombreness of the allegorical works which dominated English vernacular animal literature for centuries is replaced by the high-spirited and rather unmonastic quarrelling of birds. The descriptive mood of the *Physiologus* tradition gives way to the dramatic dialogues of the bird debates, and the protagonists are no longer exotic or even fantastic creatures, but the denizens of the native English sky. Indeed, this is the first time that the main focus is not on the animals' specific characteristics any more. The particularizing descriptions of *The Physiologus* are supplanted by a more integrated presentation of the avian protagonists. The remote and purely descriptive *Physiologus* 'natura' passages, in which the animals hardly ever interact, are dominated by the narratorial voice. In the bird poems, however, the avian characters mostly do without a narrator and, taking up the element of speaking animals from the beast fable tradition, speak and debate on their own. In the best case, the birds develop into autonomous personalities – as can be seen in *The Owl and the Nightingale*, which must be considered a milestone in the development of

---

century naturalist ULYSSIS ALDROVANDI. For a schematic overview of the *Physiologus* influence, see T.H. White (1959:233).

600 As mentioned in footnote 26 of this study, RICHARD DE FOURNIVAL (†1260) used precisely the form of the bestiary for a very secular purpose.

601 Munsterberg's (1980) collection of English bird poetry testifies to the enduring (literary) interest in 'matters avian'. The closest comparable work in time and theme to the Middle English bird debates is the Persian mystical poem *Manteq o't-tair* by FARID O'D-DIN MOHAMMAD EBN-E EBRAHIM 'ATTAR (1140-1230).

animal protagonists.[602] As far as we know, this unique poem seems to have sprung fully developed from the author's poetic genius – not unlike Pallas Athena from the head of Zeus; and even though it shares the typical characteristics of the debate poems, it seems to have no direct literary model. Its two avian antagonists are no longer mere pointers towards a hidden dimension; for most of the time, they themselves and their characteristics form the topic and subject of the poem. There is no obvious allegorical 'dissolution' on a spiritual level, and even though the poet also draws heavily on traditional booklore for his characterization of the two birds, he nevertheless succeeds in endowing them with such vivacity and verve, and thus poetic reality, that even the most lively real bird looks apathetic and lifeless alongside them. The anthropocentric elements which predominated in the older animal poems are limited to the level of the debate in *The Owl and the Nightingale*. The usefulness or uselessness of the birds to man becomes the touchstone for their respective worth, yet this criterion does not diminish the protagonists' avian status.

The Thrush and the Nightingale as well as *The Cuckoo and the Nightingale*, probably both modelled upon *The Owl and the Nightingale*, represent something of a retrograde step, if compared to the accomplishment of the older poem. For most of the time, their avian protagonists are nothing more than appropriately characterized mouthpieces for preconceived opinions, and they lack the individuality and range of their predecessor's protagonists. *The Parlement of Foulys*, finally, is, to some extent, a return to the boisterous vivacity of the first bird debate. The avian catalogue which precedes the parliamentary debate and which links up with the bookish lore of the bestiary and CHAUCER's main source, ALAN OF LILLE's *De Planctu Naturae* (Sheridan 1980), is of little importance for the overall characterization of the birds. It is again the (verbal) action which dominates the reader's perception of the avian debaters. They are not primarily ornamental and colourful bystanders, but a noisy, outspoken, and sometimes even chaotic flock that monopolizes the audience's attention in the parliamentary part of the poem. Allegorical dimensions may be detected, but it is the lively avian protagonists which loom large. CHAUCER is original, insofar as he does not let the parliamentary debate degenerate into an exchange of preconceived opinions voiced by avian mouthpieces. Thus, on a smaller scale, he repeats *The Owl and the Nightingale* poet's feat of having unmistakably individualistic characters dispute.

---

602 Burrow (1982:125-126) reminds us that medieval vernacular writers often did not know each others' works. The chronological overview of the vernacular animal poetry tradition therefore creates many connections and continuous developments which are visible only in hindsight.

Nevertheless, in general it can be said that the avian protagonists of the bird poems are used as spokespersons for the differing philosophical, social, and moral attitudes at stake. More often than not, secular topics are the subjects of the poems, and questions related to the courtly sphere of life and dealing with the relationship between man and woman stand in the centre. The function of the avian protagonists is to more or less skilfully present the various points of view to the audience, and to instigate the dialectic process of finding the truth. Simultaneously, the 'delectare' – the 'fun element', so to speak – increasingly gains in importance. This stands in contrast to the role of the rather less playful *Physiologus* animals, which are almost always used to illustrate an established and undisputed dogmatic or moral truth. Entertainment value is not their most outstanding characteristic. Yet, even though the more secular outlook and the more vivacious and playful general mood separate the bird poems and their protagonists from the works of the *Physiologus* tradition, we nevertheless notice the presence of the various allegorical and symbolic dimensions that come as the legacy of the *Physiologus* tradition to each and every animal in this world. The allegorical view of creation in general, and of creatures in particular, has enriched – or, depending on one's point of view, tainted – every later literary or artistic depiction of animals. Yet, instead of either remaining on the beaten track of allegorical interpretation or making a useless attempt to avoid any allegorical allusions, most bird poem authors decided – knowingly or not – to make cautious use of the allegorical and symbolic dimensions of their avian characters. In this way, they integrated the otherwise irritating potential and put it to use in the characterization of their protagonists – be it in the form of an 'avian catalogue', as in *The Parlement of Foulys* (Brewer 1972:80-81, ll. 330-364), or more implicitly by merely alluding to the possible allegorical dimensions, as in *The Owl and the Nightingale*. As a consequence, we have protagonists – particularly in the two poems mentioned last – with increasingly complex and multilayered characters which make the *Physiologus* allegories look comparatively straightforward and simplistic.

The Beast Fable and Beast Epic Traditions

The fact that both beast fables and many of the *Physiologus* chapters have similar aims, namely to impart a moral precept, makes the fusion of the two traditions easily possible.[603] Thus, the interpretation of the beast fable

[603] Salisbury (1994:116) writes: "What these works [i.e. fables and bestiaries] have in common, however, is that in both the actual animals were secondary to the main purpose of teaching humans a lesson."

protagonists does not remain limited to the general human level, but may include the spiritual level, too.[604] Unfortunately, of the two extant Middle English poems that have connections with the beast fable tradition, the older one, namely *The Vox and the Wolf*, shows no discernible interest in imparting a moral or in encouraging an allegorical interpretation, while the more recent *The Nun's Priest's Tale* clearly pokes fun at these very possibilities.

The poem of *The Vox and the Wolf* marks the first substantial appearance of the secular beast epic tradition within English vernacular literature. Its protagonists lack the explicit anthropocentrism with regard to theme or actors which was a major characteristic of the other poems, and the human elements and concerns are of no great importance. The animal protagonists may talk with each other and sport individualistic names, yet this is where the process of anthropomorphization ends. They primarily remain animals, whose actions revolve around the satisfaction of basic animal needs like eating and drinking. Philosophical or ethical questions are neither asked nor answered; the members of the audience are free to draw a moral from the amusing tale or to interpret it allegorically, but they are not explicitly encouraged to do so. The poet is original, insofar as he has fashioned the corresponding episode of Branch IV of the *Roman de Renart*, which is the probable source of the Middle English tale, into a short, self-contained, and rounded-off poem that exhibits traits of the beast tale, the beast fable, and, most prominently, the beast epic, without being part of a greater cycle. All these points indicate a development towards a more lighthearted and secular notion of literature, which puts greater emphasis on the aspect of 'delectare'. The usefulness of animal protagonists lies primarily in the possibility of creating a comic contrast between basic animal nature and the assumed human roles.

This idea, like so many other things, is then taken up by CHAUCER. Although he can draw upon a rich heritage of animal literature and has to be seen within the development of the various traditions, he nevertheless differs from his predecessors, since at the same time he also stands above the conventions and traditions. This becomes especially apparent in *The Nun's Priest's Tale*, which combines elements from *The Physiologus*, the animal fable, and the beast epic, together with traces of the debate. It is CHAUCER who, for the first time, eclectically makes use of what is best in the various literary traditions. His position as a secular courtly poet and clerk allows him to allude to the allegorical value of his protagonists, without limiting

---

[604] See, for example, ODO OF CHERITON's version of *The Fox and the Wolf in the Well* (footnote 462 of this study).

them to this dimension. For CHAUCER, animals are not succinctly defined and unambiguously clear elements in a spiritual scheme; he 'rediscovers' the basic ambiguity of his animal protagonists, which participate in all the various moral, allegorical, and popular traditions, so that they cannot be limited to any one category. CHAUCER's secular position allows him to apply allegorical lore without entirely having to embrace the allegorical point of view. Thus, his treatment of animals makes them, to some extent, 'free floaters' that no longer have clearly defined relations with the various traditions. In this way, he splendidly manages to accommodate the elements of the moralistic beast fable tradition within his larger and much more sophisticated narrative framework, whose basic ingredient is an episode from Branch II of the *Roman de Renart*. In *The Nun's Priest's Tale*, CHAUCER on the one hand first sabotages the traditional concepts of genre (beast fable, beast epic, and animal allegory); on the other hand, he then creates something uniquely new and amusing out of the cliché elements. The originality of his tale is not due to its subject matter, which is traditional, but rather to his masterly reinterpretation – or rather, reinvention – of the old and familiar episode of the cock that gets caught by the fox, yet manages to escape death. In contrast to the poet of *The Vox and the Wolf*, who gives us no explicit hints towards an allegorical interpretation of his tale, CHAUCER hugely enjoys and extensively exploits the various possibilities which the old tale of the cock and the fox offers him. In the guise of the Nun's Priest, he sets out to remould the raw material of the beast epic episode.

The originality of CHAUCER's achievement becomes clear when it is contrasted with *The Vox and the Wolf*. There, the anonymous poet also takes an episode from the *Roman de Renart* as his starting point and fashions it into a pleasing and funny tale; yet, in contrast to the Nun's Priest, this narrator never so much as hints at its possible allegorical or moral dimensions and thus forfeits the opportunity of ensuring that his narrative will be considered something more than 'just' a comic tale in the beast epic tradition. CHAUCER's Nun's Priest, however, rises to the challenge. The clay of the beast epic episode, while retaining and even increasing its fun element, is formed into a tale of potential moral and allegorical import, so that CHAUCER has his narrator advise the audience: "Taketh the moralitee" (Pearsall 1983:255, l. 4630). Yet, the true ingeniousness of CHAUCER's concept can be only appreciated if one realizes that the very moral and allegorical dimensions which are so hastily pointed out by the narrator concerned do not neutralize or even contradict the fundamental comic quality of the tale. On the contrary, CHAUCER puts them to use in contributing to the overall amusement of the audience. The 'delectare' is no longer merely a means towards the clearly circumscribed 'prodesse', but has become an end in itself. Thus, it took centuries and a poet of CHAUCER's stature to achieve the successful integration of the *Physiologus* heritage into secular English vernacular animal literature, but the straightforward and religiously motivated interpretation is now part of a greater and much more sophisticated view of the world.

2. The Three Traditions after 1400

As mentioned before, the *Physiologus* and the bestiary traditions remain present throughout the Middle Ages. Yet, CAXTON's translation and publication of *The History of Reynard the Fox* (1481, translated from the Dutch *Die Hystorie van Reynaert die Vos*), as well as his translation of the fables of *Æsop* (1484), mark the final emancipation of English vernacular literature from the predominance of the *Physiologus* and the bestiary traditions. Thus, even though CAXTON points out the general moralistic usefulness of the Reynard stories in his preface (Blake 1970:6), and to some extent asks his (reading) audience to 'take the moralitee', he presents unadulterated beast epic fun.[605] He may, therefore, be rightly considered a somewhat less sophisticated fifteenth century counterpart to CHAUCER's Nun's Priest. At the same time, however, the allegorical mode of thinking lives on, as can be seen in the allegorized beast fables of the Scottish poet ROBERT HENRYSON (fl. 1480).[606] Thanks to their general nature, the *Physiologus* animals also survived the decline of their original carrier. When the allegorical mode of thinking began to be replaced by the more scientific methods of experiment and first-hand observation, many of the *Physiologus* animals had already secured new territories for themselves. Thus, we find them not only in poetry (see SHAKESPEARE's *The Phoenix and the Turtle*, G.B. Evans 1974:1795-1798) and the emblematic tradition (see CAMERARIUS 1590-1604), but also, to some extent, in the treatises of the sixteenth and seventeenth century naturalists ULYSSIS ALDROVANDI

---

605 In the preface to his *Reynard the Fox* (Blake 1970:6), CAXTON writes: "In this historye ben wreton the parables/goode lerynge, and dyuerse poyntes to be merkyd, by whiche poyntes men maye lerne to come to the subtyl knoweleche of suche thynges as dayly ben vsed[.] [....] Thenne who that wyll haue the very vnderstandyng of this mater, he muste ofte and many tymes rede in thys boke and ernestly and diligently marke wel that he redeth/For it is sette subtylly[.]"

606 Thus, some of *The Morall Fabillis of Esope the Phrygian* (C. Elliott 1963:1-89) are interpreted in a religious, allegorical fashion. See, for example, *The Preiching of the Swallow* (C. Elliott 1963:49-58), *The Taill of the Foxe, that begylit the Wolf, in the schadow of the Mone* (C. Elliott 1963:67-74), and *The Taill of the Paddok and the Mous* (C. Elliott 1963:83-89).

(†1605 Bologna) and EDWARD TOPSELL (†1638?).[607] The latter based his works on CONRAD GESNER's (1516-1565) *Historia animalium*, which in turn incorporated zoological knowledge both from Antiquity and from the Middle Ages. These few, randomly selected examples illustrate the fact that traces of the *Physiologus* and the bestiary traditions survived the waning of the Middle Ages, even though the heyday of the allegorical interpretation was over; and even today, we still find relics of this once so influential tradition in art, literature, and, not least, everyday language – as expressions like 'to lick into shape' or 'like a phoenix from the ashes' testify.[608]

The bird debate tradition produced not only 'pure bird poems', such as DUNBAR's *The Merle and the Nightingale* (late fifteenth century), but also quite a few poems which have a human being and a bird as their protagonists.[609] The genre survived relatively unchanged into the Renaissance, as the two poems of *The Parliament of Birds* and *The Harmony of Birds* (both in Andrew 1984) prove.[610] It influenced later poets to varying degrees, yet seems to have disappeared from modern poetry.[611]

---

607 Thus we find, for example in ALDROVANDI's *Ornithologiae, Hoc Est de Avibus Historiae Libri XII* (Bononiae 1599), not only moral interpretations of the birds (see, for example, the "Moralia" to the vulture-chapter in ALDROVANDI 1599:257), but also whole chapters on mythological beings, like «De sirenibus» (ALDROVANDI 1599:623-628) and «De Phoenice» (ALDROVANDI 1599:816-832). In TOPSELL (1607), the moral interpretations are omitted, but some of the more fabulous beasts are still included. See, for example, the chapters «Of the Mantichora» (1607:442) or «Of the Ichneumon» (1607:448-452), which include bestiary lore.

608 The expression 'to lick into shape' originates from the *Physiologus* chapter on the bear: the she-bear supposedly gives birth to shapeless lumps and thus has to lick her offspring into the desired shape.

609 Thus, Andrew (1984:28) lists *The Dialogue between the Poet and the Bird* (c. 1460), the fifteenth century *The Clerk and the Nightingale*, LYDGATE's *The Churl and the Bird*, and *The Nichtingall and the Kynd Cheild* (c. 1500), though not all of these poems can be called debates proper.

610 Of these two poems, *The Parliament of Birds* is very close to the debate genre proper, whereas *The Harmony of Birds*, written as a kind of mass-parody, cannot be considered to be a debate any more.

611 Munsterberg's (1980) collection of bird poetry includes two later poems that seem to have been infiuenced by the bird debate tradition, namely the dialogic poem *The Turtle and the Sparrow* (Munsterberg 1980:219-220) by MATTHEW PRIOR (1664-1721) and the debate *Goose and Swan* (Munsterberg 1980:235-236) by EDWARD MOORE (1712-1757). Also THOMAS YALDEN's (1671-1736) short fable *The Nightingale and the Cuckow* (French 1967, volume 3:345) contains debate elements.

Finally, the beast fable and beast epic traditions retained their popularity in England throughout the ages into modern times. The Aesopian animal fable, in particular, attracted a host of poets, translators, and editors throughout the centuries, a development which has even continued into our century, which abounds with new translations and 'retellings' of AESOP's fables.[612]

The main representative of the beast epic was, and still is, the cycle of stories around Reynard the Fox. New creations in the beast epic vein, such as THOMAS NASH's (1567-1601) tale of the bear in *Pierce Pennilesse*, or EDMUND SPENSER's (1552-1599) adventures of the ape and the fox in *Posopopoia or Mother Hubberds Tale*, are exceedingly rare.[613] Generally, poetic effort was limited either to producing a versification of CAXTON's translation or to giving a 'moralized' version.[614]

Apart from the beast fable and the beast epic proper, animal protagonists are encountered above all in children's literature. Beginning with JOHN NEWBERY's volume *A Pretty Book of Pictures for Little Masters and Misses* (1752), there issued an unceasing flow of literary works with either animal protagonists and/or animal narrators;[615] and it is also in works belonging to children's literature that the animal fable finds its modified successor. Thus, both KENNETH GRAHAME, in his classic *The Wind in the Willows* (1908), and BEATRIX POTTER in her 'Peter Rabbit' books use "animals as types of human character, and as actors in predominantly social comedy" (Carpenter and Prichard 1984:25). Contemporary writers of 'animal children's literature' are TED HUGHES and BRIAN PATTEN, to name just two.

Yet, apart from the more 'lighthearted' genre of children's literature, there are few works of twentieth century literature which make use of animal protagonists. GEORGE ORWELL's biting political fable *Animal Farm*

---

612 The history of the fable in England up to and including JOHN GAY's translation of AESOP's fables (1726) has been dealt with in detail by Plessow (1906). On the development of both beast fable and beast epic from their beginnings to modern times, see Blackham (1985).

613 See Plessow (1906:lxvii).

614 A 'moralized' version of CAXTON's translation was anonymously published in 1629, under the title *Most Delectable History of Raynard the Fox* (see Plessow 1906:lxix-lxx). This prose work was then put into heroic verse by JOHN SHURLEY in the year 1681, and published under the title *Most Delightful History of Reynard the Fox* (see Plessow 1906:lxxiv). Three years later, an anonymous work with the title *Reynard the Fox, and Reynardine his Son* appeared (see Plessow 1906:lxxv). The year 1701 saw the publication of *The Most Delectable History of Reynard the Fox*, a revised and enlarged reprint of the 1629 edition (see Plessow 1906:lxxx).

615 For an overview of animals in children's literature, see the article «Animal stories» in Carpenter and Prichard (1984:24-25).

(1945) is probably the most important representative of this nowadays small but enduring tradition.

3. Integrated Overview of Medieval English Vernacular 'Animal Literature'

The following illustration attempts to relate the individual works of vernacular English animal literature to each other and to the different sources or influences which shaped them to various degrees. The background pattern indicates the tradition to which the text belongs, the shape of the frame expresses general relationships, and the arrows stand for specific influences.

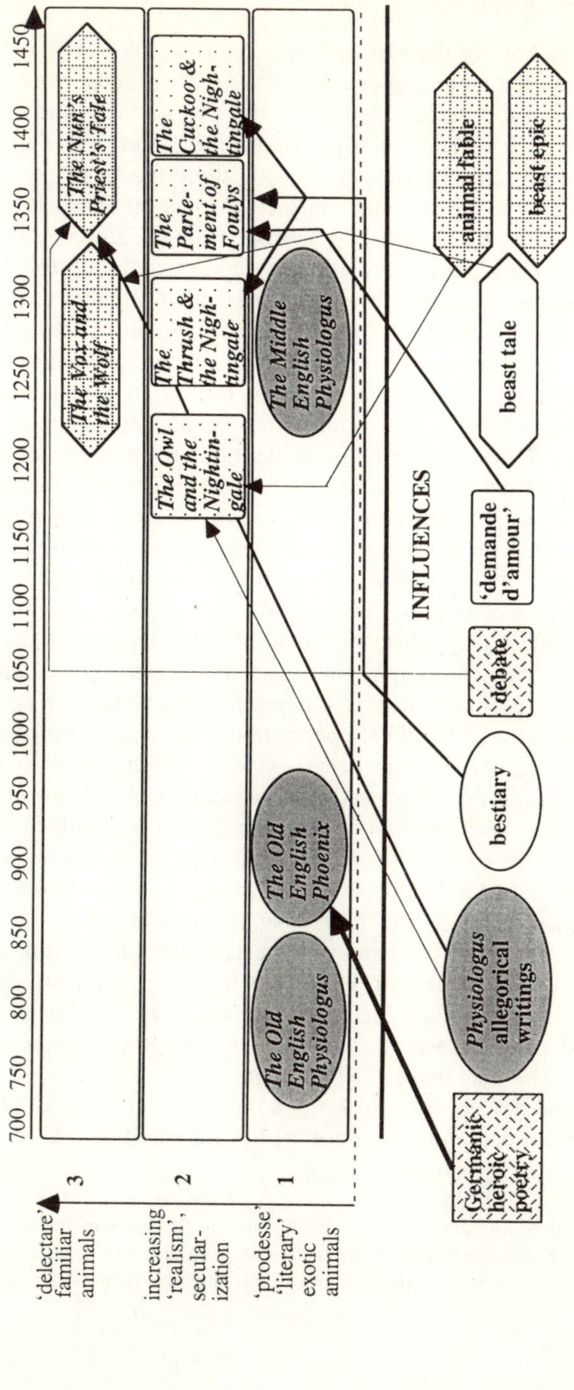
'delectare' familiar animals
increasing 'realism', secular-ization
'prodesse' 'literary' exotic animals
3
2
1
700 750 800 850 900 950 1000 1050 1100 1150 1200 1250 1300 1350 1400 1450
The Vox and the Wolf
The Nun's Priest's Tale
The Owl and the Nightin-gale
The Thrush & the Nigh-tingale
The Parle-ment of Foulys
The Cuckoo & the Nigh-tingale
The Old English Physiologus
The Old English Phoenix
The Middle English Physiologus
INFLUENCES
Germanic heroic poetry
Physiologus allegorical writings
bestiary
debate
'demande d'amour'
beast tale
animal fable
beast epic

The diagram highlights two things.

First, we can clearly discern the three main vernacular literary traditions (1 to 3), namely the animal allegories of the *Physiologus* group, the flock of bird debates, and the representatives of the animal fable and the beast epic traditions.[616] Allegorical writings in general, and *The Physiologus* in particular, are not only represented by the three works of the *Physiologus* tradition, but they also exert their influence upon other works, notably *The Owl and the Nightingale* and *The Nun's Priest's Tale*. Though neither of these poems is a straightforward allegory in the manner of *The Physiologus*, they both nevertheless make (playful) use of their allegorical potential. The situation is rather different in the case of the remaining three bird debates; they do not seem intent on exploiting the allegorical dimension of their protagonists, and yet, they make use of the avian lore provided by the bestiaries, the extended and sometimes secularized successors to *The Physiologus*. Thus, it is the bare 'facts', stripped of any allegorical interpretation, which are of importance in the bird debates that come after *The Owl and the Nightingale*. This is why I have drawn a distinction between the influence of the '*Physiologus*/allegorical writings' on the one hand, and that of the 'bestiary' on the other. The form of the debate, apart from being very well represented by the sub-category of bird debates, also makes itself felt in the debate between Chauntecleer and Pertelote in *The Nun's Priest's Tale*. Similarly, there is a strong element of the 'demande d'amour' in the 'parliamentary' section of *The Parlement of Foulys*, though this by no means turns the whole poem into a 'demande' proper. As regards *The Vox and the Wolf*, there are two facts which speak in favour of a connection between this poem and the shadowy, native 'beast tale' tradition. On the one hand, *The Vox and the Wolf* is the earliest and, for a long time, only representative of the 'beast epic' tradition, which seems to have been mostly unknown to the English vernacular up to the time of CAXTON. On the other hand, the way in which the poet structures his poem and introduces the beast epic names of the heroes suggests an attempt to link up his poem with the fox tales of the native 'beast tale' tradition. The last item on the list of influences, the 'animal fable' tradition, not only contributes to *The Vox and the Wolf* and *The Nun's Priest's Tale*, but it also plays a role in the complexity of *The Owl and the Nightingale*.

Secondly, the development towards a 'lighter' and more secular notion of animal literature becomes apparent within all traditions. This tendency is

---

616 The three poetic-literary traditions established on the basis of the medieval English vernacular texts analysed do not always coincide with the more general medieval literary categories presented in the «Introduction» to this study (see page 7ff.).

mainly due to the establishment of the royal court – and its smaller aristocratic counterparts throughout the country – as the new secular literary centres from the twelfth century on. Even though the religious allegorical way of thinking directly or indirectly exerts its influence on all subsequent works, the aforementioned rise of secular centres of learning promoted an unmistakable trend towards an attitude which attached more importance to the aspect of 'delectare' than to that of 'prodesse'. In spite of their education and cultural training, the courtly circles did not share the point of view and the erudite and scholarly literary predilections of the clerics and monks who made up the primary audience of *The Physiologus* and its ilk. This is reflected in the fact that the 'new' animal poems which are intended for a courtly circle generally exhibit a spirit of playfulness. Their hallmark is no longer the sombre learnedness of the monks, but the carefree sophistication of a cultivated secular audience, whose interests do include moral or religious issues, but not exclusively or even predominantly. This new attitude becomes noticeable even in those works that derive directly from the *Physiologus* tradition, namely the bestiaries. Many of the later European bestiaries are lavishly illustrated and place great emphasis on the curious and exotic aspects of the animals treated, while often neglecting any 'moral' or allegorical teaching. This reflects the fact that the lives of the members of a courtly audience are no longer orientated only towards eternity, but are geared to celebrating the 'hôhe muot', the ideal courtly awareness of life.[617] Of all the poems analysed, it is CHAUCER's contributions that express this new attitude best. They combine secular philosophical and moral traditions with the most recent developments in contemporary courtly literature, and at the same time, they make use of the time-honoured devices of animal protagonists.

Parallel to the increasing 'secularization' of animals in vernacular literature, we notice the growing importance of animals native to western Europe. Taking all the texts of traditions 1 to 3 into consideration, we notice a distinct development away from the 'literary' concept of animals prevalent in the *Physiologus* tradition. This means that the exotic animals which were known only from hearsay are increasingly replaced by representatives of the native animal world, whose connection with everyday reality is less tenuous than that of those beasts which exist only within the limits of a parchment page. This development is due not so much to an increasing interest in the observation of nature, as rather to the nature of the animal protagonist in the genres other than that of *The Physiologus*. Thus, almost all of the animals of the original *Physiologus* are exotic creatures from faraway lands, known

617 On the origin of courtly ideals see Jaeger (1985).

only from written descriptions; and even if less exotic beasts do gain a place among them, the original way of schematically describing each creature and focussing on one or two characteristics backed by the Scriptures or the 'auctores' is also applied to those more familiar animals. In contrast to the *Physiologus* beasts, the protagonists of the beast fables, the beast epics, and also the bird debates are known to most people in western Europe from first-hand experience. It is therefore small wonder that the original *Physiologus* animals exhibit the tendency to turn into religious icons devoid of any life, whereas the 'native' animals retain much of their original vivacity and animal spirit, and thus strike the modern reader as more 'real'. A *Physiologus* animal does not need, and indeed must not have, an individual and thus often anthropomorphic character. Neither does it really interact with the other protagonists. Its function remains limited to possessing a peculiar characteristic which points towards a more fundamental truth on a spiritual level. Yet, it is this very focussing on the additional spiritual dimension which causes the *Physiologus* animal to look comparatively one-dimensional and lifeless. In contrast to this, the protagonists of the beast fables, the beast epics, and also the bird debates often combine the best of both worlds, so to speak. The competent poet will, on the one hand, take the real-life animals as the basis for his protagonists. On the other hand, the allegorical and symbolic dimensions are also used to add additional depth to the characters of the protagonists, as well as to the meaning of the poem as a whole.[618] *The Owl and the Nightingale* and *The Nun's Priest's Tale* are prime examples of the successful combination of these elements; their authors were able to free themselves from the restrictions imposed by the traditional genres. Their gaze is no longer fixed upon eternity and morality but wanders around with a broader interest in this world, and the animal protagonists are no longer mere means of reaching a higher plane, destined to become insignificant as soon as they have served their purpose. Even though there are already signs of a certain fascination with the animals 'per se', even in the earliest texts (see, for example, *The Old English Phoenix*), it took the twin development of secularization and a return to the native animal world to shape such animal characters as 'Chauntecleer' or 'Reneuard' – characters that are able to draw the focus of the poems on to themselves, and which constitute the vital core of a literary work.

At the same time, the 'originality' of the poems increased. Many poets were no longer satisfied merely to translate or closely adapt a Latin source,

---

[618] See Salisbury's (1994:105) observation on the metaphoric use of animals: "[T]his new symbolic emphasis of animals did not displace the previous concrete day-to-day relationship people had with their real animals. That relationship always remained central to the medieval economy; the symbolism was a newly added dimension."

as did the authors of *The Old English Physiologus* and *The Middle English Physiologus*. The poet of *The Owl and the Nightingale*, for example, not only created an entirely original poem – as far as we know – but he also laid the foundation for the new sub-genre of the 'bird debate', and his successors continued and varied this newly-found tradition. Most often, however, the poets freely adapted Latin, French, or even Italian material (as in the case of CHAUCER), while staying within the limits of traditional animal symbolism and recognized genres. It is this continuous give-and-take, this testing-of-the-limits without breaking with the traditions, which is responsible for the genesis of some of the most original animal poems.

Bibliography

Ackermann, Erich. 1991. «(Un-)Tiere und Tiergestaltige in Mythos und Märchen der Antike.» In: Esterl, Arnica and Wilhelm Solms (eds.). 1991. *Tiere und Tiergestaltige im Märchen.* Veröffentlichungen der Europäischen Märchengesellschaft 15. Regensburg: Erich Röth, 48-64.

Actes Du Quatrième Congrès International De Philosophie Médiévale (Université de Montréal 1967): Arts Libéraux et Philosophique Au Moyen Âge. 1969. Montreal: Institut d'études médiévales.

Adolphus, A.E. 1907. «Chauceriana.» *Notes and Queries* 8:202-203.

Aers, David. 1981. «'The Parliament of Fowls': Authority, the Knower and the Known.» *Chaucer Review* 16:1-17.

Aiken, Pauline. 1935. «Vincent of Beauvais and Dame Pertelote's Knowledge of Medicine.» *Speculum* 10:281-287.

Aldrovandi, Ulyssis. 1599. *Ornithologiae, Hoc Est de Avibus Historiae Libri XII.* Bononiae (Bologna): Apud Franciscum de Franciscis Senensem.

- - -. 1606. *De Reliquibus Animalibus Exanguilous Libri Quator, post Mortem Eius Editi.* Bononiae (Bologna): Apud Io. Baptistam Bellagambam.

- - -. 1621. *Quadrupedum Omnium Bisulcornum Historia.* Posthumously published. Bononiae (Bologna): Apud Sebastianum Bonhommium.

- - -. 1634. *Ornithologiae Tomus Alter.* Posthumously published. Bononiae (Bologna): Apud Nicolaum Tebaldinum.

- - -. 1637. *De Quadrupedibus Digitatis Viviparis Libri Tres et de Quadrupedibus Digitatis Oviparis Libri Duo.* Posthumously published. Bononiae (Bologna): Apud Nicolaum Tebaldium.

- - -. 1638. *De Piscibus Libri V et de Cetis Liber Unus.* Posthumously published. Bononiae (Bologna): Apud Nicolaum Thebaldinum.

- - -. 1640. *Serpentum et Draconum Historiae Libri Duo.* Posthumously published. Bononiae (Bologna): Apud Clementem Ferronium.

- - -. 1642. *Monstrorum Historia cum Paralipomenis Historiae Omnium Animalium.* Posthumously published. Bononiae (Bologna): Typis Nicolai Tebaldini.

Allen, Judson Boyce. 1969. «The Ironic Fruyt: Chauntecleer as Figura.» *Studies in Philology* 66:25-35.

Allen, Mark and John H. Fisher. 1987. *The Essential Chaucer: An Annotated Bibliography of Major Modern Studies.* London: Mansell.

Allen, Richard E. 1970. «The Voices of 'The Owl and the Nightingale'.» *Studies in Medieval Culture* 3:52-58.

Allison, Alexander W. et al. (eds.). 1983. *The Norton Anthology of Poetry.* Third edition. First edition 1970. New York and London: W.W. Norton.

Anderson, J.J. (ed.). 1974. *Chaucer: The Canterbury Tales. A Casebook.* London: The Macmillan Press.

Anderson, M.D. 1954. *Misericords: Medieval Life in English Woodcarving.* Harmondsworth: Penguin Books.

Andrew, Malcolm (ed.). 1984. *Two Early Renaissance Bird Poems: The Harmony of Birds / The Parliament of Birds.* The Renaissance English Text Society and the Newberry Library. Washington: The Folger Shakespeare Library.

Atkins, J.W.H. 1940. «A Note on 'The Owl and the Nightingale'.» *Modern Language Review* 35:55-56.

- - - (ed.). 1922. *The Owl and the Nightingale.* Cambridge: At the University Press.

Augustinus, Aurelius. 1965. *The City of God against the Pagans.* Translated by Eva Matthews Sanford and William McAllen Green. The Loeb Classical Library. London: Heinemann.

- - -. 1968. *Geist und Buchstabe / De Spiritu et Littera Liber Unus.* Translated by Anselm Forster OSB. Aurelius Augustinus' Werke in deutscher Sprache 15. Paderborn: Ferdinand Schöningh.

- - -. 1983. *Über die Psalmen.* Selected and translated by Hans Urs von Balthasar. Christliche Meister 20. Second edition. Einsiedeln: Johannes.

Bäuml, Franz H. 1980. «Varieties and Consequences of Medieval Literacy and Illiteracy.» *Speculum* 55:234-265.

Baird, Lorrayne Y. 1977. *A Bibliography of Chaucer 1964-1973.* Boston, Massachusetts: G.K. Hall.

Baird-Lange, Lorrayne Y. and Hildegard Schnuttgen. 1988. *A Bibliography of Chaucer 1974-1985.* Cambridge: D.S. Brewer.

Baker, Donald C. 1968. «'The Parliament of Fowls'.» In: Rowland, Beryl (ed.). 1968. *A Companion to Chaucer Studies.* Toronto/New York/London: Oxford University Press, 355-369.

Baldwin, Anne B. 1967. «Henry II and 'The Owl and the Nightingale'.» *Journal of English and Germanic Philology* 66:207-229.

Balss, Heinrich. 1947. *Albertus Magnus als Biologe: Werk und Ursprung.* Grosse Naturforscher 1. Stuttgart: Wissenschaftliche Verlagsgesellschaft.

Barnes, Jonathan (ed.). 1984. *The Complete Works of Aristotle.* Volume 1. The revised Oxford translation. Bollingen Series 71:2. Princeton, New Jersey: Princeton University Press.

Bartas, Guillaume de Saluste du. 1981. *La Sepmaine.* Edited by Yvonne Bellenger. Original edition 1581. Paris: Librairie Nizet.

Bately, Janet M. (ed.). 1986. *MS A.* Volume 3 of *The Anglo-Saxon Chronicle. A Collaborative Edition.* Cambridge: D.S. Brewer.

Baugh, Albert C. 1948a. «The Middle English Period (1100-1500).» In: Baugh, Albert C. (ed.). 1948b. *A Literary History of England.* New York: Appleton-Century-Crofts, 109-314.

- - -. 1968. *Chaucer.* Goldentree Bibliographies in Language and Literature. New York: Appleton-Century-Crofts.

- - - (ed.). 1948b. *A Literary History of England.* New York: Appleton-Century-Crofts.

Bausinger, Hermann. 1991. «Die moralischen Tiere.» In: Esterl, Arnica and Wilhelm Solms (eds.). 1991. *Tiere und Tiergestaltige im Märchen.* Veröffentlichungen der Europäischen Märchengesellschaft 15. Regensburg: Erich Röth, 162-175.

Bazire, Joyce. 1953. «'The Fox and the Goose'.» *English Studies* 34:163-164.

Beck, Heinrich. 1965. *Das Ebersignum im Germanischen: Ein Beitrag zur germanischen Tiersymbolik*. Quellen und Forschungen zur Sprach- und Kulturgeschichte der germanischen Völker NF 16. Berlin: Walter de Gruyter.

- - -. 1970. «Die Tiere der Walstatt in den eddischen Liedern.» In: Schwab, Ute (ed.). 1970. *Das Tier in der Dichtung*. Heidelberg: Carl Winter, 55-73 and 259-267.

Benassai, Lucia. 1991. «Schlangenhaut verleiht einen klaren Blick.» *Die Waage* 30/4:149-154.

Bennett, J.A.W. 1957. *The Parlement of Foules: An Interpretation*. Oxford: At the Clarendon Press.

- - -. 1979. «Some Second Thoughts on 'The Parlement of Foules'.» In: Vasta, Edward and Zacharias P. Thundy (eds.). 1979. *Chaucerian Problems and Perspectives*. Essays presented to Paul E. Beichner. Notre Dame and London: University of Notre Dame Press, 132-146.

- - - and G.V. Smithers (eds.). 1968. *Early Middle English Verse and Prose*. Second edition. First edition 1966. Oxford: Clarendon Press.

Benson, Larry D. (ed.). 1987. *The Riverside Chaucer*. Third edition, based on Robinson, F.N. (ed.). 1966. *The Works of Geoffrey Chaucer*. Boston: Houghton Mifflin. Reprinted 1988. Oxford: Oxford University Press.

Bercovitch, Sacvan. 1966. «Clerical Satire in 'The Fox and the Wolf'.» *Journal of English and Germanic Philology* 65:287-294.

Bergner, Heinz. 1973. «'The Fox and the Wolf' und die Gattung des Tierepos in der mittelenglischen Literatur.» *Germanisch-Romanische Monatsschrift* NF 23:268-285.

Berriot, François. 1990. «Symbolisme de l'Animal dans les Traités d'Interprétation des Songes à la Fin du Moyen Age.» In: Jones-Davies, M.T. (ed.). 1990. *Le Monde Animal au Temps de la Renaissance*. Centre de Recherches sur la Renaissance, Université de Paris-Sorbonne: Jean Touzot, 173-187.

Besserman, Lawrence L. 1977. «Chaucerian Word Play: The Nun's Priest and his 'Womman Divyne'.» *Chaucer Review* 12:68-73.

Bethurum, Dorothy. 1959. «Chaucer's Point of View as Narrator in the Love Poems.» First published in *Publications of the Modern Language Association of America* 74:511-520. Reprinted in: Schoeck, Richard J. and Jerome Taylor (eds.). 1961. *Chaucer Criticism Vol. II: Troilus and Criseyde and The Minor Poems*. Notre Dame and London: University of Notre Dame Press, 211-231.

- - - (ed.). 1960. *Critical Approaches to Medieval Literature*. Selected Papers from the English Institute, 1958-1959. New York and London: Columbia University Press.

Biblia Sacra Iuxta Vulgatam Versionem. 1983. Third edition. Edited by Bonifatius Fischer OSB, Johannes Gribomont OSB, H.F.D. Sparks, and W. Thiele. First edition 1969. Stuttgart: Deutsche Bibelgesellschaft.

Birney, Earle. 1985. *Essays on Chaucerian Irony*. Edited, with an essay on irony, by Beryl Rowland. Toronto: University of Toronto Press.

Bishop, Ian. 1979. «'The Nun's Priest's Tale' and the Liberal Arts.» *Review of English Studies* 30:257-267.

Blackham, H.J. 1985. *The Fable as Literature*. London and Dover: The Athlone Press.

Blake, Norman F. 1962. «Some Problems of the Interpretation and Translation in the OE 'Phoenix'.» *Anglia* 80:50-62.

- - -. 1973. *Caxton's Own Prose*. London: Andre Deutsch.

- - -. 1975. «Reynard the Fox in England.» In: Rombauts, E. and A. Welkenhuysen (eds.). 1975. *Aspects of the Medieval Animal Epic: Proceedings of the International Conference: Louvain, May 15-17, 1972.* Leuven/The Hague: University Press/Martinus Nijhoff, 53-65.

- - - (ed.). 1970. *The History of Reynard the Fox. Translated from the Dutch Original by William Caxton.* Early English Text Society Original Series 263. London: Oxford University Press.

- - - (ed.). 1990. *The Phoenix.* Second edition. First edition 1964. Exeter: University of Exeter Press.

Blamires, Alcuin, with Karen Pratt and C.W. Marx (eds.). 1992. *Woman Defamed and Woman Defended.* Oxford: Clarendon Press.

Bloomfield, Morton W. 1958. «Symbolism in Medieval Literature.» *Modern Philology* 56/2:73-81.

- - -. 1979. «The Wisdom of the 'Nun's Priest's Tale'.» In: Vasta, Edward and Zacharias P. Thundy (eds.). 1979. *Chaucerian Problems and Perspectives.* Essays presented to Paul E. Beichner. Notre Dame and London: University of Notre Dame Press, 70-82.

Böker, Uwe, Manfred Markus, and Rainer Schöwerling (eds.). *The Living Middle Ages: Studies in Mediaeval English Literature and Its Tradition.* 'Festschrift' for Karl Heinz Göller. Stuttgart: Belser.

Bonjour, Adrien. 1957. «'Beowulf' and the Beasts of Battle.» *Publications of the Modern Language Association of America* 72:563-573.

Boone, Lalia Phipps. 1949. «Chauntecleer and Partlet Identified.» *Modern Language Notes* 64:78-81.

Boone, Laurel. 1985. «The Relationship Between 'The Owl and the Nightingale' and Marie de France's 'Lais' and 'Fables'.» *English Studies in Canada* 11:157-178.

Borst, Arno. 1991. *Lebensformen im Mittelalter.* Eleventh edition. First edition 1973. Frankfurt on the Main and Berlin: Ullstein.

Bossard, Robert. 1991. «Die Tiersymbolik im Traum.» In: Michel, Paul (ed.). 1991b. *Tiersymbolik.* Schriften zur Symbolforschung 7. Bern: Peter Lang, 13-35.

Bossy, Michel-André (ed. and trans.). 1987. *Medieval Debate Poetry: Vernacular Works.* Garland Library of Medieval Literature 52, Series A. New York and London: Garland.

Bosworth, Joseph and T. Northcote Toller (eds.). 1882. *An Anglo-Saxon Dictionary.* Oxford: At the Clarendon Press.

Bouard, Michel de. 1930. «Encyclopédies Médiévales: Sur la 'Connaissance de la Nature et du Monde' au Moyen Age.» *Revue des Questions Historiques.* Series 3/16:258-304.

Bowers, R.H. 1952. «The Middle English 'The Fox and the Goose'.» *Journal of English and Germanic Philology* 51:393-394.

Bowra, C.M. 1952. *Heroic Poetry.* London: MacMillan.

Boyd, Heather. 1978. «Chauntecleer and the Eagle.» *English Studies in Africa* 21:65-69.

Braddy, Haldeen. 1931. «'The Parlement of Foules': A New Proposal.» *Publications of the Modern Language Association of America* 46:1007-1019.

- - -. 1935. «The Historical Background of the 'Parlement of Foules'.» *Review of English Studies* 11:204-209.

- - -. 1953. «Chaucer's Comic Valentine.» *Modern Language Notes* 68:232-234.

Bradley, S.A.J. (ed. and trans.). 1982. *Anglo-Saxon Poetry.* Everyman's Library. London: Dent.

Brandl, A. and O. Zippel (eds.). 1917. *Mittelenglische Sprach- und Literaturproben.* Berlin: Weidmannsche Buchhandlung.

Breier, W. 1910. *Eule und Nachtigall: Eine Untersuchung der Überlieferung und der Sprache, der örtlichen und zeitlichen Entstehung des me. Gedichts.* Studien zur englischen Philologie 39. Halle: Max Niemeyer.

Brewer, D[erek] S. 1958. «The Genre of the 'Parlement of Foules'.» *Modern Language Notes* 53:321-326.

- - - (ed.). 1972. *Geoffrey Chaucer: The Parlement of Foulys.* Old and Middle English Texts. Second edition. First edition 1960. Manchester: Manchester University Press.

Bridges, Margaret. 1992. «Of Myths and Maps: the Anglo-Saxon Cosmographer's Europe.» In: Engler, Balz (ed.). 1992. *Writing & Culture.* SPELL 6. Tübingen: Gunter Narr, 69-84.

Bright, James W. 1902. «Minor Notes on Chaucer.» *Modern Language Notes* 17:278-280.

Brinkmann, Hennig. 1970. «Die 'Zweite Sprache' und die Dichtung des Mittelalters.» In: Zimmermann, Albert (ed.). 1970. *Methoden in Wissenschaft und Kunst des Mittelalters.* Miscellanea Mediaevalia 7. Berlin: Walter de Gruyter, 155-171.

- - -. 1974. «Die Zeichenhaftigkeit der Sprache, des Schrifttums und der Welt im Mittelalter.» *Zeitschrift für deutsche Philologie* 93:1-11.

Broek, R. van den. 1972. *The Myth of the Phoenix (According to Classical and Early Christian Traditions).* Leiden: E.J. Brill.

Broes, Arthur T. 1963. «Chaucer's Disgruntled Cleric: 'The Nun's Priest's Tale'.» *Publications of the Modern Language Association of America* 78:156-162.

Bronson, Bertrand H. 1948. «'The Parlement of Foules' Revisited.» *English Literary History* 15:247-260.

Brook, G.L. (ed.). 1968. *The Harley Lyrics.* Fourth edition. First edition 1956. Manchester: Manchester University Press.

Brosnahan, Leger. 1961. «Does the Nun's Priest's Epilogue Contain a Link?» *Studies in Philology* 58:468-482.

Brown, Carleton. 1920. «Mulier est hominis confusio.» *Modern Language Notes* 35:479-482.

- - - (ed.). 1924. *Religious Lyrics of the XIVth Century.* Oxford: At the Clarendon Press.

Brown, Emerson Jr. 1975. «Priapus and the 'Parlement of Foulys'.» *Studies in Philology* 72:258-274.

Brown, P.R., G.R. Crampton, and F.C. Robinson (eds.). 1986. *Modes of Interpretation in Old English Literature.* Essays in honour of Stanley B. Greenfield. Toronto: University of Toronto Press.

Brunner-Traut, Emma. 1968. «Ägyptische Mythen im Physiologus (zu Kapitel 26, 25 und 11).» In: Helch, Wolfgang (ed.). 1968. *Festschrift für Siegfried Schott zu seinem 70. Geburtstag.* Wiesbaden: Otto Harrassowitz, 13-44.

Bryan, W.F. and Germaine Dempster (eds.). 1941. *Sources and Analogues of Chaucer's Canterbury Tales.* Reprinted 1958. London: Routledge and Kegan Paul.

Burger, Harald, Alois M. Haas, and Peter von Matt (eds.). 1992. *Verborum Amor: Studien zur Geschichte und Kunst der deutschen Sprache.* 'Festschrift' for Stefan Sonderegger on the occasion of his 65th birthday. Berlin and New York: Walter de Gruyter.

Burrow, J.A. 1982. *Medieval Writers and Their Work: Middle English Literature and Its Background (1100 - 1500).* Oxford: Oxford University Press.

Camerarius, Joachim. 1590-1604. *Symbola et Emblemata.* Edited by Wolfgang Harms and Ulla-Britta Kuechen. Naturalis Historia Bibliae: Schriften zur biblischen Naturkunde des 16.-18. Jahrhunderts 2/1-2. Two volumes. Reprint of the original edition with an added introduction and register, 1986 (part 1) and 1988 (part 2). Graz: Akademische Druck- und Verlagsanstalt.

Cargo, Robert T. and Emanuel J. Michel Jr. (eds.). 1972. *Studies in Honor of Alfred G. Engstrom.* University of North Carolina Studies in the Romance Languages and Literatures 124. Chapel Hill: University of North Carolina Press.

Carmody, Francis J. 1938. «'De bestiis et aliis rebus' and the Latin Physiologus.» *Speculum* 13:153-159.

Carpenter, Humphrey and Mari Prichard. 1984. *The Oxford Companion to Children's Literature.* Oxford and New York: Oxford University Press.

Carson, M. Angela O.S.U. 1967. «Rhetorical Structure in 'The Owl and the Nightingale'.» *Speculum* 42:92-103.

Cawley, A.C. 1951. «Astrology in 'The Owl and the Nightingale'.» *Modern Language Review* 46:161-174.

Céard, Jean. 1977. *La Nature et les Prodiges: L'Insolite au XVIe Siècle, en France.* Geneva: Librairie Droz.

Chamberlain, David. 1970. «The Music of the Spheres and 'The Parlement of Foules'.» *Chaucer Review* 5:32-56.

Cherry, John (ed.). 1995. *Mythical Beasts.* London: The British Museum Press

Cizek, Alexander. 1981. «Ungeheuer und magische Lebewesen in der 'Epistula Alexandri ad Magistrum Suum Aristotelem de Situ Indiae'.» In: Goossens, Jan and Timothy Sodmann (eds.). 1981. *International Beast Epic, Fable and Fabliau Colloquium: 1979, Münster.* Niederdeutsche Studien 30. Cologne and Vienna: Böhlau, 78-94.

Clark, Anne. 1975. *Beasts and Bawdy.* London: J.M. Dent and Sons.

Clark, George. 1965. «Chauntecleer and Deduit.» *English Language Notes* 2, Supplement:168-171.

Clark, Willene B. and Meradith T. McMunn (eds.). 1989. *Beasts and Birds of the Middle Ages: The Bestiary and Its Legacy.* Philadelphia: University of Pennsylvania Press.

Clemen, Wolfgang. 1938. *Der junge Chaucer: Grundlagen und Entwicklung seiner Dichtung.* Kölner Anglistische Arbeiten 33. Bochum-Langendreer: Heinrich Pöppinghaus.

Clerq, Charles de. 1970. «La Nature et le Sens dú 'De avibus' d'Hugues de Fouilloy.» In: Zimmermann, Albert (ed.). 1970. *Methoden in Wissenschaft und Kunst des Mittelalters.* Miscellanea Mediaevalia 7. Berlin: Walter de Gruyter, 279-302.

Colgrave, Bertram. 1966. «'The Owl and the Nightingale' and the Good Man From Rome.» *English Language Notes* 4:1-4.

Collins, Arthur H. 1913. *Symbolism of Animals and Birds Represented in English Church Architecture.* London: Sir Isaac Pitman and Sons.

Conlee, John W. (ed.). 1991. *Middle English Debate Poetry: A Critical Anthology.* East Lansing: Colleagues Press.

Cook, Albert S. 1906. «Chaucer 'Parl. Foules' 353.» *Modern Language Notes* 21:111-112.

- - -. 1924. «Chaucer and Venantius Fortunatus.» *Modern Language Notes* 39:376-378.

- - - and Chauncey B. Tinker (eds.). 1902. *Select Translations from Old English Poetry.* Reprinted 1970. Westport, Connecticut: Greenwood Press.

Coote, Stephen. 1985. *The Nun's Priest's Tale.* Penguin Masterstudies. Harmondsworth: Penguin.

Cordasco, Francesco. 1949. «The Old English Physiologus: Its Problems.» *Modern Language Quarterly* 10:351-355.

Coss, Peter. 1993. *The Knight in Medieval England: 1000-1400.* Stroud: Alan Suton.

Coulton, G.G. 1922. «'The Owl and the Nightingale'.» *Modern Language Review* 17:69-71.

Cowgill, Bruce Kent. 1975. «The 'Parlement of Foules' and the Body Politic.» *Journal of English and Germanic Philology* 74:315-335.

Crawford, S.J. and N.R. Ker (eds.). *The Old English Version of the Heptateuch, Ælfric's Treatise on the Old and New Testament, and His Preface to Genesis.* Early English Text Society Original Series 160. Reprinted 1969. London: Oxford University Press.

Crawford, William R. 1967. *Bibliography of Chaucer 1954-1963.* Seattle and London: Washington University Press.

Creed, Robert P. (ed.). 1967. *Old English Poetry: Fifteen Essays.* Providence, Rhode Island: Brown University Press.

Cronin, Grover Jr. 1941. «The Bestiary and the Mediaeval Mind – Some Complexities.» *Modern Language Quarterly* 2:191-198.

Cross, J.E. 1967. «The Conception of the Old English 'Phoenix'.» In: Creed, Robert P. (ed.). 1967. *Old English Poetry: Fifteen Essays.* Providence, Rhode Island: Brown University Press, 129-152.

Crotch, W.J.B. 1928. *The Prologues and Epilogues of William Caxton.* Reprinted 1956. Early English Text Society Original Series 176. London: Oxford University Press.

Curley, Michael J. (ed. and trans.). 1979. *Physiologus.* Austin and London: University of Texas Press.

Curry, Walter Clyde. 1960. *Chaucer and the Medieval Sciences.* Second edition. First edition 1926. New York: Barnes and Noble.

Curtius, Ernst Robert. 1961. *Europäische Literatur und lateinisches Mittelalter.* Third edition. First edtion 1948. Bern and Munich: Francke.

Dahlberg, Charles. 1954. «Chaucer's Cock and Fox.» *Journal of English and Germanic Philology* 53:277-290.

Damon, Phillip W. 1952. «'The Parlement of Foules' and the 'Pavo'.» *Modern Language Notes* 67:520-524.

Dargan, E.P. 1906. «Cock and Fox: A Critical Study of the History and Sources of the Mediaeval Fable.» *Modern Philology* 4:38-65.

Darwin, Charles. 1966. *Die Abstammung des Menschen.* Translated by Heinrich Schmidt-Jena from the second revised edition (1874) of *The Descent of Man.* Kröners Taschenbuchausgabe Band 28. Stuttgart: Alfred Kröner.

Davies, R.T. (ed.). 1963. *Medieval English Lyrics: A Critical Anthology.* London: Faber and Faber.

Dawson, Christopher. 1934. *Mediaeval Religion (The Forwood Lectures 1934) and Other Essays.* London: Sheed and Ward.

Defourny, Michel. 1981. «'Pancatantra' et Pensée Brahmanique.» In: Goossens, Jan and Timothy Sodmann (eds.). 1981. *International Beast Epic, Fable and Fabliau Colloquium: 1979, Münster.* Niederdeutsche Studien 30. Cologne and Vienna: Böhlau, 95-101.

Dickins, Bruce and R.M. Wilson (eds.). 1951. *Early Middle English Texts.* Cambridge: Bowes and Bowes.

Dieckmann, Emma M. 1938. «Moore feelynge than had Boece.» *Modern Language Notes* 53:177-180.

Dithmar, Reinhard. 1971. *Die Fabel: Geschichte, Struktur, Didaktik.* UTB 73. Paderborn: Ferdinand Schöningh.

Doane, A.N. (ed.). 1978. *Genesis A.* Madison: University of Wisconsin Press.

Dobbie, Elliott van Kirk (ed.). 1942. *The Anglo-Saxon Minor Poems.* Volume 6 of *The Anglo-Saxon Poetic Records: A Collective Edition.* London: Routledge and Kegan Paul.

- - - (ed.). 1954. *Beowulf and Judith.* Volume 4 of *The Anglo-Saxon Poetic Records: A Collective Edition.* London: Routledge and Kegan Paul.

Donahue, Charles. 1960. «Patristic Exegesis in the Criticism of Medieval Literature: Summation.» In: Bethurum, Dorothy (ed.). 1960. *Critical Approaches to Medieval Literature.* Selected Papers from the English Institute, 1958-1959. New York and London: Columbia University Press, 61-82 and 160-162.

Donaldson, E. Talbot. 1960. «Patristic Exegesis in the Criticism of Medieval Literature: The Opposition.» In: Bethurum, Dorothy (ed.). 1960. *Critical Approaches to Medieval Literature.* Selected Papers from the English Institute, 1958-1959. New York and London: Columbia University Press, 1-26 and 155-157.

- - -. 1980. «Venus and the Mother of Romulus: The 'Parliament of Fowls' and the 'Pervigilium Veneris'.» *Chaucer Review* 14:313-318.

Donovan, Mortimer J. 1953. «The 'Moralite' of the Nun's Priest's Sermon.» *Journal of English and Germanic Philology* 52:498-508.

- - -. 1956. «The Owl as Religious Altruist in 'The Owl and the Nightingale'.» *Mediaeval Studies* 18:207-214.

Douglas, T.W. 1928. «What is the 'Parlement of Foules'?» *Modern Language Notes* 43:378-384.

Dubs, Kathleen E. and Stoddard Malarkey. 1978. «The Frame of Chaucer's 'Parlement'.» *Chaucer Review* 13:16-24.

Eadie, J. 1986. «The Authorship of 'The Owl and the Nightingale': A Reappraisal.» *English Studies* 67:471-477.

Economou, George D. 1972. *The Goddess Natura in Medieval Literature.* Cambridge, Massachusetts: Harvard University Press.

Eden, P.T. (ed. and trans.). 1972. *Theobaldi 'Physiologus'.* Mittellateinische Studien und Texte 6. Leiden and Cologne: E.J. Brill.

Eisenstein, Herbert. 1990. *Einführung in die arabische Zoographie.* Berlin: Dietrich Reimer.

Elliott, Charles (ed.). 1963. *Robert Henryson: Poems.* Oxford: At the Clarendon Press.

Elliott, Ralph W. 1965. *Notes on English Literature: The Nun's Priest's Tale / The Pardoner's Tale.* Reprinted 1982. Southampton: The Camelot Press.

Emerson, Oliver Farrar. 1910. «The Suitors in Chaucer's 'Parlement of Foules'.» *Modern Philology* 8:45-62.

- - -. 1911. «The Suitors in the 'Parlement of Foules' again.» *Modern Language Notes* 26:109-111.

- - -. 1914. «What is the 'Parlement of Foules'?» *Journal of English and Germanic Philology* 13:566-582.

---. 1923. «Some Notes on Chaucer and some Conjectures.» *Philological Quarterly* 2:81-95.

---. 1926. «Originality in Old English Poetry.» *Review of English Studies* 2:18-31.

Engler, Balz (ed.). 1992. *Writing & Culture*. SPELL 6. Tübingen: Gunter Narr.

Entzminger, Robert L. 1975. «The Pattern of Time in 'The Parlement of Foules'.» *Journal of Medieval and Renaissance Studies* 5:1-11.

Erdmann, Oskar (ed.). 1957. *Otfrids Evangelienbuch.* Altdeutsche Textbibliothek 49. Third edition, revised by Ludwig Wolff. First edition ?. Tübingen: Max Niemeyer.

Erzgräber, Willi (ed.). 1983. *Geoffrey Chaucer.* Wege der Forschung 253. Darmstadt: Wissenschaftliche Buchgesellschaft.

--- and Sabine Volk (eds.). 1988. *Mündlichkeit und Schriftlichkeit im englischen Mittelalter.* Script Oralia 5. Tübingen: Gunter Narr.

Esterl, Arnica and Wilhelm Solms (eds.). 1991. *Tiere und Tiergestaltige im Märchen.* Veröffentlichungen der Europäischen Märchengesellschaft 15. Regensburg: Erich Röth.

Evans, E.P. 1906. *The Criminal Prosecution and Capital Punishment of Animals.* London: William Heinemann.

Evans, G. Blakemore (ed.). 1974. *The Riverside Shakespeare.* Boston: Houghton Mifflin.

Everett, Dorothy. 1955. «Chaucer's Love Visions, with Particular Reference to the 'Parlement of Foules'.» In: Kean, Patricia (ed.). 1955. *Essays on Middle English Literature by Dorothy Everett.* Oxford: At the Clarendon Press, 97-114.

Farnham, Willard Edward. 1917. «The Sources of Chaucer's 'Parlement of Foules'.» *Publications of the Modern Language Association of America* 32:492-518.

---. 1920. «The Contending Lovers.» *Publications of the Modern Language Association of America* 35:247-323.

Ferguson, George. 1954. *Signs and Symbols in Christian Art.* London: Oxford University Press.

Ferruolo, Stephen C. 1984. «The Twelfth-Century Renaissance.» In: Treadgold, Warren (ed.). 1984. *Renaissances Before the Renaissance: Cultural Revivals of Late Antiquity and the Middle Ages.* Stanford: Stanford University Press, 114-143.

Fink, Hanno. 1969. *Die sieben Todsünden in der mittelalterlichen erbaulichen Literatur.* Britannica et Americana 17. Hamburg: Cram and de Gruyter.

Finkelstein, Dorothee. 1970. «On the Motion of the Heart in 'The Owl and the Nightingale'.» *Neuphilologische Mitteilungen* 71:621-635.

Fischer, Andreas. 1994. «'Sumer is cumen in': the seasons of the year in Middle English and Early Modern English.» In: Kastovsky, Dieter (ed.). 1994. *Studies in Early Modern English.* Topics in English Linguistics 13. New York: Mouton de Gruyter, 79-95.

Fischer, Nancy. 1970. «A Handlist of Animal References in Middle English Religious Prose.» *Leeds Studies in English* NS 4:49-110.

Fiske, C.F. 1913. «Animals in Ecclesiastical Literature (650-1500).» *Publications of the Modern Language Association of America* 28:368-87.

Flinn, John. 1963. *Le Roman de Renart Dans la Littérature Française et Dans les Littératures Étrangères au Moyen Âge.* Toronto: University of Toronto Press.

Flint, Valerie I.J. 1988a. *Ideas in the Medieval West: Texts and Their Contexts.* London: Variorum Reprints

- - -. 1988b. «Thoughts about the Context of Some Early Medieval Treatises 'De Natura Rerum'.» In: Flint, Valerie I.J. 1988a. *Ideas in the Medieval West: Texts and Their Contexts.* First published ?. London: Variorum Reprints, item III.

- - -. 1988c. «Monsters and the Antipodes in the Early Middle Ages and Enlightenment.» In: Flint, Valerie I.J. 1988a. *Ideas in the Medieval West: Texts and Their Contexts.* First published ?. London: Variorum Reprints, item IV.

Frank, Lothar. 1971. *Die Physiologus-Literatur des englischen Mittelalters und die Tradition.* Dissertation. Tübingen: Eberhard-Karls-Universität.

Frank, Robert Worth Jr. 1956. «Structure and Meaning in the 'Parlement of Foules'.» *Publications of the Modern Language Association of America* 71:530-539.

Fredericus II. c. 1250. *De Arte Venandi cum Avibus.* Facsimile of the Ms. Pal. Lat. 1071, Bibliotheka Apostolica Vaticana. Published 1969. Two volumes: Volume 1 facsimile, volume 2 commentary by Carl Arnold Willemsen. Graz: Akademische Druck- und Verlagsanstalt.

French, David P. (ed.). 1967. *Minor English Poets 1660-1780.* Ten volumes. A selection from Alexander Chalmer's *The English Poets.* 1810. Twenty-one volumes. New York: Benjamin Bloom.

Frese, Dolores Warwick. 1981. «The 'Nun's Priest's Tale': Chaucer's Identified Master Piece.» *Chaucer Review* 16:330-343.

Frewein, Josef (ed.). 1983. *Das Tier in der menschlichen Kultur.* Zürcher Hochschulforum 5. Zurich: Artemis.

Frey, Hermann Heinrich. 1595. *Therobiblia: Biblisches Thier- Vogel- und Fischbuch.* Leipzig. Edited by Heimo Reinitzer. Naturalis Historia Bibliae: Schriften zur biblischen Naturkunde des 16.-18. Jahrhunderts 1. Reprint of the original edition with an added introduction and register, 1978. Graz: Akademische Druck- und Verlagsanstalt.

Friedman, John Block. 1972. «The 'Nun's Priest's Tale': The Preacher and the Mermaid's Song.» *Chaucer Review* 7:250-266.

- - -. 1981. *The Monstrous Races in Medieval Art and Thought.* Cambridge, Massachusetts: Harvard University Press.

Friedman, William F. and Elizabeth S. Friedman. 1959. «Acrostics, Anagrams, and Chaucer.» *Philological Quarterly* 38:1-20.

Friedmann, Herbert. 1946. *The Symbolic Goldfinch: Its History and Significance in European Devotional Art.* The Bollingen Series 7. Washington: Pantheon Books.

- - -. 1980. *A Bestiary for Saint Jerome: Animal Symbolism in European Religious Art.* Washington: Smithsonian Institution Press.

Fromm, Hans, Wolfgang Harms, and Uwe Ruberg (eds.). 1975. *Verbum et Signum.* Beiträge zur mediävistischen Bedeutungsforschung. 'Festschrift' for Friedrich Ohly. Two volumes. Munich: Wilhelm Fink.

Gadow, Wilhelm. 1909. *Das mittelenglische Streitgedicht 'Eule und Nachtigall'.* Palaestra 55. Berlin: Mayer und Müller.

Gallacher, Patrick. 1976. «Food, Laxatives and Catharsis in Chaucer's 'Nun's Priest's Tale'.» *Speculum* 51:49-68.

Gallick, Susan. 1975. «A Look at Chaucer and His Preachers.» *Speculum* 50:456-476.

- - -. 1977. «Styles of Usage in the 'Nun's Priest's Tale'.» *Chaucer Review* 11:232-247.

Gallo, Ernest. 1971. *The 'Poetria Nova' and Its Sources in Early Rhetorical Doctrine.* The Hague and Paris: Mouton.

Ganzenmüller, Wilhelm. 1914. *Das Naturgefühl im Mittelalter.* Beiträge zur Kulturgeschichte des Mittelalters und der Renaissance 18. Leipzig and Berlin: B.G. Teubner.

Gardner, John. 1977. *The Poetry of Chaucer.* Carbondale and Edwardsville: Southern Illinois University Press.

Gaston III Phoebus, Comte de Foix. c. 1391. *Le Livre de la Chasse.* Facsimile of the MS. Français 616 of the Bibliothèque Nationale Paris. Published 1976. Two volumes: Volume 1 facsimile, volume 2 commentary by Marcel Thomas and François Avril. Translated by Eberhard König and Pierre Comte de Brissac. Codices Selecti Phototypice Impressi: Facsimile 53, Comentarium 53*. Graz: Akademische Druck- und Verlagsanstalt.

Gattiker, Ernst and Luise Gattiker. 1989. *Die Vögel im Volksglauben: eine volkskundliche Sammlung aus verschiedenen europäischen Ländern von der Antike bis heute.* Wiesbaden: Aula.

Gellinek-Schellekens, Josepha E. 1984. *The Voice of the Nightingale in Middle English Poems and Bird Debates.* New York: Peter Lang.

George, Wilma and Brunsdon Yapp. 1991. *The Naming of the Beasts: Natural History in the Medieval Bestiary.* London: Gerald Duckworth.

Gerhardt, Christian. 1981. «Der Phönix auf dem dürren Baum.» In: Harms, Wolfgang and Heimo Reinitzer (eds.). 1981. *Natura loquax.* Mikrokosmos 7. Frankfurt on the Main: Peter D. Lang, 73-108.

- - -. 1988. «Gab es im Mittelalter Fabelwesen?» *Wirkendes Wort* 38:156-171.

Gerhardt, Mia I. 1965. «The Ant-Lion: Nature Study and the Interpretation of a Biblical Text, from the Physiologus to Albert the Great.» *Vivarium* 3:1-23.

- - -. 1970. «Zoologie Médiévale: Préoccupation et Procèdés.» In: Zimmermann, Albert (ed.).1970. *Methoden in Wissenschaft und Kunst des Mittelalters.* Miscellania Mediaevalia 7. Berlin: Walter de Gruyter, 231-248.

Gibbons, Robert F. 1954. «Does the Nun's Priest's Epilogue Contain a Link?» *Studies in Philology* 51:21-33.

Glauche, Günter. 1970. *Schullektüre im Mittelalter: Entstehung und Wandlungen des Lektürekanons bis 1200 nach Quellen dargestellt.* Münchener Beiträge zur Mediävistik und Renaissance Forschung 5. Munich: Arbeo-Gesellschaft.

Godden, M.R. 1985. «Anglo-Saxons on the Mind.» In: Lapidge, Michael and Helmut Gneuss (eds.). 1985. *Learning and Literature in Anglo-Saxon England.* Studies Presented to Peter Clemoes on the occasion of his 65th birthday. Cambridge: Cambridge University Press, 271-295.

Goffin, R.C. 1936. «Heaven and Earth in the 'Parlement of Foules'.» *Modern Language Review* 31:493-499.

Goossens, Jan and Timothy Sodmann (eds.). 1981. *International Beast Epic, Fable and Fabliau Colloquium: 1979, Münster.* Niederdeutsche Studien 30. Cologne and Vienna: Böhlau.

Gordon, R.K. (ed. and trans.) 1926. *Anglo-Saxon Poetry.* Reprinted 1976. Everyman's Library. London/New York: Dent/Dutton.

Gottschalk, Jane. 1966. «'The Owl and the Nightingale': Lay Preachers to a Lay Audience.» *Philological Quarterly* 45, Supplement:657-667.

Grahame, Kenneth. 1991. *The Wind in the Willows.* Illustrated by Ernest H. Shepard. First edition 1908. London: Dean, in association with Methuen.

Grant, Edward (ed.). 1974. *A Source Book in Medieval Science.* Cambridge, Massachusetts: Harvard University Press.

Grattan, J.H.G. and G.F.H. Sykes (eds.). 1935. *The Owl and the Nightingale.* Early English Text Society Extra Series 119. London: Oxford University Press.

Greenfield, Stanley B. 1955. «The Formulaic Expression of the Theme of 'Exile' in Anglo-Saxon Poetry.» *Speculum* 30:200-206.

- - - and Fred Robinson. 1980. *A Bibliography of Publications on Old English Literature to the End of 1972.* Toronto and Buffalo: University of Toronto Press.

Greither, Aloys (ed.). 1986. *Pancatantra: Die fünf Bücher indischer Lebensweisheit.* Based on the translation by Theodor Benfey (1859). Munich: C.H. Beck.

Griffith, Dudley David. 1955. *Bibliography of Chaucer 1908-1953.* Seattle: University of Washington Press.

Grimm, Jacob. 1834. *Reinhart Fuchs.* Berlin: Bei Reimer. Reprinted 1974. Hildesheim and New York: Georg Olms.

- - -. 1875-78. *Deutsche Mythologie.* Three volumes. Fourth edition. First edition 1835. Reprinted 1992. Wiesbaden: Drei Lilien.

Grinda, Klaus R. and Claus-Dieter Wetzel (eds.). 1993. *Anglo-Saxonica.* Beiträge zur Vor- und Frühgeschichte der englischen Sprache und zur altenglischen Literatur. 'Festschrift' for Hans Schabram on the occasion of his 65th birthday. Munich: Dieter Fink.

Grubmüller, Klaus. 1975. «Etymologie als Schlüssel zur Welt? Bemerkungen zur Sprachtheorie des Mittelalters.» In: Fromm, Hans, Wolfgang Harms, and Uwe Ruberg (eds.). 1975. *Verbum et Signum.* Beiträge zur mediävistischen Bedeutungsforschung. 'Festschrift' for Friedrich Ohly. Two volumes. Munich: Wilhelm Fink, volume 1:209-230.

- - -. 1977. *Meister Esopus: Untersuchungen zu Geschichte und Funktion der Fabel im Mittelalter.* Münchener Texte und Untersuchungen zur deutschen Literatur des Mittelalters 56. Zurich and Munich: Artemis.

- - -. 1978. «Wahrheitsanspruch des 'Physiologus' im Mittelalter.» *Frühmittelalterliche Studien* 12:160-178.

- - -. 1981. «Semantik der Fabel.» In: Goossens, Jan and Timothy Sodmann (eds.). 1981. *International Beast Epic, Fable and Fabliau Colloquium: 1979, Münster.* Niederdeutsche Studien 30. Cologne and Vienna: Böhlau, 111-134.

Guerin, Richard. 1973. «The Nun's Priest and Canto V of the 'Inferno'.» *English Studies* 54:313-315.

Gumbrecht, Hans Ulrich (ed. and trans.). 1973. *Marie de France: Äsop.* Klassische Texte des romanischen Mittelalters in zweisprachigen Ausgaben 12. Munich: Wilhelm Fink.

Gupta, R.D. 1975. «Indian Parallels of the Fox Story.» In: Rombauts, E. and A. Welkenhuysen (eds.). 1975. *Aspects of the Medieval Animal Epic: Proceedings of the International Conference: Louvain, May 15-17, 1972.* Leuven/The Hague: University Press/Martinus Nijhoff, 241-249.

Haas, Alois M. 1991. «Ichthys: Fischsymbolik im frühen Christentum.» In: Michel, Paul (ed.). 1991b. *Tiersymbolik.* Schriften zur Symbolforschung 7. Bern: Peter Lang, 77-89.

Hässler, Herbert. 1939. *'The Owl and the Nightingale' und die literarischen Bestrebungen des 12. und 13. Jahrhunderts.* Dissertation. Frankfurt on the Main: Johann Wolfgang Goethe Universität.

Hamer, Richard (ed. and trans.). 1970. *A Choice of Anglo-Saxon Verse*. Reprinted 1985. London and Boston: Faber and Faber.

Hamm, Victor M. 1954. «Chaucer: 'Heigh Ymaginacioun'.» *Modern Language Notes* 69:394-395.

Hammond, Eleanor Prescott. 1908. «A Parliament of Birds.» *Journal of English and Germanic Philology* 7:105-109.

- - -. 1916. «Chaucer and Dante and their Scribes.» *Modern Language Notes* 31:121.

Hanford, James Holly. 1911. «Classical Eclogue and the Mediæval Debate.» *Romanic Review* 2:16-31 and 129-143.

- - -. 1913. «The Mediæval Debate Between Wine and Water.» *Publications of the Modern Language Association of America* 28:315-367.

Hardison, O.B. Jr. 1965. *Christian Rite and Christian Drama in the Middle Ages: Essays in the Origin and Early History of Modern Drama.* Baltimore: The John Hopkins Press.

Harf-Lancner, Laurence. 1985a. «De la Métamorphose au Moyen Âge.» In: Harf-Lancner, Laurence (ed.). 1985b. *Métamorphose et Bestiaire Fantastique au Moyen Âge.* Collection de l'École Supérieure de Jeunes Filles. Paris: 48, Boulevard Jourdan, 3-25.

- - - (ed.). 1985b. *Métamorphose et Bestiaire Fantastique au Moyen Âge.* Collection de l'École Supérieure de Jeunes Filles. Paris: 48, Boulevard Jourdan.

Hargraves, Joyce. 1990. *Hargraves New Illustrated Bestiary.* Glastonbury: Gothic Image Publications.

Harkort, Fritz. 1970. «Tiergeschichten in der Volksüberlieferung.» In: Schwab, Ute (ed.). 1970. *Das Tier in der Dichtung.* Heidelberg: Carl Winter, 12-54 and 244-258.

Harms, Wolfgang. 1975. «Der Eisvogel und die halkyonischen Tage. Zum Verhältnis von naturkundlicher Beschreibung und allegorischer Naturdeutung.» In: Fromm, Hans, Wolfgang Harms, and Uwe Ruberg (eds.). 1975. *Verbum et Signum.* Beiträge zur mediävistischen Bedeutungsforschung. 'Festschrift' for Friedrich Ohly. Two volumes. Munich: Wilhelm Fink, volume 1:477-516.

- - - and Heimo Reinitzer (eds.). 1981. *Natura loquax.* Mikrokosmos 7. Frankfurt on the Main: Peter D. Lang.

Harrison, Thomas P. 1956. *They Tell of Birds: Chaucer, Spenser, Milton, Drayton.* Reprinted 1969. Westport, Connecticut: Greenwood Press.

- - -. 1960. «Bird of Paradise: Phoenix Redivivus.» *Isis* 51:173-180.

Hatto, A.T. 1957. «Snake-swords and Boar-helms in 'Beowulf'.» *English Studies* 38:145-160 and 257-259.

Hatton, Thomas J. 1967. «Chauntecleer and the Monk, Two False Knights.» *Papers on Language and Literature* 3, Summer Supplement:31-39.

Heberer, Gerhard. 1966. «Charles Darwin's Werk über die Abstammung des Menschen.» In: Darwin, Charles. 1966. *Die Abstammung des Menschen.* Translated by Heinrich Schmidt-Jena from the second revised edition (1874) of *The Descent of Man.* Kröners Taschenbuchausgabe Band 28. Stuttgart: Alfred Kröner, vii-xxii.

Helch, Wolfgang (ed.). 1968. *Festschrift für Siegfried Schott zu seinem 70. Geburtstag.* Wiesbaden: Otto Harrassowitz.

Hemingway, Samuel B. 1916. «Chaucer's Monk and Nun's Priest.» *Modern Language Notes* 31:479-483.

Henderson, Arnold Clayton. 1981. «Animal Fables as Vehicles of Social Protest and Satire: Twelfth Century to Henryson.» In: Goossens, Jan and Timothy Sodmann (eds.).

1981. *International Beast Epic, Fable and Fabliau Colloquium: 1979, Münster.* Niederdeutsche Studien 30. Cologne and Vienna: Böhlau, 160-173.

- - -. 1982. «Medieval Beasts and Modern Cages: The Making of Meaning in Fables and Bestiaries.» *Publications of the Modern Language Association of America* 97:40-49.

Henkel, Nikolaus. 1976. *Studien zum Physiologus im Mittelalter.* Hermaea NF 38. Tübingen: Max Niemeyer.

Henking, Karl H. 1983. «Das Tier im Schamanentum.» In: Frewein, Josef (ed.). 1983. *Das Tier in der menschlichen Kultur.* Zürcher Hochschulforum 5. Zurich: Artemis, 19-28.

Hennig, Ursula and Herbert Hennig (eds.). 1970. *Mediævalia litteraria.* 'Festschrift' for Helmut de Boor on the occasion of his 80th birthday. Munich: Beck'sche Verlagsbuchhandlung.

Henning, Standish. 1965. «Chauntecleer and Taurus.» *English Language Notes* 3:1-4.

Hermes, Eberhard (ed. and trans.). 1977. *The 'Disciplina Clericalis' of Petrus Alfonsi.* Title of the German edition which provided the basis for the English translation: *Die Kunst, vernünftig zu leben. (Disciplina Clericalis).* 1970. Zurich: Artemis. Translated into English by P.R. Quarrie. London: Routledge and Kegan Paul.

Herzfeld, George (ed.). 1900. *An Old English Martyrology.* Early English Text Society Original Series 116. Reprinted 1981. London: Kegan Paul, Trench, and Trübner.

Hieatt, Constance. 1967. *The Realism of Dream Visions: The Poetic Exploitation of the Dream-Experience in Chaucer and His Contemporaries.* The Hague and Paris: Mouton.

- - -. 1968. «The Subject of the Mock-Debate Between the Owl and the Nightingale.» *Studia Neophilologica* 40:155-160.

- - -. 1970. «The Moral of 'The Nun's Priest's Tale'.» *Neophilologus* 42:3-8.

Higuchi, Masayuki. 1987. «On the Language of 'The Owl and the Nightingale': How Language Becomes a Weapon for a Verbal Duel.» *Poetica* 25/26:73-92.

Hildegard von Bingen. 1991. *Heilkraft der Natur 'Physica': Das Buch von dem inneren Wesen der verschiedenen Naturen der Geschöpfe.* Translated by Marie-Louise Portmann. Augsburg: Pattloch.

Hilgers, Sister Mary. 1973. *A Study of the Middle-English Bird Debate: Backgrounds, Form, Matter, and Characterization.* PhD. Indiana: University of Notre Dame.

Hinckley, Henry Barrett. 1919. «The Date of 'The Owl and the Nightingale'.» *Modern Philology* 17:247-258.

- - -. 1929. «The Date, Author, and Sources of the 'Owl and the Nightingale'.» *Publications of the Modern Language Association of America* 44:329-359.

- - -. 1932. «Science and Folk-Lore in 'The Owl and the Nightingale'.» *Publications of the Modern Language Association of America* 47:303-314.

- - -. 1937. «A Note on the 'Owl'.» *English Literary History* 4:299-300.

Hirsh, John C. 1974. «Classical Tradition and 'The Owl and the Nightingale'.» *Chaucer Review* 9:145-152.

Hoad, T.F. (ed.). 1986. *The Concise Oxford Dictionary of English Etymology.* Oxford: Oxford University Press.

Holmes, Urban Tigner. 1972. «The Monster in Mediaeval Literature.» In: Cargo, Robert T. and Emanuel J. Michel Jr. (eds.). 1972. *Studies in Honor of Alfred G. Engstrom.* University of North Carolina Studies in the Romance Languages and Literatures 124. Chapel Hill: University of North Carolina Press, 53-62.

Holtei, Rainer. 1990. *Norm und Spiel in The Owl and the Nightingale.* Studia humaniora 18. Düsseldorf: Droste.

Holthausen, F. 1919. «Der me. Streit zwischen Drossel und Nachtigall.» *Anglia* 43:52-60.

Holy Bible: The New Scofield Reference Bible – Authorized King James Version. 1967. Edited by C.I. Scofield. London: Oxford University Press.

Horgan, Frances (ed. and trans.). 1994. *Guillaume de Lorris and Jean de Meun: The Romance of the Rose.* The World's Classics. Oxford and New York: Oxford University Press.

Hotson, Leslie J. 1924. «Colfox vs. Chauntecleer.» *Publications of the Modern Language Association of America* 39:762-781.

Hoult, Janet. 1990. *Dragons: Their History and Symbolism.* Second edition. First edition 1987. Glastonbury: Gothic Image Publications.

Howard, Donald R. 1976. *The Idea of the Canterbury Tales.* Berkley: University of California Press.

- - -. 1987. *Chaucer and the Medieval World.* London: Weidenfeld and Nicolson.

Hoy, Michael. 1969. «The Nun's Priest's Tale.» In: Hoy, Michael and Michael Stevens (eds.). 1969. *Chaucer's Major Tales.* London: North Bailey, 133-162 and 171-172.

- - - and Michael Stevens (eds.). 1969. *Chaucer's Major Tales.* London: North Bailey.

Huganir, Kathryn. 1931. *The Owl and the Nightingale: Sources, Date, Author.* PhD. Philadelphia.

- - -. 1937. «Equine Quartering in 'The Owl and the Nightingale'.» *Publications of the Modern Language Association of America* 52:935-945.

Hulbert, James R. 1941. «'The Nun's Priest's Tale'.» In: Bryan, W.F. and Germaine Dempster (eds.). 1941. *Sources and Analogues of Chaucer's Canterbury Tales.* Reprinted 1958. London: Routledge and Kegan Paul, 645-663.

Hume, Kathryn. 1975. *The Owl and the Nightingale: The Poem and Its Critics.* Toronto: Toronto University Press.

- - -. 1984. *Fantasy and Mimesis: Responses to Reality in Western Literature.* New York and London: Methuen.

Huppé, Bernard F. and D.W. Robertson Jr. 1963. *Fruyt and Chaf: Studies in Chaucer's Allegories.* Princeton, New Jersey: Princeton University Press.

Hutchinson, Judith. 1977. «'The Parliament of Fowls': A Literary Entertainment?» *Neophilologus* 61:143-151.

Iser, Wolfgang. 1959. «'The Owl and the Nightingale': Versuch einer formgeschichtlichen Ortsbestimmung.» *Deutsche Vierteljahresschrift für Literaturwissenschaft* 33:309-323.

Jacobs, John C. (ed. and trans.). 1985. *The Fables of Odo of Cheriton.* Syracuse: Syracuse University Press.

Jaeger, C. Stephen. 1985. *The Origin of Courtliness: Civilizing Trends and the Formation of Courtly Ideals, 939-1210.* Philadelphia: University of Pennsylvania Press.

Janson, H.W. 1952. *Apes and Ape Lore in the Middle Ages and in the Renaissance.* London: The Warburg Institute University of London.

Jantzen, Hermann. 1896. *Geschichte des deutschen Streitgedichtes im Mittelalter mit Berücksichtigung ähnlicher Erscheinungen in anderen Litteraturen.* Germanistische Abhandlungen 13. Breslau: Wilhelm Koebner. Reprinted 1977. Hildesheim: Georg Olms.

Jauss, Hans Robert. 1959. *Untersuchungen zur mittelalterlichen Tierdichtung*. Beiheft zur Zeitschrift für Romanische Philologie 100. Tübingen: Max Niemeyer.

- - -. 1977. *Alterität und Modernität der mittelalterlichen Literatur. Gesammelte Aufsätze 1956-1976*. Munich: Wilhelm Fink.

Jauss-Meyer, Helga (ed. and trans). 1965. *Le Roman de Renart*. Klassische Texte des Romanischen Mittelalters in zweisprachigen Ausgaben 5. Munich: Wilhelm Fink.

Jeger, Urs and Ian Lässig. 1992. *The Owl and the Nightingale*. Seminarpaper. University of Zurich.

Johnson, Lynn Stanley. 1985. «'To Make in Som Comedye': Chauntecleer, Son of Troy.» *Chaucer Review* 19:225-244.

Jones, H.S.V. 1912. «'Parliament of Fowls' 693 F.» *Modern Language Notes* 27:95.

Jones-Davies, M.T. (ed.). 1990. *Le Monde Animal au Temps de la Renaissance*. Centre de Recherches sur la Renaissance, Université de Paris-Sorbonne: Jean Touzot.

Jordan, Robert M. 1977. «The Question of Unity and the 'Parlement of Foules'.» *English Studies in Canada* 3:373-385.

Kaimakis, Dimitris (ed.). 1974. *Der Physiologus nach der ersten Redaktion*. Beiträge zur klassischen Philologie 63. Meissenheim on the Glan: Anton Hain.

Kantrowitz, Joanne Spencer. 1964. «The Anglo-Saxon 'Phoenix' and Tradition.» *Philological Quarterly* 43:1-13.

Kaske, R.E. 1960. «Patristic Exegesis in the Criticism of Medieval Literature: The Defense.» In: Bethurum, Dorothy (ed.). 1960. *Critical Approaches to Medieval Literature*. Selected Papers from the English Institute, 1958-1959. New York and London: Columbia University Press, 27-60 and 158-159.

Kastovsky, Dieter (ed.). 1994. *Studies in Early Modern English*. Topics in English Linguistics 13. New York: Mouton de Gruyter.

Kaylor, Noel Harold Jr. 1989. «'The Nun's Priest's Tale' as Chaucer's Anti-Tragedy.» In: Böker, Uwe, Manfred Markus, and Rainer Schöwerling (eds.). 1989. *The Living Middle Ages: Studies in Mediaeval English Literature and Its Tradition*. 'Festschrift' for Karl Heinz Göller. Stuttgart: Belser, 87-102.

Kean, Patricia (ed.). 1955. *Essays on Middle English Literature by Dorothy Everett*. Oxford: At the Clarendon Press.

Kelley, Michael R. 1979. «Antithesis as the Principle of Design in the 'Parlement of Foules'.» *Chaucer Review* 14:61-73.

Kennedy, Charles W. (ed. and trans.). 1952. *Early English Christian Poetry*. London: Hollis and Carter.

Kenyon, John S. 1913. «Notes on 'The Owl and the Nightingale'.» *Journal of English and Germanic Philology* 12:572-592.

- - -. 1916. «Further Notes on the Marriage Group in the 'Canterbury Tales'.» *Journal of English and Germanic Philology* 15:282-288.

Ker, N. R. (ed.). 1963. *The Owl and the Nightingale*. Reproduced in facsimile from the surviving manuscripts Jesus College Oxford 29 and British Museum Cotton Caligula A. IX. Early English Text Society Original Series 251. London: Oxford University Press.

King, Helen. 1995. «Half-human Creatures.» In: Cherry, John (ed.). 1995. *Mythical Beasts*. London: The British Museum Press, 138-167.

Kinneavy, Gerald B. 1967. «Fortune, Providence and the Owl.» *Studies in Philology* 64:655-664.

Kinsley, James (ed.). 1979. *The Poems of William Dunbar.* Oxford: At the Clarendon Press.

Klaeber, Friedrich (ed.). 1950. *Beowulf and the Fight at Finnsburg.* Third edition. First edition 1922. Boston: D.C. Heath.

Klingender, Francis. 1971. *Animals in Art and Thought to the End of the Middle Ages.* London: Routledge and Kegan Paul.

Klopsch, Paul. 1966. «Prosa und Vers in der mittellateinischen Literatur.» In: Langosch, Karl (ed.). 1966. *Mittellateinisches Jahrbuch.* Cologne: Selbstverlag, 9-24.

Knowlton, Edgar C. 1920. «The Goddess of Nature in Early Periods.» *Journal of English and Germanic Philology* 19:224-253.

- - -. 1921. «Nature in Middle English.» *Journal of English and Germanic Philology* 20:186-207.

Koch, John. 1877. «Ein Beitrag zur Kritik Chaucers.» *Englische Studien* 1:249-293.

König, Roderich and Gerhard Winkler (eds. and trans.). 1973-1994. *C. Plinius Secundus der Ältere: Naturkunde.* Thirty-seven volumes. Latin-German. Darmstadt: Wissenschaftliche Buchgesellschaft.

Kohl, Stephan. 1988. «Fingierte Mündlichkeit: Erzähler in mittelenglischer Literatur.» In: Erzgräber, Willi and Sabine Volk (eds.). 1988. *Mündlichkeit und Schriftlichkeit im englischen Mittelalter.* Script Oralia 5. Tübingen: Gunter Narr, 133-146.

Kolb, Herbert. 1970. «Der Hirsch, der Schlangen frisst.» In: Hennig, Ursula and Herbert Hennig (eds.). 1970. *Mediævalia litteraria.* 'Festschrift' for Helmut de Boor on the occasion of his 80th birthday. Munich: Beck'sche Verlagsbuchhandlung, 583-610.

Konstantinowa, Alexandra. 1929. *Ein englisches Bestiar des zwölften Jahrhunderts in der Staatsbibliothek zu Leningrad.* Berlin: Deutscher Kunstverlag.

Krapp, George Philip (ed.). 1931. *The Junius Manuscript.* Volume 1 of *The Anglo-Saxon Poetic Records: A Collective Edition.* London: Routledge and Sons.

- - - (ed.). 1932a. *The Vercelli Book.* Volume 2 of *The Anglo-Saxon Poetic Records: A Collective Edition.* London: Routledge and Kegan Paul.

- - - (ed.). 1932b. *The Paris Psalter and the Meters of Boethius.* Volume 5 of *The Anglo-Saxon Poetic Records: A Collective Edition.* New York: Columbia University Press.

- - - and Elliott Van Kirk Dobbie (eds.). 1936. *The Exeter Book.* Volume 3 of *The Anglo-Saxon Poetic Records: A Collective Edition.* London: George Routledge and Sons.

- - - and Elliott Van Kirk Dobbie (eds.). 1931-53. *The Anglo-Saxon Poetic Records: A Collective Edition.* Six volumes. New York/London: Columbia University Press/Routledge and Kegan Paul.

Kreisler, Nicolai von. 1970. «Satire in 'The Vox and the Wolf'.» *Journal of English and Germanic Philology* 69:650-658.

- - -. 1971. «The 'Locus Amoenus' and Eschatological Lore in the 'Parliament of Fowls' 204-210.» *Philological Quarterly* 50:16-22.

Lange, Hugo. 1940. «Die Nordnordwest-Stellung der Venus und der Nordwestwind in Chaucers 'Vogelparlament'.» *Anglia* 64:196-204.

Langosch, Karl (ed.). 1966. *Mittellateinisches Jahrbuch.* Cologne: Selbstverlag.

Lapidge, Michael and Helmut Gneuss (eds.). 1985. *Learning and Literature in Anglo-Saxon England.* Studies presented to Peter Clemoes on the occasion of his 65th birthday. Cambridge: Cambridge University Press.

Lauchert, Friedrich. 1889. *Geschichte des Physiologus.* Strassburg: Karl J. Trübner.

Law, Robert Adger. 1922. «'In Principio'.» *Publications of the Modern Language Association of America* 37:208-215.

Lawton, David. 1985. *Chaucer's Narrators.* Chaucer Studies 13. Cambridge: D.S. Brewer.

Leclercq, Jean OSB. 1963. *Wissenschaft und Gottverlangen: Zur Mönchstheologie des Mittelalters.* Translated by J. and N. Stöber. French original published in 1957. Düsseldorf: Patmos.

Lecompte, I.C. 1917. «Chaucer's 'Nonne Prestes Tale' and the 'Roman de Renart'.» *Modern Philology* 14:737-749.

Lecouteux, Claude. 1977. «Das bauchlose Ungeheuer: Des Strickers 'Daniel vom blühenden Tal', 1879ff.» *Euphorion* 71:272-276.

- - -. 1979a. «Der Drache.» *Zeitschrift für deutsches Altertum und deutsche Literatur* 108:13-31.

- - -. 1982. *Les Monstres dans la Littérature Allemande du Moyen Âge.* Göppinger Arbeiten zur Germanistik 330/1-3 (1=Étude, 2=Dictionnaire, 3=Documents). Göppingen: Kümmerle.

- - - (ed.). 1979b. *De Rebus In Oriente Mirabilius (Lettre de Farasmanes).* Edition synoptique accompagnée d'une introduction et de notes. Beiträge zur klassischen Philologie 103. Meisenheim on the Glan: Anton Hain.

Lehmann, Elmar and Bernd Lenz (eds.). 1992. *Telling Stories.* Studies in honour of Ulrich Broich on the occasion of his 60th birthday. Amsterdam: John Benjamins.

Lehmann, Paul. 1963. *Die Parodie im Mittelalter.* Second edition. First edition ?. Stuttgart: Anton Hiersemann.

Leibfried, Erwin. 1976. *Fabel.* Third edition. First edition 1967. Stuttgart: J.B. Metzlersche Verlagsbuchhandlung.

Lenaghan, R.T. 1963. «The Nun's Priest's Fable.» *Publications of the Modern Language Association of America* 78:300-307.

LeSaux, Françoise. 1987. «Song and Harmony in 'The Owl and the Nightingale'.» *Études des Lettres* ?:3-9.

- - -. 1990. «Of Desire and Transgression in the Middle English 'Vox & Wolf'.» *Reinardus* 3:69-79.

Lessing, Gotthold Ephraim. 1759. *Fabeln: Drey Bücher. Nebst Abhandlungen mit dieser Dichtungsart verwandten Inhalts.* Berlin: Voß. Reprinted 1979. Hamburg: Maximilian-Gesellschaft.

Levy, Bernard S. and George R. Adams. 1967. «Chauntecleer's Paradise Lost and Regained.» *Mediaeval Studies* 29:178-192.

Lewis, C. S. 1938. *The Allegory of Love.* Second edition. First edition 1936. London: Oxford University Press.

- - -. 1964. *The Discarded Image.* Reprinted 1988. Cambridge: Cambridge University Press.

Lewis, Gertrud Jaron. 1974. *Das Tier und seine dichterische Funktion in Erec, Iwein, Parzival und Tristan.* Kanadische Studien zur deutschen Sprache und Literatur 11. Bern and Frankfurt on the Main: Herbert Lang.

Lindahl, Carl. 1987. *Earnest Games: Folkloric Patterns in the Canterbury Tales.* Boomington and Indianapolis: Indiana University Press.

Lindsay, W.M. (ed.). 1911. *Isidori Hispalensis Episcopi Etymologiarum Sive Originum Libri XX.* Two volumes. Reprinted 1987. Oxford: At the Clarendon Press.

Linzey, Andrew and Tom Regan (eds.). 1988. *Animals and Christianity.* London: SPCK.

Lord, Albert Bates. 1960. *The Singer of Tales.* Harvard Studies in Comparative Literature 24. Cambridge, Massachusetts: Harvard University Press.

Lowes, John Livingston. 1927. *The Road to Xanadu: A Study in the Ways of Imagination.* London: Constable.

Loyn, H.R. (ed.). 1989. *The Middle Ages: A Concise Encyclopædia.* Reprinted 1991. London: Thames and Hudson.

Lumiansky, R. M. 1948. «Chaucer's 'Parlement of Foules': A Philosophical Interpretation.» *Review of English Studies* 24:81-89.

- - -. 1953a. «Concerning 'The Owl and the Nightingale'.» *Philological Quarterly* 32:411-417.

- - -. 1953b. «The Nun's Priest in 'The Canterbury Tales'.» *Publications of the Modern Language Association of America* 68:896-906.

- - -. 1955. *Of Sondry Folk: The Dramatic Principle in the Canterbury Tales.* Illustrated by Malcolm Thurgood. Austin: University of Texas Press.

Luria, Maxwell S. and Richard L. Hoffman (eds.). 1974. *Middle English Lyrics.* New York and London: W.W. Norton.

Maag, Viktor. 1983. «Das Tier in den Religionen.» In: Frewein, Joseph (ed.). 1983. *Das Tier in der menschlichen Kultur.* Zurich: Artemis, 7-18.

MacDiarmid, Hugh (ed.). 1973. *Henryson.* Poet to Poet. Harmondsworth: Penguin Books.

Macdonald, Emslie. 1955. «Codes of Love and Class Distinctions.» *Essays in Criticism* 5:1-17.

Maes-Jelinek, Hena, Pierre Michel, and Paulette Michel-Michot (eds.). 1987. *Multiple Worlds, Multiple Words.* Essays in honour of Irène Simon. Liège: English Department of the University of Liège.

Magoun, Francis P. Jr. 1955. «The Theme of the Beasts of Battle in Anglo-Saxon Poetry.» *Neuphilologische Mitteilungen* 56:81-90.

Manly, John Matthews. 1913. «What is the 'Parlement of Foules'?» 'Festschrift' for Lorenz Morsbach. *Studien zur Englischen Philologie* 50:278-290.

- - -. 1926. «Chaucer and the Rhetoricians.» *Proceedings of the British Academy* 12:95-113. Reprinted in: Schoeck, Richard and Jerome Taylor (eds.). 1960. *Chaucer Criticism.* Two volumes. Reprinted 1982. Notre Dame and London: University of Notre Dame Press, volume 1:268-290.

- - -. 1934. «Three Recent Chaucer Studies.» *Review of English Studies* 10:257-273.

- - -. 1935. «Response to: The Historical Background of the 'Parlement of Foules'.» *Review of English Studies* 11:209-213.

Mann, Jill. 1975. «The 'Speculum Stultorum' and the 'Nun's Priest's Tale'.» *Chaucer Review* 9:262-282.

- - - (ed.). 1987. *Ysengrimus: Text with Translation, Commentary and Introduction.* Mittellateinische Studien 12. Leiden and New York: E.J. Brill.

Manning, Stephen. 1960. «The Nun's Priest's Morality and the Medieval Attitude toward Fables.» *Journal of English and Germanic Philology* 59:403-416.

Manzalaoui, Mahmoud. 1962. «Ars Longa, Vita Brevis.» *Essays in Criticism* 12:221-224.

Martin, B.K. 1971. «Notes on 'The Owl and the Nightingale'.» *Notes and Queries* NS 18:407-408.

Martin, Ernest Whitney. 1914. *The Birds of the Latin Poets.* Leland Stanford Junior University Publications 25. University Series 13. California: Stanford University.

Martin, Ernst. 1908. «Zur Geschichte der Tiersage im Mittelalter.» *Prager deutsche Studien* 8/1:273-287.

Maurer, Friedrich. 1967. *Der altdeutsche Physiologus: Die Millstätter Reimfassung und die Wiener Prosa (nebst dem lateinischen Text und dem althochdeutschen Physiologus).* Tübingen: Max Niemeyer.

Mayr-Harting, Henry. 1972. *The Coming of Christianity to Anglo-Saxon England.* London: Batsford.

McCulloch, Florence. 1960. *Mediaeval Latin and Fench Bestiaries.* University of North Carolina Studies in the Romance Languages and Literatures 33. Chapel Hill: University of North Carolina Press.

McDiarmid, Matthew P. 1981. *Robert Henryson.* Scottish Writers Series. Edinburgh: Scottish Academic Press.

McDonald, Charles O. 1955. «An Interpretation of Chaucer's 'Parlement of Foules'.» *Speculum* 30:444-457.

McGall, John P. 1970. «The Harmony of Chaucer's 'Parliament'.» *Chaucer Review* 5:22-31.

McGarry, Daniel D. (ed. and trans.). 1955. *The Metalogicon of John of Salisbury.* Berkley: University of California Press.

McKeehan, Irene Pettit. 1926. «'Guillaume de Palerne': A Medieval 'Best Seller'.» *Publications of the Modern Language Association of America* 41:785-809.

McKenzie, Kenneth. 1905. «Unpublished Manuscripts of Italian Bestiaries.» *Publications of the Modern Language Association of America* 20:380-433.

McKnight, G[eorge] H. 1908. «The M.E. 'Vox and Wolf'.» *Publications of the Modern Language Association of America* 23:497-509.

Mehl, Dieter. 1988. «'The Owl and the Nightingale': Mündlichkeit und Schriftlichkeit im Streitgespräch.» In: Erzgräber, Willi and Sabine Volk (eds.). 1988. *Mündlichkeit und Schriftlichkeit im englischen Mittelalter.* Script Oralia 5. Tübingen: Gunter Narr, 75-84.

Meier, Christel. 1978. «Argumentationsformen kritischer Reflexion zwischen Naturwissenschaft und Allegorese.» *Frühmittelalterliche Studien* 12:116-159.

Meier, Hans H. 1987. «Old English Style in Action: The Battle Scene (With a Hint on 'Hildebrand').» In: Simon-Vandenbergen, A.M. (ed.). 1987. *Studies in Honour of René Derolez.* Gent: Seminarie voor Engelse en Oud-Germaanse Taalkunde R.U.G., 334-350.

- - -. 1992. «Writing and Medieval Culture.» In: Engler, Balz (ed.). 1992. *Writing & Culture.* SPELL 6. Tübingen: Gunter Narr, 33-52.

Mellinkoff, Ruth. 1986. «Serpent Imagery in the Illustrated Old English Hexateuch.» In: Brown, P.R., G.R. Crampton, and F.C. Robinson (eds.). 1986. *Modes of Interpretation in Old English Literature.* Essays in honour of Stanley B. Greenfield. Toronto: University of Toronto Press, 51-64.

Meredith, George. 1862. «Modern Love.» In: Allison, Alexander W. et al. (eds.). 1983. *The Norton Anthology of Poetry*. Third edition. First edition 1970. New York and London: W.W. Norton, 801-803.

Meredith, Peter. 1970. «Chauntecleer and the Mermaids.» *Neophilologus* 54:81-83.

Mermier, Guy R. 1989. «The Phoenix: Its Nature and Its Place in the Tradition of the 'Physiologus'.» In: Clark, Willene B. and Meradith T. McMunn (eds.). 1989. *Beasts and Birds of the Middle Ages: The Bestiary and Its Legacy*. Philadelphia: University of Pennsylvania Press, 69-85.

Mertens-Fonck, Paule. 1987. «Tradition and Feminism in Middle English Literature: Source Hunting in the Wife of Bath's Portrait and in 'The Owl and the Nightingale'.» In: Maes-Jelinek, Hena, Pierre Michel, and Paulette Michel-Michot (eds.). 1987. *Multiple Worlds, Multiple Words*. Essays in honour of Irène Simon. Liège: English Department of the University of Liège, 175-192.

Metcalf, Allan A. 1963. «Ten Natural Animals in 'Beowulf'.» *Neuphilologische Mitteilungen* 64:378-389.

- - -. 1970. «Ornamentale Tiermotive in der altenglischen Versdichtung.» In: Schwab, Ute (ed.). 1970. *Das Tier in der Dichtung*. Heidelberg: Carl Winter, 74-90 and 268-71.

Metlitzki, Dorothee. 1977. *The Matter of Araby in Medieval England*. New Haven and London: Yale University Press.

Michel, Paul. 1979. *Tiere als Symbol und Ornament*. Wiesbaden: Dr. Ludwig Reichert.

- - -. 1991a. «Anhang: Einige Grundbegriffe der mittelalterlichen Bibelauslegung.» In: Michel, Paul (ed.). 1991b. *Tiersymbolik*. Schriften zur Symbolforschung 7. Bern: Peter Lang, 205-217.

- - - (ed.). 1991b. *Tiersymbolik*. Schriften zur Symbolforschung 7. Bern: Peter Lang.

- - - and Alexander Schwarz. 1978. *unz in obanentig: Aus der Werkstatt der karolingischen Exegeten Alcuin, Erkanbert und Otfrid von Weissenburg*. Studien zur Germanistik, Anglistik und Komparatistik 79. Bonn: Bouvier Verlag Herbert Grundmann.

Migne, Jean-Paul (ed.). 1844-1900. *Patrologiae Cursus Completus, seu Bibliotheca universalis [...] omnium ss. patrum, doctorum, scriptorumque ecclesiasticorum, sive Latinorum, sive Graecorum*. Series Latina. Twohundred-twenty-one volumes. Quotation title: *Patrologia Latina*. First edition Paris: Garnier. Reprinted 1956-?. Turnholti: Brepols.

Miller, Robert P. (ed.). 1977. *Chaucer: Sources and Backgrounds*. New York: Oxford University Press.

Misch, Manfred. 1974. *Apis est animal – apis est ecclesia: Ein Beitrag zum Verständnis von Naturkunde und Theologie in spätantiker und mittelalterlicher Literatur*. Europäische Hochschulschriften 107 (Reihe 1). Bern/Frankfurt: Herbert Lang/Peter Lang.

Mitterer, Pater Sigisbert (ed. and trans.). 1925. *Des heiligen Kirchenvaters Aurelius Augustinus ausgewählte praktische Schriften homiletischen und katechetischen Inhalts*. Bibliothek der Kirchenväter 8. Munich: Josef Kösel and Friedrich Pustet K.G.

Mode, Heinz. 1974. *Fabeltiere und Dämonen in der Kunst: Die fantastische Welt der Mischwesen*. Stuttgart: W. Kohlhammer.

Mölk, Ulrich. 1993. «Fuchs und Wölfin. Über eine Episode des 'Ysengrimus' und ihre englische Quelle.» In: Grinda, Klaus R. and Claus-Dieter Wetzel (eds.). 1993. *Anglo-Saxonica*. Beiträge zur Vor- und Frühgeschichte der englischen Sprache und zur altenglischen Literatur. 'Festschrift' for Hans Schabram on his 65th birthday. Munich: Dieter Fink, 515-525.

Mooney, Linne R. 1993. «The Cock and the Clock: Telling Time in Chaucer's Day.» *Studies in the Age of Chaucer* 15:91-109.

Moore, Arthur K. 1949. «'Somer' and 'Lenten' as Terms for Spring.» *Notes and Queries* 194:82-83.

Moore, Samuel. 1911. «A Further Note on the Suitors in the 'Parliament of Fowls'.» *Modern Language Notes* 26:8-12.

Moran, Irene. 1978. «Two Notes on 'The Owl and the Nightingale'.» *English Studies* 59:499-507.

Morris, Richard (ed.). 1868. *Old English Homilies and Homiletic Treatises.* Early English Text Society Original Series 29 and 34. Originally published London: N. Trübner. Reprinted 1969. New York: Greenwood Press.

Moseley, C.W.R.D. (ed. and trans.). 1983. *The Travels of Sir John Mandeville.* Harmondsworth: Penguin.

Mosher, Joseph Albert. 1911. *The Exemplum in the Early Religious and Didactic Literature of England.* New York: Columbia University Press.

Mossé, Fernand. 1951. «Le 'Roman De Renart' Dans L'Angleterre Du Moyen Âge.» *Langues Modernes* 45:70-84.

- - -. 1969. *Handbuch des Mittelenglischen.* Translated by Herbert Pilch and Ursula Siewert. Original French edition published 1949. Munich: Max Hueber.

Müller, Gunter. 1968. «Germanische Tiersymbolik und Namengebung.» *Frühmittelalterliche Studien* 2:202-217.

Munsterberg, Peggy (ed.). 1980. *The Penguin Book of Bird Poetry.* Harmondsworth: Penguin.

Murphy, James J. 1978a. «Rhetoric and Dialectic in 'The Owl and the Nightingale'.» In: Murphy, James J. (ed.). 1978b. *Medieval Eloquence: Studies in the Theory and Practice of Medieval Rhetoric.* Berkley: University of California Press, 198-230.

- - - (ed.). 1978b. *Medieval Eloquence: Studies in the Theory and Practice of Medieval Rhetoric.* Berkley: University of California Press.

Muscatine, Charles. 1957. *Chaucer and the French Tradition.* Berkley: University of California Press.

Myers, D.E. 1972. «Focus and 'Moralite' in the 'Nun's Priest's Tale'.» *Chaucer Review* 7:210-220.

Naumann, Hans-Peter. 1991. «Altgermanische Tiersymbolik und Probleme ihrer Deutung.» In: Michel, Paul (ed.). 1991b. *Tiersymbolik.* Schriften zur Symbolforschung 7. Bern: Peter Lang, 49-76.

Nims, Margaret F. (trans.). 1967. *Poetria Nova of Geoffrey of Vinsauf.* Medieval Sources in Translation 6. Toronto: Pontifical Institute of Mediaeval Studies.

Noelle, H. 1870. *Die Sprache des altenglischen Gedichts von der Eule und Nachtigall.* Göttingen: Dietrich'sche Universitätsbuchdruckerei.

North, J.D. 1969. «Kalenderes Enlumyned ben They: Part III.» *Review of English Studies* NS 20:418-422.

- - -. 1988. *Chaucer's Universe.* Oxford: Clarendon Press.

Ogilby, John. 1668. *The Fables of Aesop Paraphras'd in Verse.* Reprinted 1965. Los Angeles: William Andrews Clark Memorial Library.

Ogilvy, J.D.A. 1967. *Books Known to the English, 597-1066.* Cambridge, Massachusetts: Mediaeval Academy of America.

Ohly, Friedrich. 1958. «Vom geistigen Sinn des Wortes im Mittelalter.» Reprinted in: Ohly, Friedrich. 1977. *Schriften zur mittelalterlichen Bedeutungsforschung.* Darmstadt: Wissenschaftliche Buchgesellschaft, 1-31.

- - -. 1968. «Probleme der mittelalterlichen Bedeutungsforschung und das Taubenbild des Hugo de Folieto.» Reprinted in: Ohly, Friedrich. 1977. *Schriften zur mittelalterlichen Bedeutungsforschung.* Darmstadt: Wissenschaftliche Buchgesellschaft, 32 -92.

- - -. 1976. *Diamant und Bocksblut: Zur Traditions- und Auslegungsgeschichte eines Naturvorgangs von der Antike bis in die Moderne.* Berlin: Erich Schmidt.

- - -. 1977. *Schriften zur mittelalterlichen Bedeutungsforschung.* Darmstadt: Wissenschaftliche Buchgesellschaft.

Olson, Paul A. 1980. «'The Parlement of Foules': Aristotle's 'Politics' and the Foundations of Human Society.» *Studies in the Age of Chaucer* 2:53-69.

Olsson, Kurt. 1977. «Character and Truth in 'The Owl and the Nightingale'.» *Chaucer Review* 11:351-368.

Oruch, Jack B. 1981. «St. Valentine, Chaucer, and Spring in February.» *Speculum* 56:534-565.

- - -. 1983. «Nature's Limitations and the 'Demande d'Amour' of Chaucer's 'Parlement'.» *Chaucer Review* 18:23-37.

Owen, Charles A. Jr. 1953. «The Crucial Passages in Five of the 'Canterbury Tales': A Study in Irony and Symbol.» *Journal of English and Germanic Philology* 52:294-311.

Owen, Lewis J. 1969. «'The Thrush and the Nightingale': The Speaker in Lines 94-96.» *English Language Notes* 7:1-6.

Owst, G.R. 1966. *Literature and Pulpit in Medieval England.* Second edition. First edition 1933. Oxford: Basil Blackwell.

Paffard, M.K. 1957. «Pertelote's Prescription.» *Notes and Queries* NS 4:370.

Patrick, David. 1930. «The Satire in Chaucer's 'Parliament of Birds'.» *Philological Quarterly* 9:61-65.

Paul, Jean. 1990. *Vorschule der Ästhetik.* Edited by Wolfhart Henckmann. Philosophische Bibliothek 425. First edition 1804. Hamburg: Felix Meiner.

Payne, Ann. 1990. *Medieval Beasts.* London: The British Library Board.

Payne, Anne F. 1975. «Foreknowledge and Free Will: Three Theories in the 'Nun's Priest's Tale'.» *Chaucer Review* 10:201-219.

Pearcy, Roy J. 1968. «The Epilogue to 'The Nun's Priest's Tale'.» *Notes and Queries* NS 15:43-45.

Pearsall, Derek. 1977. *Old English and Middle English Poetry.* The Routledge History of English Poetry 1. London: Routledge and Kegan Paul.

- - -. 1980. «Chaucer, the 'Nun's Priest's Tale', and the Modern Reader.» *Dutch Quarterly Review of Anglo-American Letters* 10:164-174.

- - - (ed.). 1983. *The Nun's Priest's Tale.* A Variorum Edition of the Works of Geoffrey Chaucer. Volume 2, part 9. Norman: University of Oklahoma Press.

- - - and R.A. Waldron (eds.). 1969. *Medieval Literature and Civilization.* Studies in memory of G.N. Garmonsway. London: The Athlone Press.

Peebles, R.J. 1911. «The Anglo-Saxon 'Physiologus'.» *Modern Philology* 8:571-79.

Pelen, Marc M. 1979. «Form and Meaning of the Old French Love Vision: the 'Fableau dou Dieu d'Amors' and Chaucer's 'Parliament of Fowls'.» *Journal of Medieval and Renaissance Studies* 9:277-305.

Perry, B.E. 1941. «Physiologus.» In: Wissowa, Georg (ed.). 1894-1972. *Paulys Realencyclopädie der classischen Altertumswissenschaft.* Revised edition begun by Georg Wissowa, continued by Wilhelm Kroll and Karl Mittelhaus. Stuttgart: J.B. Metzlerscher Verlag, volume 39:1074-1129.

Perryman, Judith. 1984. «Lore, Life, and Logic in 'The Owl and the Nightingale'.» *Dutch Quarterly Review of Anglo-American Letters* 14:97-109.

Petersen, Kate Oelzner. 1898. *On the Sources of The Nonne Prestes Tale.* Radcliffe College Monographs 10. Boston: Ginn, The Athenaeum Press.

Peterson, Douglas L. 1956. «'The Owl and the Nightingale' and Christian Dialectic.» *Journal of English and Germanic Philology* 55:13-26.

Pfeffer, Wendy. 1985. *The Change of Philomel: The Nightingale in Medieval Literature.* Bern: Peter Lang.

Pfister, Manfred. 1992. «'Man's Distinctive Mark': Paradoxical Distinctions between Man and His Bestial Other in Early Modern Texts.» In: Lehmann, Elmar and Bernd Lenz (eds.). 1992. *Telling Stories.* Studies in honour of Ulrich Broich on the occasion of his 60th birthday. Amsterdam: John Benjamins, 17-33.

Pichaske, David Richard. 1969. «The Reynardian Tradition in Medieval and Renaissance English Literature.» *Dissertation Abstracts International A: The Humanities and Social Sciences.* March 1970, volume 30/9, 3953-A.

Piltz, Anders. 1982. *Die gelehrte Welt des Mittelalters.* Translated from the Swedish by Sybille Didon. Original edition published 1978. Cologne: Böhlau.

Plessow, Max. 1906. *Geschichte der Fabeldichtung in England bis zu John Gay (1726).* Palaestra 52. Berlin: Mayer and Müller.

Polzella, Marion L. 1975. «'The Craft so Long to Lerne': Poet and Lover in Chaucer's 'Envoy to Scogan' and 'Parliament of Fowls'.» *Chaucer Review* 10:279-286.

Poole, Austin Lane (ed.). 1958. *Medieval England.* Two volumes. Oxford: At the Clarendon Press.

Pope, John C. (ed.). 1981. *Seven English Poems.* Second edition. First edition 1966. New York and London: W. W. Norton.

Potts, Richard. 1991. «Untying the Knot: Evolution of Early Human Behavior.» In: Robinson, Michael H. and Lionel Tiger (eds.). 1991. *Man and Beast Revisited.* Washington and London: Smithsonian Institution Press, 41-59.

Powell, Marianne. 1983. *Fabula Docet: Studies in the Background and Interpretation of Henryson's 'Morall Fabilis'.* Odense University Studies in English 6. Odense: Odense University Press.

Pratt, Robert A. 1947. «Chaucer's Use of the 'Teseida'.» *Publications of the Modern Language Association of America* 62:598-621.

- - -. 1949. «The Classical Lamentations in the 'Nun's Priest's Tale'.» *Modern Language Notes* 64:76-78.

- - -. 1972. «Three Old French Sources of the 'Nonnes Preestes Tale': Part I and II.» *Speculum* 47:422-444 and 646-668.

- - -. 1977. «Some Latin Sources of the Nonnes Preest on Dreams.» *Speculum* 52:538-570.

Ranke, Kurt et al. (eds.). 1977ff. *Enzyklopädie des Märchens.* Berlin and New York: Walter de Gruyter.

Reale, Nancy M. 1984. «Rhetorical Strategies in 'The Owl and the Nightingale'.» *Philological Quarterly* 63:417-430.

Reiss, Edmund. 1969. «Conflict and Its Resolution in Medieval Dialogues.» In: *Actes Du Quatrième Congrès International De Philosophie Médiévale (Université de Montréal 1967): Arts Libéraux et Philosophique Au Moyen Âge.* Montreal: Institut d'études médiévales, 863-872.

Renoir, Alain. 1976. «Crist Ihesu's Beasts of Battle: A Note on Oral-Formulaic Theme Survival.» *Neophilologus* 60:455-459.

Renwick, W.L. and Harold Orton. 1966. *The Beginnings of English Literature to Skelton 1509.* Third edition, revised by Martyn F. Wakelin. First edition 1939. Introductions to English Literature 1. London: The Cresset Press.

Rickert, Edith. 1920. «A New Interpretation of 'The Parlement of Foules'.» *Modern Philology* 18:1-29.

Robertson, D.W. Jr. 1968. «The Concept of Courtly Love as an Impediment to the Understanding of Medieval Texts.» Reprinted in: Robertson, D.W. Jr. 1980. *Essays in Medieval Culture.* Princeton: Princeton University Press, 257-272.

- - -. 1980. *Essays in Medieval Culture.* Princeton: Princeton University Press.

Robin, Percy Ansell. 1932. *Animal Lore in English Literature.* London: John Murray.

Robinson, F.N. (ed.). 1966. *The Complete Works of Geoffrey Chaucer.* Second edition. First edition 1933. Oxford: Oxford University Press.

Robinson, Michael H. and Lionel Tiger (eds.). 1991. *Man and Beast Revisited.* Washington and London: Smithsonian Institution Press.

Röhrich, Lutz. 1991. «Der Herr der Tiere.» In: Esterl, Arnica and Wilhelm Solms (eds.). 1991. *Tiere und Tiergestaltige im Märchen.* Veröffentlichungen der Europäischen Märchengesellschaft 15. Regensburg: Erich Röth, 30-47.

Rombauts, E. and A. Welkenhuysen (eds.). 1975. *Aspects of the Medieval Animal Epic: Proceedings of the International Conference: Louvain, May 15-17, 1972.* Leuven/The Hague: University Press/Martinus Nijhoff.

Rooney, Anne. 1993. *Hunting in Middle English Literature.* Rochester: The Boydell Press.

Ross, Werner. 1954. «Die 'Ecbasis Captivi' und die Anfänge der mittelalterlichen Tierdichtung.» *Germanisch-Romanische Monatsschrift* NF 4:266-282.

Rossiaud, Jaques. 1989. *Dame Venus: Prostitution im Mittelalter.* Translated from Italian by Ernst Voltmer. Munich: C.H. Beck.

Rothschild, Victoria. 1984. «'The Parliament of Fowls': Chaucer's Mirror up to Nature?» *Review of English Studies* NS 35:164-184.

Rowan, Andrew N. 1991. «The Human-Animal Interface: Chasm or Continuum?» In: Robinson, Michael H. and Lionel Tiger (eds.). 1991. *Man and Beast Revisited.* Washington and London: Smithsonian Institution Press, 279-289.

Rowland, Beryl. 1962. «Chaucer's 'Throstil old' and Other Birds.» *Mediaeval Studies* 24:381-384.

- - -. 1963. «Chaucer and the Unnatural History of Animals.» *Mediaeval Studies* 25:367-372.

- - -. 1965. «'Owles and Apes' in Chaucer's 'Nun's Priest's Tale' 3092.» *Mediaeval Studies* 27:322-325.

- - -. 1968. «'A sheep that highte malle' (NPT, VII, 2831).» *English Language Notes* 6:84-87.

- - -. 1971. *Blind Beasts: Chaucer's Animal World.* Chatham: The Kent State University Press.

- - -. 1974. *Animals with Human Faces.* Second edition. First edition 1973. London: George Allen and Unwin.

- - -. 1981. «The Wisdom of the Cock.» In: Goossens, Jan and Timothy Sodmann (eds.). 1981. *International Beast Epic, Fable and Fabliau Colloquium: 1979, Münster.* Niederdeutsche Studien 30. Cologne and Vienna: Böhlau, 340-355.

- - -. 1985. «Seven Kinds of Irony.» In: Birney, Earle. 1985. *Essays on Chaucerian Irony.* Edited, with an essay on irony, by Beryl Rowland. Toronto: University of Toronto Press, xv-xxx.

- - - (ed.). 1968. *A Companion to Chaucer Studies.* Toronto/New York/London: Oxford University Press.

Ruggiers, Paul G. 1965. «'The Nun's Priest's Tale'.» Reprinted in: Anderson, J.J. (ed.). 1974. *Chaucer: The Canterbury Tales. A Casebook.* London: The Macmillan Press, 222-236.

Russell, J.C. 1969. «The Patrons of 'The Owl and the Nightingale'.» *Philological Quarterly* 48:178-185.

Sachs, Hannelore, Ernst Badstübner, and Helga Neumann. ?. *Erklärendes Wörterbuch zur christlichen Kunst.* Hanau: Verlag Werner Dausien.

Sakanishi, Shio. 1932. «A Note on the 'Nonne Preestes Tale'.» *Modern Language Notes* 47:150-151.

Salisbury, Joyce E. 1994. *The Beast Within: Animals in the Middle Ages.* New York and London: Routledge.

Salzmann, L.F. 1913. *Mediæval Byways.* London: Constable.

Sanders, Willy. 1975. «Die unheile Welt. Zu einer christlichen Etymologie des Mittelalters.» In: Fromm, Hans, Wolfgang Harms, and Uwe Ruberg (eds.). 1975. *Verbum et Signum.* Beiträge zur mediävistischen Bedeutungsforschung. 'Festschrift' for Friedrich Ohly. Two volumes. Munich: Wilhelm Fink, volume 1:331-340.

Sauer, Hans (ed. and trans.). 1983. *The Owl and the Nightingale / Die Eule und die Nachtigall.* Middle English/German. RUB 7992. Stuttgart: Philipp Reclam jun.

Sbordone, Franciscus (ed.). 1936. *Physiologus: Singulas Variarum Aetatum Recensiones.* Milano: Dante Alighieri Society.

Scattergood, V.J. 1964. «The Authorship of 'The Boke of Cupide'.» *Anglia* 82:137-149.

- - - (ed.). 1965. *The Works of Sir John Clanvowe: The Boke of Cupide and The Two Ways.* Reprinted 1975. Cambridge: D.S. Brewer.

Schaller, Dieter. 1970. «Lateinische Tierdichtung in frühkarolingischer Zeit.» In: Schwab, Ute (ed.). 1970. *Das Tier in der Dichtung.* Heidelberg: Carl Winter, 91-113 and 272-276.

Scheiber, Alexander. 1979. «Berechja ha-Nakdan.» In: Ranke, Kurt et al. (eds.). 1977ff. *Enzyklopädie des Märchens.* Berlin and New York: Walter de Gruyter, volume 2 (1979), columns 135-137.

Scheps, Walter. 1970. «Chaucer's Anti-Fable: 'Reductio ad Absurdum' in the 'Nun's Priest's Tale'.» *Leeds Studies in English* NS 4:1-10.

Schleusener, Jay. 1973. «'The Owl and the Nightingale': A Matter of Judgment.» *Modern Philology* 70:185-189.

Schlotterose, Otto (ed. and trans.). 1908. *Die altenglische Dichtung 'Phœnix'*. Bonn: Peter Hanstein.

Schmidtke, Dietrich. 1968. *Geistliche Tierinterpretation in der deutschsprachigen Literatur des Mittelalters (1100-1500)*. Two volumes. Volume 1 text, volume 2 notes. Dissertation. Berlin: Freie Universität Berlin.

Schnur, Harry C. (ed. and trans.) 1978. *Fabeln der Antike: Griechisch und Lateinisch*. Munich: Heimeran.

Schoeck, Richard and Jerome Taylor (eds.). 1960-1961. *Chaucer Criticism*. Two volumes. Reprinted 1982. Notre Dame and London: University of Notre Dame Press.

Schöpf, Hans. 1988. *Fabeltiere*. Reprinted 1992. Wiesbaden: VMA.

Schubel, Friedrich. 1973. «Der ags. 'klagende' Kuckuck.» In: Stanzel, Franz K. and Franz Zaic (eds.). 1973. *Festschrift Prof. Dr. Herbert Koziol zum siebzigsten Geburtstag*. Wiener Beiträge zur englischen Philologie 75. Stuttgart: Wilhelm Braumüller, 280-296.

Schwab, Ute. 1992. «Lebendige Schwerter und lateinische Schlachtvögel.» In: Burger, Harald, Alois M. Haas, and Peter von Matt (eds.). 1992. *Verborum Amor: Studien zur Geschichte und Kunst der deutschen Sprache*. 'Festschrift' for Stefan Sonderegger on the occasion of his 65th birthday. Berlin and New York: Walter de Gruyter, 3-33.

- - - (ed.). 1970. *Das Tier in der Dichtung*. Heidelberg: Carl Winter.

Seel, Otto (ed. and trans.). 1992. *Der Physiologus*. Lebendige Antike. Second edition. First edition 1960. Zurich and Stuttgart: Artemis.

Seelmann, W. 1888. «Die Vogelsprachen (Vogelparlamente) der mittelalterlichen Literatur.» *Jahrbuch des Vereins für niederdeutsche Sprachforschung* 14:101-147.

Segre, Cesare (ed.). 1957. *Li Bestiaires d'Amours di Maistre Richart de Fornival e li Response du Bestiaire*. Milan: Riccardo Ricciardi.

Selvin, Rhoda Hurwitt. 1965. «Shades of Love in the 'Parlement of Foules'.» *Studia Neophilologica* 37:146-160.

Severs, J. Burke. 1946. «Chaucer's Originality in the 'Nun's Priest's Tale'.» *Studies in Philology* 43:22-41.

Shackford, Martha Hale. 1916. «The Date of Chaucer's 'House of Fame'.» *Modern Language Notes* 31:507-508.

Shallers, Paul A. 1975. «The 'Nun's Priest's Tale': An Ironic Exemplum.» *English Literary History* 42:319-337.

Shaver, Chester Linn. 1943. «Chaucer's 'Owles and Apes'.» *Modern Language Notes* 58:105-107.

Sherbo, Arthur. 1949. «Chaucer's Nun's Priest Again.» *Publications of the Modern Language Association of America* 64:236-246.

Sheridan, James J. (ed. and trans.). 1980. *Alan of Lille: The Plaint of Nature*. Medieval Sources in Translation 26. Toronto: Pontifical Institute of Mediaeval Studies.

Simek, Rudolf. 1992. *Erde und Kosmos im Mittelalter: Das Weltbild vor Kolumbus*. Munich: C.H. Beck.

Simon-Vandenbergen, A.M. (ed.). 1987. *Studies in Honour of René Derolez*. Gent: Seminarie voor Engelse en Oud-Germaanse Taalkunde R.U.G.

Sisam, Kenneth (ed.). 1927. *Chaucer: The Nun's Priest's Tale*. Reprinted 1989. Oxford: Oxford University Press.

Skeat, Walter W. (ed.). 1873. *The Vision of William Concerning Piers the Plowman, Dowel, Dobet, and Dobest, by William Langland. The 'Whitaker' Text; or Text C. / Richard the Redeles by the Same Author. / The Crowned King by Another Hand.* Reprinted 1910. Early English Text Society Original Series 54. London: Kegan Paul, Trench, and Trübner.

- - - (ed.). 1894. *The Complete Works of Geoffrey Chaucer.* Six volumes. Oxford: Clarendon Press.

- - - (ed.). 1897. *Chaucerian and Other Pieces: Being a Supplement to the Complete Works of Geoffrey Chaucer.* Oxford: Clarendon Press.

Sklute, Larry M. 1981. «The Inconclusive Form of the 'Parliament of Fowls'.» *Chaucer Review* 16:119-128.

Slaughter, E.E. 1931. «'Every Vertu at his Reste'.» *Modern Language Notes* 46:448-453.

Smalley, Beryl. 1983. *The Study of the Bible in the Middle Ages.* Third edition. First edition 1952. Oxford: Basil Blackwell.

Smith, Roland M. 1951. «Five Notes on Chaucer and Froissart.» *Modern Language Notes* 66:27-32.

South, Malcolm (ed.). 1987. *Mythical and Fabulous Creatures: A Source Book and Research Guide.* New York: Greenwood Press.

Spearing, A.C. 1976a. *Medieval Dream Poetry.* Cambridge: Cambridge University Press.

- - -. 1976b. «Chaucer: The Parliament of Fowls.» In: Spearing, A.C. 1976a. *Medieval Dream Poetry.* Cambridge: Cambridge University Press, 89-101.

- - -. 1976c. «Clanvowe: The Cuckoo and the Nightingale.» In: Spearing, A.C. 1976a. *Medieval Dream Poetry.* Cambridge: Cambridge University Press, 176-181.

Spillemaeckers, Diederik Lodewijk. 1970. «Reynard the Fox: The Evolution of His Character in Select Medieval Beast Epics.» *Dissertation Abstracts International A: The Humanities and Social Sciences.* November 1970, volume 31/5, 2355-A/2356-A.

Squires, Ann (ed.). 1988. *The Old English Physiologus.* Durham Medieval Texts 5. Durham: School of English.

Standop, Ewald. 1980. «Zur allegorischen Deutung der 'Nonnes Preestes Tale'.» Original version 1961. This revised version reprinted in: Erzgräber, Willi (ed.). 1983. *Geoffrey Chaucer.* Wege der Forschung 253. Darmstadt: Wissenschaftliche Buchgesellschaft, 409-421.

Stanley, Eric Gerald (ed.). 1972. *The Owl and the Nightingale.* Old and Middle English Texts. Second edition. First edition 1960. Manchester: Manchester University Press/Barnes and Noble.

Stanzel, Franz K. and Franz Zaic (eds.). 1973. *Festschrift Prof. Dr. Herbert Koziol zum siebzigsten Geburtstag.* Wiener Beiträge zur englischen Philologie 75. Stuttgart: Wilhelm Braumüller.

Steadman, John M. 1959. «Chauntecleer and Medieval Natural History.» *Isis* 50:236-244.

- - -. 1965. «Champier and the 'Altercatio Hadriani': Another Chaucer Analogue.» *Notes and Queries* NS 12:170.

Steiger, Christoph von and Otto Homburger (eds.). 1964. *Physiologus Bernensis: Voll-Faksimile-Ausgabe des Codex Bongarsianus 318 der Burgerbibliothek Bern.* Basel: Alkuin.

Stillwell, Gardiner. 1950. «Unity and Comedy in Chaucer's 'Parlement of Foules'.» *Journal of English and Germanic Philology* 49:470-495.

- - -. 1954. «Chaucer's Eagles and their Choice on February 14.» *Journal of English and Germanic Philology* 53:546-561.

Stone, Brian (ed. and trans.). 1988. *The Owl and the Nightingale / Cleanness / St. Erkenwald.* Second edition. First edition 1971. Harmondsworth: Penguin.

Stoob, Carola. 1991. «Der Beitrag der Ethologie zum Verständnis der menschlichen Auffassung vom Tier.» In: Michel, Paul (ed.). 1991b. *Tiersymbolik.* Schriften zur Symbolforschung 7. Bern: Peter Lang, 171-203.

Suchier, Walter. 1922. «Tierepik und Volksüberlieferung.» *Archiv für das Studium der neuen Sprachen und Literatur* 143:223-236.

Sundby, Bertil. 1950. *The Dialect and Provenance of the Middle English Poem 'The Owl and the Nightingale'.* Lund Studies in English 18. Lund: Gleerup.

Swanton, Michael. 1987. *English Literature before Chaucer.* Longman Literature in English Series. London and New York: Longman.

Sylvester, Joshua (trans.). 1979. *The Divine Weeks and Works of Guillaume de Saluste Sieur du Bartas.* Edited by Susan Snyder. Two volumes. Original French edition 1578-1584. Complete translation first published 1605. Oxford: At the Clarendon Press.

Tatlock, John S.P. 1914. «Notes on Chaucer: 'The Canterbury Tales'.» *Modern Language Notes* 29:140-144.

- - -. 1966. *The Mind and Art of Chaucer.* New York: Gordian Press.

ten Brink, Bernhard. 1877. *Geschichte der englischen Literatur.* Two volumes. Berlin: Robert Oppenheim.

Thurber, James. 1945. *The Thurber Carnival.* New York and London: Harper.

Timmer, B.J. (ed.). 1948. *The Later Genesis: Edited from MS. Junius 11.* Oxford: The Scrivener Press.

Tolkien, J.R.R. and E.V. Gordon (eds.). 1967. *Sir Gawain and the Green Knight.* Second edition revised by Norman Davis. First edition 1925. Oxford: At the Clarendon Press.

Toller, T. Northcote (ed.). 1921. *Supplement to the Anglo-Saxon Dictionary.* Oxford: At the Clarendon Press.

Toops, Connie. 1990. *The Enchanting Owl.* Shrewsbury: Swan Hill Press.

Topsell, Edward. 1607. *The Historie of the Foure-Footed Beastes.* London: William Iaggard. Reprinted 1973. The Early English Experience 561. Amsterdam: Theatrum Orbis Terrarum.

- - -. 1608. *The Historie of Serpents. Or, the Second Booke of Liuing Creatures.* London: William Jaggard. Reprinted 1973. The Early English Experience 562. Amsterdam: Theatrum Orbis Terrarum.

Torre Bueno, Lillian de la. 1934. «A Note on the Date of 'The Owl and the Nightingale'.» *Anglia* 58:122-130.

Toynbee, J.M.C. 1983. *Tierwelt der Antike.* Kulturgeschichte der antiken Welt 17. Translated from the English by Maria R. Alföldi and Detlef Misslbeck. Mainz on the Rhine: Verlag Philipp von Zabern.

Treadgold, Warren (ed.). 1984. *Renaissances Before the Renaissance: Cultural Revivals of Late Antiquity and the Middle Ages.* Stanford: Stanford University Press.

Treu, Ursula (ed. and trans.). 1981. *Physiologus: Naturkunde in frühchristlicher Deutung.* Hanau: Werner Dausien.

Trevisa, John (trans.). 1975. *On the Properties of Things.* John Trevisa's translation of *Bartholomæus Anglicus: De Proprietatibus Rerum.* A critical text in two volumes. Date of the Latin original c. 1230. Trevisa's translation first published 1398/9. Oxford: At the Clarendon Press.

Trillitzsch, Winfried (ed. and trans.). 1964. *Ecbasis cuiusdam captivi per tropologiam. Die Flucht eines Gefangenen (tropologisch).* Text and German translation. With historical notes by S. Hoyer. Leipzig: B.G. Teubner.

Tupper, Frederick. 1912. «The 'Physiologus' of the Exeter Book.» *Journal of English and Germanic Philology* 11:89-91.

- - -. 1921. «Chaucer's Tale of Ireland.» *Publications of the Modern Language Association of America* 36:186-222.

- - -. 1934. «The Date and Historical Background of 'The Owl and the Nightingale'.» *Publications of the Modern Language Association of America* 49:406-427.

Twiti, William. c. 1327. *The Art of Hunting.* Edited by Bror Danielsson. 1977. Cynegetica anglica I. Stockholm: Almqvist and Wicksell International.

Unterkircher, Franz. 1986a. *Tiere, Glaube, Aberglaube: Die schönsten Miniaturen aus dem Bestiarium.* Graz: Akademische Druck- und Verlagsanstalt.

- - - (ed. and trans.). 1986b. *Bestiarium: Die Texte der Handschrift MS. Ashmole 1511 der Bodleian Library Oxford in lateinischer und deutscher Sprache.* Graz: Akademische Druck- und Verlagsanstalt.

Utley, Francis Lee. 1944. *The Crooked Rib: An Analytical Index to the Argument About Women in English and Scots Literature to the End of the Year 1568.* Colombus: Ohio State University.

Varnhagen, Hermann. 1881. «Zu dem streitgedicht zwischen drossel und nachtigall.» *Anglia* 4:207-210.

Varty, Kenneth. 1964. «The Pursuit of Reynard in Medieval English Literature and Art.» *Nottingham Mediaeval Studies* 8:62-81.

- - -. 1966. «The Death and Resurrection of Reynard in Mediaeval Literature and Art.» *Nottingham Mediaeval Studies* 10:70-93.

- - -. 1967. *Reynard the Fox: A Study of the Fox in Medieval English Art.* Leicester: Leicester University Press.

- - -. 1975. «Further Examples of the Fox in Medieval English Art.» In: Rombauts, E. and A. Welkenhuysen (eds.). 1975. *Aspects of the Medieval Animal Epic: Proceedings of the International Conference: Louvain, May 15-17, 1972.* Leuven/The Hague: University Press/Martinus Nijhoff, 251-256.

- - -. 1991. «La datation des contes de Renart le Goupil et la branche IV: 'Renart et Isengrin dans le puits'.» In: *A la Recherche du 'Roman de Renart'.* Two volumes. New Alyth: Lochee Publications, volume 2, 330-343.

- - -. «'Renart et Ysengrin dans le puits': la version courte, la version longue, et la version plus longue de la branche IV du 'Roman de Renart'.» Unpublished manuscript.

Vasta, Edward and Zacharias P. Thundy (eds.). 1979. *Chaucerian Problems and Perspectives.* Essays presented to Paul E. Beichner. Notre Dame and London: University of Notre Dame Press.

Volkert, Wilhelm. 1991. *Adel bis Zunft: Ein Lexikon des Mittelalters.* Munich: C.H. Beck.

Walther, Hans. 1920. *Das Streitgedicht in der lateinischen Literatur des Mittelalters.* Quellen und Untersuchungen zur lateinischen Philologie des Mittelalters 5/2. Munich: C.H. Beck'sche Verlagsbuchhandlung.

Ward, C.E. 1929. «The Authorship of 'The Cuckoo and the Nightingale'.» *Modern Language Notes* 44:217-226.

Warnke, Karl (ed.). 1898. *Die Fabeln der Marie de France.* Bibliotheca Normannica 6. Halle: Max Niemeyer.

Watkins, Charles A. 1969. «Chaucer's 'Sweete Preest'.» *English Literary History* 36:455-469.

Watson, Charles S. 1964. «The Relationship of the 'Monk's Tale' and the 'Nun's Priest's Tale'.» *Studies in Short Fiction* 1:277-288.

Wehrli, Max. 1969a. *Formen mittelalterlicher Erzählung: Aufsätze.* Zurich: Atlantis.

- - -. 1969b. «Vom Sinn des mittelalterlichen Tierepos.» In: Wehrli, Max. 1969a. *Formen mittelalterlicher Erzählung: Aufsätze.* Zurich: Atlantis, 113-125.

Weidhorn, Manfred. 1967. «The Anxiety Dream in Literature from Homer to Milton.» *Studies in Philology* 64:65-82.

Weimann, Klaus (ed.). 1975. *Middle English Animal Literature.* Exeter Medieval English Texts. Exeter: University of Exeter.

Wellmann, Max. 1930. *Der Physiologus: Eine religionsgeschichtlich-naturwissenschaftliche Untersuchung.* Philologus Supplement 22/1. Leipzig: Dietrich'sche Verlagsbuchhandlung.

Wells, John Edwin. 1916. *A Manual of the Writings in Middle English: 1050-1400.* New Haven: Yale University Press.

Wentersdorf, Karl P. 1980. «'Heigh Ymaginacioun' in Chaucer's 'Nun's Priest's Tale'.» *Studia Neophilologica* 52:31-34.

- - -. 1982. «Symbol and Meaning in Chaucer's 'Nun's Priest's Tale'.» *Nottingham Mediaeval Studies* 26:29-46.

Westhuizen, J.E. van der (ed.). 1974. *John Lydgate: The Life of Saint Alban and Saint Amphibal.* Leiden: E.J. Brill.

White, Beatrice. 1954. «Medieval Animal Lore.» *Anglia* 72:21-30.

- - -. 1969. «Saracens and Crusaders: from Fact to Allegory.» In: Pearsall, D.A. and R.A. Waldron (eds.). 1969. *Medieval Literature and Civilization.* Studies in memory of G.N. Garmonsway. London: The Athlone Press, 170-191.

White, Lynn. 1947. «Natural Science and Naturalistic Art in the Middle Ages.» *American Historical Review* 52:421-435.

White, T. H. (ed. and trans.). 1959. *The Book of Beasts: Being a Translation from a Latin Bestiary of the Twelfth Century.* Fourth edition. Reprinted 1969. First edition 1954. London: Jonathan Cape.

Whitesell, Frederick R. 1947. «Fables in Mediaeval Exempla.» *Journal of English and Germanic Philology* 46:348-366.

Whiting, B.J. 1934. «Ac He Kan Hongi Bi þe Boȝe: 'Owl and Nightingale', l. 816.» *Anglia* 58:368-373.

Whittingham, A.B. 1981. *Norwich Cathedral Bosses and Misericords.* Norwich: Jarrold and Sons.

Williams, Elizabeth. 1981. «Blossom in the Breach: Some Comments on the Language of Spring in 'The Owl and the Nightingale'.» *Leeds Studies in English* NS 12:163-183.

Wilson, R.M. 1958. «The Contents of the Mediaeval Library.» In: Wormald, Francis and C.E. Wright (eds.). 1958. *The English Library before 1700.* London: The University of London/The Athlone Press, 85-111.

- - -. 1968. *Early Middle English Literature.* Third edition. First edition 1939. London: Methuen.

- - -. 1970. *The Lost Literature of Medieval England.* Second edition. First edition 1952. London: Methuen.

Windeatt, B.A. (ed. and trans.). 1982. *Chaucer's Dream Poetry: Sources and Analogues.* Chaucer Studies 7. Cambridge and Totowa, New Jersey: D.S. Brewer and Rowan and Littlefield.

Winny, James. 1973. *Chaucer's Dream-Poems.* London: Chatto and Windus.

Wirtjes, Hanneke (ed.). 1991. *The Middle English 'Physiologus'.* Early English Text Society Original Series 299. Oxford: Oxford University Press.

Wissowa, Georg (ed.). 1894-1972. *Paulys Realencyclopädie der classischen Altertumswissenschaft.* Revised edition begun by Georg Wissowa, continued by Wilhelm Kroll and Karl Mittelhaus. Stuttgart: J.B. Metzlerscher Verlag.

Witt, Michael A. 1981. «'The Owl and the Nightingale' and English Law Court Procedure of the Twelfth and Thirteenth Centuries.» *Chaucer Review* 16:282-292.

Wormald, Francis and C.E. Wright (eds.). 1958. *The English Library before 1700.* London: The University of London/The Athlone Press.

Wright, H. Bunker and Monroe K. Spears (eds.). 1959. *The Literary Works of Matthew Prior.* Two volumes. Oxford: At the Clarendon Press.

Wright, Thomas (ed.). 1863. *Alexandri Neckam: De Naturis Rerum Libri Duo. With the Poem of the Same Author: De Laudibus Divinae Sapientiae.* Rerum Britannicarum Medii Aevi Scriptores (Rolls Series) 34. London: Longman, Green, Longman, Roberts and Green.

Yates, Donald N. 1983. «Chanticleer's Latin Ancestors.» *Chaucer Review* 18:116-126.

Zimmermann, Albert (ed.). 1970. *Methoden in Wissenschaft und Kunst des Mittelalters.* Miscellanea Mediaevalia 7. Berlin: Walter de Gruyter.

Index